Miraculous Images and Votive Offerings in Mexico

Miraculous Images and Votive Offerings in Mexico

FRANK GRAZIANO

OXFORD
UNIVERSITY PRESS

OXFORD
UNIVERSITY PRESS

Oxford University Press is a department of the
University of Oxford. It furthers the University's objective
of excellence in research, scholarship, and education
by publishing worldwide.

Oxford   New York
Auckland   Cape Town   Dar es Salaam   Hong Kong   Karachi
Kuala Lumpur   Madrid   Melbourne   Mexico City   Nairobi
New Delhi   Shanghai   Taipei   Toronto

With offices in
Argentina   Austria   Brazil   Chile   Czech Republic   France   Greece
Guatemala   Hungary   Italy   Japan   Poland   Portugal   Singapore
South Korea   Switzerland   Thailand   Turkey   Ukraine   Vietnam

Published in the United States of America by
Oxford University Press
198 Madison Avenue, New York, NY 10016

Library of Congress Cataloging-in-Publication Data
Graziano, Frank, 1955–
Miraculous images and votive offerings in Mexico / Frank Graziano.
pages   cm
Includes bibliographical references and index.
ISBN 978-0-19-979086-9 (cloth: alk. paper)
ISBN 978-0-19-979085-2 (pbk. : alk. paper)
1. Christianity-Mexico.   2. Mexico-Religious life and customs.   I. Title.
BR610.G73 2015
246'.550972—dc23   2015017547

The epigraph to "Seeing Through Faith" is from Richard S. Lazarus, "Cognitive and
Coping Processes in Emotion," in Stress And Coping: An Anthology, edited by Alan Monat
and Richard S. Lazarus. Copyright © 1977 Columbia University Press. Reprinted with
permission of the publisher.

1 3 5 7 9 8 6 4 2
Typeset in Scala Pro
Printed in the United States of America
on acid-free paper

for Rickie Lee Jones,
a lifetime of inspiration.

It takes close attention to see what is happening in front of you. It takes work, pious effort, to see what you are looking at. He was mesmerized by this, the depths that were possible in the slowing of motion, the things to see, the depths of things so easy to miss in the shallow habit of seeing.

—DON DELILLO

Contents

Marco

Remedios

Chalma

Preface

MIRACULOUS IMAGES AND *Votive Offerings in Mexico* is written in two voices. One is analytical and at times descriptive; it consolidates, applies, and advances a broad range of previous scholarship relevant to petitionary devotion. The other voice is primarily narrative. It conveys the fieldwork in more creative prose to illustrate the analytical chapters and to bring the reader closer to experiences at the shrines. Chapters written in these two voices alternate throughout the book to provide interlocking, mutually enhancing perspectives.

In the narrative chapters I trust instinctively that "the mood is more important than the theme," or at least equally important. The narratives explore the richness, beauty, strangeness, and emotive power that are patent in devotion but underrepresented in scholarship. I create as best I can a sense of ambience, the feel of the devotions, and the experience of studying them. The wonder and awe I could not always capture at the sites is approximated—generated—by the recollections carried on the rhythms of the prose. These narratives contrast with the analytical chapters in voice but also in tempo, pausing for moments "lost at normal speed" and for a sense of place conveyed through imagery.[1]

In the analytical chapters I am mindful of "the insincere neutrality that is the scholarly norm," particularly as it pertains to representing accurately and sensitively the devotees' points of view while at once going beyond them to develop my secular understanding of devotions. Much of the book is written by the "principle of prolonged empathetic immersion" to relate the perspectives of devotees. Rather than modifying "miracle" with "perceived" or putting words in scare quotes, for example, I state simply, "The Virgin of Zapopan granted the miracle." The qualifier "this statement is true within the devotions" is implicit throughout the book. When I intervene for secular analysis the transition is apparent in context. At times a given topic is treated twice to represent both devotee perspectives and my own. In the section "Faith, Presence, and Power," for example, I provide devotee views regarding the empowerment of miraculous images, and in "Projective Animation" I explore the same topic in secular perspective.[2]

I draw from scholarship—sometimes incompatible scholarship—in several disciples, reading as widely as possible on a given topic and then articulating as clearly and as briefly as possible an integrated interdisciplinary analysis. I am less interested in the comprehensive validity of a theory or the global intent of an ethnography than I am in the knowledge and insights that I can derive and apply to my topics of study. My intent is not to converse with my sources in the text nor to faithfully interpret the world as a given theorist would see it, but rather to learn what I can from each source and then to assimilate and synthesize that knowledge into an approach of my own. I also intentionally avoid such conventions as a thesis statement, a methods statement, an explicit hypothesis, a review of previous scholarship, an overview of chapters, routine summaries, and a conclusion. I make my points on the move and revisit them as appropriate, particularly in the narrative chapters, and I aspire to a cumulative effect.

My sources are itemized in extensive endnotes that sometimes include quoted passages to provide evidence, broaden context, and support arguments. The endnotes are intended as a bibliographic resource and an enrichment supplement. To simplify references in the notes, I use "from" when quoting directly from a textual source ("the quoted passage is from") and "in" for a secondary citation ("the quoted passage is in," rather than "the quoted passage is quoted in"). To facilitate reading, the notes are consolidated and numbered at the ends of paragraphs.

Subject matters like devotion are rebelliously resistant to organization. I hope to have maintained echoes while eliminating redundancy, but in the end any divisions for the convenience of exposition are provisional. In studying devotions one is reminded that "human experience, in its immediacy, is profoundly oblivious of the internal partitions that gerrymandering theorists impose on it." Another challenge was to describe and interpret without imposing contrived coherence on the imprecision, ambiguity, and simultaneity of contradictory meanings that abound in devotions and contribute to their complexity.[3]

Word choice, particularly pronoun choice, was sometimes difficult. A miraculous image as a statue or painting is attributed the neuter pronoun "it" (*I went to see it*), but for devotees miraculous images are also quasi-human and superhuman, and as such are attributed personal pronouns

(*I went to see him or her*). In view of this, I allowed the context of given passages to dictate the pronoun that seemed most appropriate. In Mexico, as elsewhere in Latin America, miraculous images are often referred to as *santos* (saints), which has certain advantages as a word choice because it collapses hierarchy and clouds the distinction, as devotees do, between a material image in a church and a sacred figure in heaven. Ultimately, however, I opted for "image" and "miraculous image" to avoid confusion, and also for accuracy because my research focuses almost exclusively on images of Christ and the Virgin. In reference to people I use "devotee" as the general term, with the subcategories of "votary" in the context of petitionary devotion and "pilgrim" in the context of pilgrimage. To avoid the term "ex voto," which I find unfortunate, I use "votive offering."[4]

Informants are identified by first names only, some of which are pseudonyms, and quotations without endnotes are from my fieldwork. All translations from Spanish are mine, and all bible translations are from the New American Bible, Revised Edition, unless otherwise noted. Following Vatican usage, I translate the Spanish *santuario* to "shrine," which Canon 1230 defines as "a church or other sacred place to which numerous members of the faithful make pilgrimage for a special reason of piety."[5]

All photographs in the book were taken by me during the fieldwork. Most of these are reproduced in color, together with an expansive image gallery and archive, on the book's companion website: miracles-in-mexico.com.

Acknowledgments

MY FIRST THANKS go out to the reader, or perhaps more accurately to the motivating anticipation—imagination—of a sympathetic implied reader. A sense of presence, of resonating with another mind and engaging in an empathetic understanding, mitigated the loneliness of a solitary enterprise and inspired my best effort. In this context I am particularly grateful to the colleagues who read the manuscript and participated in a workshop organized by the Kenan Institute for Ethics at Duke University. Many of their comments were incorporated into the final draft.

I am also grateful to have presented my research and dialogued with colleagues in the history department at Columbia University, in religious studies at Duke University, in Latin American studies at Princeton University, and at the Center for Religion and Civic Culture at the University of Southern California.

The development of this project was supported by a research fellowship from the National Endowment for the Humanities; by a Humanities Writ Large Visiting Faculty Fellowship at Duke University, funded by the Andrew W. Mellon Foundation and hosted by Religious Studies and the Kenan Institute for Ethics; and by the dean of the faculty and the John D. MacArthur chair at Connecticut College. No words can express my deep gratitude for this support, which provided funds for the fieldwork and unencumbered time for writing the manuscript. At Duke I most gratefully acknowledge the kindness and support of Srinivas Aravamudan, Laura Eastwood, David Morgan, Noah Pickus, and Suzanne Shanahan.

My gratitude to the many devotees and priests who graciously accommodated my endless questions, sometimes for hours, has already been expressed to each individually, but I reiterate it here formally and for the collective.

Finally, I extend my enduring gratitude again to my editor, Cynthia Read, especially for her kindness, guidance, solidarity, and remarkable efficiency.

Señor del Rayo

First you notice the floor, its tired beauty, an aisle eroded by centuries of need. The stones are veined in shapes that seem meaningful if badly enough you need some meaning. An abused maroon, footworn and dulled, a deep black fading toward its fate. The chapel is solemn, even somber. A life-size crucified Christ presides; the muscles in the arms look twisted. People come and go, mostly women, some peaceful and prayerful, maintaining relations, and others agitated and working through petitions. Everyone is comfortable, feels at home, knows what to do. A man moves a few pews closer to the altar; a woman leans forward, into the prayer; a baby coos between sips through a straw. The world outside muffles through the wall: traffic, voices, "All By Myself" interrupted by a hawker with a mic. No one seems to notice. The chapel's silence pushes back, insulates a sense of closure. A silence too heavy to hover, like a dense fog, oppressive, a silence that spreads itself out between the bare walls, over the pews, that cushions the noise to a mute bass background, a tonal prelude for prayer and song. Every once in a while you hear a coin drop. Metal on metal, the deep clunk after the fall.

Lourdes, the president of the Señor del Rayo devotional association, said people find peace and tranquility in the chapel. One can see that on many faces: meditation, absorption, relaxation. Other devotees come with urgent purpose and their demeanor is far from tranquil. A woman in the first pew is pleading aloud and finally she stands up and gestures, paces, overwhelms the chapel's dulled visuals with her wild gray hair half-tamed in a ponytail that swings a beat behind her bright blue dress. She kneels at the altar, stands up, paces, kneels again, lifts her arms, pleads, cries, recomposes, and cries again while praying. The whole body is involved. Her anguish is apparent. It takes a while to finish. And the spectacle seems double directional, addressed forward to the Señor del Rayo—who remained stoically indifferent, like a statue—and backward to the audience in the pews.

Emilia's devotion was also emotional and corporal, but without the the-atrics. She had come from her village with her daughter, Rebecca, who remained in a pew, to pray at the altar in her native language, Zapotec. Emilia began visiting the chapel in 2010 because her son, undocumented in the United States, was struggling to survive economically. With help from the Señor del Rayo the son's earnings eventually improved enough to build a modest house for the family, so Emilia and Rebecca return peri-odically to give thanks and to renew their bond with the miraculous image that provides for and protects them.

Luz, also an indigenous devotee, stressed the happiness one feels when miracles mitigate the uncertainties of subsistence. A gift from God, she explained, "is when you're asking for a crop you're going to plant, that you're given the harvest, that you don't lose it, so you get happy because you're given the fruit of what you've planted, no? And you're happy, it's a gift, the whole family has something to eat. You get happy. God gave us what we asked for." In matters of health, miracles are valued in themselves but also because they supplement or substitute unaffordable health care. "You keep spending money that you don't have," Luz explained, "and you're trying to find the money and taking the drugs. And if you don't get better you have to pay back whoever lent you the money and are even

Luz, on the right, with family members. "You get happy."

poorer and sadder, and you're still sick." With a miracle, conversely, "you're cured, you're happy, you're cured with a little money."[1]

Lourdes stressed how miracles take time, how an initial nonresponse to a petition is a call to perseverance. Her devotion to the Señor del Rayo began in earnest when she had a problem several years ago. "I came a lot and would say to him, 'Help me, Lord,' but at first he didn't grant me the miracle." The problem got worse, and Lourdes, confused, would ask, "Why don't you listen, why don't you help me, why don't you grant me the miracle?" Then she came to understand that a miracle is a process, not an instantaneous remedy, and that patience is integral to faith. "With time I realized that He does listen, that his powerful hand touches you little by little, little by little, until your miracle is completed." As an example Lourdes explained that she was unable to get pregnant and repeatedly asked the Señor del Rayo for children, until finally the miracle was granted. "I got married when I was sixteen and had my son when I was thirty-four."

More recently, in 2010, Lourdes felt "on the verge of a stroke and heart attack." Her position as the president of the devotional association affords intimate access to the Señor del Rayo, and, consequently, more expeditious

Lourdes, president of the Señor del Rayo devotional association.

results. Every year on October 21 the cathedral pillars are adorned with flowers—"it looks like paradise"—and the Señor del Rayo is moved from his chapel to the cathedral's main altar for high mass on October 23. "He's carried by men who have a lot of faith in him, who are in pain, who have cancer," and whose ailments improve through contact with this sacred power. Lourdes is present too, and on one occasion, while fearing the stroke and heart attack, she took the opportunity to make her petition: "I whispered in his ear and he cured me. I also had vertigo and he cured that too."

In many cases miracles provide a solution when there is nowhere else to turn, when desperation becomes so intense that it alchemizes into the faith that makes miracles happen. I met Margarita while she was mopping in the Chapel of the Holy Sacrament. She carried herself with a heavy sadness that seemed to radiate down her arms, into the mop, and over the floor that held hidden meaning if badly enough you needed some meaning. That heaviness was compounded by the specific gravity of her fatigue. "Thirteen years ago my husband left me with three children, one twelve, one six, and one five months old. He went to the United States, got married to another woman, and didn't send me a single peso." Margarita struggled through hard times. She was unable to find work, unable to support the children—"how could I feed them, how could I dress them?"—and succumbed finally to hopelessness, resentment, bitterness, and defeat. "I was desperate and wanted to take it out on the children, beating them, hitting them a lot because of their father, because I was alone and hurting, because I felt desperate." She wanted to flee, to escape, "to go far away," but there was nowhere to go, no money for flight, and Margarita was trapped together with her hopelessness and rage and three hungry children.

That's when she gravitated toward an exit as extreme as it was absolute: "to kill myself and my children, that's what I had in my head." She had gotten the idea from a murder-suicide reported in the news. I asked Margarita why she would kill the children too and not just herself, and she explained, "Because at the same time I thought and said to myself, 'How am I going to kill myself and leave my children alone?' No. I thought I'd take them with me and we'd go together." The plan to murder the children, however misguided and horrible objectively, was Margarita's expression of desperate maternal protection, a liberation from crisis as a family. She would not abandon the children as her husband had abandoned them earlier.

Margarita. "I'm O.K. now, I made it."

Margarita went to the church in her village, confided her plan to a woman there, and was advised to visit the Señor del Rayo. Devotion thus began as a search for relief from desperation and its dreadful impending consequences. The miracle that Margarita requested and received, employment, resolved the family's immediate crisis but also resulted in knowledge and solidarity that alleviated Margarita's alienation. "I asked God to help me, and what he helped a lot with was getting out to work. Getting out to work, because I met women who are alone like me and I never knew it because I had never gone out to work. So I would go to work and people would ask me why I was crying and they said to me, 'Listen, Señora, you're not the first or the last woman to be left. Look at us here, we're all widows and abandoned women, and you see how we keep going and are moving forward? You have to keep on going.'"

So Margarita got work, met people, and found her way. At first she made and sold tortillas—"my father helped me with corn, helped me with firewood"—and her brother in the United States helped with modest support. Later Margarita got her current job, cleaning in Oaxaca's cathedral, and is never far from the Señor del Rayo who saved her. Thirteen years have passed since the husband abandoned the family, the children are grown (I met the oldest daughter, who seemed close to her mother), and Margarita says, "I'm O.K. now, I made it. But I suffered a lot."

According to tradition, a ship sailed from Spain with a statue of the crucified Christ destined for Oaxaca (then called Antequera), but was blown off course. The ship landed at a remote location rather than at the port in Veracruz, and the image never reached its destination because it was intercepted by local natives who had converted to Catholicism. (This image is now venerated in Otatitlán.) The king and queen of Spain, informed of this confiscation and duly concerned, sent another image of the crucified Christ, which arrived safely in Oaxaca around 1550. Construction of the cathedral began a few years later. The image was situated on the altar early in the cathedral's development, when the walls were bare adobe and the roof was straw. On one occasion a bolt of lightning struck the roof and ignited a fire that destroyed the cathedral's interior, but the Christ image "was respected by the fire" and miraculously remained intact. Thus the Señor del Rayo (literally, Lord of the Lightning Bolt) acquired his name.[2]

Today the Señor del Rayo's chapel, the last on the left in Oaxaca's cathedral, has decorative columns, gilded woodwork, painted biblical scenes, and, as its centerpiece, the crucified Christ on a gold cross, in a glass case, and backed with red cloth displaying votive hearts. A statue of the Virgin is beside the Señor del Rayo and floral arrangements color the foreground.

On the twenty-third day of each month the image's waistcloth is changed with the greatest deference and solemnity. When I witnessed this changing, Lourdes's husband and another man carefully moved the flowers aside and slid the glass door open, revealing the Señor del Rayo to gathered devotees. The mood in the chapel approached awe. One man looked on with a face completely abandoned to astonishment, as though he were witnessing something impossible. The waistcloth was changed with a gentleness of gesture that indexed deep respect and devotion. One waistcloth or the other shielded the image so that its nakedness was never visible. Afterward the waistcloth that had absorbed sacred power over the course of a month was ceremoniously displayed on a table before the altar. A line formed up the aisle and devotees approached to touch, to kiss, to rub themselves against the cloth while acoustic guitars lifted the emotion to a higher register and then another when the voices came in with a naïve beauty so moving and sincere that even the wooden pews seemed to soften. Those harmonies going up to God went sideways too and cohered us as a group. Some people lined up again to have another pass at the waistcloth; an older couple holding hands began to cry. Eventually, after the waistcloth had been taken away and the music had stopped, it felt like something was wrong in the world, an emptiness, as though someone had drained the mood from the building.

"The music really enhances...," I said to Lourdes, and was going to finish the sentence with "emotion," but she filled the blank first with "faith." Through emotion the music enhances faith and creates a sense of sacred presence. "I know the Lord is here," Lourdes said, "listening to what I am asking for." What we were feeling and believing was cued by music in context, resonating in the chamber of that chapel, and the ambient tone also cued the pitch of our voices, the pace of our step, the gentleness and measure of our gestures. Through the music we accessed emotions that we couldn't get to on our own.

At morning mass the guitarists, the packed pews, and the charismatic priest imbue the chapel with an upbeat mood unlike the somberness of petitionary devotion at other times. The crowd feels different too; more men and children, families. Expectation builds as mass time approaches. The sacristan checks the mic, lights the candles, and eventually the mostly retired Father Ernesto arrives, walks up the aisle to the altar, and wrestles into an over-the-head white robe as a guitarist sets the mood. Most of the mass is music and most of the music is joyful. The regular guitarist standing at the back of the chapel is accompanied by teenage volunteers in the pews. Father Ernesto is a pleasure to watch as he masterfully orchestrates the mass, pointing now to the guitarists who miss their cue, now to the nervous first-communionist, holding a candle, so that she'll takes her place on the altar. He pivots her body to the appropriate angle, about forty-five degrees, then leads a song with his hands lifted heavenward at an odd angle, the torso tilted, as though God were in a particular area of the sky.

I had come to mass with the hope of interviewing Father Ernesto afterward. During the service, however, something took hold of my emotions, a slow accumulation that I couldn't control, until finally I was overwhelmed by all of the humility and honesty and vulnerability and need, the choral voices and innocent faces and O-shaped mouths, the bad guitar chords and the nervous, composed girl trying to hold the candle right, timid in her wedding dress, with God inside her body, drinking the blood from that chalice. I was overwhelmed and envious of these people completely absorbed in faith, completely invested in their belief that something is sacred, that something transcends the habituated pettiness that in my world is sacralized so that we have, at least, a contrived sense of meaning, contrived like this meaning but less moving, less miraculous. I felt completely depleted, as though everything had drained away until there was nothing left but an emotion stronger than my ability to control it and a sense of being pathetic and condemned to absurdity and broken because I couldn't invent something to believe in. It was like an epiphany, except it happened in my emotions. I struggled for composure while Father Ernesto cleaned out the chalice and everyone else was praying.

After mass Father Ernesto came up the aisle with the overturned lid of a doughnut box to collect contributions for the musicians. As he made his way he greeted and blessed people, rubbing the earlobes of women—a form of *limpia* or ritual cleansing—as they conversed. Most of the collected money, including all of the bills, was given to the regular guitarist; the teenagers shared the coins. I feared that Father Ernesto would leave when he reached the back of the chapel—Margarita had told me that he departs right after mass—so I approached, shook his hand, explained my business, and asked if we could meet when he was free. He nodded and directed me toward the altar. The chapel was still half full, even though the mass had ended some ten minutes earlier. The communion girl, her parents, and some others were standing on the altar. I sat in the second row of pews, beside some of the guitarists, and was relieved to have time to compose myself while Father Ernesto attended to those awaiting him.

A moment later, however, Father Ernesto called me onto the altar. That seemed strange; I thought we would talk when he had finished with his obligations. He asked me to repeat what I wanted, indicating with a finger that he didn't hear well. I got close to his ear and explained my purpose but not too loudly; I was self-conscious about my intrusion. The communion girl's father was standing nearby, and some others, drawn by curiosity, were on approach and closing the gap.

Then, inexplicably, Father Ernesto put his hand on my shoulder and pulled me in closer to the ear, saying he would take my confession. I couldn't make sense of what was happening. Everything was moving too quickly. "Tell me your sins," he was saying, but I wouldn't know where to begin with sins, or if I had sins, or if it was all a sin. All I wanted was an interview. I remembered that as a boy I invented sins for confession, then added one to the count of lies. Father Ernesto was waiting for an answer, the others on the altar were waiting for an answer, Christ was bleeding so patiently behind us, and I was stunned mute and didn't know what to do.

I had the idea—completely incorrect—that Father Ernesto wanted to exchange an interview for bringing me back to the church, so into that ear that seemed too big, that seemed imposing enough to make demands of its own, my mouth delivered the awkward phrase, "Let's talk later." Father

Ernesto nodded, as though in agreement, and I was relieved. A reprieve. But then he pulled me in again by the shoulder, hugging me close, for an unexpected, unearned, unorthodox absolution: "I forgive all of your sins, past, present, and future. You can eat the body of Christ in any church in the world."

Afterward I wandered dazed through the streets of Oaxaca, trying to walk off the mood of the mass and my strange exchange with Father Ernesto. In some sense I had shared in a devotion that rocked the vacuous pretense of my world, but at the same time I was an impostor, a spy, the undercover infiltrator who had no faith in miraculous images or in anything, really, not even pious surrender or the absolution that Father Ernesto had so generously—so mysteriously—granted.

"Without faith in something life has no meaning," Mayuela later told me, and Miguel said, "if you lose faith you don't have anything." So there I was: no meaning and no anything, doomed to the empty routine of disbelief. But the feeling was strong, and I wondered if devotees were drawn back to church less by the meaning than the feeling of devotion, the woeful joy, the solemn serenity, the gentle sense of solace that carries implicit significance. The meaning comes through feeling, in the same way that the miracle comes through faith. It must be something like a novel or film that summons you back, that draws you toward it not with the pull of its content—you've forgotten that—but rather with a lingering feeling that you've lost and want to regain. You go back for the feeling, you re-enter through the mood, and once inside you rediscover that you love the plot and characters too.[3]

Miraculous Images

Ambiguity

Statues and paintings like the Señor del Rayo, the Virgen de Guadalupe, the Señor de Chalma, and countless others in Mexican churches are miraculous by virtue of a sacred presence that empowers them. They belong to a long tradition of empowered objects that spans centuries of pre-Christian and Christian devotion on both sides of the Atlantic and that encompasses objects as disparate as indigenous fetishes and the consecrated eucharist. Medieval bone relics are a notable precedent; like miraculous images today, they maintained ambiguous relations between an object on earth and a sacred figure in heaven. An inscription on the tomb of St. Martin of Tours is characteristic: Martin's soul is with God, "but he is entirely here, present and manifest in all the grace of his virtues." Relics concentrated sacred power and made it accessible to human purposes; today miraculous images do the same.[1]

Sacred presence is interpreted literally in popular devotion, to the degree that relics "*were* the saints, continuing to live among their people." The theology of relics (like that of the eucharist) provided that the whole was present in any part, which in turn resulted in proliferations as the distributed body parts acquired independent cults in separate regions. An arm bone was the saint in one town and a leg bone was the saint in another. The cult of relics thereby anticipated the local, multiple, sometimes competing image devotions that are so common in Mexico today. A prototype Christ or Virgin is usually in the background, but in the foreground are discrete images that are entities—almost deities—in themselves. Relics and images are associated with a heavenly person but also dissociated insofar as the connection is distended and the sacred object becomes more or less autonomous. Petitions and votive offerings are made not to the heavenly Christ or Virgin, but rather to a local Christ or Virgin, the one among and for the people of a particular place.[2]

This tendency toward local and petitionary devotion is also indebted
to religious conquest and the syncretic adaptations that it initiates. The
sequence repeats in changing contexts: In early medieval European Catholicism forbidden pagan deities were replaced by relic-based sacred presences, and in postconquest Mexican Catholicism forbidden indigenous
deities were replaced by image-based sacred presences. In both cases the
catechism may have been largely unintelligible to new converts, but Christianity was nevertheless amenable insofar as it provided a substitute supernatural power source adaptable to immediate needs.[3]

The transition from relic to miraculous image was sometimes mediated by reliquaries that took human form. The reliquary of Sainte Foy, a
late tenth-century image at the Cluniac monastery in Conques, is a great
example. The skull of Sainte Foy was housed in the head of an enthroned,
gold-gilded, bejeweled statuette. The statuette's lifelike eyes facilitated the
belief among monks and lay devotees that Sainte Foy was present, vigilant,
and receptive to petitions. The relic empowered the statuette, the statuette's human attributes contributed a sense of presence, and the two—
relic and statuette—interacted and mutually enhanced one another until
ultimately they fused into a composite.[4]

Such integration of relics and images continues today when bone fragments are used to authenticate or empower a given statue. In Mexico
City's cathedral, for example, a disturbing image of the dead St. Felicitas is
displayed in a glass coffin. The statue is opened at the chest and the left
forearm to reveal the bone relics inserted there. Red paint gives the impression of blood around a wound in the forearm, as though the statue
were a real corpse cut to reveal the miraculous bone inside. The statue thus
serves as a reliquary, while from the opposite direction the integration of
bones into their lifelike (or deathlike) body authenticates and empowers
the statue. The sacred essence of most images is invisible and presumed,
like the soul in a body, but through these x-ray apertures devotees see the
power source that guarantees this statue's miraculous potential.

Eventually medieval statues and paintings acquired an independent
claim to sacred presence and power, thereby achieving a status that previously had been restricted to relics. Images, like relics, became "the highly
actual presence of a saint." Works of art enhanced the sense of a living
sacred presence in ways that bone relics could not. These included resemblance (however contrived) with the depicted heavenly figure, representation of emotional and physical states (suffering, mourning, affection,

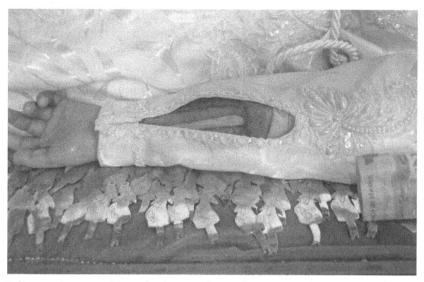

Relics are integrated into the image of St. Felicitas in Mexico City's cathedral. The milagritos in the foreground indicate a specialization in pregnancy and childbirth.

ecstasy), implicit or explicit narrative, and the capacity to elicit the emotion, empathy, and devotional engagement of viewers.[5]

The most conspicuous predecessors of miraculous images as we know them today are the icons of Byzantium (the Christian, East Roman empire governed from Constantinople between 330 and 1435). These paintings of holy figures (Christ, the Virgin) were "the visible images of invisible presences" through which God's graces were made manifest in this world. Icons were divine imprints on matter and, accordingly, were imbued with sacred presence and power that one could experience sensually. These attributes were unique to specific images and not distributed equally even among sacred icons themselves, and consequently those images that evidenced (through miracles) high spiritual concentrations attracted huge cults and massive pilgrimages. The same is true of miraculous images in Mexico today.[6]

Throughout the ages devotees and especially votaries have sought immediacy, simplicity, and unmediated sensual access to material objects of devotion. When these objects are paintings and statues, the distinction between the image in the church and the prototype in heaven tends to break down and yield finally to devotion to the images themselves. This is most explicit in petitionary devotion when miracle petitions and votive offerings are directed specifically to an image, not to the heavenly figure that it ostensibly represents. Theologians across the centuries have expressed their concern with this tendency: "some more learned people can avoid worshipping the images themselves and can venerate that to which they refer. But for the ignorant they constitute a scandal, for they worship only what they see"; "there are many simple folk also in our day who make no distinction in their prayers between the images of saints and the saints themselves"; and "when images are put up the customs of pagans do the rest."[7]

Such concerns contributed to the iconoclast controversy of 730 to 843. The iconoclasts (those who advocated the elimination of imagery from churches) maintained that images are powerless, that there is no spirit dwelling in their matter, and consequently that images "are not to be worshiped because they have allegedly performed signs or miracles." The iconoclasts also argued that to paint an image of Christ was to circumscribe (confine) God's infinite, immaterial divinity.[8]

The iconophiles (those who advocated the inclusion of imagery in churches, also known as iconodules) argued in reply that divinity had circumscribed itself when spirit united with matter, the Word became flesh, and the invisible God became visible in Christ. This argument was championed early in the debate by the first theologian of images, St. John of Damascus (circa 690–750), who bridged from the incarnation to a justification of sacred imagery. "I do not worship matter; I worship the Creator of matter who became matter for my sake, who willed to take His abode in matter; who worked out my salvation in matter," John wrote. "You, who refuse to worship images, would not worship the Son of God, the Living Image of the invisible God, and His unchanging form."[9]

John then pursued this argument into the prohibition of imagery in Exodus 20:4–5: "You shall not make for yourself an idol or a likeness of anything." He did so by following a Pauline concept developed in Galatians 3, which argued that "we were held in custody under law" until Christ came, and then were liberated by faith. Old Testament laws kept order until they were superseded; they were interim injunctions against false similitudes until the true one, the Word incarnate, established the precedent for subsequent imagery. "God himself had suspended his own commandment by 'violating' it—or, to put it not only more reverently but also more precisely, by fulfilling it—when he provided a genuine icon of himself in the history of Christ, an icon of which it was now legitimate to make an icon in turn." When John of Damascus rhetorically asks "Who first made an icon?" his ready answer is that God himself was the first to do so: "In the beginning He who is God begot His only Son, His Word, the living image of Himself, the natural and precisely similar likeness of His eternity." God became human and therefore representable, providing a precedent and protocol for later images that would emulate the incarnation as spiritual presence integrated into the material world. Pagan idols could not claim this authentication; they depicted gods who had no prototype to justify their representation. There was nothing behind them.[10]

John's argument is careful to distinguish between prototype and copy—"The image is one thing, the person represented another"—with devotion proper only to the prototype. His use of the incarnation as justification for image-making, however, extended the union of spirit and matter to icons, thereby implying their sacred presence and power. Later iconophile theologians ultimately responded to iconoclast challenges by repairing to a more modest, nonessentialist theory of the icon. The prototype in heaven and the image on earth are united in form or appearance, they argued, but not in essence. The icon is the likeness, not the presence, of its prototype.[11]

Following a period of iconoclasm and then the Synod of Hiereia (754), which forbade the use of holy images, the Second Council of Nicea (787) restored imagery to Catholic churches and ritual. The use of holy images was permitted and indeed encouraged "to remember and long for those who serve as models," with the caveat that the veneration is proper only to the person represented, not to the representation itself. In 1563 the Council of Trent (1545–1563) reaffirmed and clarified this position: images should be revered in churches, "not because some divinity or power is believed to lie in them as reason for the cult, or because anything is to be expected from them, or because confidence should be placed in the images as was done by the pagans of old; but because the honour showed to them is referred to the original which they represent." This position is still current in the Catholic catechism today: "The image is not venerated in itself, but rather for what it represents."[12]

In Byzantium as in Mexico today, however, practice diverts from theory. Despite centuries of theological debate, dogma, and catechesis, devotees remain firm in their conviction that certain images are imbued with sacred presence and have the power, volition, and independent agency to perform miracles. These beliefs are tenable and endure in Mexico because devotees are not attuned to or restricted by theological nuance; because forced conversion and later inculturation were conducive to syncretism;

because devotion to images has been instituted by tradition and habituated by common practice; because images are the founding principles (as
relics were earlier) of churches, shrines, and basilicas; and because devotion is primarily petitionary, which is to say motivated more by management of hardships and compensatory satisfaction of worldly needs than
by salvation of the soul after death.[13]

It is also occurs because devotees receive mixed messages from priests,
who in turn receive a cloudy theological mandate. John of Damascus distinguished clearly between prototype and image, but at once situated one
inside the other: "An image is a likeness and representation of some one,
containing in itself the person who is imaged." He argued that "the honor
given to an image is given to the one portrayed in the image," but the
honor is still given to the image. The same inherent ambiguity is maintained in current Catholic teachings: "the image is not venerated for itself,
but rather for what it represents," but the image is still venerated. Along
the same lines, the Council of Trent permitted and indeed encouraged the
use of holy images "to remember and long for those who serve as models,"
with the caveat that veneration is proper only to the person represented,
not to the representation itself. The lingering ambiguity of presence is
nevertheless maintained: "The honour paid to an image traverses it, reaching the model; and he who venerates the image, venerates the person represented in that image."[14]

The Trent decrees and current doctrine situate image devotion at the
nuance where passionate devotional engagement with images (praying,
pleading, crying, expressing gratitude) is acceptable insofar as devotees
remain aware that the image is a visual aid for venerating sacred figures in
heaven. Abidance by such nuance is uncharacteristic of devotional practice, however, and were it not the passion of devotion before images would
be reduced to a form of improvised theater, a make-believe, an emotional
performance for a mannequin when prayer could venerate more authen-
tically. A prop recognized as such cannot inspire or accommodate emotional intensity; devotion wants its object to be real.

The same ambiguities obtain in pastoral practice. In their sermons
and private counseling priests instruct explicitly that Christ, the Virgin,
and the saints are not present in the images that represent them, that
images are not to be venerated in and of themselves, that petitions should
not be made to images, and that the power to perform miracles is exclusive to God. After this dutiful message discipline, however, informal discourse and everyday devotion reveal that many priests accommodate the

realities of inculturated devotion and to varying degrees share its beliefs. Fray Hugo, a Franciscan affiliated with the shrine of the Virgen del Pueblito, is characteristic. He catechizes against inappropriate devotion to images, but also explains that "God chooses and manifests his grace through certain images, not all of them." Images are not miraculous, except some are. For Fray Hugo and many other priests, the power is not inherent to the image but rather "God spreads his grace through images" that he has chosen for this purpose. The images are identifiable by their miracles but also by animations of their lifelessness and expressions of emotion, so that human and supernatural attributes coalesce with matter to consolidate a compound identity.[15]

The belief in supernaturally invested images is reinforced by ritual care that seems more appropriate to a sacred presence than to a work of art intended as a visual aid. The lavish rituals of procession, fiestas, and everyday glorifications (candles, flowers, vestments) contradict the discourse that limits images to the status of reminders. The ceremonial pomp of clergy in priestly garments and devotional deference to the tiny, dressed-up, doll-like Virgins of Remedios, Zapopan, or Juquila, for example, is completely ridiculous unless the image itself is sacred. The same point is illustrated in the extreme by papal coronations. On October 17, 1946, the bishop in Querétaro, as mandated by a papal brief and acting as the pope's delegate, solemnly coronated the Virgen del Pueblito. Many other images were also coronated by papal mandate: the Virgen de San Juan de los Lagos in 1904; the Virgen de la Soledad in 1909 and again on its fiftieth anniversary (the 1959 crown was stolen in 1991); the Virgen de Zapopan in 1921; the Virgen de Talpa in 1923; the Virgen de Izamal in 1993; and the Virgen de Juquila in 2014. Less sensational but more compelling is the simple fact that shrines and basilicas are founded on miraculous images themselves, thereby establishing a sacred material presence with a tenuous relation to its heavenly prototype.[16]

For all of these reasons, popular devotion resists the distinction between a statue or painting and the heavenly figure that it represents. When I asked Father Juan Manuel, the former rector of the Virgen de Soriano basilica, to what degree devotees distinguish between the statue in the church and the Virgin in heaven, he gave a common and unambiguous response: "They don't distinguish." But nor do they equate. There is a range of belief regarding the relation between a miraculous Virgin image in a church and the Virgin in heaven, but generally the image acquires an identity that is derived from but independent of the heavenly Virgin.

A local, inculturated idea of the Virgin provides an essence and a core of attributes that endow the variations—the Virgen de Talpa, de Zapopan, de Tonatico—with authenticity and legitimacy, but these variations are autonomous miraculous entities in and of themselves. The image on earth and the prototype in heaven form a composite something like a ragged duet, an inexact overlap of separate, identifiable components that by their very dissonance enrich one another. The heavenly Virgin hovers in ambiguous relation to her representations, thereby generating the mystery, intrigue, and tension of an absence whose presence is suggested. The referent is and must remain cloudy, because the power of this ambiguity, like any other, is in its unresolved potential and the dynamic interaction of its possibilities.

On September 8, 1556, a Franciscan friar named Francisco de Bustamante gave a sermon in Mexico City to discourage devotion to the Virgen de Guadalupe. He argued that indigenous converts had been instructed to venerate only what images represented, not the images themselves, and that now the Indians were being confused and their faith was being misguided by church reports that the Virgen de Guadalupe was performing miracles. Bustamante tried quite unsuccessfully to advocate precisely what Catholic doctrine required: that devotion be directed away from the image and toward the Virgin and God in heaven. Nearly five hundred years later miraculous images—and especially the Virgen de Guadalupe—are so deeply institutionalized and so integral to everyday devotion in Mexico that any theological challenges are easily overwhelmed. When we say that the Virgen de Guadalupe is the Patroness of the Americas, as designated by Pope Pius XII in 1946, we forget that the Virgen de Guadalupe is a painting.[17]

Attributes

The sacred presence and power of miraculous images are expressed through a complex of attributes that signal aliveness, humanness, and personhood. Among these attributes are emotion, cognition, volition, intentionality, agency, subjectivity, perspective, desires, values, preferences, corporal vitality and animation, and the need for recognition and care. Miraculous images also have less admirable human qualities—vengeance, jealousy, wrath—and human limitations, such as exhaustion. They are susceptible to flattery, bribes, and enticements. And they get overcommitted:

"I know that you must be very busy," a votary wrote to the Santo Niño de Atocha.[18]

The human attributes create an approachable, like-us, individualizable source of sacred power. Each devotee has the sense of a personal relationship with this construct. The blank stare looks at no one in particular; it might as well be you. At the same time, humanizing the image fulfills the greater, counterintuitive purpose of establishing the nonhumanity, the superhumanity of the image, because the aliveness of inert matter is perceived as evidence of sacred presence. The miraculous image becomes another social person among the community of people who create it, but a specially endowed superperson. Devotees confer upon the image-person a status that is sacred and greater than their own, and consequently they satisfy their needs through petitions but also feel guilt and fear before their own creation when they transgress or fail to fulfill votive promises. In one perspective they have created an empowered, capable patron amenable to remedying their problems, and in another they are subordinate to, indebted to, and fearful of their own creation.[19]

Once the image's human identity has been established, the maintenance of attributes occurs on two fronts: the actions of the image itself, and the perceptions and comportment that the image receives from devotees. The two fronts collapse into one and the same insofar as the image's actions are attributed. When I asked Adriana if the Señor de Chalma expressed emotions, she replied, "sometimes he seems light and sometimes he seems dark. I came here about three months ago and he looked coffee-colored." On another visit "he looked sort of black," and "sometimes he looks light, transparent." Do these complexion changes indicate changes in his emotions? Pause. "I think it also depends on us." Pause. "I'd say that my emotions are the ones that keep changing."[20]

The intermixing of emotions, facial expression, and changing complexion is common. "A person devoid of emotion is considered 'lifeless,' unable to make human connections, and superficial," so visual changes in an image's countenance at once enliven it and make it sentient and socially interactive. Colonial texts are particularly nuanced in perceptions of physiognomy. The Virgen de los Remedios "does not always have the same expression, like a living person." Her face is "sometimes pale, others white, occasionally flushed, often cheerful and smiling, and not infrequently sad with pity"; "and it seems to me, if I am not deceiving myself, that it is true. I especially noticed it the night that we carried the Holy Image to her house this year, 1616, when the Indians were offering her flowers and incense. The Virgin wore a face so pleasant and cheerful that I looked at it many times." On a wall at the Virgen de los Remedios basilica today a brief, illustrated history describes the Virgin's changing expressions as "majestic and noble, angry and terrible, kind and understanding, smiling and cheerful." The image's emotions are responsive, for better or for worse, to devotee behavior, and the pleasure or displeasure registered on the face is also communicated through allotment of miracles or punishment.[21]

Much the same is said of the Virgen del Pueblito. In the mid-seventeenth century "they saw her cry many times," and at other times "her eyes were very fiery and her face so terrible that more than reverence it caused horror and fear in those who looked at her. On twenty-two occasions they saw her sweat so copiously that it soaked the cloths used to clean her." Fray Hugo was close to the Virgen del Pueblito for six years and described how she closes her eyes, sometimes seems angry, and has a changing complexion that gets darker or redder. These animations and expressions of emotion are formalized—historicized—in prayers published in a devotional booklet distributed at the Virgen del Pueblito shrine.[22]

Vitality is also suggested by other corporal qualities. Many devotees report that the hair of Christ and Virgin images is growing (some sacristans attribute the change to a periodic rotation of wigs). Gabriela, who tends the store at the shrine in Tepatitlán, enthusiastically described the Señor de la Misericordia as alive, "like a person," with eyes that open and close and also a tongue, both of which she thinks might be human. She also thought of the skull as a bone relic. The aliveness of other images, including the Señor del Sacromonte in Amecameca, is theatrically enhanced by articulated limbs. In Atlatlahucan there are two articulated Christs, one the Cristo de las Tres Caídas—"of the three falls," which during reenactments are skillfully choreographed with hidden ropes—and the other one entombed. When the dead Christ is removed from his coffin, "he is carried like a person, putting one arm under his neck and the other under the bent knees; carried in this way, the head falls backward and the arms dangle uncontrollably, in an impressive realism."[23]

This mobilization of compounded lifelessness—once because the image is an image, and again because it represents a death—is also suggested when crucified Christs change position. The changes generally concern the head. Marta, who tends to visitors in an office beside the votive offerings at Chalma, said that the Señor de Chalma's head has fallen, so that his beard is now pressed against his chest. "Pilgrims tell me that he doesn't look good," she said, and added that the head lowered gradually over a period of time. Some devotees attribute fallen heads to the heavy load of petitions and sorrows and problems that the image has to bear. As Matthew 8:17 has it, "He took away our infirmities and bore our diseases." One woman said the Señor de Chalma's head was bowing "because of our sins," and added, "he's sad, crying." In Otatitlán, the Cristo Negro's head falls due to the heavy load of votary hardships during pilgrimages but subsequently recovers.

In other cases an image's head moves upward, usually in relation to its gaze. The Cristo de las Tres Caídas in San Andrés Teotilalpam "used to look downward," Karina said, "but suddenly he looked upward." Other images make similar adjustments to better see—watch over—their devotees. The Virgen de Tonatico, conversely, broke visual contact, but in order to look heavenward for the benefit of devotees. "Her eyes, which used to look at the floor, toward where her devotees were, turned so that she was looking at the sky. In this way the image sealed its pact with men, by showing them its intercessory role before the Most High."[24]

In previous centuries the ambience of candlelit and lamplit churches contributed to the sense that images were alive. Flickering candlelight before images otherwise enveloped in darkness created a sense of movement, as did the wavering heatrise from the candles and the flame disruptions caused by devotee approach, movement, and breathing. Today most images are out of range and sometimes protected behind even bombproof plexiglass, but the ambience still contributes to a sensuous experience that can be conducive to perceptions of aliveness and movement. Flowers, incense, music, oral prayer, crying, the crush of the crowd, the sacred architecture, the aura of holiness, and the exhausted exhilaration after pilgrimage all make their contributions.[25]

A precedent for image movements, and for aliveness generally, is established by myths of origin and by stories of deteriorated images that self-renovate miraculously. The Virgen de Talpa was originally made of *pasta de caña* (cornstalk paste) but in 1644 transubstantiated to wood. Miraculous renovation is also attributed to the Señor de Tila in Chiapas, the Cristo de Ixmiquilpan, the Virgen de San Juan de los Lagos, and the Virgen del Rayo, among others.[26]

An exceptional renovation narrative published in 1699 begins with a statue of the crucified Christ, subsequently known as the Cristo Renovado (Renovated Christ), in a lamentable state of decomposition, "lacking a mouth, nose, and eyes, so that only the beard remained, in which mice were nesting in a hole at the top." The archbishop ordered the image's dis-assembly and burial with the next deceased Christian. The order was not carried out, however, and for the next years "on many nights loud moans were heard in the Church," together with music, sighs, sobs, and banging. At one point, "the Holy Image, old and destroyed as it was, detached from the Cross, left the Church by itself through the air, and following behind it was the Holy Cross separately and at a distance of more than twelve feet." Later, "they saw that the Holy Image was returning in the air back-ward and the Holy Cross in the same way, until reaching the place where it was, nailing itself again in the same place." Then, on May 19, 1621, the vicar, while praying the rosary, heard a lament that brought him to tears, together with "such great knocks and moans that it seemed like the church would be knocked down." Finally the image began to perspire so copiously that sweat ran on the floor, and the priests who investigated this myste-rious phenomenon discovered to their surprise that the image had mirac-ulously renovated, with "the Head whole and sound," and "the whole Holy Face and Body so radiant that they seemed like a mirror, and the Eyes open."[27]

The dual nature of miraculous images as human and superhuman is also registered in expressions—and sometimes enforcements—of volition. Images interact willfully and intelligently with their social world. They communicate silently but sometimes insistently through signs and infer-ence, and they impose their will when resisted. This is clearest when images decide where they wish to reside and which people they wish to favor with their graces. Many myths of origin describe images resisting transport to their intended destinations and choosing instead to reside among a given community. Today the members of that community are aware that they have been chosen. Authorities on earth may dismiss them for their insignificance, but a Christ or Virgin made a willful choice and sometimes detour to be among them, to sacralize their territory, and to offer patronage, protection, and the miracles that alleviate their suffering. Sometimes the site is chosen by apparition: the Virgen de Guadalupe is a clear example. Other images, such as the Virgen de Soledad in Oaxaca and the Virgen de Izamal in Yucatán, become too heavy to move from their chosen destinations. The Señor del Sacromonte, actually made of very light cornstalk paste, arrived by a lost mule that buckled under its burden when the image reached its chosen home in Amecameca.[28]

The Virgen de Tonatico's narrative is well developed in this regard. As related in a brochure distributed at the shrine, the image was originally on a domestic altar and was later moved to a local Franciscan church. The church was damaged by fire, repairs were made, and afterward the Virgen de Tonatico was returned to her place. Mysterious occurrences began shortly after. One day the image was found at the foot of the altar and another day outside the church, until finally it disappeared completely. "Everyone was very sad, until one day a shepherd who was watching over his sheep far from town saw with great surprise under a palo blanco tree the Image that all had searched for." The image was ceremoniously returned to the church, "but Our Lady no longer wanted to be in that place, and by dawn the next day was again under the palo blanco." The cycle repeated until finally the villagers understood that the Virgin had chosen her place beside the tree, so they built her a church there. "And so it was that people began to abandon their homes and they moved to this place founding a new TONATICO where it is currently located." All of this happened around 1650. From the shrine's bell tower today, on clear days, one can imagine the old town ruins in the distance.[29]

The same motif gains more nuanced expression when otherworldly artists are commissioned to make one image but instead make another. In the early seventeenth century a Yucatec priest hired one of these artists to sculpt an image of the Virgin of the Immaculate Conception. The artist locked himself in a room with no tools and by the next day had disappeared, leaving behind not a Virgin but rather the crucified Christ known as the Señor de las Ampollas, which is now in Mérida's cathedral. An almost identical story is told of the Cristo Negro de Otatitlán. The angelic artist sculpts not what a community has chosen, but rather a Christ who has chosen them.[30]

The personhood of images is often suggested indirectly by referring to the shrine as an image's house or home. In their native language Otomíes in central Mexico say that the image *lives* in the church, but the pew *is* in the church. While he was being beaten and feared for his life, a Purhépecha man pleaded, "Señor de Carácuaro, save me, help me, and I promise that I will go to see you there where you live." These ideas of residence are supported more generally by the common pilgrimage concept of paying the image a visit at his or her home, as though the image were a friend or relative living in a nearby or distant village. In reference to the Señor de Chalma one pilgrim said, "Just as I have a house where I live, this is where he lives." Common are phrases like "tomorrow I am going to visit the Virgen de Juquila." During research I visit shrines; devotees visit the person who lives there. The image receives the visit and the protocol is reciprocated when a traveling image, known as an *imagen peregrina*, leaves the shrine to visit devotees at their home churches.[31]

The comfortable familiarity between devotees and miraculous images replaces the unapproachable awe of deity with a "very colloquial coexistence," as Gaby put it. Devotion transforms images into social persons with stable but evolving identities and legitimates their participation in the social life of devotees. Such rapport is particularly useful in votive contexts, where petitions are addressed not to an indifferent outsider but rather to a trusted patron and confidant. Intimate conversations, loving nicknames, and a sense of solidarity establish bonds. Many devotees, especially women, think of an image, especially a Virgin, as their closest friend or a family intimate. "I want you to be my principal guest at my Wedding," one woman wrote to the Virgen del Pueblito. Some devotees think of an image as a member of the family. Among colonial Nahuas converted to Catholicism, "sacred images were not purely physical parts of a house complex; they were considered to be more like actual residents." The images had a dual status, "a tangible object as well as a sort of human being, another member of the family." In modern Chatino culture an image purchased for a home altar, once baptized by family members, is "ritually treated as if it were their child."[32]

The Virgin's motherhood is regarded literally in image-devotee relations when devotees consider and refer to a Virgin as their own mother. In a petition to the Virgen de Talpa for restored health of her father and sister, the votary described herself as "your daughter who loves you as my holy mother that you are. Mother of God and my mother." This perception affords a sense of intimacy but also implicitly obligates the image with the corresponding maternal responsibilities. In a textual petition to the Virgen del Pueblito one woman made a gently coercive request for employment and concluded emphatically with "YOU ARE MY MOTHER," almost to suggest that a favorable response were required by that relation. Respectful requests for commended care are more common: "you protect me as much as a real mother," as it is worded in a prayer to the Virgen de Tonatico. Others appeal to the Virgin's maternal understanding more generally; as a suffering mother herself she will understand. In a petition to the Virgen de Tonatico a woman dying of a terminal illness asked for more time "to take care of my two daughters because they are very young and can't take care of themselves mother and who will take care of them for me? Losing me would be a very very great blow." This mother-to-mother appeal asks for more time not for the votary herself but rather for continuity of responsible motherhood. A petition to the Virgin of Pueblito sounds the same note and concludes with a sense of comotherhood. The votary asks for help with an anticipated difficult childbirth, then promises, "if you give me the opportunity to have my son, on the day I leave the hospital I will come to you to deliver your son."[33]

The personhood of miraculous images is also developed when images are considered relatives among themselves. Many of the Christ images in Oaxaca, for example, are brothers. The Virgins of Talpa, Zapopan, and San Juan de los Lagos are sisters. Some images are twins, or one is the offspring of the other, or they are feuding rivals. Before pilgrimage to Otatitlán, pilgrims from one region visit the Virgen del Carmen in Catemaco to request permission to visit her son. During fiestas an image from one town is often brought to another so the two related images can hear mass together, and one of the original purposes of pilgrimages was precisely to transport the image from one town to another so the two images could enjoy a visit.[34]

Social relations between devotees and images are coterminous and interactive with social relations between images among themselves. Also operative in this same sphere are social relations between devotees that are to some degree defined and mediated by images. Miraculous images conform most literally to an "anthropological theory in which *persons* or 'social agents' are, in certain contexts, substituted for by *art objects*." Miraculous images are centerpieces that cohere and contribute to the identities of local, regional, and even national communities. They bring into contact people with common beliefs, needs, and purposes. Their presence enriches meanings, strengthens relationships, sets the agenda, establishes the tone, and defines the parameters. They have social roles, community rights and responsibilities, and a unitive function that consolidates natural and supernatural, sacred and profane, material and spiritual, civil and religious. Vertically they unite this world with the next and horizontally they unite communities. Bonds are formed with miraculous images through commended care and votive contracts, and with other devotees through oral tradition, votive offerings, and miracle narratives that relate the common story of crisis and resolution through a shared sacred resource available at times of need.[35]

Faith, Presence, and Power

Devotees hold varying views on why certain images are miraculous, but they all agree that faith—deep, sincere, even desperate faith—is required to receive a miracle. Karina, a Cuicateca from San Andrés Teotilalpam, said that the miraculous image there, the Señor de las Tres Caídas, grants all of the miracles requested by "people who have faith in him." If you have faith, "nothing is impossible." I pressed by asking why some people do not receive petitioned miracles, and she replied consistently, saying "Because they don't have faith. They don't come with faith. For lack of faith." The idea that miracles are contingent on and implemented through faith has clear biblical precedent in, for example, the story of the hemorrhaging woman in Mark 5:25–29. "If I but touch his clothes, I shall be cured," the woman said to herself, and with that faith she reached out. After she was cured Jesus located the miracle in her faith, not in his power. As the Amplified Bible has it, "your faith (your trust and confidence in Me, springing from faith in God) has restored you to health."

In the simplest understanding, faith is required to make one deserving of a miracle. Miraculous images think like humans, narcissistically: If you don't believe in me, why should I give a miracle to you? "It's like with people," Mayuela said, and Antonio developed the idea: "It's like with people. You have to express your faith by doing something for them, so that they do something for you." Miracles in this view are negotiated through reciprocity. The idea is clearest when informants use "devotion" rather than "faith" to explain the commodity exchanged for the miracle. One visits, prays, makes offerings, and makes sacrifices, and the miraculous image reciprocates with miracles. The devotional gestures must be sincere and cannot be feigned: "If you don't have faith in them, they know it."[36]

Faith and devotion are often intensified incrementally when a petitioned miracle is not granted. One must persevere (devotees use the verb *insistir*) and perhaps increase or enhance what is offered in exchange for a requested miracle. Marta related how her brother's vague faith evolved finally to "surrendering in body and soul to the Señor de Chalma." The brother wanted a child and his wife could not get pregnant, so after five years of trying the brother petitioned a miracle from the Señor de Chalma. "I want a child," the brother said, but without devotional conviction and commitment. The miracle was not granted. He tried again and the miracle was not granted. Marta continued: "'I'm requesting a miracle and not receiving it.' Five more years go by. Now that's ten. And nothing. He goes again and says—but no longer like it was with 'I want you to give me a child,' no—now inside him, from deep in his heart, he pleads, 'Oh, God, give me a child,'" until finally the miracle was granted. The brother's devotion increased in tandem with his desperation until the strength of the devotion, the power of the devotion, the "surrender in body and soul," were rewarded. Miracles are dependent on "dispositions of the heart," as worded on a banner in Nuestra Señora de Las Mercedes church in downtown Guadalajara; "it is not something magical or fast." Perseverance is critical. As the Amplified Bible expands Luke 11:9 to stress the point, "Ask and keep on asking and it shall be given you; seek and keep on seeking and you shall find; knock and keep on knocking and the door shall be opened to you."[37]

In more complex understandings, God endows certain images with miraculous power in proportional relation to the faith addressed to these images. When asked where miraculous images get their sacred power, almost all devotees say "from people's faith" and even "it's people's faith." Images are empowered by faith, because God directs sacred power to where it is needed and summoned. John of Damascus was unambiguous on this point: "Matter is endued with a divine power through prayer made to those who are depicted in image." The same was true in early modern Catholicism—the Virgin "was where her image was being worshipped"— and is also apparent in other religious traditions: "supernatural beings derive a large share of their power from the worship and sacrifices they receive from their followers. We can posit that the benevolence of the supernatural beings is proportionate to their followers' devotion."[38]

Devotees in Mexico say that God invests power in a given image when faith, devotion, and petitions demonstrate the need. Just as miraculous images appear among people in need of supernatural support, so God's grace gravitates to these images to provide the resources. On rare occasions the idea of empowerment through faith is registered in votive offerings, such as a 2013 petition to the Virgen de Tonatico that includes, "you who with our faith can do anything." The sacristan at the Cristo Negro de Otatitlán shrine also summed up succinctly when I asked where the image got its power: "from all the miracles that people ask of him." Rather than a depletion, as devotees relate in other contexts, here petitions are an empowerment. Eventually a cumulative enhancement maintains and increases the power: new pilgrimages and petitions are constantly generated as the news of miracles disseminates, and this growing demand results in ever greater deposits of God's grace.[39]

As Father Paco in Oaxaca elaborated these ideas, "one image has more devotees, and this results obviously from what God has done or does through that image, based on people's faith." Then he added, "In other words, devotion like that is not gratuitous. Because if devotion to an image grows, then it is because people have found a response, in accord with their faith, in accord with their needs. That devotion grows, keeps growing, the word spreads. It's not simply because it's an image, but rather really because if people come and that devotion keeps growing and growing, it is because there is a response, that is, there is sufficient faith to find the response of God." The two critical points are God and faith; "the image is in the middle and can change, one for another." Only God can perform miracles, but "they are realized thanks to the faith of the person who asks for them" and "the image is an intermediary." Ultimately, for Father Paco, the image drops out of the schema, because the source of the miracle "is God, through faith. The faith of the person who asks."

Devotees would agree with Father Paco regarding the centrality of faith, but most assign the protagonal role to images themselves. The power that images have to perform miracles is generally attributed in two ways: either the power is inherent to the image, or else the power originates in heaven and flows through the image. Some devotees hold both positions, either simultaneously (despite the contradiction) or alternately. The two perspectives are illustrated implicitly by the contrasting beliefs of Otomíes who make pilgrimages to Chalma and other shrines. Some believe "that images are alive," while others believe "that images are nothing but wood" and that the saints "live in heaven" and "descend to churches for ceremonies." The idea that images are visual aids for devotion to heavenly figures is more or less moot in practice.[40]

Most devotees believe that images have inherent power to perform miracles. The phrase *de sí mismo/a* (from him-/her-/itself) is the common response to questions regarding the source of an image's miraculous power. The same is explicit in votive offerings that make attributions to "the infinite power of such a miraculous image," as it is worded in one retablo, rather than to a heavenly figure. Such belief is sometimes based on degrees of nondifferentiation between Christ or the Virgin in heaven and a painting or statue on earth. Just as Christ "is the image of the invisible God" (Colossians 1:15), so devotees want the Señor de Chalma, for example, to be the image of the invisible Christ. When I asked Lourdes if the Señor del Rayo itself performed miracles or if God performed the miracles through the image, she responded, "God, through his son. This image is his son." A female devotee from Malinalco said the Señor de Chalma got his power "from himself, because he is crucified"; the sacristan at Otatitlán said "the living Christ is here"; and Father Juan Manuel in Querétaro said devotees view a miraculous image as a "virtual presence" or "living image." When I asked Karina if the Cristo de las Tres Caídas was alive in some way, she looked at me with astonished incredulity and finally said, "What do you mean?" and then, "He is God. He can do whatever he wants."[41]

Despite the seeming conflation of prototype and image, most devotees maintain a simultaneous belief in the separate existence of God and the Virgin in heaven. In colonial works written by priests the apparent contradiction is remedied through spiritual presence or ubiquity. Two separate Virgins—one spiritual, one material—in some sense become one but nevertheless, like the three persons of the holy trinity, maintain their individuality. As the Jesuit Francisco de Florencia explained it, "By the miracles that are worked through images of MARY, one must deduce the presence of MARY in them by replication of her person, without ceasing to be in Heaven." Referring to the Virgin images of Zapopan and San Juan de los Lagos, he wrote, "And if one has these two Sacred Images, of Zapopan and San Juan, how does one not have MARY? Because she is in these two images, like their souls, through which MARY animates them." Florencia also scripted discourse for the Virgin herself to explain her figurative incarnation in images: "By the grace of my Lord Jesus Christ I will also be corporally with you until the end of the world, not in the Sacrament of the altar, as is my Son, because that is not fitting, nor decent, but rather in my Images...and so you will know that I am in them, when you see that miracles are done through them."[42]

The inherent power of miraculous images is often established by myths of origin, but devotees rarely make the connection explicitly. Agustín, an older man at the Virgen de Talpa shrine, was an exception. He told the Virgen de Talpa's apparition story and then explained how God invested the image with miraculous power and sent it to Talpa, a small city in Jalisco, to help the people there. The Virgen de Talpa is thus reminiscent of *enviados de Dios*, which are people (or in this case an image) sent by God for the benefit of humanity. She is also one of many images "not made by [human] hands," as such images are called in translation of a Greek term, meaning "not a part of this material creation." These images appear miraculously or are produced under mysterious circumstances often attributed to angels, and they are sent to a particular location as a sacred presence and source of divine grace.[43]

In Mexico there are several examples: the Señor de Chalma, who appeared miraculously to dethrone an indigenous god in a cave; the Señor de los Milagros in Michoacán, brought by an image vendor who was really an angel; the Señor de la Misericordia in Tepatitlán, whose apparition in a tree was announced by intense illuminations and whose image was then refined by mysterious, vanishing strangers; the Señor de las Ampollas in Mérida, whose story is similar to that of the Señor de la Misericordia; the Virgen de Ocotlán, who appeared inside a tree on fire; and the Virgen de Soledad in Oaxaca, who appeared in a trunk on the back of an unowned mule that insinuated itself into a mule driver's camp and then died on the spot where the church was to be built. All of these images are works of art, but "the artifice, the illusion of art, must disappear so that the miraculous image is 'real.'" In this sense images not made by hands are visual complements to textual religious doctrines and myths that are "authorless, timeless, and true." The authorship disappears and the texts and images are attributed an indisputable authenticity and veracity. There is similar appeal to anonymity when informants qualify their responses with "people say that…" or "according to tradition," which diverts ownership of the discourse and endows it with the vague, distant authority of scripture while at once suggesting the speaker's uncertainty.[44]

Mexican not-made-by-hands images belong to a long tradition that includes works of art attributed to the apostle Luke. The legend of Luke as painter may have originated in the sixth or eighth century (sources vary) to legitimate icon veneration by implying apostolic origins and divine approval of images. Luke was the first to paint the Virgin, thereby providing a true likeness and a sacred material presence as partial compensation for the lack of relics. (The Assumption of Mary, a dogma of the Catholic Church, holds that upon death the Virgin "was assumed body and soul into heaven.") Luke's icons include the Virgin of Smolensk and the Hodegetria ("she who gives sight"), thus named because she restored the sight of two blind men. Like not-made-by-hands images in Mexico, the quasi-divine origin of these images endows them with special powers. During a plague in Rome, an image of the Virgin painted by Luke was taken out in procession, and the image "brought about a wonderful serenity and purity in the air" because "the poisonous uncleanness of the air yielded to the image as if fleeing from it and being unable to withstand its presence."[45]

The outstanding not-made-by-hands example in Mexico is the Virgen de Guadalupe, who appeared miraculously as a painting on Juan Diego's tilma. A remarkable eighteenth-century Mexican painting depicts God the Father seated on his throne, with a palette in one hand and a paintbrush in the other, painting the image of the Virgen de Guadalupe on a cloth that angels hold before him. Christ, at his right side, looks on in admiration. A similar origin is captured in prose regarding the Señor de Chalma, who received so much devotion and is "so perfect, so well proportioned...so superior to what art can achieve, so that in the judgment of the best sculptors it seems that it was carved, assembled, and incarnated by the omnipotent hand of the Lord, creating it as a miracle of his power and his wisdom."[46]

By all of these means miraculous images are endowed with sacred power that separates from its source, becomes autonomous, and is viewed as inherent.

The other option for empowerment of miraculous images—that they are channels of divine grace, "leading us through matter to the invisible God"—is more amenable to Catholic doctrine. God acts "through the mediation of the image," as Father Paco put it. In this view, shared at least in theory by better-instructed lay Catholics, miraculous images are focal points through which sacred power flows. Manuela said that priests "try to instill in us that we should not believe it is the image" that performs the miracle, but rather that "God does the miracle through the image." Karina said that an image "is something that God sends us so that we can have a means to talk with him or with her, the Virgin." When I asked Carlos if images were alive in some way he responded "no" without hesitation, then added, "If I buy an image it has no life. But if I take it home and the Virgin wants to send me a message, the Virgin manifests herself in that image." Adriana said similarly that at home one can request miracles of shrine-acquired images blessed by a priest, and most votaries share this belief. Pedro clarified that faith, not the particular image, is the critical factor: If you have faith the miracle will be granted by a reproduction at home, and if you lack faith the miracle will not be granted by the original at the shrine. Some miraculous images also channel the powers of indigenous deities. Teofilio, a Mazateco curandero from Veracruz, does healing rituals before the Cristo Negro de Otatitlán, because through this image the mountain and earth spirits speak and send the curandero his healing powers.[47]

Lourdes explained at length the idea of images as channels of sacred power. In the background of her argument is the belief noted above that sacred power accrues in proportion to devotion. Lourdes pointed to a broom and said, "If your faith is in that made into a cross, and if you are in pain, and if you focus on that, it will perform the miracle. Why? Because miracles are wherever you look for them." Later she added, "All images are miraculous, you just have to focus on one. God is in everything, you focus on an image to get to God." With faith, need, and concentration one can tap into God's power through images that are not explicitly miraculous, such as reproductions or images in one's local church. Similar conclusions are reached by another route in a medieval argument regarding false relics. How could a cripple be cured by the bones of some anonymous sinner dug up from a graveyard and peddled as the relics of a saint? Caesarius of Heisterbach had an answer: "It is certain that this is true, since sometimes the Lord works miracles through false relics to honour the saints to whom they are ascribed and for those who do them honour in good faith."[48]

Consequently a given image is not inherently empowered or even special, but rather is a potential site for activation by devotion that transforms it into a repository for or channel of sacred power. Reynaldo, from Tuxtepec, made his first pilgrimage to Otatitlán as a boy in 1975, "before there were cars." He explained that "you connect with the power of Christ" through the image of the Señor de Otatitlán. Reynaldo believes that the image itself performs miracles, not with inherent power but rather with the power of God that channels through it, and he then bridged to the concept of images as intermediaries. "God is not personal," Reynaldo said, "God always works through an intercessor." The only exception is the consecrated eucharist, transubstantiated into the body of Christ, which provides unmediated access. "You talk directly with him," Reynaldo said in reference to the eucharistic Christ. "That's another way to get the message to him."

In Catholic dogma only God has the power to perform miracles. The Virgin, the saints, and—in the present context—miraculous images intercede on our behalf, but the granted miracle comes from God alone. When the role of images is configured into the arrangement, miracles happen through "special interventions before God by the Virgen in her Image." Such nuance is usually lost in everyday devotion, but occasionally petitions and votive offerings to images do credit God for the miracles, sometimes indirectly with phrases like "I know you will intercede before God." One offering gives thanks for "the many miracles that Our Lady has performed through the most miraculous Image of Our Lady of San Juan," thereby attributing the miracles to a mediated heavenly source, but erring in attribution of the miracle to the Virgin rather than to God. More attuned to dogma are the offerings to the Virgen de Tonatico that include the phrase, "thanks to God and for your intercession." One of this type says, "I ask you I beg you to intercede for me before God our Lord through your son Jesus." Another falls somewhere in the middle: "I request with true faith and devotion that you ask your loving son that together you perform a miracle."[49]

Some devotees think of miraculous images as advocations of Christ or the Virgin. The image in these cases is not so much a channel for sacred power as it is a localized manifestation of a heavenly figure. One characteristic offering gives thanks to God "through your advocation as the Holy Niño Manuelito del Arenal." In a written petition at Otatitlán a mother asks "Jesus Christ in the advocation of the Cristo Negro" to help her son with alcoholism and drug addiction. An image as advocation is also suggested by an extra explicit offering made in gratitude after the cure of a baby daughter. Thanks were given to "our ALL POWERFUL GOD through the BLESSED FIGURE OF OUR LORD JESUS CHRIST in the version of the MOST HOLY NIÑO DE MEZQUITIC (NIÑO DEL CACAHUATITO)."

In all cases, whether sacred power is inherent to images or flows through them, devotees maintain their belief in God, the Virgin, and the saints in heaven. In everyday devotion these heavenly figures recede into distant otherworldly abstraction as devotion is directed primarily, if not exclusively, to miraculous statues and paintings. The heavenly figures are something like the silence under sound. They are always present imperceptibly but necessarily, as guarantors, as background that makes the foreground possible.

Perhaps the better analogy is the relation between paper currency and the reserves that establish its value. A gold-standard monetary system is based on a stable quantity of gold (heavenly figures) that guarantees the value of the currency (miraculous images) used in everyday transactions. Bills are pieces of paper with little inherent value, but they represent the gold behind them and as symbols of that gold accrue value that seems inherent to the currency itself. In our daily transactions we are indifferent to the monetary system's theoretical operations (theology), because in practice (devotion), in our earning and spending, our debts and our savings, the bills are all that we need and need to know. The gold becomes insignificant in practice because the symbol displaces what is symbolized. Eventually the gold can be eliminated. No country in the world still uses a gold standard as the basis for its monetary system. Currency floats on an illusion of value but nevertheless remains valuable in itself.

Projective Animation

If one conjectures that sacred power is not inherent to miraculous images and does not flow through them from heaven, then what is the source of this power? I think devotees' association of power with a subjective investment—

faith—is essentially correct and I explore that empowerment here in secular terms. As inert matter a painting or statue has no power, but the
perception of power, and the perception of miracles realized through this
power, are generated by a complex of interacting factors: faith, emotive
cognition, devotional culture, needs in pursuit of relief, and miracle precedents documented in votive offerings. The agency that these factors together generate and attribute to miraculous images is efficacious and is not
(or not only) illusory. In some sense miracles happen. A miraculous image
"is real, factual, and forceful, but only as long as there exists a community
of persons whose beliefs, desires, emotions, purposes, and other mental
representations are directed at it, and are thereby influenced by it."[50]

I organize an understanding of this phenomenon using the structure
of reification, which I divide for expository convenience into three stages
labeled metaphorically as projection, absorption, and retrieval. Devotion
creates its object; the object consolidates and mediates personal and social
agency; and that agency is perceived as proper to the object (miraculous
image), is retrieved, and is exercised to the benefit of devotees. One might
say that power channels through miraculous images, but that the source
of the power is human rather than divine.[51]

Reification is the perception of human productions—institutions,
nations, values, miraculous images—as though they had nonhuman origin
and independent ontological validity. Whether their origin is attributed to
the laws of nature, the will of gods, or some other extrahuman abstraction,
we experience such entities as objective realities that conform to their
ideal as exactly as the redundant propositions of a tautology—the law is
the law—in an order of things that precedes us and is taken for granted.
We inherit this unchallenged reality at birth and learn socially to interpret
within its parameters and under its paradigm, unless eventually a collective struggles against it sufficiently to implement a change of paradigm.
A conservative American man in the early nineteenth century, for example,
would find the idea of female suffrage preposterous, against the natural
laws of gender hierarchy. He would live and die with this absolute conviction shared at least tacitly by his social group, and he would remain completely unaware that a century later, in 1919 and 1920, quite the opposite
view would result in a constitutional amendment. The unawareness is
critical to reification. The connection between the human producer and
world as product must remain imperceptible or at least deniable, so that
we do not recognize our externalization into the world and take for granted
the objectivity and autonomy of our productions. Consequently, someone

born a century after the nineteenth amendment would view the idea of universal suffrage as natural, inherently valid, and obviously the way things should be done.[52]

Projection

Insofar as miraculous images are concerned, by projection I mean that a statue or painting is in some sense animated by the needs, desires, beliefs, and emotions that devotees invest in it. Without this intermingling of projecting subject and receptive object the image remains lifeless and inert. In psychoanalytical terms, the phenomenon occurs in transitional space as an intermediate area of experience between imagination and reality, where inner and outer worlds intermingle. The miraculous image belongs to the world of things, but also in another register to an inner reality, individual and collective, that invests things with meanings and powers. A statue of the crucified Christ is a piece of wood, but also more than wood when complicated by devotee projections and attributions. "Consequently, the objects as religious symbols are neither exclusively perceived in real and objective terms, nor simply produced by subjective creation. Rather, they evolve from the amalgamation of what is real, material, and objective as it is experienced, penetrated, and creatively reshaped by the subjective belief and patterns of meaning attributed to the object by the believer." Miraculous images are "paradoxical subjective constructions of me- and not-me-objects."[53]

In this view miraculous images represent less a heavenly prototype than collective need and religious resource development. Devotee intentions are objectified by images. The objectification is active, which is to say that the image comes alive and performs to fulfill the needs of projecting devotees. The animated image illustrates in the extreme "the very ordinary tendency to attribute one's emotional experience to objects and events rather than to psychological processes." Transitional phenomena are also particularly suggestive in their use of symbols, in this case images, "in the sense that some extrinsic object or form is adopted as a vehicle for expressing something from the subjective realm."[54]

Once the image is given a name—the Señor del Rayo, for example—it assumes an identity as a quasi-human, sacred, social object-subject with a history. The identity is enriched by retroactive mythopoesis "as a form of cultic accretion," but also accreditation. Tradition creates the object of devotion according to collective norms and needs and the object's fixed but flexible identity is then customized for personal use by individual devotees. The less

the lifeless image has to give on its own, because its cultural-construct repository is weak, the more devotees can invest subjectively to customize or compensate. The Virgen de Guadalupe has a lot to offer, a rich and well-known
cultural foundation; the Niño del Arenal has a weaker claim and consequently requires greater investment in identity construction. Miraculous
images with established identities seem, on their own, to elicit or demand
devotion, which attests again to their sacred aliveness.[55]

The relationship with a statue or painting is largely an intrasubjective
affair. It exemplifies in the extreme the idealizations that are also characteristic of romantic love. We fall in love not with an actual person, but
rather with a representation of the person as we construct him or her in
our minds. This creation of love objects is particularly evident in Internet
relations, in which the parties have never met and market to one another
an idealized self-identity that in turn is idealized in the minds of the respective lovers along the contours of their needs and desires. The monological relationship with a statue or painting manifests these dynamics in
high complexity because the image is mute and inert and can only contribute what it is given, but also because the devotee is cognizant that the
image is mute and inert and nevertheless experiences its presence, aliveness, and interactions with sufficient emotion for both parties. Devotees
establish an "affective bond with the sacred" and engage with the perceived responsiveness that they attribute to an image.[56]

Similar ideas emerge if one considers miraculous images as selfobjects,
which are either "used in service of the self" or are "themselves experienced
as part of the self." "The concept of a selfobject refers not to an object in the
social sphere, to an object in the interpersonal sense of the word, but to an
inner experience of an object." ("Objects" in this usage include people, that
is, whatever is not the subject). These representations can be shared socially, as is apparent in devotion to miraculous images. The selfobject is not
the physical statue or painting, the wood or canvas, but rather is the shared
inner experience of the statue or painting, which is to say its identity as an
empowered, quasi-living entity in service to a community. In the selfobject, or miraculous image, opposing vantage points meet and interact. The
painting or sculpture maintains its objectivity because devotees recognize
that it is a thing in the world, and at the same time the painting or sculpture
is a subjective extension of devotees who engage with it in fulfillment of
their needs. "Satisfaction is obtained from illusions, which are recognized
as such without the discrepancy between them and reality being allowed to
interfere with enjoyment." The object (statue, painting) becomes a mental

construct (miraculous image) that has ontological validity within a devotional community, while continuing to be an object.[57]

Much the same arguments are made in art history: "We are concerned here with material images, of course, but ones that are invested with mental images." A miraculous image is a work of art cocreated or doubly created: first by an artist who made the statue or painting, and then by the devotees who invest it empathetically, animate it, and transform it into a sacred presence. Devotees enliven images with emotions and intentions that seem inherent to the images themselves. The process is similar to how works of fictions are activated by reading. A dialogue ensues between a work of art and an imagination, or, in the present case, a work of art and faith. The perception of miraculous images is a creative act that endows a statue or painting with new properties but at once remains restricted by what the image's appearance and identity can accommodate.[58]

Absorption

Projected faith, need, and emotion accumulate on and around a miraculous image—I am speaking metaphorically—and infuse it, saturate it together with absorptions from the sacred ambience (music, prayer, laments, ritual care), from the image's history, and from the proof of miraculousness established by reputation and votive offerings. The image absorbs the passion of devotion around it and these accruals accumulate and concentrate and confuse with one another and with the image itself. The image is already saturated when each new votary arrives to activate, contribute, and draw from this composite. This saturation contributes to votary expectation that a miracle will be granted, which in turn contributes to the miracle itself. The image has been "modified over the history of its incorporation into goal-directed human action," and consequently it becomes a resource and a tool, "an embodiment of purpose." Devotees are producers and consumers of their endowments to miraculous images but remain largely unaware of their role in production. When they explain that miracles are contingent on faith, however, they express an understanding that sacred presence and power are generated by devotion.[59]

Retrieval

Recent scholarship in psychology and cognitive science has stressed "how thought shapes emotion and how emotion, in turn, shapes thought."

Through a "reciprocal causality," emotion and cognition mutually regulate, motivate, and reform one another. Emotions like love and guilt, for
example, affect how we think, and these thoughts then work back reciprocally on the love and guilt to moderate or intensify them.[60]

Such interactions are critical in the context of devotion, where what
one feels affects what one thinks and believes. Powerful emotions are
aroused by faith, and these emotions, in mutual interaction, reinforce the
faith that aroused them: "Just as emotional expressions convey emotional
information to other people, emotional experience conveys such information to oneself." Faith emerges from feelings that return to validate faith.
The strong emotions generated by devotion are used as evidence to substantiate the reality of miraculous images and their agency. If I am moved
this deeply, how could it not be real? Devotees do not feel emotion because
they experience an image's sacred presence and power, but rather experience the image's sacred presence and power because they feel emotion.
The two components—emotion and experience—then engage dialectically. Ambient emotional cueing (music, smells, the devotional mood),
thought content (miracle precedents, sermons, a miraculous image's history and identity), and the consensus of a community intensify what one
feels at a shrine and cycle back through cognitions to affirm the reality and
validity of beliefs. One's convictions might have low verisimilitude but
nevertheless have high truth value because faith, like love, is beyond tests
of truth, grounded in intuitive certainty by a deep inner feeling that is in-
subordinate to reason or conditions reason to support its designs. The
feelings are also somatized in sensations, postures, gestures, and perceptions. I feel a certain way when I kneel and put my hands like this in
prayer, when I look at that image looking back at me, when I hear my voice
singing together with the others, so that the feelings and the performance
likewise become interactive and mutually enhancing.[61]

Retrieval occurs when a projection bounces back from a saturated
image. It is extended human subjectivity returning to votaries as though it
were the subjectivity of a miraculous image. Votaries project faith and
need, and the projection returns as miraculous power. Projecting subjects
reciprocate their own devotion with rewards attributed to an autonomous
other. The content of the returning projection includes inversions of what
the votary projected (need becomes satisfaction), intermingled with—
confused with—other absorptions (sacred context, reputation as miraculous) that contribute to a sense of aliveness, receptivity, and, eventually, to
a miracle. Through votary projections "the product acts back upon the

producer." Retrieved projections, because they are so heavily laden with antecedents, endow each individual experience with verisimilitude and complexity.[62]

In simple terms a votary approaches with a need, engages an image with an expectation, and eventually experiences the need's inverted return as miraculous fulfillment. Miraculous images are something like mirrors that return inverted whatever is projected onto them. These reflections are dependent on their originals, like the images in any mirror, but miraculous images distort benevolently. A problem reflects as a solution; desperation as solace. We see ourselves as we would like to be. Petitions are made by votaries in states ranging from mild anxiety to desperation, and such conditions bias perception. "The assumptions and expectation we start out with will influence the evidence that we find, the interpretations that we make and ultimately, the judgments we arrive at."[63]

When Elia visited the Señor de Carácuaro in Michoacán she had already received her miracle, so her primary concern was the image's recognition of her votive offering in exchange. Elia approached the Señor de Carácuaro, looked at him, touched him, gave thanks, and could feel, as she told an anthropologist, "that he knew she had arrived, recognized her, and thanked her for her effort in keeping her word." In such encounters both roles of the drama are played by devotees but nevertheless feel dialogical, generate strong emotion, and are satisfying (in Elia's case because the offering was recognized). The votary's subjectivity becomes ambiguous as it is shared with the image, bounced off the image, and retrieved. In this doubled monologue the votary engages not with wood or canvas but rather with an internal construct in all of its awesome presence and power. Images speak a collaborative discourse derived in part from the cultural content of this internalized representation, which knows what the images should say, and in part from the votary's subjective contributions (such as Elia's desire that her offering be acknowledged). Even in the act of speaking the image is voiceless —"one is spoken rather than speaking," a "subject being spoken by the myth"—and this cocreated internal representation lives within a self-affirming cycle, a closed chamber in which a votary's voice meets its echo. The image's silence is activated by faith, and votaries know their petitions have been heard because miracles are granted in response. The actions speak louder than words.[64]

Silence has similar meanings in a higher register of Christian theology. By giving his son, as San Juan de la Cruz explained it, God "spoke everything to us together and at once in this single Word" and "has become as

though mute and has nothing more to say." The silence of God is articulated by the presence of Christ. What sounds like silence is the aftermath
of transition from abstraction to incarnation, from spirit to flesh, discourse to action. Once the Word—the power and the grace of God—is
incarnate, God speaks through presence and deed, and through images.[65]

Florencia tells the story of a painter who was hired to make a copy of
the Virgen de San Juan de los Lagos. The painter had difficulty with the
project, spent a long time, and could not get it right, until finally "he came
back very happy, saying: Now, praise be to God, it is copied; and showing
the Portrait that he had made, one discovered that he had painted himself,
with all of his features, even the moustache."

Among the many interpretations this narrative accommodates is one
that is resonant in the present context: when we look at miraculous images
we see ourselves, our own projected subjectivity. That idea is illustrated
uniquely by a wall collage in the courtyard of the Virgen de los Remedios
basilica, where hundreds of photographs of individual votaries are arranged to form the mystical body of Christ. Christ is the head of the
Church that is his mystical body, built in this case of photographs representing votaries whose faith makes miracles happen. When we look at this
Christ we see ourselves, or more precisely our subjective contribution to a
congregation that composes the image that coheres us. My photograph is
not primarily about me, as it would be if posted elsewhere at the basilica,
but rather about me as a member of a collective that together builds the
sacred image that serves us. I can point to myself, as in a group shot of a
team or class, but the picture is about the whole, the constitutive horizontal solidarity and coidentity, the congregation that has the power to
make images and make them miraculous.[66]

In another collage beside this Christ hundreds of *milagros* or *milagritos* (tiny metal representational offerings) are arranged collectively to
form the image of the Virgen de los Remedios. (The same Spanish word,
milagros, is used for miracles themselves and for these offerings.) In this
case the sacred image is built not of votary images but rather of miracles
that are validated because they are represented. The miraculous image is
made of attributed miracles. The collage of the Virgin is collectively constructed to emphasize the founding principle—miraculousness—that
gives the congregation its resource and purpose. The two collages, of
Christ and the Virgin, are united by a sign above them that reads, "The
Virgin Mary continues forming the mystical body of her son Jesus with
her 'miracles.'"[67]

The mystical body of Christ at the Virgen de los Remedios basilica. A sign on the wall invites devotees to include themselves by posting a photograph.

Poetic Faith

Samuel Coleridge, referring to supernatural characters envisioned for *Lyrical Ballads*, sought a "transfer from our inward nature a human interest and a semblance of truth sufficient to procure for these shadows of imagination that willing suspension of disbelief for the moment, which constitutes poetic faith." This transfer is reminiscent of the projective animation that enlivens miraculous images, but in devotion the duration is ongoing rather than momentary and devotees seem as much inclined to a willing construction of belief as to a willing suspension of disbelief. Devotees' engagement with miraculous images is nevertheless structurally similar to readers' engagement with fictional characters in novels and films. "You are invited to enter into your religious commitment the way you enter into a novel, except you are invited to imagine that it is real."[68]

When we engage with fictions we allow ourselves degrees of absorption and identification, even though we are aware that the plot and characters are not real in the same way as the world and people around us. We maintain a commonsense distinction between actor and character and understand that the characters—words on a page or images on a screen— have no real presence. Marlon Brando is not Don Corleone, we know that, but at the same time we allow character and actor to fuse so that the fiction can move us with its powers. We temporarily accept fiction as reality while at once we maintain an awareness that it is fiction, and through this qualified suspension of disbelief fictions elicit our emotions. Sam knows that the green slime coming toward him on the screen is not real, but nevertheless he responds with real fear, together with the corporal reactions that generally accompany fear, but he does not run out of the theater. The theatrical context—darkness, giant screen—and shared audience experience contribute to this sense of reality and corresponding emotion. Some scholars understand these phenomena through compartmentalization or limited cross-reference of mutually inconsistent "belief dossiers." In Sam's case a dominant dossier that knows the danger is not real recedes and yields the foreground to a temporary, subordinate dossier that accepts the fictional reality of the film.[69]

Devotees inclined to utilitarian devotion might harbor doubt about the reality of miraculous images, but as needs arise the doubt yields to belief. The shrine ambience facilitates suspension of disbelief and devotees resume a familiar plot, interact with the characters, and feel the validating emotion that imbues their petition with an oddly optimistic probability. By acting as if they believe they acquire a sense of genuine belief, however transient and contingent on need, so that the devotion becomes self-affirming. This performance is accompanied by a cognitive shift—a change of dossiers— by which everyday disbelief is subordinate to a devotional script that they know almost innately and can reactivate. "Participants practicing ritual act as if the world produced in ritual were in fact a real one. And they do so fully conscious that such a subjunctive world exists in endless tension with an alternate world of daily experience."⁷⁰

More interesting, however, are the devotees with deep faith who maintain simultaneous beliefs in miraculous images as inert objects; as autonomous quasi-human, quasi-divine beings imbued with sacred presence and power; and as related to or identical with Christ and the Virgin in heaven. These three components of a compound identity are paradoxically differentiated, unified, and interactive. What is perceived as miraculous power, or at least mysterious otherworldliness, is partially indebted to the tension generated by these incompatible identities. The power of miraculous images dissipates if one separates the compound into it its discrete components. When priests enforce a distinction between a statue of the Virgin and the Virgin in heaven, for example, the power of the statue is undermined. The statue becomes nothing more than a devotional aid, a reminder of a figure in heaven. If the free play is lost to sacred presence, conversely, so that the wood disappears and the statue comes alive, then belief collapses into delusion. The tension, and thus the power, are contingent on ambiguity, "a continuous generation of internal relations," an "internal resonance," an ontological imprecision. The paradox must remain unresolved, "knowing and at the same time not knowing," but the paradox must also be recognized.⁷¹

Simulacra

The identities of the Virgin evolved in stages: 1) The biblical Virgin, as established in a nonspecific mention in Galatians; brief appearances in Mark, John, and Acts; and the infancy narratives in Matthew and Luke. 2) The Catholic Virgin, as gradually elaborated over centuries to include the Virgin's divine motherhood (which is based in scripture) and the other three dogmas—perpetual virginity (649), immaculate conception (1854), and assumption into heaven (1950)—that the Catholic Church introduced later. 3) The Virgin as represented in multiple advocations (such as the Virgins of Candelaria, of Sorrows, and of the Immaculate Conception) that developed textually and iconographically and that diversified the prototype with interrelated subidentities. And 4) statues and paintings of the Virgin that localize a specific advocation (such as the Virgen de Ocotlán and the Virgen de San Juan de los Lagos as manifestations of the Immaculate Conception), and that in turn are reproduced and elaborated in devotional imagery. Petitions and votive offerings are made to specific images at this this fourth stage.[72]

The identity of what is generically referred to as "the Virgin" is modified in the progression through these stages, particularly in the transitions from the biblical to the Catholic Virgin and from the advocations to their local manifestations. The result is a complex that integrates multiple and sometimes competing identities, so that finally references to the Virgin specify not a historical or heavenly figure or even a local construct fully present to itself, but rather the top layer of a palimpsest that accumulates diverse forms (advocations, inculturations) in response to similarly diverse contexts and needs. Statues and paintings as representations of a prototype Virgin are factitious insofar as the prototype itself is subsequent to—created by—the very images that purport to represent it. "The relationship between the image and its model has been reversed," so that the representations precede and produce the prototype.[73]

Ultimately claims to resemblance are circular: the image resembles the prototype Virgin whose identity is established by the image. A local Virgin's identity is negotiated in this projection and retrieval: "The image has only to resemble itself: it is its own point of reference." When devotees envision the Virgin in prayers, dreams, or apparitions, they reabstract the image—the material image becomes a mental image—and in doing so repeat the self-confirming cycle: The Virgin in the vision is identical to the one in the church. Autonomy is established by this tautological loop. The Virgin is self-resembling, which attests to the validity her identity.[74]

Advocations and images of the Virgin may differ considerably in identity, but they share a claim to the Virgin's sacred presence and power. This is their common denominator, the essence that consolidates their differences. The heavenly Virgin may be displaced as local images are projected heavenward to become their own prototypes, but the Virgin's nonvisual, spiritual essence remains separate and vital, like a soul awaiting a body or the sacred something that enlivens and empowers statues and paintings and that networks the Virgin in all of her guises—Tonatico, Guadalupe, Remedios—to their single, common attribute.

In this perspective, miraculous images seem metonymies that represent the heavenly Virgin more by contiguity (in its broadest sense, including causal and part-to-whole relations) than by similarity or substitution. Metonymies also tend to concretize abstractions, often by the reduction "of some higher or more complex realm of being to the terms of a lower or less complex realm of being," in order "to convey some incorporeal or intangible state in terms of the corporeal or tangible." The displacement from intangible to tangible allows for significant representational liberty, so that multiple advocations and images selectively derive what they need from the ideal—the Virgin's presence and power, and thus the part-to-whole relation—but can be considerably different one from the other in appearance and in their local identities. It is not that an original Virgin construct has a priori authenticity and the local Virgins are inauthentic or inexact copies, but rather that the original construct yields to multiple variations on a theme that share a "practical identity" and remain in "ontological communication" with their power source.[75]

Similar ideas regarding prototype and reproductions are approachable through theory pursuant to Plato's simulacrum, meaning "the identical copy for which no original has ever existed." Here again miraculous images are not representations of an original prototype but rather are self-referential copies with only a void behind them. Among the successive phases of the image—"it is the reflection of a profound reality; it masks and denatures a profound reality; it masks the *absence* of a profound reality; it has no relation to any reality whatsoever: it is its own pure simulacrum"—miraculous images tend toward the latter phases. The simulacrum "subverts the cherished dichotomy of model and copy, original and reproduction, image and likeness," and consequently, with nothing behind it, nothing to resemble but itself, the simulacrum "calls into question the ability to distinguish between what is real and what is represented." Ultimately the issue is not how a miraculous image represents a prototype but rather how a prototype is produced by an image and then loops back to validate and empower the image that produced it. The empowerment occurs "in an uninterrupted circuit without reference," except circular reference between prototype and copy.[76]

How do we account for something like a miraculous image without regarding it as a fraud, an aberration, or a semipagan and superstitious illusion? The categories we have to classify phenomena and things—the phenomena of things—cannot accommodate ambiguous artifacts that are "material embodiments of nonmaterial intentionality." The very question of whether a painting or statue can be miraculous is dependent on a dichotomous separation of spirit and matter that nevertheless allows for union in privileged exceptions like the incarnation and consecrated eucharist, as well as in such broadly held conceptions as the soul within the body. What is supernatural is socially constructed in opposition to what is natural, but this dominant construct is inadequate when it confronts flexible ontological boundaries that tend more toward integration, toward embed-dedness of spirit and matter, of human and nonhuman, and of this world and the next.[77]

Most Mexican Catholics take for granted that presence and power are somehow integral to miraculous statues and paintings and that these images are endowed with consciousness capable of considering and responding to petitions. These devotees do not feel bound by dogma that dismisses or denigrates their beliefs. They have not read the decrees of the ecumenical councils. What matters to them are miracles, not the theology of how miracles happen, and their miracle has no less a claim to truth or falsity than, for example, the Virgin's immaculate conception or assumption into heaven. The validity of miraculous images is not dependent on verifiable inherent agency; the exercise and outcomes of attributed agency are sufficient.

Adolfo, a pilgrim from Mexico City, is an educated professional de-voted to the Señor de Chalma. "It is a solid image," he said, meaning a wooden one, "but for us it exists as a human being, to whom we com-mend ourselves here at his home." What Adolfo is expressing is not a psychotic delusion that mistakes a statue for a person, but rather a com-monly held concept of being that cannot be accommodated by current ontological categories. A miraculous image must be either a statue or a person but it cannot be both, and nevertheless for millions of people on three American continents it is both. The Catholic Church, too, is on both sides of the fence, with a theory of images as visual aids and a prac-tice of God channeling through images enlivened by sacred power. Realities are validated by consensus and rehearsal, and a visit to miracu-lous-image churches in Mexico on a Sunday more than establishes the critical mass necessary to validate an operative, nondichotomous on-tology amenable to image devotion. Mexican Catholics want their images to be, like Christ, a living fusion of spirit and matter. In a world of human projections reified into the realities we live by, what are the criteria for exclusion?

In addition to miraculous images, "a great range of other entities—perhaps even the majority of entities in our everyday world—fall between the cracks of standard category systems." These include laws, theories, works of literature, and other abstract human creations with ontological ambiguity, but also "concrete artifacts such as sculptures, churches, dollar bills, and pieces of real estate [that] cannot be identified with those real entities on which they depend without missing some of the essential characteristics that distinguish them, as cultural artifacts, from mere physical entities. The failure of standard ontological categories to cope with such a wide range of entities suggests the need for a broader, more varied ontology." Without such an "adequate ontology of the everyday world" the validity of miraculous images is deferred, even for centuries, and even as shrines and basilicas are founded on these same images.[78]

Otatitlán

A humid illumination, subdued, not quite bright enough to qualify as light. The low road is flanked by miles of plantation, sugarcane in stillness that makes it seem uncomfortable, bound to a palette of competing greens, almost swathed in hues, as though the leaves would be grateful for some wind. On one side the Papaloapan borders the plantations; its waters are greenish brown or, in higher sun, brownish green. Reynaldo is driving; his face is peaceful. When the morning light finds a break in the clouds it makes the leaves seem strangely excited.

We arrive in the calm between masses. Birds outside, a woman selling herbs for *rameadas*, the dry swoosh of the sacristan's broom. The day feels endless and lethargic, heatbound, so that you're not sure if you're stupid or just recoverably benumbed. Reynaldo kneels on the floor and prays in Chinantec, then sits among rows of empty pews. A damp breeze enters almost imperceptibly, reluctantly, as though in conspiracy for discomfort with the mosquitoes. The herb vendor, curious, comes inside, pauses, looks me over with her lowland gaze. She sits near Reynaldo and asks if he's Catholic; he responds "proudly"; they talk. The acoustics feel dead, muffled despite the emptiness and stark wooden pews. Candles burn on the floor before the Cristo Negro's decapitated head enshrined under glass near the altar. The flames hardly move. The glass is cloudy. A whitish plaque, an uneven veneer of salt, archives the prints of sweaty hands. Something like fog on shadow, but greasier.[1]

The head was sawn off in 1931, during an assault on Catholicism pursuant to the 1917 Mexican constitution and, particularly, the Law for Reforming the Penal Code ("Calles Law") of 1926. The mayor of Otatitlán at the time well summarized a goal of the reformers: "to redeem the masses from the ignorance with which a religious sect [Catholicism] has plagued their consciousness and souls and for many years has confused the thought of humanity." On or around September 6, 1931, soldiers under orders of the governor of Veracruz entered and secured Otatitlán. The following night five soldiers led by local officials broke into the church, stole the Cristo Negro and escaped along the dirt road that parallels the Papaloapan. One can imagine the polished statue brilliant in moonlight, with the crucified body banging on the cart wood against wood to the staccato rhythm of a trot. The soldiers tried to burn the image on the riverbank but the fire was insufficient to the density of the wood. Finally they sawed off the head and took it upriver, first to the town of Papaloapan and then to Xalapa, where it was exhibited to substantiate the victory. The body was left beside the river.[2]

The abduction and murder, as many devotees describe this profanation, was discovered the following morning. Otatitlán Catholics organized in the plaza, divided into groups, and began a search. They discovered the Cristo Negro headless but otherwise intact, save the scorching on one side of the ribs. Families brought sheets and blankets to wrap the naked body and the Cristo Negro was carried back to town on a metal bedspring. Devotees took turns at the sides of this improvised litter, much as they

A painting in the church illustrates the profanation.

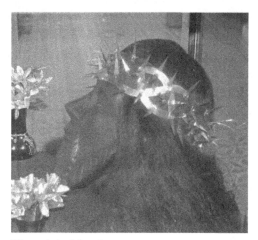

The original head.

would during a procession. The image remained headless for over a year until a new head was sculpted by an artist from Mexico City. Decades later, in the 1950s, the original head was returned to Otatitlán. Thus began the current dual devotion: to the restored image of the Cristo Negro and to the recovered head now under glass.[3]

A woman is wedging a folded piece of paper into a seam where the sides of the glass case meet. Proximity to the head would improve her chances for a miracle but the slit is too thin and the paper too limp to force the petition inside. Finally she gives up, rubs the paper on the glass and then on herself, puts it in her pocket, and picks up her infant daughter. The daughter seems sleep-dazed but shakes off the slumber, lifts her gaze with precocious determination and tries to keep the head from bobbing. She would like the head to look where she directs it. Her chubby arm, barely long enough to be jointed, connects with the head's direction and momentum and succumbs to some magnetic attraction, some primordial clumsy infant intention to bridge the distance and—like her praying mother—touch the glass in which the head is encased.

I asked Reynaldo why the Cristo Negro didn't use his power to prevent the decapitation, and he replied that Christ, in Otatitlán as in the bible, surrenders to his enemies and endures their torments. Christ does so patiently, serenely, and even gratefully, because suffering is redemptive. The Cristo Negro's profanation (like ubiquitous crucifixion imagery generally) is a testament to ongoing tribulation and as such resonates with devotees' own enduring hardship. It provides a localized rehearsal of the biblical prototype, a catalyst for empathetic identification, a precedent that gives meaning to suffering, and a suggestion of an unstated salvific exchange: the Cristo Negro saved us, but we also saved him. Also implicit in the profanation and the rescue is a cultural reversal: in colonial Mexico images of Christ were profaned during indigenous rebellions, but in the present case indigenous and indigenous-identifying peoples are the defenders and rescuers of Christ after a profanation by mestizos.[4]

Unlike Reynaldo, some Chinanteco and Mazateco devotees argue that the Cristo Negro did deploy his miraculous power when abducted; that's why the body didn't burn. He also used the soldiers as agents of his own designs. As one informant explained, "They cut off the Lord's head because he ordered his enemies to do it; they didn't realize that they did it under orders. And they cut it off because his children [devotees] saw him from the sides and their necks got twisted, because He had his head twisted to one side. It would be better to look at him from the front, that's why he ordered them to cut off his head, so that his children would not be harmed, but his body didn't burn because he didn't want that." Some miraculous images, such as the Virgen de Talpa, self-renovate spontaneously, without assistance; in this narrative, however, the Cristo Negro opts for a secondary cause—his enemies—to carry out his plan.[5]

Devotees visit the riverside site of the Cristo Negro's decapitation for devotional purposes and ritual cleansings, but also to acquire the sacred, curative dirt there. Reynaldo and I drove in search of the site on the dirt

Reynaldo in conversation with the herb vendor.

road beside the river. Driftwood and debris were cradling downriver in a slow flow with the humid humus compost of everything that had decomposed to sludge too thick even to ripple. A boy on a bicycle had told us that the site was another kilometer up the road, and when we arrived in half that distance Reynaldo lit up with an innocent joy because the Cristo Negro "enlightened us to find it; it's a miracle." We should commend ourselves to God and let him guide us, Reynaldo added after a pause.

Before the area had been cemented over, a simple monument, thought to be a tomb, marked the site of the decapitation. Devotees dug beneath and collected dirt at a place that would correspond to the neck or head were the tomb, like Christ's, not empty. As one devotee explained, "this land is holy because the blood of the Lord was spilled here." The earth was infused with sacred power when the neck was severed; others say excavations get to the ashes left when the image was burned. The dirt is collected to sprinkle in homes, fields, or wells, or to make a tea that is ingested for its curative properties. "We don't use doctors or anything, so what we take home is this dirt to make a holy remedy," a female devotee explained. During fiestas, when thousands of pilgrims arrive, the monument was undermined to the point of collapse; perhaps for this reason the concrete slab was added. Now devotees excavate at the edge and underneath the concrete, getting as close as they can. They loosen the earth with sticks, gather the dirt with cupped hands, and carry it away in plastic bags, pieces of newspaper, or whatever receptacles are at hand.[6]

Devotion to the Cristo Negro of Otatitlán probably began in the seventeenth century and has always been notably multiethnic, with devotees from indigenous groups including at least Chinantecos, Mazatecos, Cuicatecos, Mixtecos, Nahuas, Popolucas, Chatinos, and Zapotecos, in addition to mestizos. Everyday devotion is largely petitionary but also common are ritual cleansings (limpias or rameadas), and, for some, rituals done at the shrine by indigenous curanderos who use the Cristo Negro's power in their healings. Miracle requests include community petitions regarding collective problems and crises, as well as the more common individual petitions regarding health, employment and economic stability, love and family, and realization of life goals. One man left a simply illustrated note to ask for success with his carpentry business, for peace and tranquility, and for "the love of my life," followed by her full name. Another man asked the Cristo Negro to "move the hearts" of "those people who work in the embassy as consuls, as ambassadors…so that they grant me a pardon and give me a visa, be it for tourism, work, or residence." Many other petitions concern agriculture, including blessings at planting and harvest, reproduction of domestic animals, and petitions relating to water and irrigation (wells, springs, and rain). Seeds, beans, ears of corn, and poultry feathers are common offerings in thanks for agricultural patronage.[7]

Also frequent are petitions made by concerned wives and mothers. One woman in a twenty-year marriage and with three children "who are really lost" made her request on behalf of the family, "which is on the verge of disintegrating and I ask that my husband does not leave our home." Another mother petitioned the Cristo Negro on behalf of her son: "that you cleanse his mind so that he changes the way he is" and stops getting into trouble with his friends. The petition also included a secondary request derived from a perceptive, self-reflective insight: "give me strength and fortitude to have with him the same patience that you have with me."

Some petitions solicit the Cristo Negro's power for revenge against adversaries. In these cases, which are perceived by the votaries as pleas for protection or justice, an affront (envy, evil, crime) is deflected or reverted back to the perpetrator, and the boomeranged harm often coerces the adversary to apologize. The petitions are generally made anonymously but include some explanation of the offense, a requested punishment, and a name and other specifics to help the Cristo Negro identify the adversary. The following phrases are characteristic: "they are never going to enjoy that money they stole from me. Punish them wherever they go"; make "everything she says about me happen to her"; and "help me so he doesn't kill me, I ask for him to die, I ask for forgiveness and that he doesn't kill me."[8]

In Otatitlán the Cristo Negro's fiesta is celebrated on May 3, a date derived from the image's myth of origin. According to the myth, three wooden sculptures of the crucified Christ arrived from Spain in 1596. The Spaniards transporting the images temporarily left one tied to a tree, and on May 3 a Mazateco couple discovered it and brought it home. The image became the object of community devotion. A year later a flood and cholera epidemic decimated the village, and the survivors migrated in search of a better place to live. They built a raft to transport the Cristo Negro and headed downriver. At one point the clouds opened unexpectedly and a cone of sunlight illuminated the image, while at the same time an eddy threw the raft toward the riverbank. It was understood that the Cristo Negro had chosen the place where he wished to live. The raft landed near a tamarind tree (*otate* in Mazatec, thus the town's name) on a September 14. Centuries later a chapel was built on the site of this landing and mass is still celebrated there periodically.[9]

"Just like the Virgen de Guadalupe chose Tepeyac, the Cristo Negro chose Otatitlán," Jorge explained. "People needed that and he wanted to stay here." Jorge and his two companions elaborated the motif by adding that the image was twice removed from Otatitlán and, discontent with that displacement, on both occasions returned again by raft. Their elaboration does not conform to the standard version of the myth but does stress the common motif of miraculous images choosing where they wish to remain and returning of their own volition when removed. Other devotees extend the motif of return by river to the decapitated head. In one version, when the soldiers threw the head onto a raft there was a brilliant light as the current drove the raft ashore. In another, the head floated home on the Papaloapan.[10]

The two principal dates in the origin narrative —May 3 and September 14—coincide with the Catholic Feast of the Cross. Versions of the Feast of the Cross were originally celebrated on both dates, but in 1960 Pope John XXIII eliminated the duplication and consolidated the two feasts into what is known as Exaltation of the Holy Cross. The formal date in the liturgical calendar is now September 14, but in Mexico and other parts of Latin America the feast is still celebrated on May 3. The key events of the Otatitlán myth that are assigned to these dates (discovery on May 3 and arrival to Otatitlán on September 14) suggest how temporal structure is often retroactively applied in ways that enhance meaning and integrate syncretic devotions into the Catholic calendar. Early May also coincides with local corn planting and the beginning of the agricultural cycle.

A separate myth attributes the Cristo Negro to supernatural origin. An Indian from Otatitlán cut a trunk of cedar with the intention of finding someone to sculpt an image of the Virgin. The search was fruitless, but a few years later two mysterious "handsome young men of gallant presence" showed up at his home, saying they were sculptors. The Indian set them up to work, lodged them in a hut, paid them in advance, and returned the following day to see if their work had begun. What he discovered instead was that the sculpture had been completed, not of the Virgin but of the crucified Christ. The sculptors had vanished ("they must have been angels") and had left behind the money paid to them.[11]

When the two myths are overlapped, they combine the common site-choice motif (which, by extension, designates a chosen people) with the also common not-made-by-hands motif (which provides a basis for sacred power).

The May 3 arrival of the Cristo Negro is commemorated annually with a procession of the image on the river. Crowned, bound, covered with a white sheet, surrounded by flowers, and with a face of bewilderment, the Cristo Negro is carried to the river and then majestically floats down the Papaloapan on a raft, followed by a procession of boats. The spectacle is extraordinary in its devotional beauty. Pilgrims arrive on this and other occasions through a highly organized pilgrimage system headed by spiritual leaders, and they pause at crosses stationed at the town's entry points for ritual cleansing before continuing to the church.[12]

Once inside they pray, sing, touch, cleanse, and fulfill the obligations of their vows. The area beneath the Cristo Negro is covered with flowers and candles burn on the floor. The barrenness of the empty shrine is populated and enlivened but the mood remains solemn, almost mournful. The women especially have come to this sacred reprieve from their difficult lives to together cry off some anguish. An intermittent wail rises and falls with hypnotic, reassuring, repetitive measure. The room fills with a tension that you think might escalate but instead maintains a mournful monotony with off-key singing—nasal, toneless—that mixes with prayers in lonesome collective pleading, a dirge-like moan of deep pain in slow alleviation, a cathartic sadness. A patience. Some people sit expressionless, as though long ago their capacity for sorrow had been depleted. Others hold burning candles, a few in each hand, as long as it takes, offering the pain from the melting wax as sacrifice. Incense and body heat, babies crying, women in braids crying while praying with shawls on their heads and hands on their faces, absorbed in an overwhelming sense of succumbing, of unloading, a solemn spectacle that no one notices because, for them, it is entirely unspectacular, a traditional devotion that they actualize.[13]

Miraculous images are not accessible at most shrines; devotees must view them from a distance, often through glass. In Otatitlán, the decapitated head is encased but the Cristo Negro himself is unprotected and may be touched directly. This facilitates transmission of sacred power through tactile contact and also facilitates petitionary devotion by, for example, allowing votaries to pin milagritos on the image's waistcloth. Direct access to the image is particularly efficacious for ritual cleansings, done at this shrine in the form of rameadas, and for the related healing rituals of curanderos, which include rubbing candles on the Cristo Negro and then on the patient.

In everyday rameadas, a bundle of fresh herbs—basil is common, sometimes adorned with a few gardenias—is swept over the miraculous image and then over oneself or a family member. The purpose of this cleansing is broadly defined but essentially is a purification of body and soul, including the elimination of illness. A separate bundle is used for each cleansing to avoid the transferal of impurities through contact. The woman selling basil bundles outside of the church had a broad, good-for-business conception of rameadas as an all-purpose remedy. Rameadas are done, she said, to strengthen devotees, to protect them from enemies, to cure sicknesses, to improve earnings, and to silence gossipers, among other purposes.

As explained by a pilgrim, the rameada relieves exhaustion but is also a means of offering, because you sweep the image and yourself and say, "Lord, here is my tiredness, I offer it to you." The implicit message is, in effect, *I offer you the sacrifice of my pilgrimage.* That message is more explicit in comments that describe the purpose of pilgrimage as "to offer your suffering, your sweat, your tears, your blood." "The dust and the sun are our blessing," and pilgrimage as an "act of purification" is "the joyful acceptance of the deprivations, the tiredness, the hardship."[14]

But the phrase "here is my tiredness, I offer it to you" is also taken literally. The devotional transfer is bidirectional because devotees give the Cristo Negro their exhaustion, their weariness, their problems, their needs, and their illnesses, while at once deriving from him sacred power—"give me strength and fortitude," as many petitions put it—before returning home to resume their burdens. For this reason pilgrims say that the Cristo Negro's head is high when they arrive but by the time they leave has fallen, hanging in exhaustion. "You are tired," a woman said to the Cristo Negro, after "so many troubles that we came here to leave." One sees in his face a weariness and depletion, as though this piece of wood wished it had been carved into something else, something other than the crucified Christ, so that people wouldn't expect so much from it.[15]

Petitionary Devotion

Votive Exchange

Devotion to miraculous images is little concerned with salvation of the soul or with amending one's ways to lead a more virtuous Christian life. It is rather concerned almost exclusively with petitioning sacred power for purposes that range from banal desires to resolution of life-threatening crises. It is a practical, goal-directed, utilitarian devotion; a survival strategy; a way of interpreting reality; and a resource enhancement realized through collaboration with a sacred patron. Miracles are petitioned above all for health-related matters, but also for matters concerning employment, family, pregnancy and childbirth, romantic love, education, migration, and agriculture, among others. Miraculous images assist with passing an exam, crossing a border, healing a wound, surviving a war, getting out of prison, kicking an addiction, preventing a separation or divorce, silencing gossipers, finding lost pets and livestock, and enhancing self-esteem. Petitions thrive in social contexts characterized by deprivation and vulnerability, poor access to basic social services (including education and health care), a loss of trust in institutions and government, and a sense that it would take a miracle to survive this inhospitable world.[1]

Petitionary devotion consists primarily of making miracle requests together with promises to offer something in exchange. "You ask him to do the miracle for you and in return you are going to give him something," as Adriana put it in reference to the Señor de Chalma. In written petitions the promises, or vows, are sometimes explicit, like a signed agreement instead of a handshake, but usually the reciprocation remains unspecified. Promises may be made in prayer, before or after the miracle, but votaries also—and often—petition miraculous images without explicitly obligating themselves. Reciprocation is nevertheless always required, and when no terms are stated it is likely to take the form of a shrine visit to give thanks in person. Votaries have little to lose in these arrangements, known as votive contracts, because they themselves establish the terms and are under no obligation unless the miracle is granted.[2]

In theory one may request anything of a miraculous image, but tacit conventions establish parameters. A diabetic may petition that a limb not be amputated, but knows not to petition the regrowth of an amputated limb. Old people may ask for a few more years, but not for restoration of youth. These conventions are relatively stable in current devotion. In previous centuries the parameters were wider, and miracles attributed to Sainte Foy, for example, included the replacement of gouged-out eyes, the regrowth of a bald man's hair, and several resuscitations of the dead, including of a mule and other animals.[3]

Petitions are usually made by the intended beneficiary of the miracle, but sometimes they are made on one's behalf. Female relatives—mothers, wives, grandmothers, aunts—are the most common proxies. A mother might petition a miracle for a son in the hospital, in prison, or in the United States, and if the miracle is granted both mother and son, when possible, will visit the shrine to give thanks. Some votaries mail letters of petition or gratitude, often from abroad. The shrine at Plateros receives about four thousand letters a year addressed to the Niño de Atocha. The majority are petitions by mothers on behalf of sons with drinking, drug, or legal problems. The recipients of the miracle might even be nonbelievers, because the miracles are indirectly granted to the mothers who petitioned and will reciprocate them.[4]

Among clergy and votaries it is also acceptable that a third person make an offering on behalf of a miracle beneficiary who is unable to fulfill a promise (due to sickness, for example). In a few cases proxies share the responsibility: "I made a promise so that my niece would recover from a tumor, but her mom and I are paying back the promise together." A petition to the Virgen de Talpa is written in two hands: the first is the primary petitioner's to request the cure of her intestinal problem, and the second is her mother's to reinforce the petition. If the miracle is granted, mother and daughter will reciprocate together.[5]

An emotional space opens between the petition and the anticipated miracle. Petitionary devotion is a way of anticipating. One waits and hopes, and as time passes one might reiterate the petition and make interim offerings or additional promises to strengthen it. Miracles are contingent on faith, but faith exercised in devotion as an active engagement and pursuit.

Insufficient faith is the primary reason cited by devotees for the failure of petitions, but miracles are also denied because God and miraculous images know what is best for us. In reference to the Señor de Chalma, Marta explained that "Sometimes we ask for something material that will harm us. God won't grant it. I might ask, 'Dear God, give me a lot of money,' but if that money is going to do me a lot of harm, if it's going to change me, I'm going to be different with people, I'm going to look down on them, the Lord is not going to grant me that." When I asked Adriana why some miracles are not granted, she gave another reason: "I'm just me, there are a lot of people." Everyone thinks their problem is critical and worthy of attention, but "some people come with problems much worse than others. God knows that. My santito [Señor de Chalma] goes by that, granting the bigger favors before one that is small." The same reasons occasion delays in granting miracles.

After a miracle is received, the votary must make the promised offering. The promise or vow (*voto*) is followed by the votive offering (*ex voto*). The Spanish phrase used to describe this reciprocation, *pagar la manda*, denotes the idea of paying up, of canceling a debt or fulfilling a promise. A *manda* itself is a commitment established by a promise. Common material offerings (in addition to cash and gifts) include photographs, homemade collages, textual offerings (letters, miracles narratives, poems), clothing, hair cuttings and braids, votive candles, flowers, and *milagritos* (tiny metal representational offerings). Votive gifts and practices often combine in a votive process or complex that might include, for example, a visit, a mass of thanksgiving, and a handwritten expression of thanks, all of which together fulfill the vow. A woman helped through a difficult pregnancy might enter the shrine on her knees, present the newborn, and leave a photograph and hair cutting.[6]

Votaries view an unfulfilled promise to a miraculous image as an encumbrance, a precarious state of incompletion, an open debt. This creates a burden of conscience and a certain urgency to fulfill the obligation. Negative experiences in the interim are interpreted as punishments. Problems arise when desperate devotees overextend and find themselves incapable of fulfilling their promises. Some votaries negotiate extensions. A letter to the Virgen de San Juan de los Lagos includes, "I'm writing you today because a year ago I made a promise and you know that I will not be able to keep it, I asked you to intercede so that Martín would survive and you did that, you saved him from so much pain, and I thank you. This year I will not be able to visit you but from my heart and from here I am writing this letter with all of my faith."

There is a sense of alleviation when the offering is made, but the closure is only of this particular account, this outstanding debt, not of the ongoing reciprocity that most votaries will maintain with the image. The benefit is acknowledged and the cycle closes, but the relationship remains active and new cycles are initiated as the need arises. It is an open-ended contract maintained in increments and installments. "I'm very devoted," said an older woman at the Niño de Atocha shrine. "I've petitioned him my whole life. I come whenever I can. I came with my neighbor, we're going back today too, we came for nothing other than what we came for, to visit him and that's it." Two teen-aged girls said: "We come every year just to give thanks, and every once in a while we come to pagar mandas." Many devotees have commended themselves to the care of a particular image, or were commended in infancy by their parents, and consequently they periodically affirm, renew, and maintain a lifelong relationship that intensifies as needs and crises occasion. As one devotee put it, "I keep coming so that he keeps helping me."[7]

Often priests object to petitionary devotion to miraculous images, and for many reasons. One concerns precisely the idea of cyclical encounter, an episodic Catholicism structured on petition and pilgrimage. Father Paco in Oaxaca expressed an assessment shared by many priests when he argued that a devotee with uninstructed faith sins at will—he mentioned infidelity, negligence as a father, alcoholism, and criminality—"but has the faith to go there and visit an image to ask for whatever he wants." "He does it with a lot of faith, even walking to those places [shrines] and the sacrifice it implies," but "it's a kind of momentary satisfaction, a way to calm his conscience, and then he returns to his ordinary life." Others stress how devotees work off sins in showy displays, have faith that emerges only in times of need, and get all of their being Catholic done at the annual fiesta. An Augustinian friar is characteristic in his assessment of pilgrims to the Señor de Chalma: "They are limited to markedly external aspects: the visit, the offering, the praying aloud, but there is no internal renovation, no true conversion; they come and go again and again with the same defects, the same flaws, the same misfortunes," and "they reduce the faith to a commercial transaction with God: I give you so that you give me."[8]

Women are generally more steadfast than men, but nevertheless the priests' critique obtains insofar as the sincerity of devotion is subordinate to utilitarian goals, the offerings intend to manipulate an image's will to one's needs, and the petitions outweigh the devotional gratitude. A devotional pamphlet distributed at the Virgen de Juquila shrine advises that "true devotion is disinterested" and that "the faithful devotee does not love Mary for favors received or expected, but rather simply because she is worthy of love." "Ask, ask, ask, almost without gratitude," Father Daniel complained at the Remedios basilica. Father Paco explained that "petitionary prayer is important but not the most important. The greatest and best prayer that one can offer is a prayer of thanksgiving." And Fray David at Chalma, like many other priests, disapproves of votaries' idea that "God exists to remedy their worldly problems."[9]

These objections have a certain validity insofar as liturgical and sacramental Catholicism are concerned, but at the same time Christian teachings encourage petitionary devotion. A stone plaque above the main entry to Chalma's church is inscribed with a passage from Matthew 11:28: "Come to me, all you who labor and are burdened, and I will give you rest." At the Remedios basilica a panel of stained glass reads, "jesus is the remedy to all of our troubles, that is why we call you mother of our remedies"; and a prayer inside the glass case of the Niño de los Remedios includes, "Remedy all of my troubles, Answer all of my petitions, Console all of my sorrows." A prayer distributed at the Señor de la Misericordia shrine in Tepatitlán begins, "With so much trust I appeal to You, my most kind Jesus, to ask you for the remedy of all of my needs." The Lord's prayer in Matthew 6:5–13 and Luke 11:1–4 includes "Give us each day our daily bread"; in Matthew 7:7 Jesus says, "ask and it will be given to you"; and in John 16.23–24 Jesus says, "whatever you ask the Father in my name he will give you" and "ask and you will receive, so that your joy may be complete." Etymologically "to pray" is derived from the Latin *precari* ("ask earnestly, beg"), and this concept is carried also in the Spanish *rogar*, which means both to beg (plead) and to pray. "We are in the house of our mother, but in the presence of God," a priest said during a sermon at the Zapopan basilica. Then he called for silent prayer with the preface, "What will you ask God for?" Clerical objection to petitionary devotion is grounded ultimately in a nuance of degree and a subtlety of protocol that are irrelevant to most devotees. The message is mixed because priests must balance a theological ideal with the reality—poverty, need, tradition—that it confronts.

Petition

Requests for miracles are made in oral or mental prayer, in written petitions, and sometimes with miniatures that represent a desired object or circumstance. The tone and content of written petitions vary widely. Some are wish lists with little sense of humility, devotion, gratitude, or reciprocation. One woman presented the Señor de la Misericordia with a list of seven requests, each beginning with "I ask you for." The requests included her mother's health; itemized petitions for love, work, well-being, and health for herself and other members of the family; and protection of her dogs Wero, Chola, and Mitzi. A note to the Virgen de los Remedios in its entirety reads: "1. Confidence. 2. Overcome fear. 3. A husband. 4. Health." Another, to the Virgen de Talpa, is also in the form of a numbered request: "1. For Yola's cancer 2. For my marriage 3. For my daughters 4. For my sons-in-law 5. For all of our needs 6. For my husband's work 7. For my health 8. For forgiveness 9. For my freedom 10. For protection against the devil and Rosalda's brujería." When I discussed such petitions with Antonio, he said, "they sound like letters to Santa Claus." The miraculous image is perceived as a magical source of benefits and relief, and the results are likely to be disappointing.[10]

In other cases the petitions are more developed but the tone remains nondeferential, gratitude is lacking, and in lieu of a mutually binding votive contract the emphasis falls heavily on the unilateral obligations that the votary imposes on the image. "My name is Nelly," one woman wrote to the Virgen de los Remedios, "and although I am not a devotee of this church nor of my religion I hope that my faith serves as proof that I want to change...and I only ask you that my family never lacks anything, neither physical, moral, affective, or social."

Another petition, to the Virgen del Pueblito, is in the same spirit. It announces three requests, makes four, and, like Nelly, prefaces its wish list with "only." "Holy Virgencita I only want to ask you for 3 things that I consider very important and they are: that you give me a job whatever it might be but that pays well and I feel good there, 2 To find the love of my life and there are no misunderstandings, 3 That there is peace in my family and lastly reserve me my trip to the United States." In a well-developed petition to the Virgen de Talpa, Rosalinda begins with "Help me with all of my needs" and then itemizes them: freedom from prison for her brother and for the father of her daughter; love, health, and work for all members of her family; and forgiveness for another brother who had problems with his employer. She also made a request for financial assistance—"if you can, give me money at least to get on top of the house expenses"—before concluding with a presumption and a request to subsidize an anticipated shrine visit: "Give me the means necessary to go to thank you personally for the favors that I am going to receive from you."

The sense of entitlement in these petitions graduates in another to mild coercion. Rosalía petitioned the Señor de la Columna in Santa

Catarina Yosonotú because she was unable to get pregnant, and her remarks illustrate how strength of faith can yield to expectation and demand. "My Santo is going to perform the miracle of giving me a child, because it is the wish of my husband and myself. We have petitioned it with a lot of faith and he is not going to let me down."[11]

Such petitions contrast sharply with those that have a humble and devotional tone devoid of egoistic entitlement. "My Niño del Cacahuatito I ask you with all of my heart to eliminate the poverty from my home forever please bless my family, my husband, and my son. I ask that my husband has work and money and that my son behaves well in school and is obedient." The request in this petition is essentially for income, but income to alleviate the financial and emotional hardships of poverty, to strengthen the family, and, as the votary puts it later, "to give my son a future."

Written petitions often include thanks for previous miracles, requests for forgiveness, and arguments of worthiness. Votaries negotiate. One petition to the Virgen de los Remedios includes a separate plea for clemency addressed to God. "Father, I know that maybe we are not the ideal couple or perfect but there are so many imperfect people who can procreate children. Why not me? I beg you Lord to guide us and teach us to strengthen our love, union, affection, and to be a normal couple like so many others. We are sinners but we are also humans and would like a baby. Thank you Lord for listening to us." Deprivation of the desired miracle (pregnancy) engenders reflection—why not me?—and then the fruits of those reflections become arguments of worthiness. Some petitions have an apologetic, self-deprecating tone, particularly when votaries who view themselves as undeserving arrive humbly in desperation on behalf of a loved one, usually a child. "Maybe you are very busy with better people but if you have a chance I'm asking for my baby, he is barely seven weeks old and there is something that has us worried it's called hematoma, that's our fear, Señor de Chalma have pity on this son of yours that I am asking for he is all that I have and I live for him day to day."

Many petitions ask only for perseverance: "Continue giving me strength and health to keep on going." In a few cases strength and wisdom are petitioned to tolerate hardships sent by God. On behalf of himself, his wife, and his daughter, a father wrote to the Virgen de Tonatico regarding the imminent birth of twins. "Now I ask that although we are aware that one of the babies supposedly is not well give each of us the resignation to accept what you have planned for us.... We know your power and your will and that if you want it you are going to give it to us but also if your will is not for that I want to thank you for everything because you know what you are doing and although it is difficult to accept we want your will to be done, and I want to ask you for a lot of strength and intelligence for Carolina, Abigail, and Alejandro [mother, daughter, and father] so that we can accept what is coming." Votaries such as this father subordinate their will to that of God or a miraculous image, and rather than advocating a change of destiny they petition forbearance to tolerate the burdens of the Lord's mysterious ways.

Priests instruct votaries to conclude their petitions with "thy will be done," which is to say to express their needs but entrust the outcome to God's wisdom and designs. A few votaries do so—"that your will be done, not mine," a woman wrote to the Virgen de los Remedios—but the great majority advocate only their own interests with little consideration of their patron's intents. One "thinks and imagines that when he prays, the important thing, the thing he must concentrate upon, is that *God should hear what* he *is praying for*. And yet in the true, eternal sense, it is just the reverse: the true relation in prayer is not when God hears what is prayed for, but when *the person praying* continues to pray until he is *the one who hears*, who hears what God wills." An offering to Niño del Cacahuatito includes a prayer by Rabindranath Tagore that asks for strength for various purposes, and then concludes, "And give me the strength to surrender my strength to thy will with love." The same principle is expressed in everyday speech when devotees say "if God wills it" not as a formulaic expression, but rather with a sincere sense of contingency. Deferent votaries are more attuned to devotion as proscribed by priests, but the deference also fosters reciprocal empathy and ultimately can be a strategy of persuasion.[12]

Even votaries who are barely literate make an effort to textualize petitions. Their reasons for doing so underscore their preference for material immediacy and for interpersonal relations with a miraculous image. Petitions are written and posted at a shrine, as a sacristan put it in reference to the Cristo Negro de Otatitlán, "so that he sees them." The same is sometimes registered in the text itself: "For you, read it my Lord." Petitionary objects and practices are regarded similarly. As explained by a mayordomo of the Señor de Tila fiesta in Chiapas, "I think that when I organize the fiesta in honor of the Lord he sees it and looks at it, he takes it into account so that from there he can give his blessing, because people are fulfilling their obligations to him." Reynaldo, who tends to view miraculous images as channels to God, said that the Cristo Negro de Otatitlán

Textual petitions and votive offerings to an image in Oaxaca's Franciscan church.

reads petitions and "carries the message, passes it to God the Father and God the Son."[13]

Some votaries, particularly those more familiar with Catholic teachings, are opposed to textual petitions. Juana at the Remedios basilica said, "You're not going to talk to God on a cell phone, and not by writing either. Many people do it through a letter, but it doesn't work like that. The reality is with faith, with devotion, and asking the Virgin with words," meaning prayer. Marta agreed. She sees hundreds of devotees at the Chalma shrine daily and explained how the practice of writing petitions proliferates through observation and imitation. One devotee sees another posting a petition, Marta said, and thinks, "'I'm going to write one too.' They go around trying to find paper, trying to find a pen, in order to leave a piece of paper." This contributes to the highly improvised nature of media, with petitions written on scraps of paper, a Styrofoam take-out tray, a prayer card to Juan Soldado taken out of someone's wallet, and whatever else is at hand. In reality, Marta said, "it's better just to ask him by praying." These same ideas extend to Marta's beliefs regarding photographs. "He knows us, he sees us, it is not necessary to leave a photo for him to know what I asked him for, he already knows, he looks after all of us."

Others are similarly aware that miraculous images are omniscient and know what we need before we request it, even before we know it, but

nevertheless these votaries write petitions and integrate their awareness—
"you know that…" or "you know my problem"—into their petitionary
texts. Eugenia wrote to the Señor de las Tres Caídas, "you know Lord what
I feel in my heart, you know what is happening in my house, in my home,"
but her awareness of this omniscience does not affect her impulse to
write.[14]

Miracles are also petitioned using representational objects, particularly
in Oaxaca, where miniature houses, children, cars, trucks, livestock, and
other desired acquisitions are offered. Devotees fabricate these at home
(of wood or cardboard) or, usually, on site at *pedimentos* (from the verb
pedir, to ask for). The outstanding example is the pedimento affiliated with
the Virgen de Juquila shrine, where petitionary objects are molded using
the clay-rich dirt there. Votaries also offer wooden models of houses and
cars that are sold at the pedimento, and petitions to the Señor de la
Columna in Santa Catarina Yosonotú are made with plastic miniatures.
Other petitionary objects are more ambiguous. At the church in Astata,
leaves from a medicinal plant known as *cordoncillo* (Piper amalago L.) are
left on the altar before an image when making petitions. An offering at the
Cruz del Monte pedimento in Huatulco had smooth white stones and
large, deep-red seeds beautifully arranged inside a seashell on top of leaf.
Complex representation was most ingenious in an offering made by a
Huatulco woman who petitioned pigs. She collected shells known as
cochinitos (literally piglets), brought a handful of these to the Cruz del
Monte, and, in a kind of inverted rebus, used the homonym to bridge from
the offered objects (shells) to the desired ones (pigs).[15]

Elsewhere in Mexico, milagritos are commonly used to request miracles. Petitions are also made with inscribed photographs and lengths of
ribbon (known as *listones*, and sometimes called *reliquias* or relics) that are
growing in popularity, perhaps due to their use in widespread devotion
to San Charbel Makhuf. Objects, such as baby clothes, are sometimes
inscribed with petitions, and on occasion models—like those common in
Oaxaca—represent or are related to petitions. Some of these are inscribed.
A small wooden truck offered by a child reads, "take care of my dad, who
is a tractor-trailer driver," and on the roof of a model house offered at
Chalma the votaries wrote, "we ask that you give us the good fortune of
having a house." Votaries who wish to shut the mouths of gossipers leave
locks as petitionary objects to San Ramón Nonato in Mexico City's cathedral. At Chalma I saw simple chalk drawings on rock faces beside the Cave
of the Apparition, representing houses and a truck at downward angle.

Clay miniatures are used to make petitions to the Virgen de Juquila.

Votary-made models, like this house offered to Niño del Cacahuatito, are sometimes used to represent petitions.

I interpreted these as petitions and Marta agreed, but the boys who attend the cave thought the truck represented a bus with pilgrims that went off a cliff en route to Chalma (thus the angle). On very rare occasions the votive paintings known as retablos, which are usually offered following a miracle, are commissioned in advance to make petitions. A 1949 retablo presented to the Virgen de Tonatico, for example, petitions relief from chronic intestinal problems.[16]

All of these textual and visual representations evidence a need to make petitions present tangibly before miraculous images. When the miracle-maker is itself material (unlike a sacred figure in heaven), prayer alone seems too abstract. Represented petitions are monuments to needs and desires but also are reminders that emit quietly but constantly in the votary's absence so that the petition is heard and not forgotten. "I am leaving you this baby suit so when you see it you remember us and do the miracle for us," a woman explained to St. Toribio Romo in a note attached to the clothing. In this sense petitionary objects are reminiscent of the ear images on many Egyptian stelae, especially those addressed to Ptah, which represented the act of hearing in order to facilitate it, even enable it, by suggesting the god as a hearer of prayers. Mexican offerings represent emission rather than receipt of a petition and are more explicit, either because a text itemizes the needs or because representative objects are implicitly narrative—*I need a house, protect our cows, my infant daughter is sick.*

Promise

The promise (or vow) commits a votary to reciprocation but is conditional, because the votary is not obligated unless the miracle is granted. Sometimes the condition is explicit. One votary promised a retablo "provided that" her pregnant daughter had a safe delivery. A man with migraines prayed for cure "and made the vow that, if he were cured, he would make the offer of a silver head." Porfiria, with a seriously injured leg, promised the Señor del Hospital "that soon she would put a retablo in his Church if he granted her alleviation." The *if* clauses that are explicit in these cases are usually only implied, but the wording in votive offerings sometimes connects the conditional reciprocation to a granted miracle. In July 2010, a baby boy was born with a heart problem, the parents petitioned a miracle from the Señor de la Misericordia, and the miracle was granted. "And just as you granted the miracle that we asked you for and did not fail us for that reason we also fulfill the promise that we made to bring you his hair which was never cut until now." The text of a 2013 offering to the Señor de Chalma is similar: "Thank you for having helped Enrique because thanks to you Father he is well and alive. You helped him combat between life and death and gave him a lot of strength to fight," and consequently, "I come to fulfill what I promised you, THANKING YOU with my hair."[17]

The commitment is binding after granted miracles and sometimes after fortuitous events—unexpected income, minor injury after serious accidents—that are perceived as miracles, especially by votaries who have commended their care to a particular image. Most votaries feel obligated to fulfill their promises expeditiously. A nineteenth-century miracle narrative regarding the Virgen de San Juan de los Lagos concludes with a warning: "Don't postpone your promise, because the one who miraculously gave you health can by the same token take it away if you are slow in fulfilling your promise." Votaries have the liberty to reciprocate however they chose—and prudent devotees chose carefully—but once committed cannot breach the agreements that they themselves have initiated and defined. Reciprocity with miraculous images is an obligation but also a matter of honor, social responsibility, and correct behavior, and as long as promises remain unfulfilled votaries are motivated by a growing sense of unease to close the cycle and restore equilibrium. "You're not going to rest until you fulfill the promise," Antonio said, because "you're in debt to the Virgin." You fulfill the obligation as soon as possible "to feel like you're free—you kept your promise and it's over." Fulfillment frees you from the bondage of debt, as suggested by the phrase "to redeem a vow" and the Spanish saying *lo prometido es deuda* (what is promised is a debt).[18]

A conscientious sense of urgency is intensified by fear of punishment for unfulfilled promises. Among some indigenous groups the consequences include death, but generally the punishments are more moderate (accidents, broken bones, illness, things go badly) or entail reversal of the miracle (restored sight reverts to blindness). A retablo text relates how a man delayed fulfillment of his promise, suffered accidents as a consequence, and was not left in peace until finally he paid up a year and a half later. Timely reciprocation is also motivated by the belief that heaven is not open to votaries with unpaid debts. As Mayuela put it, "there are people who are about to die and before dying ask their family to fulfill the promise for them," because they feel "obligated by the fear that the Lord is going to punish them." One dead woman channeled a message to her family members gathered for this purpose, telling them that she had unfulfilled promises and asking that the debts be paid by proxy so she could rest in peace in heaven. Some offerings suggest an eleventh-hour fulfillment of the promise, precisely to avoid such problems. In 1913 a man was robbed and shot by four men, survived thanks to an intervention by the Virgen de la Luz, and many years later, in 1938, when he was eighty-three years old, made his offering.[19]

As is evident in this last example, there is great latitude in the conception of timely repayment and sometimes lassitude in fulfillment of promises. Votaries in this class reap the benefits, minimize the cost, and postpone the repayment. Francisca from Jalisco petitioned the Virgen de San Juan de los Lagos during pregnancy complications, promising a shrine visit with the child if the birth were successful. A daughter was born without complications, but about five years later, when the family moved to Dallas, Texas, the promise had still not been fulfilled. A miraculous solution presented itself years later when the Virgen de San Juan de los Lagos visited Dallas for a week in October 2013. This visit provided immigrants with the opportunity to fulfill their promises and to pay their debts in person, but Francisca's motivation was low and she made no preparations. "My idea was to find out where the church was but, I thought, 'I don't think I will go,' because I didn't know where the church was." She and the daughter, now twenty-five, then came upon the church accidentally because it was near a clinic where the daughter had a mammography appointment, "as though the Virgin accommodated me so that I would come here." Her daughter added, "We didn't know where it was and got here by chance." The indifference to fulfilling the promise was consequently reconceived as a bestowal of additional miracles—the visit to Dallas, the proximity to the clinic—and a facilitation: if Francisca doesn't go to the Virgin, then the Virgin comes to Francisca. The meaning of events, including reciprocation, is defined by votary perceptions.[20]

In Mexican tradition as in devotions in other regions and periods, gods and saints are believed to be punitive. This is particularly true for breach of votive contracts—"we must fulfill our vows punctually, if we do not want to experience punishment," as a colonial priest put it—but Mexicans are also penalized for lack of faith, for mocking miraculous images, and for unacceptable behavior during pilgrimages. One nonbeliever's tortilla-making machine was supernaturally disabled. Another man went blind for a disparaging remark regarding the beauty of the Virgen de San Juan de los Lagos, and a bandit was saved from a firing squad by the Cristo Negro de Otatitlán and then banished to hell for his incredulity regarding the miracle. In colonial Spanish America all calamities—epidemics, earthquakes, floods, droughts, volcano eruptions, pirate attacks, indigenous rebellions—were understood as divine punishments and often resulted in processions of miraculous images to placate divine wrath.[21]

The Catholic Church today nevertheless teaches that God does not punish humans. As Monseñor Francisco explained, Christ "always gives love to lift us up from the lack of love. He teaches us to love by loving us. That is God. That is the doctrine of the Church. God is mercy and does not punish." Laura, who has spent twenty years in the association that cares for the Virgen del Pueblito, said, "Our own actions cause negative things, it is not because God wants to hurt us." Padre Paco elaborated that point: "The punishment of a person is a consequence of one's own sin. It is not that God punishes, but rather the Christian faith teaches that if I commit a wrongdoing the damage can fall back on me. Not because God is punishing me but rather because of the very damage of the sin itself." Along the same lines Fray Hugo said that devotees often get angry at God and question why he has punished them with disease, but "God does not send us diseases." To think otherwise, as a less tolerant Chalma friar put it, is the work of "false devotees, superstitious and pusillanimous," who would convert the shrine into "a place of terror" and the Lord of Chalma into "an object of noxious fear," when in fact the image "is talking to us only about kindness and love."[22]

Marta, who is well instructed in Catholic doctrine, applied these ideas to petitionary devotion. Many votaries "fulfill their promises out of fear. They are afraid of the Lord, because they say 'he is going to punish me.' But I don't think he's going to punish anyone. If I can't fulfill what I promised him, then I'll pay him with a mass, a mass of thanksgiving. If I can't go to the shrine, he knows that and I'll fulfill my promise in another way."

Despite Church teachings and educated opinions like Marta's, most devotees persevere in the belief that miraculous images punish those who do not fulfill their promises. The more convenient position would be to follow Catholic doctrine and embrace a God who helps us when we need it but does not punish us when we deserve it. Devotees perhaps remain with their punishing God and images because the idea better conforms to their common sense, because the tough love is love nevertheless and further proof of sacred presence in everyday life, and because Christ on the cross has taught them that their suffering is meaningful and redemptive. Punishment is the flipside, the inverted complement, that reinforces miraculous benevolence. It provides evidence that God and the images are vigilant and participatory in everyday life, for better or worse. One man gave thanks to the Señor de la Misericordia "for those pleasant moments and also for the difficulties because I know that you have been with me." If punishment is removed from the equation it disrupts the balance, weakens the sense of ubiquitous oversight. And the fear, because it is transient, is compatible with affective familiarity and endows miraculous images with human complexity.[23]

Votary reciprocations presume that miraculous images, because they are like us, value what we offer them. It is taken for granted that images desire attention, recognition, deference, popularity; that they enjoy visits and recognize sacrifices made on their behalf; that they are flattered by the lavish and bejeweled accoutrements, the ambience worthy of royalty, the processions, and the extravagant fiestas; that they appreciate the offerings— clothing, ears of corn, braids, collages—made to them; and, above all, that they need devotion. This need is essential to votary and clerical conceptions of image empowerment: no devotion, no power. The power is allotted not in proportion to the exemplary Christianity of devotees, but rather to the outpouring of devotion in all of its ceremonial and material manifestations.[24]

What petitions and offerings would miraculous images desire if their identities were consistent with Catholic theology? One should give thanks to God for what he has given us, Father Paco said, and also "ask him that we be good, that we obey his will, that we obey his commandments. What we do here is precisely to deserve the rewards of eternity." Along the same lines Marta said, "How beautiful it would be if I said to him, 'Lord, grant me this miracle and I promise you that I will change and be a good person.' No one does that."

But a few votaries actually do, like a man who petitioned Niño del Cacahuatito for the restored health of a young boy and concluded his petition, "I promise you I will be a better person"; a stabbed man who promised to amend his ways; and a mother who in gratitude for childbirth wrote on a photographic offering to the Virgen del Pueblito, "I promise to be a good Christian and never lose the faith."

Beyond such exceptions the offerings appeal to an image's needs and desires as established by consensus and tradition. Foremost is the image's need for devotion. The market is competitive, so the image must excel in providing for devotees who have other options. If you grant my wish "I promise to pray only to you," as it is worded in a petition to the Virgen de los Remedios. The same presumption of a need or desire for devotion is carried in offerings whose explicit purpose is to expand a cult by publicizing miracles. In a characteristic offering dated 1745, parents explain to Oaxaca's Virgen de la Soledad that if she cured their sick son they would place a votive painting in her church to increase devotion by propagating the miracle. It does not occur to these votaries that "She does not need our praise. It is we who need her glory." If we conceive of her as needing our praise, then we open an access to that glory through exchange. A votary's subordinate role as the one in need is elevated to a parity when the needs becomes mutual: the votary needs the miracle and the image needs the devotion. In this configuration the hierarchy remains intact abstractly (because the image is sacred) while at once it is leveled or even inverted by votary practice (because the sacred image is dependent on devotion).[25]

Once miraculous images become dependent on devotion, their volition is manipulable to votary purposes. Miraculous images have the power—no one doubts that—but are they willing to deploy it for you? Votary promises and offerings are "part of a persuasive strategy" that appeals to the compassion and generosity of miraculous images but also to their vanity and self-interest. The votive exchange, captured in the formula *do ut des* ("I give that you might give"), is as much a balance of reciprocal self-interest as it is of reciprocal altruism. In votary perspective the formula is especially appropriate when advance offerings obligate an image to reciprocate, in the same way that votaries feel obligated after miracles that were not requested. The votary cannot compel the image's reciprocity, but devotion entitles one to miracles and experience can be interpreted in such a way that the reciprocal obligation is fulfilled by attribution even where others might not recognize miracles. The unilaterality of the arrangement is likewise registered in the image's need for devotion and susceptibility to persuasion, both constructs built by votaries to their own advantage.[26]

In previous centuries and other regions advanced offerings sometimes seemed bribes that motivated a sacred figure to grant a miracle. A woman suffering from a polyp promised a silver nose to the Virgin in exchange for restored health, and "after the woman made this vow, or rather as she was in the act of making it, the Lady of Heaven cured her, as if greedy for gain." In Mexican offerings the sequence is rarely so explicit, but on occasion the idea of an offering as incentive is suggested. A man with a swollen foot ordered from silversmiths "a silver foot, as big as his own foot" so that in the Virgen de Guadalupe basilica "they would hang it, commending himself to her with his whole heart so she would heal him." Another offering, to the Virgen de Tonatico, was used to advance or accelerate a miracle in progress: "Now I am almost well but I trust that upon making your miracle public you will grant me complete health." The suggestion in these instances is not that the images are greedy for offerings, but rather that they might be motivated to reciprocate, or to expedite, by the diligence of faithful votaries who make public offerings in advance. The second example is noteworthy for its explicit connection of publicizing the miracle and completing it.[27]

Manipulation is illustrated in the extreme when miraculous images are punished to coerce miracles. In Oaxaca some devotees "leave the Saint [image] under the burning sun when he has not sent the rain petitioned in rituals, so that 'he knows how it feels.'" Similar punishments occur in other regions, and images are also whipped and dragged. San Antonio is inverted to an uncomfortable upside-down position and remains there until he delivers a boyfriend or girlfriend to a votary, and when an animal is lost villagers incarcerate the saint in a box tied closed with a string until the animal is found. The incarcerated San Antonio is particularly suggestive as a hyperbolic trope for the situation of miraculous images generally. Venerated but controlled, under luxurious house arrest in their chapels and chambers, the images are entitled to servile devotion insofar as they remain with a community and satisfy its needs with miracles. The most dedicated female devotees of the Virgen de Talpa consider themselves slaves of the Virgin, but nevertheless their purpose is petitionary and their enthroned queen is expected to serve them.[28]

Offerings

Textual and material offerings are made for many reasons. Fundamental is fulfillment of one's promise to reciprocate: "I fulfill my promise by paying with this retablo," "in payment and debt of said miracle the García Quinteros dedicate this humble retablo," "here is my offering for the miracle that you did for me." Votaries sometimes use the phrase *en recompensa* (in recompense or compensation, with allusions to reward) to describe their motivation for an offering. A textual or material votive offering is at once payment and documentation of payment, a votary-issued receipt posted publicly before the image, so that the reciprocation will be acknowledged and credited to the right account. In Mexico this function is implied, but ancient Greek votive inscriptions sometimes made explicit a votary's satisfaction of obligations. "Know that you have received the debt, Asklepios, which Akeson owed you because of his prayer for his wife

Demodike: were you to forget it and claim it a second time, the votive tablet will serve as evidence."[29]

Another primary purpose of textual and material offerings is to give thanks. Reference to gratitude is commonly made in phrases like "in testimony of gratitude" and "in proof of eternal gratitude," as well as variations of "thank you" and "many thanks." Gratitude is a positive emotional response to a miracle, a heartfelt desire to acknowledge and reciprocate, and it strengthens the relationship between a votary and an image. Indebtedness, in contrast, is bound to obligation and the protocols of reciprocity. "Gratitude and indebtedness can be dissociated," and consequently some votaries experience one, some the other, and some combinations of the two, either simultaneously or successively over the long-term of votive interactions. Sincere gratitude gives us something to do with relief and joy, it shares co-ownership of emotions with the benefactor who made them possible and by doing so enhances them for ourselves. Just as faith is made manifest in devotion, gratitude is made manifest in expression. It feels good to be grateful. In a psychological experiment, the descriptive statements most selected to describe gratitude were "there is an inner warm glow, a radiant sensation," "a sense of well-being," "there is a renewed appreciation of life," and "I'm optimistic about the future."[30]

Votive offerings also aspire to a sense of permanence or at least longevity, to memorializing the fleeting miraculous moment in an enduring document or object. Such phrases as "for perpetual memory" and "I leave the miracle painted for memory" evidence an intent to objectify the miracle so that it will endure and be reactivated, in effect, by the perception of devotees who view its representation. In 1865 Feliciana, suffering from a fever "and finding no recourse in medicine," invoked the Señor de la Misericordia, was cured, and posted a retablo "to immortalize this wonder."[31]

The idea of permanence or longevity also extends to outcomes. A miraculous solution will not revert to a problem because the miracle has been fixed or frozen by objectification in an offering. A grandfather petitioned the Señor de Chalma to modify the intolerable behavior of a grandson who came home, presumably drunk, "at one or 2 in the morning, fighting with the whole family." The petition was successful, the grandson's behavior improved, and the grandfather made his offering: "I am sure that you did this powerful miracle for us, for which I dedicate 2 masses and this retablo." The grandfather identifies a miraculous cause for a perceived effect and implicitly registers the presumption that after proper action on his

part (the offerings) the problem is resolved and the improvement is permanent. The family's practical actions (disapproval, admonitions) failed,
but symbolic actions (petition, miracle, votive offerings) were successful,
closed the cycle, and seem binding on the grandson.

A miracle remedies the out-of-control situation, the offering objectifies
a sense of closure, and one's faith in the image's ongoing vigilance makes
the remedy seem permanent. The votive offering serves as a kind of insurance, or assurance, that the positive change will endure. At the shrine of
the Virgen del Pueblito there is a photograph of a couple posing in front
of the Virgen de Guadalupe basilica. The photograph had been torn in
half, with the husband on one side and the wife on the other, and later
taped back together. The text on the back reads: "Many thanks for having
made my husband reconsider and that no one not even with their lies has
been able to separate what God united forever. Keep watching over our
marriage and don't let anyone come between us or separate us I ask you
for my children Holy Mother keep watching over my marriage so only
death separates us." The text gives thanks and at once petitions ongoing
protection, until death do they part, so that the past miracle will be consolidated and defended by future interventions. The miracle and votive offering are mutually necessary and interdependent components working
together to reunite what had been torn apart.

When votaries and priests are asked why offerings are made publicly
rather than simply giving thanks in prayer, they almost exclusively respond that offerings demonstrate an image's miraculousness to others, so
that devotion will increase. Antonio, referring to the Virgen de San Juan
de los Lagos, said, "So that people realize that the Virgin really is miraculous," and "so that more people find out and become devoted to her." In
reference to the Señor del Rayo, Lourdes said similarly, "so that people
see," and "to make people aware that he does do miracles, so that people
believe in him more, get closer to him, and don't lose faith." Fray David
made the same observation—offerings "increase faith in the image"—and
then added insightfully that offerings are also made "to assure oneself of
one's own conviction," because to some degree the reality of the miracle is
dependent on representing it. Fray Hugo added that votive offerings are
motivated by a desire to inform others of a granted miracle, but also to
demonstrate that *this* particular image—the stress is his—is highly miraculous, which benefits the image in itself but also in competition with
images from other churches and regions.[32]

Gaby took these ideas in a different direction by saying that "a miracle is a gift, and you want to share the gift with others." If someone gives you jewelry, she said, you want to show it to others to express your pride in the gift. Showing it to others also quietly evidences your love worthiness. Sometimes votaries seem inclined simply to the happy announcement of their gains: "I give thanks to the Holy Niño de Atocha because I have three sisters and I'm the ugliest and I got married first, to a good man." Fray David explained that votaries publicize miracles due to "a certain altruistic sentiment" that is expressed orally as well as in offerings. "If that image did a miracle for me, I have relatives, I have friends, many people with the same needs that I have, and I'm going to tell them, 'Do what I did, the results were very positive, he did the miracle for me.'"[33]

Miguel also stressed dissemination of miracles by word of mouth. You request a miracle, receive it, and make your offering. "People ask you why you're doing it. You tell them the story, and they tell others," and consequently other people's faith is strengthened by what happened to you. Such circulation of miracle stories is enhanced by more formal opportunities for witnessing, and by textual outlets in church publications and local newspapers. The newsletter of the Virgen del Pueblito's shrine solicits information in a carefully worded announcement: "Have you received a grace or favor through the intercession of the most holy Virgen de El Pueblito? Share your testimony with us." One can do so in the church office, on the shrine webpage, or by email, and some of the testimonies are reproduced in this same publication. Shrine visits, petitions, and, in turn, miracles can increase exponentially after promotion of an image, particularly when high-profile miracles are reported by mainstream press.[34]

In this context the primary objective of votive offerings is testimonial: "In proof of the miracle," "in testimony of such a great miracle," "I make public testimony," "I dedicate the present offering in testimony of her great miracles." A probative intent is suggested too by uninscribed offerings that are made not so much in reciprocation and thanksgiving as they are to document the occurrence of a petitioned miracle. Such offerings would include, for example, a photocopy of a visa, an entrance letter to a university, an x-ray or medical report, and a photograph of a newborn child.

A secret offering is an offering half wasted: the proof must be public so that the miracle inspires others. "Niño del Cacahuatito I want everyone to see the great miracle that you did for me," one votary wrote. Another, in a message to the Virgen de San Juan de los Lagos, wrote "by means of this retablo I make known to everyone who sees it the great miracle that she did for me." A primary purpose of such proof, as worded in a Talpa offering, is to demonstrate to others "that miracles *do exist!*" No one thought this female votary would survive, but after four kidney operations her health improved and she made her offering with the specific purpose of affirming the reality of miracles to reassure other devotees. In this same spirit a handwritten text to the Señor de la Misericordia begins with a plea: "Please, I ask everyone to read my story so that they see how great God is and always have confidence in Him, he guides us along the path of goodness, let's be grateful to Him by believing in Him." Many other petitions sound the same theme: "with this I fulfill my promise for the greater glory of God"; "so that all devotees of Most Holy Mary of Solitude do not leave Their Holy devotion this Miracle is made Public."[35]

As suggested by all of these passages, "Each miracle that is produced strengthens devotees' faith and that strengthened faith facilitates the multiplication of miracles." Votive messages are addressed to miraculous images, but devotees are ratified recipients too. Reading a posted offering is something like invited eavesdropping, because the miracle recipients are purposefully communicating at once with an image and a devotional community. The offering is like a published open letter, or like saying something to one person when the intent is simultaneously (or primarily) to make an impression on others who overhear. If miraculous images lack the capacity to read, see, or appreciate offerings, then images drop out as interlocutors and we are left with devotees who communicate indirectly with one another through the mediation of images and offerings.[36]

Votive offerings, in short, are multiply efficacious: they fulfill promises, pay debts, express gratitude, bear witness, document and commemorate, strengthen faith, and mediate discursive exchanges between votaries. Some offerings tend more to one function than another, and many combine functions in various configurations: "we came to pay this promise and to give thanks"; "with this testimony I fulfill my promise and make public"; "to make this miracle public and...I give infinite thanks."[37]

Reciprocity

The exchange between miraculous images and votaries is asymmetrical. A votary's ability to reciprocate is incommensurate with a miraculous image's ability to give. This imbalance is presumed in votive contracts, which might specify a visit and photograph in exchange for the successful outcome of a difficult pregnancy. One is cured of cancer and offers a hospital wristband in exchange. In the perspective of sincerely grateful votaries, such offerings are tokens or symbols of gratitude for a gift—the miracle—that cannot be reciprocated. At times the symbolic nature is explicit in offerings: "This baby cap is the symbol of our gratitude." The offering endeavors not to equitably reciprocate but rather to represent "the sincere gratitude you feel in your heart," as Teresa put it, and the gratitude you may have expressed in prayer. The exchange relation is something like giving mom flowers on mother's day, either in sincere gratitude or in dutiful but loveless compliance. The same two-peso milagrito can be offered with heartfelt gratitude or pinned up to fulfill one's obligation.

Such imbalanced reciprocity is characteristic of patron-client relations, which are hierarchical and without pretense to equity. A patron is someone with status, power, influence, authority, and resources that he or she is willing to share under certain circumstances, and a client is someone in a lesser position who is in need and accepts the subordinate, respectful, and sometimes obedient position required for eligibility to these benefits. As Gaby put it, people say to miraculous images, in effect, "you're very powerful—will you give me a hand?" Petitionary devotion in this perspective seems a transcendentalized variation of proxy control, by which "people try to get those who wield influence and power to act on their behalf to effect the changes they desire."[38]

The protocols of reciprocity are generally derived from norms among humans within the votaries' cultures. The closest social model is the godparent-godchild relationship in the ritual kinship system known as *compadrazco*. Like relationships between miraculous images and votaries, these arrangements are "more flexible than kinship and more enduring than friendship" and "are both vertical and horizontal, both intensive and extensive." They are adaptable to diverse circumstances, from the "formal posture of respect (respeto) to the most informal, personal stance of mutual trust (confianza)." An "affectionate dependence" develops particularly when devotees commend themselves to images with which they feel a special connection or affinity. Constant protection at low intensity is activated by need and crises that trigger specific, targeted interventions. Despite the hierarchical arrangement and acknowledged dependence, devotees can perceive the relation as mutually beneficial, binding, and reciprocal.[39]

The asymmetrical reciprocity of petitionary devotion in some cases is nothing more than a consequence of ingratitude, selfishness, or lack of generosity. One man's father survived two risky operations thanks to the

Virgen de San Juan de los Lagos. In his note of thanks the man said, "How will I be able to thank you?" and without answering the question added, "I will continue asking you [for miracles] on behalf of my whole family, so that we will always remain united." A similar attitude toward reciprocity was expressed by a man who was approved for a visa to the United States after petitioning the help of St. Toribio Romo. An interviewer asked the man how he thanked the saint for the favor, and the man responded, "Well, just thanking him, I just went to Santa Ana and left him a piece of paper on which I wrote my gratitude."[40]

Often the difference between adequate and inadequate reciprocity is a matter of tone, insofar as tone is indicative of disposition. In a petition to the Virgen de Tonatico a woman with a terminal illness made a moving plea and then offered an apology, "with my whole heart and with tears in my eyes mother because I have nothing to give except to ask you." In content this text is similar to that of the man who gave thanks by requesting more miracles, but the woman's tone and emotional investment evidence the sincerity of her gratitude. Many votaries offer only notes or milagritos in exchange for miracles, but they do so with humility, reverence, and genuine appreciation. Father Juan Manuel gave the example of a rural couple who had nothing but one horse. The horse was attacked by African bees, was stung countless times, and was sure to die. As the horse rolled on the ground in agony the couple petitioned the intervention of the Virgen de Soriano ("in the country you scream it"), the horse survived, and the couple offered a tiny horse milagrito at the basilica. The milagrito is a symbolic token of the deep and probably ineffable gratitude that the couple feels and feels the need to express. The implicit discourse behind the offering is, *Here is our horse that you saved. We give it to you so you can see our gratitude.* Something of high symbolic value is exchanged for something of high practical or material value.[41]

Consequently petitions from votaries who have little to offer materially are often made with a devotional tone deeply imbued with emotion that itself constitutes an offering. On the back of a photograph showing a grandmother holding a baby, the grandmother wrote a note asking the Virgen de Pueblito to help her daughter find work. The note concluded with "I have nothing to offer you only my love and faith." A collage offered to the Virgen de Zapopan shows an older woman beside a still older, emaciated, seemingly moribund woman lying in bed. In barely literate prose the former gives warm, almost desperately grateful thanks to the Virgin and God for the mother's discharge after two months in the hospital, and says, "I have no way to pay you for all of this." In these cases, as in the offering of the horse milagrito, the balance of trade depends to a great degree on the value that the votary places on the offering and on the feelings (love, gratitude, faith) with which the offering is invested.

Visits to shrines are a good example. Their intent is not to balance the scale, although long-distance trips are an expense and a sacrifice, but rather to be physically present before a miraculous image. A high value is placed on paying respects and giving thanks in person. This very human encounter is a courtesy call to a social superior and at once an intimate visit with a dear friend. It confers upon images the desire to be visited and the capacity to receive visits, and it renews the relationship between votary and image, as visits do in secular social life. The visits are also double-directional, because miraculous images—like the Virgen de San Juan de los Lagos who went to Dallas—travel to visit devotees. This is generally done by procession of a replica image (known as a *peregrina*, literally pilgrim) to visit regional parishes and other local images.

On occasion images also venture out on their own. In a typed textual offering accompanied by a photograph a mother explained that her twins were born prematurely and that their survival was uncertain. Just when it was needed an image of Niño del Cacahuatito could not be found in the house, and after an unsuccessful search everyone realized that the missing image had gone to the hospital to take care of the twins. Near the end of the message the mother expressed her desire to reciprocate the visit: "I hope that someday I will be able to take my girls to meet you at your temple and bring you flowers. Just as you made that long trip in December I hope one day to be able to do the same."

The young Ramón was cured after falling from a truck because Carmen petitioned the Niño de la Cruzada on his behalf. When Ramón was convalescing Carmen told him "to offer his first steps to the Niño. I'm not telling you to bring him votive candles, I'm not telling you to bring him anything, what he wants are your steps. That you go there and give him thanks." The implicit discourse is something like, *Look, here I am, I can walk now thanks to you.* Sharing this joy with the image is better than any material offering. When Chela gives instructions regarding shrine visits, she says: "When you go to the church, talk with him, and ask him to help you. You just have to enter and greet him: 'Lord, I'm here now, I came to see you from so far, to greet you here where you are.' Then all you have to do is ask him to help you and protect you, so that nothing bad happens to you again." Others prefer to commemorate their visit or to document their fulfillment of a

promise. When a boy's hospital treatment was successful thanks to a miracle from Niño del Cacahuatito, his grandmother brought him to the
shrine and in a written message narrated what was happening: "Today I
bring him here in your presence, fulfilling my promise of faith."[42]

Shrine visits, including pilgrimage, are in themselves and as components of votive complexes the most common form of offering. Visits have
multiple purposes: to fulfill a promise, maintain relations, express gratitude, make a material or textual offering, make a new petition, request
forgiveness, enact faith, recharge faith, attend mass, make confession,
make a juramento, be in proximity of or contact with sacred power, get
blessed with holy water, acquire relics, participate in fiestas, socialize with
other devotees, and generally immerse in the sacred ambience. "I went to
the Virgin's house," Carlos said, referring to the Virgen de Guadalupe
basilica in Mexico City, and when he came out, he added with emotion,
gesturing with his hand over his body, "I felt very protected." Pilgrimages share
all of these functions and in addition purge sins, make sacrifices in thanks for
or anticipation of a miracle, break routine, foster solidarity and camaraderie,
and provide opportunities for testing oneself, succeeding, and arriving to a
shrine in cathartic joy and worthy of a miracle. Pilgrimage is a difficult, life-
enriching, moving experience that many pilgrims describe as beautiful.[43]

It is also one of many offerings that require a physical or financial sacrifice. Others include walking to a shrine on one's knees, wearing a crown
of thorns, carrying a cross, and other penitential practices; abstaining
from food, drink, or drugs; offering hair or a braid, sometimes grown for
this purpose; participating in a ritual dance troupe when it requires frequent rehearsal and physical challenge; and making a financial sacrifice
through expensive gifts to images and shrines or by hosting fiestas or
subsidizing an associated expense (for a band, food, or fireworks, for example). Sometimes suffering in itself is an offering. From her hospital
bed a young woman wrote to the Señor de la Misericordia, "I have nothing
to offer you except the sufferings of my flesh and the sadness of these
bitter days." When doctors found a tumor in a Mexican American's woman's kidney, she said, referring to her suffering, "God, I give it to you. It
was nothing compared to what you suffered."[44]

Priests encourage votaries to make reasonable and nonsacrificial vows,
perhaps with the idea that God prefers our well-being to our suffering and
indebtedness. In the third century B.C.E. the Greek philosopher Theophrastus
was already asking, "What do the gods prefer—a rich sacrifice or little
given in the right spirit?" and opted for the latter. Most contemporary

Mexican devotees opt similarly, or sometimes for little given in the wrong spirit, but many also choose penitential sacrifice precisely because—despite the priests' admonitions—it emulates their crucified God. You have to experience it "in your own flesh," a pilgrim explains, and adds "that's the reality of life."[45]

Pilgrimage is an extension, an amplification, and a metaphor of the hardship of everyday life, but hardship given new meaning, made purposeful en route to miracles. Walking a distance on one's knees, similarly, exaggerates and concentrates quotidian sufferings and offers them as an inducement to favorable responses from miraculous images. Penitents fight fire with fire; they suffer purposefully as a means to alleviate suffering. A similar inversion is evident in material votive offerings. A wall of offerings relates a history of crises and misfortunes, but the suffering, fear, vulnerability, and tragedy are ultimately redirected toward the happy ending afforded by miraculous intervention. Unlike the iconography of Christ, which suggests patient suffering as redemptive, votive offerings subordinate suffering to the miracle of alleviation. A community's trials are transformed into success stories and are thereby conducive to hope and perseverance through faith.

The Miracle of Everyday Life

Giving thanks always and for everything.
Ephesians 5:20

Petitions and votive offerings archive the evolving concerns of Mexican Catholics across centuries, regions, and social groups. While in some periods maritime travel and war generate the need for miracles, in others employment and safe migration are predominant concerns. While urban youth give thanks for miracles regarding successful studies or resolution of personal problems, the rural poor are concerned with harvest and sick or lost livestock. A collective of petitions and offerings reflects the social context in which it is produced, documenting an evolving catalog of problems and perils. Some of these are constant (illness, accidents, consequences of violence) and others vary by period, region, class, gender, ethnicity, and the predominating values and challenges of a given social group. In Mexico as in other regions, miracles concerning health are prominent and range from minor ailments ("help me to close my hand completely please") to life-threatening diseases ("I trust in you and know that the tumor will disappear").

The world "miracle" in English suggests an extraordinary event that bends or breaks the laws of nature, like a resurrection from the dead or the spontaneous remission of a terminal disease. Mexican usage of the same word—*milagro* in Spanish—also encompasses such spectacular events, as evidenced particularly in retablos and narratives from the colonial period. A man hit accidentally by an arrow died and was resuscitated by the Virgen de Guadalupe, and dead children were resuscitated by the Virgen de Zapopan and the Virgen de Talpa. On occasion resuscitations still occur, and include for example the girl María José, who was revived after drowning by the Virgen de los Dolores in Soriano. A retablo from the shrine of San Francisco de Asís in Real de Catorce shows a man murdered by stabbing who "came back to life after three hours"; and in a votive text a mother gave thanks to the Virgen de los Remedios for resuscitating her son, Raúl, who "was born again" after an accident. Miraculous cures of life-threatening illnesses occur with far greater regularity than resuscitations, and, like miracle narratives supporting canonization processes, generally include variations of the phrase "the doctors were surprised by the miracle."[46]

In addition to these extraordinary occurrences, the word "miracle" in Mexico and throughout Spanish America encompasses a broad range of phenomena, from the most banal daily events to near fatal accidents. The word *favores* (favors) is sometimes used, particularly at the lower end of the scale, and less frequently *la gracia* (grace), which is the most theologically accurate term. Miracles are integrated into everyday life deeply imbued with sacred presence. Devotees live their faith, and this lived faith is integral to their social world—family, work, love, community—but also to their orientation, interpretations, access to resources, and sense of control. A miracle in popular devotion "is one that exceeds not the laws of nature but rather the real possibilities of a devotee, which are frequently very limited by people's low educational level, by poor medical and sanitary conditions because of structural poverty in Latin America, and by a lack of savings to respond to unforeseen situations."[47]

In popular Catholicism throughout Spanish America material and spiritual worlds are not bordered realms separated by the sky, but rather are interacting dimensions of a single holistic reality. One talks to the dead, cares for them, makes requests of them for practical help and guidance. A sixty-seven-year-old Mexican American woman, when asked if her dead parents visited her, said, "Yes, I love it. It makes me very happy." Another older woman, also in reference to a deceased mother, said "I would see her. I would feel that she sat on my bed and she would lie down with me and hug me." Others similarly reported visual and tactile contact with the dead. "I feel like they pat me on the shoulder," a woman said of her dead relatives, "like they are telling me, 'You are doing a good job.'" A loving reciprocity is maintained because the two realms, here and hereafter, are interdependent. "They help us and we help them," as another Mexican American woman put it in reference to her dead parents.[48]

Sacred presence likewise engages socially with humans. It is concentrated in miraculous images but is also diffuse, pervasive, and perceptible in a supple emotive certainty that lends sense and security to a chaotic world. As the Latin American Episcopal Council (CELAM) explained it, "Popular piety delicately penetrates the personal existence of each devotee.... At different moments of the everyday struggle, many turn to some small sign of God's love: a crucifix, a rosary, a candle lit to accompany a sick child, an Our Father mumbled among tears, an affectionate gaze at a loved image of Mary, a smile directed to Heaven," and all of this "in the midst of a simple joy."[49]

The sense of sacred presence is implemented when devotees commend themselves to a particular miraculous image. Through such commended care and its daily renewal in prayer one's self-efficacy is reinforced by vigilant, potential agency that intervenes imperceptibly but constantly at low frequency and then more actively when summoned by urgency or need. Votaries' attributions of success and well-being to miraculous images are sometimes comprehensive: "Everything that we are, do, and have we owe to you," as a family expressed it to the Señor de Chalma. Offerings are often made not in response to a specific miracle but rather for this ongoing support, reinforcement, and protection. Miraculous images are thanked for guidance, strength, fortitude, perseverance, tranquility, happiness, insight, wisdom, and the stamina to tolerate adverse circumstances. "Thank you for giving me the strength to keep on going" is common, as are variations of this sentiment: "Thank you for keeping us strong, positive, happy, and full of hope." Another votary wrote, "I implore you to enlighten my understanding, strengthen my will, purify my heart, and sanctify my soul." Images are also thanked for miracles that were not requested, because the commended votaries know the source. One man gave thanks to the Señor de Otatitlán for "all of the favors granted without asking you for them."

The stakes are higher when miraculous images intervene for narrow escapes from precarious situations, sometimes without being asked. A 1903 broadside narrates the story of Fidencio, whose father converted to a Protestant church and later threw him into a fired oven as punishment for praying to the Señor de Chalma. Fidencio emerged unharmed the following day, accompanied by angels, and his father returned to the Catholic faith. A colonial narrative similarly relates a miraculous rescue but now through direct intervention of an image, the Virgen de la Bala (Virgin of the Bullet), which thereafter carried the feat in her name and pedestal. A husband who wrongly accused his wife of infidelity and was enraged by jealousy "one day decided to kill his innocent wife, picked up a pistol, and shot her." The wife was helpless but took "as defense and shield a small image of the Virgin," and "the bullet was stopped miraculously by the image."[50]

This motif of corporal shielding repeats with some frequency. On December 14, 1921, a vandal hid dynamite in flowers that he offered to the Virgen de Guadalupe. The explosion caused massive destruction, but the Virgin was unharmed because a metal image of the crucified Christ took the blast to protect her. That crucifix, known now as the Cristo del Atentado, was completely bent in an arc from the impact it sustained. Marta tells a related story. Her sister and an infant son lived on a hill in Ixtlahuaca, and during a thunderstorm a bolt of lightning struck the house. The sister had images of the Señor de Chalma and Virgen de Guadalupe on her dresser, "and the lightning hit the Christ, here in this part of his back [she points], and it made a hole, the whole room was clouded with dust, with smoke," and "for me it was a miracle of the Señor de Chalma, who took the lightning hit to protect them."[51]

At moments of peril devotees instantly, almost instinctively, petition protection from the images to which they are commended. Manuela's lifelong care is entrusted to Oaxaca's Virgen de la Soledad, so when an earthquake began Manuela knew what to do: "Instead of thinking anything else the first thing I did was commend myself to her, and, miraculously, the ceiling didn't fall on me, it fell all around but I remained intact." Others make similar spontaneous petitions during or after car collisions and other accidents. In a votive text a woman explains that while on the highway with her husband "a trailer carrying 20 tons of soda came toward us without brakes and crashed into our truck totally destroying it. At the moment when we were about to crash I screamed to you, HOLY VIRGEN DE TONATICO SAVE US." The husband was seriously injured and was not expected to survive, but "little by little he was getting better miraculously." Commended care provides blanket coverage, and urgent requests (referred to by the same verb, *encomendar*) catalyze quick responses during impending crises.[52]

Pilgrims give thanks for stamina and safety en route to shrines and for the very privilege of traveling to visit a miraculous image. In the broader view their gratitude is for the health and means that made the journey possible, together with the honor and benefits of being in the image's presence. As a couple wrote to Niño del Cacahuatito, "thank you for permitting us to come another year despite everything, what we faced wasn't an obstacle to being here today." Two handwritten notes left for the Virgen de Talpa are also characteristic: "Today I come to your altar to give you thanks for permitting me to be able to come to see you"; and "Thank you for permitting us to come to see you on our first visit as husband and wife." In a message to the Virgen del Pueblito, a votary gave thanks "for leading my footsteps to your shrine in order to meet you and praise you." He then petitioned a related miracle: "I ask you Virgencita regarding my legs you know that they hurt and I can barely walk."[53]

The everyday miracles that are acknowledged in petitions and offerings can seem trivial or even ludicrous (thanks for relief from a hangover; or "for returning my cat Mimy who got lost," written on the back of a photograph depicting the happy reunion) but are often highly significant to the votary's perceived well-being. As a girl María Isabel petitioned the Señor de Villaseca because the tortillas she made always turned out poorly formed or burned. The petition seems banal, but within her family—the center of her universe—the miracle was highly meaningful because it restored María Isabel's self-esteem and status (her mother complimented rather than mocking her, her father and brother had lunch). In thanks for "so great a miracle that he did for me," as she put it decades later, María Isabel offered her first well-made tortilla at the Villaseca shrine. Other adolescent petitions likewise index concerns that seem trivial but, when you are fourteen, have a life-and-death feel to them. One young girl asked the Virgen de la Paz for good grades "and that Carmen stops gossiping."[54]

Throughout the history of Christianity miracles pertaining to health have always been prevalent, and they are as well in Mexico today. In a typology derived from processes of canonization between 1201 and 1417, an average of 85 percent of miracles were health-related. In another study of more than 1,400 miracles from the sixteenth to the twentieth centuries, about 92 percent were healing miracles (of physical or mental illness). Perhaps in these cases and certainly in Mexico today, the attribution of medical miracles depends largely on how healing is defined. In biomedical usage healing connotes a clearly identifiable positive outcome after treatment, but in miracle-related usage this meaning is complemented by healing as a medical or folk-medical intervention regardless of the result, and by a process, sometimes long-term, in which partial recovery, improving health, or lessened pain are worthy of miracle attributions.[55]

Psychological disorders range from stress, phobias, and depression to suicide attempts and schizophrenia. One retablo shows a man lying down with his bloody head on a rock; a hand and hammer are posed above for another strike. The text relates that Pablo, "despaired by the death of his mother, resorted to suicide, hitting himself with a hammer 6 times over a rock," until the Virgen de San Juan freed him of self-destructive thoughts.[56]

The medical miracles of miraculous images are usually performed through human agency. Such collaborations are well summarized in an offering to Niño del Cacahuatito "for restoring the health of my godmother," who had "cancer in a breast and by means of treatments and chemotherapies it was eradicated completely." After repeated clinical treatment some votaries petition images in specifically biomedical terms like "cerebrospinal meningitis." "Take good care of her lungs, her bronchia, and all of her organs," one votary wrote to the Virgen del Pueblito. On occasion a miracle is performed directly by a miraculous image, particularly when resort to medical doctors is unsatisfactory. After several fractures resulting from an automobile accident doctors advised leg amputation as the only solution. The patient went instead to the Señor de Amula in Jalisco, and after four months "was completely cured and without need of any surgery at all."[57]

Rescue from near-fatal accidents of all sorts is prominently represented in votive offerings. With variation by period these include transit accidents (car, bus, truck, train, horse, carts, carriages), attack by bulls and other animals, near-drownings, workplace accidents (particularly mining), and falling (from trees, buildings, bridges, cliffs). Motifs that repeat with relative frequency in earlier offerings include pedestrians run over by horse carts and carriages, and survival after prolonged dragging when a horse rider's foot gets caught in a stirrup. Votive offerings after transit accidents today include photographs and sometimes news articles that illustrate the destroyed vehicles from which votaries miraculously emerged alive.[58]

Accidents by falling often depict children mid-air in free-fall from buildings, but workers (particularly in construction) and other adults are also represented. The detailed narrative of a retablo offered to the Virgen de Tonatico relates that in 1938 a man fell from a cliff into a river, "hitting his head on a rock and breaking his forehead on the right side." His death seemed certain, but when he was carried home his daughter commended him to the Virgin and "Our Lady granted him health in a short time."

A range of other accidents—perhaps as many types as there are humans to suffer them—include a thumb almost cut off by a saw; a mother shot by her son playing with shotgun; a twisted ankle; and a man on a bicycle hit by a truck ("luckily he only hurt his arm"). Many are workplace accidents, particularly in mines and on farms. Nineteenth-century bullfighting accidents are represented by retablos at the Señor de la Misericordia shrine; and at San Juan de los Lagos there is a homemade 2002 offering from a circus trapezist. The collage includes a circus-tent drawing, a photograph of the votary in her costume, and a narrative that includes, "I was trampled by an elephant, crushing my thorax, bursting my interior, spending 3 days in which I felt like I was in a dark tunnel, I saw two angels who showed me the road I should take," until thanks to doctors and the Virgen de San Juan de los Lagos, "I was born again."

Gratitude is also expressed frequently for relief from natural disasters including floods, earthquakes, fires, and storms. Lightning strikes stand out, perhaps because they are easily—and beautifully—representable. In a 1943 retablo offered to the Virgen de San Juan de los Lagos, a lightning strike killed two horses but not the boys riding them. A retablo dated 1923 shows a bolt of lightning striking a church in Chamacuaro, where "many women fell to the ground and one of the fallen women invoked the Miraculous San Nicolas and none of them died."[59]

Votaries are also rescued from assault, armed robbery, attempted murder, gang violence, and sexual violence. A fourteen-year-old girl recovered after being shot in the head, a family was saved during a home intrusion, passengers survive the armed robbery of a bus, and men in a truck were unharmed when the car behind them opened fire. In an offering at Chalma, two men who look like cartel traffickers in made-for-television movies asked for protection from their enemies and gave thanks "for letting us live another year." Such protection, particularly in indigenous contexts, sometimes takes the form of petitioning the elimination or punishment of one's enemies. "My Mother here I deliver my enemies," a woman wrote to the Virgen del Pueblito, and a list of names followed. In San Andrés Teotilalpam, white listones are tied to an image of an entombed Christ to petition the death of enemies.[60]

Other forms of armed violence, notably war, are represented in battle scenes, miraculous survivals, and pardons from execution, often during the Mexican Revolution. Framed portraits represent uniformed soldiers in current conflicts, with militarily disciplined faces, and upon safe return many of these soldiers express their gratitude with a visit and offering. One such portrait at the Señor de la Misericordia shrine had a note taped onto it: "I give thanks to the Lord for being alive after the grenade attack that I suffered in Iraq."

Miraculous images are also petitioned and given thanks for the return of friends and family members who have been abducted by drug traffickers and kidnapping rings or who have been disappeared by government forces. This is particularly apparent at San Juan de los Lagos. One framed offering has a drawing of two abducted men tied to chairs, and thanks are given for their survival. A missing-person poster, headed "Disappeared" above the name and photograph of the victim, with phone numbers for reporting, is the backdrop for a handwritten petition for safe return. At other shrines an offering gives thanks for safe release after a carjacking and short detention; a sister petitions the return of two disappeared brothers; and a family (they all sign on) gives thanks because the young Francisco was "rescued and liberated alive, safe and sound" after being kidnapped by drug traffickers. Another offering narrates the story of a homecoming: a son missing for twenty-five years returns, the father accused of murdering him is exonerated, and the Virgin is thanked. In some cases, such as a handwritten note to the Virgen de Zapopan, the longing for an absent person is evident but the cause of the absence is unspecified: "Here I ask that you bring me my son Germancito. I promise to come every year on the day of your fiesta."

Migration themes are prominent at many shrines and include absence, safe journey, evasion of Border Patrol, economic success, family reunification, and immigration status and documents. The petitions are made by the migrants themselves and by concerned family members. "As his wife I want to ask," wrote a woman to Santiago Apóstol in Coroneo, "that he crosses [the border] and nothing happens to him on the way." Longing is evident in many reunification petitions: "I beg you to help me get my papers so I can meet my granddaughter and see my son (in the United States)." Inscribed copies of US visas and other immigration documents are sometimes accompanied by photographs of happy families reunited. There are also many petitions for release of a relative in immigration detention, and on occasion there are references to return migration. A young boy, just learning how to write, asked the Virgen de la Paz, to "take care of my dad so he arrives healthy and with gifts for everyone."[61]

Votaries are predominantly poor, and consequently income- and subsistence-related petitions are common. In addition to more generic petitions to find jobs or repay debts, votaries make profession-specific requests: to protect a claim to a market stand, heal a sick calf, assure "that the cheese sells," or, when things go better, acquire a truck for a construction business. The less fortunate make petitions concerning homelessness, acquiring a home, improving housing, and protection from losing a current residence. "I hope you give me a home for me and my parents," a young girl wrote to the Señor de Chalma. A 2013 petition to the Virgen de los Remedios addresses poverty more comprehensively, including the intergenerational transmission of disadvantage. The votary first recalls a better past and then refers to "homes with prevailing poverty, overcrowding, ignorance that make the cycle of emotional and economic poverty repeat. Now that I'm a mother I'm aware of the marginalization that surrounds us but that more so is created by us. Take care that my children don't repeat that story, and not mine either."

Income-related fortuitous events are generally interpreted as miracles. Manuela unexpectedly received a six-hundred-peso tip at a moment of financial desperation and reacted to the windfall by breaking into prayer. Juan Manuel was stressed and depressed by expenses and debts when suddenly a hundred-peso bill appeared on the street in front of him. "God is not going to abandon us when we need him," his wife told him when she learned of the episode. Adriana had a similar story. She and her husband were completely broke and unable to get support from family. They asked the Señor de Chalma for help and shortly after Adriana saw a hundred pesos blowing in the wind. "Do you see what I see," she asked her husband, he applied in the affirmative, they caught up with the pesos, and together they gave thanks. "We can eat today," Adriana said to her husband, and to me she concluded: "You ask and just like that, as if it were something illogical, a hundred pesos come blowing by. God is with me, yes, yes, God is with me." Nevertheless Adriana and her husband are still broke and struggling for economic survival. When I met her at Chalma she was petitioning another miracle—a job for her husband—so the couple could escape the tiny room at her in-laws' house where she felt trapped ("it's like a prison") and deprived of freedom, privacy, and dignity.

In rural areas miraculous images are petitioned for the health, safety, and procreation of livestock; and for rain, protection from natural disasters, abundant harvest, and other matters concerning agriculture. "I am grateful and very happy to have received the great favor ... that she granted me by increasing the number of my turkeys," one woman wrote in reference to the Virgen de Tonatico, and others made offerings in thanks for finding a lost pig together with its piglets, for return of a team of oxen, for recovery of a sick mare, and "for having done for me the miracle of having saved my animals from a strong infestation of lice." Such petitions and offerings are frequently made with milagritos in the form of crops and farm animals, and with representational offerings like ears of corn and turkey feathers. On occasion, such as the October 7 fiesta of the Virgin of the Rosary in Talpa, there are collective petitions for good harvest. Corn stalks line the aisles of the church, the harvest is blessed during mass, and afterward, over a route carpeted with flowers, there is a procession of the Virgen de Talpa. About the same time in San Juan de los Lagos, the altar is covered in apples when a pilgrimage arrives from Puebla, where the apples are grown, to make an offering in thanks for a bountiful harvest.[62]

Also prominent are petitions concerning self-improvement. These range from "I want to change" to "help me accept myself as I am." Many such petitions are from adolescents and young adults. One wrote to the Virgen del Pueblito: "Help me to find the right way to be able to be who I want to be." A framed collage dated 2004 was offered to Niño del Arenal: "I offer you with all respect and devotion my braid and I ask you that you take good care of me and that you make me a good, respectful, studious girl, and that you protect my parents from all bad things in body and soul." Another girl, Judith, wrote to the Virgen de la Paz, "I want to ask you that you help me to accept myself as I am and that my happiness does not depend on other people. I ask that you give me peace, love, happiness, tranquility, and a lot of confidence in myself." An adolescent indigenous girl from the Oaxacan village of San Andrés Teotilalpam wrote, "I want you to help me to speak Spanish." Also prevalent among adolescents are social-conscience petitions regarding "peace on earth" and global warming, and to benefit the poor, drug addicts, migrants, sick people, and souls in purgatory.

Votaries who err or backslide from self-improvement often petition second chances, and in a range of situations. These petitions are sometimes related to the common belief that God saved given votaries because he had a plan for them, and then the common practice of ignoring the plan. One woman asked the Virgen de San Juan de los Lagos for forgiveness and another chance—another baby—after a previous daughter died in unexplained circumstances. A man pictured in a hospital bed, badly injured, with a tube in his mouth, wrote to the same Virgin, "Thank you Virgencita for giving me another opportunity to live and be better to myself." In a handwritten note a mother pleaded to Niño del Cacahuatito so that "they don't seize my house and that they give me the opportunity to pay"; and a young man struggling with a compulsion wrote to the Virgen de Tonatico, "I can't stand that I do it more and more please I ask you to make me stop doing those things because I feel bad when I do them, so many times I have promised you that I'm not going to do them anymore and I always do." He asked for forgiveness and that the Virgin "tell God to give me a last chance."

School and university students make frequent petitions and offerings related to academic advancement and performance. Petitions or thanks for admission to universities, training programs, and academies are common, as are requests for diligence, intelligence, good grades, and success in competitions. At the Virgen del Pueblo shrine a university grade report is inscribed with "I give thanks to our most holy mother and to the holy spirit for the great help they gave me to satisfactorily finish the semester." At the Cruz del Monte in Huatulco some school children posted their homework, and at the bottom of language exercises one boy wrote, "today my brother did his homework very well, I hope he keeps studying like this."

Many parents likewise make petitions regarding education. On a ribbon offering to the Señor del Sacromonte a mother wrote, "Lord with all respect and humility I ask if it is possible that you help my daughter in her studies give her the clarity to get ahead." Another mother petitioned the Virgin del Pueblito to help a son who "has learning problems"; and a third posted at the same site a photograph of two children, asking for their protection and that one of them, Dany, "tries harder in school."

Adults also request self-improvement and quality-of-life enhancements for themselves. The topics covered in a packet of pilgrim petitions wrapped together and left at the Remedios basilica are characteristic. These votaries petitioned a sense of security and confidence, strengthening of positive emotions (one asked for humility), elimination of negative emotions (anger, fear), and development of love relations (including "I want to give love"). One in this group requested "Desire to live; Strength to continue with my life." Another wrote, "More understanding and discernment in my studies; I need acceptance of myself and the faith that you gave me; I need to get rid of my fears." In similar petitions elsewhere, a woman asked the Virgen de Soriano for help with her nervousness, so that "I will be capable of expressing myself in front of anyone." A man at Villaseca wrote, "not fighting and not abusing"; another, at Remedios, "so that I'm no longer afraid of heights"; and another petitioned the Virgen de Tonatico, "because I'm so desperate that I sometimes think of doing bad things to get money, but I always remember you and prefer to eliminate those thoughts."

Many other petitions, often made by wives and mothers, request that a loved one stop drinking or taking drugs. A message to the Virgen de Tonatico, written by a wife concerned about her husband and her family, is characteristic. The wife petitioned that the husband "becomes a good person who no longer has vices please now more than ever I want him to change we are going to have a baby and what has happened before I don't want to continue."

Predominant among other family matters are petitions and offerings concerning pregnancy, childbirth, and children. Many parents give thanks simply for the blessing of having a child or another child, "for sending us our baby safe and sound," as parents put it at San Felipe Torres Mochas. A votive text at Otatitlán gives thanks for a new pregnancy after a miscarriage. Others ask for miracles to get through a difficult pregnancy or are concerned with the survival of a premature or unhealthy newborn. Many of these petitions are illustrated with photographs of infants in incubators or in other hospital settings. Parents also request health and longevity miracles for themselves, but in order to be with their children. In a petition to the Virgen de Tonatico a sick mother asks "let me live with my children many more years," and a husband and father thanks Niño del Cacahuatito "for having permitted me to be with my family because you gave me health."

Other family-related petitions and offerings concern marital discord, problems with adolescents and young adults, abuse (usually by drunk husbands, fathers, and stepfathers), intrafamiliar dysfunction, alcoholism and drug addiction, paternal abandonment, and a gamut of other negative matters pertinent to family life. A note from an adolescent boy to the Señor de Chalma reads, in its entirety, "that my parents stop beating me and that my dad finds work and my mother keeps trying." In a petition to an image of St. Rita in Guadalajara, an adolescent girl asked for the return of her mother: "I miss her a lot everyone misses her sometimes I feel very alone and sad we need her a lot. Bring her back to us please." Legal matters, such as divorce and child custody disputes, are also represented.

Positive efforts and accomplishments of families are likewise common in petitions and offerings. A father asked the Virgen de Tonatico for "courage to meet with my son"; a young man gave thanks to the Virgen de San Juan de los Lagos for a great mother, "full of virtues, love, and with a heart of gold"; and a man asked the Señor del Sacromonte "that you give me the tranquility that comes with having work and tranquility with my wife." Newlyweds give thanks for their marriage, often with a wedding photograph integrated into a collage or else inscribed with petitions for happy and procreative lives together. Faith itself is a gift worthy of gratitude— "thank you for making me believe in you," a woman wrote to the Virgen de Tonatico—and under siege by secularization and Evangelical churches a few wives and girlfriends ask for the conversion or religious tolerance of their partners as a basis for a strengthened relationship.

Matters concerning love, together with loneliness and longing, are frequently petitioned and are especially addressed to Virgins. Some people seek the love of a specific person: "Please grant me the love of Juan, that he fall in love with me," one wrote, and another opened with "I ask you the following favor" and then, "that you move the heart of Hector [full name] so that he loves me, wants me, and respects me, as I do him." An adolescent girl asked the Virgen de la Paz "that Daniel be my boyfriend," then crossed out "boyfriend" and went instead with "best friend in the world." (At the Remedios basilica Omar asked "that we never lack love," then crossed out "we" and replaced it with "I.")

Other votaries seek not a specific person but rather love in general or someone to love. "I would like to find that woman who gives my life meaning, I don't want to be alone, I want her to become my reason for being," a man wrote to the Virgen de Tonatico. Some want to alter the status of a relationship in one direction ("I love him. Make him return") or the other ("Get rid of that woman Carmen for me... help me to not be with her any more"). Concerned mothers also get involved: "Because of the difficulties in which my son Gregorio found himself with the woman who was going to be his wife for a first and second time they changed their minds, and seeing him in those moments of danger I asked Our Lady of San Juan for a good companion to appear and she conceded the miracle, we give infinite thanks."[63]

Petitions and offerings concerning criminal incarceration are primarily of two types: votaries who have been falsely accused and petition or give thanks for resolution of the injustice; and votaries who acknowledge guilt and are grateful for release from prison, usually early release. Characteristic of the first type is a 2013 handwritten note that gives thanks to the Señor de la Misericordia "for having freed me from a false accusation that could have taken me to prison unjustly." Many others concern last-minute salvation from execution, but without specifying guilt or innocence. A 1918 textual offering to the Virgen de Tonatico relates that a man was scheduled to be executed the following morning, "but on that same night God granted him the miracle of escaping." Often a retablo represents a firing squad aiming or a noose around a neck when a miraculous image intervenes just in time.[64]

The second type is well illustrated by a simple offering—red text roughly painted on wood—to the Virgen de los Remedios, in which the votary, sentenced to seven years, gives thanks for release after eleven months. Some of the petitions and offerings are made by the inmates themselves but many, due in part to access and in part to faithlessness, are made on their behalf by a family member, usually a mother. In a painted retablo to the Señor de la Misericordia a mother gave thanks because her son was sentenced to five years and was released after a month and a half. Another retablo, offered to the Virgin de Tonatico, relates that a husband was imprisoned for involvement in a murder and was scheduled for transfer to a distant prison. His grateful wife gave thanks because instead "he was released from prison and stayed as a servant in the house of the Official who arranged it." A similar concern with visitation is expressed in a graffiti petition at the shrine of Santiago Apóstol in Coroneo, which asks for a short sentence for Jovani and that he not be transferred to a distant prison.

In a related, less common category, votaries gives thanks for escaping deserved punishment. Exemplary is an embroidered offering that depicts a scene outside a bar in which a husband, with another woman, is shot in the chest by his wife. The text reads, "I give thanks to the Divino Rostro of Acapulco because I killed my husband and they didn't do anything to me." The situation is similar in a retablo that depicts a man outdoors between two cacti, with a text that explains, "grieving because I injured my wife, with her in the hospital and me in hiding, I invoked the Most Holy Virgen de San Juan, promising her to make this retablo public if she freed me from the Authorities and she [the wife] returned to my side."[65]

In some votive offerings the dominant urge seems simply a desire to do something with one's gratitude after a fortuitous event. Labor came sooner than anticipated and a husband gave thanks for "having permitted me to take care of my wife during childbirth, which came unexpectedly without time to take her to the indicated place." The husband does not necessarily view the event as a miracle, but feels deeply grateful that he was able to be present at the childbirth and finds an outlet for expression of his gratitude through votive offering. A woman gave thanks to the Señor de Chalma for healing her leg after an accident, and at the end of her offering wrote, "I want to take advantage of this space to thank my whole family" for their support and solidarity after the accident. She then itemized the thanks one by one—mother, father, siblings, niece. A man similarly gave thanks to the Virgen de San Juan de los Lagos and to the doctor who saved his leg after it was crushed by a truck, and he added, "Thanks to my friends, to my family that accompanied me in difficult moments." In these cases the votive process is a means of counting one's blessings and expressing gratitude for the friends and family members—in which miraculous images are included—who stand by one's side through crises and who make life meaningful.[66]

Sometimes an offering expresses relief, like a long grateful sigh released because a potential tragedy has been averted. After an infant daughter, Irene, was almost burned, her mother offered a votary-made painting showing the infant beside flames and the mother with a face of consternation. By making the offering the mother attributed prevention of the accident to the Virgen del Pueblito, but the votive process also spared the mother the miserable situation of having nothing to do with her gratitude and relief, no outlet for their expression. From the creation of the painting to its offering at the shrine, the votive process fulfilled a function something like venting to a friend who says, at the end, "It's over now, Irene is fine. It wasn't your fault."

Juquila

Light catches waves curling before the break and in the green-blue translucence one can see momentarily, before the whitewater falls, schools of
big fish that eat little fish and attract pelicans that eat medium fish, and
the bird activity attracts fishermen too and they come for the big fish with
baited hooks at the end of filament on spools but the pelicans have better
luck. Pelicans divebomb just past the breakline, their wings piloting in
gentle lifts and flinches and then folding quickly for sleek entry behind the
beak. One pelican pulled out of a dive, corrected course, braked mid air,
and plummeted in ninety-degree downward gravity before emerging tri-
umphant for a contented chew, the head lifted to swallow, and then took
flight for more deadreckoned plunge.

   The coast seems a world away from the mountains around Juquila. In
rhythmic seclusion on a stretch of beach my feet fit their prints and the
prints are erased and I'm thinking how we don't hear what informants tell
us, how we build a world for them—for us, in their name—within a paradigm that locks them out. There is no better example than discounting as
unsatisfactory or evasive devotees' common response, "It's the tradition."
Why do you make this or that offering, touch an image while you pray, do
limpias with herbs? "It's the tradition." We ask them to articulate a practice that is intuitive and consequently difficult to explain, and then analyze
past their response until the evidence conforms to our categories, priorities, and presumptions. Devotion to the Virgen de Juquila happens at two
sites: the shrine, which is in the town of Juquila and houses the miraculous image; and the pedimento, which is on a hilltop about four miles
above the shrine. At the pedimento votaries form miniatures representing
what they request—a car, a house—using the clay-rich dirt at the site.
When I asked why this was done rather than simply making a request in
prayer, I expected that votaries might explain, as they had at other sites,
that the petition was represented so that the miraculous image could see
it. Instead they responded uniformly, "It's the tradition."[1]

I have heard this seemingly empty refrain from countless devotees over decades in many Latin American countries, and in its composite, if we hear what the repetition is trying to tell us, it is among the most profound statements that informants can make. What they are saying, in effect, is *I don't have a personal reason for doing this; I do this, and in this way, because it is what someone in my culture does in this context;* and *I'm interested in the effects of my ritual actions, not in the reasons for doing them.*

As I discussed these ideas with Rafael in Juquila he made an insightful association—"It's like with food"—to suggest that many behaviors, including taste preferences, are taken for granted. People don't question why they eat tortillas, baguettes, or Wonder Bread, they just eat it, because that is what is eaten in their family or their world. It's the tradition. It would be difficult to explain why, or to separate our tastes from the context in which they were acquired and internalized—naturalized—as integral to who we are and how we do things. Cultural traditions provide us with the motivations, intuitions, skills, resources, beliefs, values, and shared meanings with which we negotiate everyday life, and by being who we are the traditions continue and evolve. "We should be at the church, where God's representatives are," Ofelia said, alluding to a more orthodox devotional tradition, "but instead we are here [at the pedimento] because of tradition."

Through tradition devotees acquire their sense of faith and its miraculous potential, and this sense, together with its enactment in devotion, has a constitutive role in their subjectivity and self-understanding. In devotions, as in human behavior generally, certain actions at certain times and places become habituated and self-perpetuating. When you visit Juquila you make creations out of clay mud, and when you visit Chalma you wear a garland and dance at Ahuehuete. Some actions, like the pelican dive, feel natural and innate; others feel more acquired. The learning and doing bring a sense of pleasure and belonging, and being competent brings a sense of fulfillment. Tradition provides a devotional model that can be emulated and enacted even by casual devotees who form the clay or do the dance simply because that is what one does in these contexts.[2]

With the exception of the chapel, where devotional fervor is apparent, the mood at the pedimento is more playful than devout. Making the clay models is a cultural as much as a petitionary tradition, and many visitors make the models for the experience itself rather than for serious petitionary purposes. There is a certain pleasure in getting your hands dirty to create something, especially with children, and the creation is meaningful because it is an extension of oneself or one's family left behind with the Virgin. Even among committed devotees one senses a petitionary breadth that suggests more *Why not give this a try?* than a deep need and heartfelt petition. "If you have some need," Pedrito said in the context of clay miniatures, "or a dream that has never been realized, and you would like to do it but don't have the resources to do it, but you have faith, you can go and ask the Virgin for it."

When traditions are internalized and assimilated as our own they become cognitive structures known as scripts. A script (or event schema) is a mental structure that organizes knowledge about behavioral norms and provides a sequence of actions and causal relations—first the devotion, then the miracle—to guide people through an experience. A full-visit sequence in Juquila might include bringing flowers or another offering; waiting on line with proper reverence and, when one's moment before the Virgin comes, praying, touching, offering, and perhaps making a petition or giving thanks; forming a clay petitionary object on the hillside outside the chapel; walking the four miles downhill to the shrine in town, perhaps doing the last stretch, however one defines it, on one's knees; praying in the church to the original image of the Virgen de Juquila; and offering a votive candle. This sequence or parts of it can be done with sincere devotion, by rote, or as an obligation. Faces often reveal the intent, but even nondevotional enactment of the script can trigger emotional engagement that feels like faith.[3]

Many descriptions of devotion to the Virgen de Juquila relate that petitions are made with clay models and a year later the happy recipients of miracles return to offer crosses on trees. Even a glance around the shrine's two locations—the pedimento and the in-town complex—is sufficient to see that neatly ordered protocols have little to do with actual practice. Votaries customize rather than standardize, and devotional scripts are realized in countless variations. Participants are not slaves to scripts or tradition, but rather implement and modify the devotion in accord with their own understanding and disposition. Many petitions are made at the pedimento and the in-town shrine without making clay miniatures, and many miracles are reciprocated without offering crosses. The petitionary options include texts, votive candles, fake money, purchased models, milagritos, and simple prayer, and the votive options include at least the range of material offerings found at all shrines, as well as pilgrimage and visits. Petitions also tend to be redundant, so that before or after modeling a clay miniature a votary might request the miracle in other ways from the Virgin in town, the replica in the pedimento chapel, or both.

The in-town church is the primary Virgen de Juquila shrine, but the pedimento is the primary site for making petitions and offerings. Preference for the pedimento seems to violate the need for proximity, for getting as close as possible to a miraculous image and its power. In the perspective of Juquila devotees, however, the pedimento provides all the advantages of the in-town shrine without the disadvantage of devotional restrictions. A replica image at the pedimento is a surrogate Virgen de Juquila that, unlike the original, is accessible for touching, kissing, and attaching petitions and offerings. In its sacred essence the replica is also indistinguishable from the original for the purposes of petitionary devotion. "The priest blessed it, said a mass for it, so that this Virgin might be a replica but is very significant as if it had the same value as the original." When I asked Pedrito if the replica had the power to perform miracles, he added, "It's the same thing, going to the pedimento or to see the Virgin, it's the same because you do it with faith. The power is the faith."

Particularly since the papal coronation of the Virgen de Juquila on October 8, 2014, the in-town shrine has an immaculate, orderly, religious-tourism ambience. Monitors situated throughout the church give visitor guidance. The pedimento, in contrast, has the playfully chaotic feel of a folk-saint shrine, and petitions and offerings are made throughout the complex. "You can't give anything in the church," Rafael said, meaning the

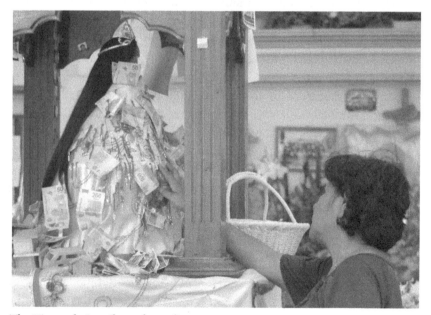

The Virgen de Juquila, at the pedimento.

in-town church, but at the pedimento you can pin things to the Virgin's vestments, leave offerings on the walls and tables beside her, write graffiti on huge votive walls, make petitionary miniatures on the hillside, and leave crosses in trees. On a random Saturday in January there were long lines and an hour or two wait to visit the replica Virgin in the pedimento, while at the same time the church with the original image had few visitors, and many were casual devotees or religious tourists. At other shrines, similarly, pilgrims make their journeys to visit images and petition miracles, not to attend mass.

The candle room at the in-town shrine is something of a hybrid space. It has the aesthetics, feel, and general orderliness of the church, but at the same time accommodates petitionary devotion by providing places for offerings. At the feet of several stone reproductions of the Virgen de Juquila votaries leave fake money, hair cuttings and braids, wooden house models, written messages, baby clothes, votive candles, and other offerings, all of which are cleared away regularly. Milagritos are pinned to the replica Virgins' vestments.

The image known today as the Virgen de Juquila was originally owned by a Dominican friar named Jordán de Santa Catarina, who in the seventeenth century evangelized among Chatinos in southern Oaxaca. When he was called back to Oaxaca city Fray Jordán gave the image—a small statue, about a foot in height—to his Chatino assistant, who took it home to his village, Amialtepec. The image was revered in a *santocale* ("house of the saints"). Devotion spread throughout the region when indigenous Christians reported miracles and, especially, when the image survived a fire that destroyed the village, including the santocale. In 1633 the priest at the parish seat in Juquila sought the transfer of the image to the church there, which he regarded as more suitable for devotion to a miraculous image with a growing cult. The Chatinos in Amialtepec resisted the loss of their object of devotion but also of the income acquired through lodging and sales to pilgrims. The priest nevertheless forced the transfer to Juquila, but soon after the image returned miraculously (or by *furta sacra*) to its original site in Amialtepec. The transfer and return occurred on three separate occasions, until finally the priest gave up. Several years later his successor resumed the effort to enshrine the image in Juquila, and he strengthened his authority by acquiring a decree of transfer from the bishop. In 1719 a ceremonial procession led by barefooted priests transported the image, and it was situated on the main altar of Juquila's church. The fugues back to Amilatepec ceased.[4]

These historical events are meaningfully modified in the oral tradition of devotees. The primary intent of the elaborations is to associate the pedimento with the Virgin. Some simply say that the pedimento was where the Virgin appeared; others have well-developed narratives. Ofelia had come from Puebla and together with her husband and son was forming petitionary objects with the clay dirt. She said that the Virgen de Juquila escaped three times not to Amialtepec, but rather to the pedimento. The Virgin did not want to be removed against her will as though she were property, so the priest asked (the Spanish verb is *pedir*) if he and the devotees could move her to Juquila in a dignified manner, with a formal procession. The Virgin granted the request. Bridging from the verb *pedir* to the noun *pedimento* (in this context, an "asking place"), Ofelia thus made two important links between the Virgin's history and current devotion: first, that the clay out of which petitionary objects are formed is sacred because the Virgin chose to reside there; and second, that petitions are still made at this site because it is where the Virgin grants requests, beginning with the priest's.

Local devotees relate the Virgen de Juquila's origins in a version that follows the historical account more closely, but like Ofelia they endow the pedimento with special meaning and importance. Pedrito, from Bajos de Chila on the coast, was characteristic. On three occasions the Virgin was brought to Juquila and returned to Amialtepec, so during a new transfer attempt the group paused at the site of the current pedimento "and they asked the Virgin to stop going back" to Amialtepec. A priest is not explicitly mentioned in this version; Pedrito stresses instead a great number of devotees who all walked barefooted in the procession as a sign of humility, sacrifice, and reverence. "The pedimento is called 'pedimento' because that's where they asked the Virgin not to go back. It's the right place to ask the Virgin for something because that's where they asked her. She was asked there and she is asked there. It's a tradition."

One of the informal, open-air restaurants near the pedimento has, in addition to dried beef and sausage links hanging over a wooden pole, a framed illustration of important moments in the Virgin's history. One picture shows the image at the base of a pine tree and in a circle before it are two priests and several devotees making their successful petition for the transfer to Juquila. The legendary event is to some degree historicized by representing it visually, and the restaurant owner continued in the same direction by literalizing and grounding the story to its place: "That tree used to be here." At a table in the semidarkness near the illustration an

Pedrito. The power is faith.

older man shook my hand and said something in Chatino that sounded like "vulnerability is a virtue." Another man lifted a bowl to finish the black water leached from black beans, a cat made a sound reminiscent of Coltrane growling his sax, and I was thinking that the framed pictures and the variant versions of the transfer narrative attest to people's need for a history that authenticates their traditions, that grounds them and explains them to themselves.

Association with the Virgen de Juquila makes the dirt at the pedimento sacred, and consequently some devotees take home samples for curative and other purposes. Devotees also rub mud on their bodies, particularly in a sign of the cross on the forehead. I had barely arrived on my first visit to Juquila when I saw some señoras coming toward me widthwise, like an offensive line, with a flat glaze of clay mud caked on their foreheads as though coming from an Ash Wednesday that had gone terribly wrong. As they approached the crowd made an instinctive flank maneuver expedited by common will, like nervous sheep shifting their huddle, and the señoras continued on their way with a dog trotting sideways behind them.

The petitions made today with clay miniatures vary in style and sophistication. Some are simple slabs with names, messages, or petitionary images etched into the clay. Many of these slabs are attached to the walls, like plaques, and a few have fake money wedged beneath the corners. One flat image represented a book. Fully three-dimensional miniatures are on the hillside, in sheds, and on square wall receptacles provided for this purpose. Votaries make the miniatures using the clay earth together with whatever else is at hand—sticks, leaves, paper, cardboard, bottle caps,

The model on the right represents a farm or ranch; a car is behind it. Another house is on the rock face, and on top of the rock there is a book and, beyond it, a human form.

pieces torn off a Styrofoam take-out container. These creations are necessarily limited to petitions that are visually representable, and consequently the great majority of the miniatures are of houses, vehicles, and people, sometimes together in composite arrangements. Farm or ranch complexes with multiple buildings, corrals, walls, and sometimes animals are also common. One miniature showed a human figure with a smaller human figure etched on the stomach area, presumably to represent pregnancy. A few had explanatory texts, like captions, to explain what was ambiguously represented: a piece of paper with "Clemente Factory" on a simply formed model building, and "twins" written in clay beneath two children, a boy and a girl, also modeled in clay. The vendors at the pedimento sell miniature wooden houses and cars that some votaries use instead of the clay creations. Some of them have a message at the top, "Virgen de Juquila, grant me a house." One votary began her offering with a purchased wooden house and then customized it using clay.

The walls in this same area of the pedimento are covered with mud-drawn figures and texts. The figures include houses, hearts, children, crosses, animals, and handprints. A few of these are written with mud letters in relief, including one that reads, "Medicina, UNAM," to petition or give thanks for studies in medicine at the national university. There is also extensive graffiti in ink. One asked for "a colt with more spirit than any other horse and that reflects my character and nobleness." Other messages written in various media include common petitions for health, family, children, prosperity, protection, and love. Votaries also wrote "I ask you to enlighten my wife, so that she changes the way she is"; "grant one more year of life to my uncle"; and "make happiness invade my life." Many votaries give thanks for the opportunity to visit the shrine, and several mention the number of times that their pilgrimage group had made the journey. In a text written on a wooden cross offering, a votary gave thanks "for letting me fulfill my promise." That sentiment, which is common in votive texts nationally, underscores the beautiful humility of reciprocation as gratitude rather than obligation, in addition to the value that devotees place on visiting images and paying respects in person.

The pine trees and other areas on these hillsides are covered with crosses, usually made of wood or wrought iron. These crosses are the traditional votive offering to the Virgen de Juquila and they are often inscribed with messages of gratitude. Also unique to Juquila are huge vinyl photo banners that give thanks for health, work, family, and the material gains acquired through the Virgin's miracles. These banners have the name and often a picture of the votaries—families are common—or of the gains. Many parents give thanks for their children, "for the miracle of our daughter," as one put it. Others show cars and houses, or express gratitude for successful surgeries.

Offerings inside the chapel, on and around the image of the Virgin, are similar to those found at other shrines—collages, letters, photos—and include an exceptional number of degree and education-related documents. Pinned on the Virgin's vestments are real bills, miniature fake bills, photographs, votive texts, and milagritos representing body parts, pregnant women, houses, animals, love (represented by kissing children), sobriety (represented by a bottle), and health (represented by a praying votary). One votary offered a bread roll, and another offering consisted of an image of the Virgen de Juquila made out of shells, with the hair provided by the votary.

The offering of fake money, which is uncommon in Mexico, is generally regarded as petitionary, to request money, work, or economic stability. Just as a clay miniature house represents a real house, so the fake money represents the real money that is petitioned by the votary. The votary proposes the exchange of a symbol for what it represents. The votary provides the clay house or fake money (the symbol) and the miraculous image

Votaries forming petitionary objects in clay. Note the votive crosses offered on the tree.

reciprocates with a real house and real money (what the symbol represents). The miracle happens through a process of desymbolization when
a petition is represented figuratively and a miracle literalizes what was
represented. This petitionary exchange between symbols and their referents inverts the order of votive exchanges. In votive exchanges, a miracle
provides a real gain and the votary reciprocates by offering that gain in
symbolic form. A wounded arm is healed miraculously, for example, and
the votary reciprocates by offering a miniature, a milagrito, that represents
the arm.[5]

    Pedrito had a different view of fake-money offerings. Some people give
real money, he said, "but there are people who don't have the necessary
resources to give real money. They don't have it, so they buy game
money—it's like a symbol that I am offering my money." In Pedrito's understanding the fake bills are a votive offering rather than a represented
petition, like the real bills pinned to the Virgin's vestments. The offering
says, in effect, *This is the best I can do; it represents the real money that I
would offer if I could afford it.* When I pressed the point with Pedrito, saying

that the fake money might be viewed as a petition rather than a votive offering, he made an amazing comment that captures precisely the discretionary nature of devotion. "It's a petition, it's a form of thanks, or whatever
meaning one gives it. I give it the meaning of asking, others give it the
meaning of thanks. It doesn't depend on the thing itself, it depends on
each person." Votive objects do not have inherent or fixed meanings, but
rather are invested with subjective meanings as votaries put them to use.

Seeing Through Faith

People select the environments to which they must respond;
they shape their commerce with it, plan, choose, avoid, tolerate,
postpone, escape, demolish, manipulate their attention, and
also deceive themselves about what is happening, as much
as possible casting the relationship in ways that fit their
needs and premises about themselves in the world.

RICHARD S. LAZARUS

Faith as a Cognitive Filter

Institutions and traditions sanction behaviors that in other contexts might seem bizarre. Praying to a dressed-up statuette wearing a crown, screaming in ecstasy because a batted ball went all the way to the wall, and going faster because a light turned yellow are all dependent on their contexts for meaning. A sense of validity—that a given phenomenon corresponds by consensus to some aspect of reality—is critical to meaningful action. Our institutions and traditions provide that validity and allow us to comfortably habituate, knowing that our practices in given contexts are appropriate. The cultures we share provide models, precedents, interpretive rubrics and restrictions, common goals, common sense, resources, and the certainty that our values, beliefs, and behaviors are legitimate and correct. We assimilate these cultural givens, take them for granted, and incorporate them into our sense of self so that we uphold them and reproduce them just by being ourselves in cultural context. This does not imply a mindless robotization, however, because we choose selectively and apply innovatively and idiosyncratically the resources that culture provides. We also bend them and invest them with meanings as we adapt them to specialized contexts and subjective needs, and we thereby contribute to their range, repertoire, and ongoing evolution.[1]

When religion is integrated into everyday life, as it is in Mexican Catholicism, it guides devotees on their excursions into a socially constructed world. There they find what their faith anticipates. The system is self-corroborating—miracles happen where miracles are perceived—and consequently also corroborates the validity of a devotional identity, a way of being and feeling, an aesthetic, a mode and mood of interpretation. A CELAM document captured the essence of this lived faith: "It is a true cultural ethos that gives intellectual and affective meaning to the encounter with God, and this experience remains engraved in the consciousness of a person, a family, a village, and even a State, as is the case in many Latin American countries. We can affirm that Popular Piety is a place of identity, insofar as it constitutes a coffer that stores events meaningful for the construction of identity" and actualizes the construct constantly "by being present in the reality of a consciousness that becomes conscious of itself." As one becomes aware of one's own identity, one discovers this ethos inside oneself, as part of one self, inalienable, and one discovers also one's position in a religious tradition preserved—treasured—in the people who hold its beliefs.[2]

Devotion to miraculous images infuses life in its crises and its banalities; in family, relationships, employment, and enjoyment; in love and marriage, pregnancy and childbirth; in youth and aging; in sickness and health; in subsistence and success, home and homelessness, migration and remittances; in addiction and sobriety; in crime and punishment; and in the countless daily details—food for children, the wellness of a calf, sales at a market—in which devotees view commended care in action. What is considered miraculous depends less on the events themselves, because almost anything qualifies, than on perceived meanings not inherent to the events. "Thus a miracle attribution takes place within the larger system of meaning that the person uses to negotiate the world."[3]

Events are ambiguous signifiers, and we each make—one might say impose—an interpretation based on our respective points of view. The announcement that the president will visit a given city to speak about a controversial policy, for example, might evoke various meanings and emotions. For a supporter, happiness, anticipation, and perhaps pride; for a nonsupporter, indifference or resentment; for an opponent, dissonance or anger; for the business community, an opportunity; for protesters, a forum; for the police commissioner, a headache; for the president and staff, another routine obligation; and for residents of a neighboring city, disappointment or relief that the visit did not come to them. The same event evokes a range of responses depending on its appraisal, meaning how the interpreters relate the event to their subjective interests, beliefs, and needs. It is not that the event can mean anything at all, but rather that it can accommodate multiple conflicting readings as each individual or interest group privileges its own perspective. "Humans are meaning-oriented, meaning-creating creatures who constantly evaluate events from the perspective of their well-being and react emotionally to some of these evaluations."[4]

The face of Jesus that appeared on a comal in San Andrés Teotilalpam is a simple example. Karina and Reynaldo are both devout Catholics; Karina is a rural Cuicateca and Reynaldo is an urban Chinanteco. For both of them there were only two options to explain this mysterious apparition: either it was a miracle, or else it was a deception that someone had cleverly perpetrated. Among those options they both readily agreed that the apparition was a miracle, because a fraud could never achieve such an exact likeness to Jesus.

In my worldview a coincidence is the primary, if not the exclusive, explanation for the apparition: burn marks on the comal happened to form in a pattern that had a moderate resemblance to a face that could be considered the face of Jesus as it is represented in Roman Catholic iconography. I do not entertain the possibility of a miraculous apparition and the possibility of fraud seems to me unlikely. In the worldview of Karina and Reynaldo, conversely, the idea of a coincidence is never entertained, even after I introduce it to test their resolve. Once the possibility of fraud is dismissed as impossible, because the image on the comal too perfectly resembles Jesus, Karina and Reynaldo celebrate the conviction that Jesus has chosen an essential artefact of their culture (just as the Virgen de Guadalupe chose a tilma) to manifest himself among them and to open a local access to his grace.

Such beliefs are viable and secure within the enclosure of a religious culture but are threatened at its edges and beyond. "All socially constructed worlds are inherently precarious," and any given one is dependent on "the particular social context within which that world can retain its plausibility." A religious culture is particularly vulnerable because its validity is contingent on faith. Karina explained Jesus's apparition on the comal in the context of divisions resulting from Catholic conversions to Evangelical and Pentecostal churches. Extensive, nationwide defections from Catholicism are challenging the stability of truths—including the truth of miraculous images—that are deeply embedded culturally and for centuries have been taken for granted. The apparition on the comal occurred during San Andrés Teotilalpam's annual fiesta on the fifth Friday of lent, which is centered on devotion to the town's miraculous image, the Señor de las Tres Caídas. Protestants do not participate in these image-centered events, and consequently a tradition that once cohered the community now divides it. As Karina explained, the apparition on that particular day, during the fiesta, was a sign that Jesus was choosing sides and demonstrating his alliance with the one true faith. Thus, in addition to the dissemination of grace, the apparition validates the beliefs that reciprocally validate the apparition and miraculous images.[5]

Even in a strongly Catholic country like Mexico beliefs are besieged not only by the counterdiscourse of Protestants but also by secularization and interaction with nonbelievers among devotees' own families, friends, coworkers, and associates. The challenges range from polite dismissal to mocking condescension and ridicule. When beliefs are challenged many devotees to miraculous images learn that doubt and faith are complements, thesis and antithesis, that work out a compromise through which faith ultimately prevails and then engages again with doubt at a higher and less-threatening level. Many believers maintain an "epistemological double register," a "self-conscious combination of reification and qualification" in which miracles are at once essential realities and subject to doubt. Faith is a volatile cognition, and the doubt tends to decrease at times of need. When it is challenged and the challenge is defeated, the devotee experiences relief within a worldview that remains intact. Faith must be protected, even in bad faith, because—we recall Miguel—"if you lose faith you don't have anything." Without faith the world comes apart and leaves one helpless in the ruins, completely vulnerable with no protection, resource, or recourse. That frightening demolition is averted by faith-affirming interpretations, by miracles that prove daily that nonbelievers are incorrect, and by the consensus of cobelievers expressed orally in testimony and silently in votive offerings that communicate the message "miracles do exist," sometimes even explicitly.[6]

Family is also critical to the maintenance of religious tradition. Children are born and raised into devotions and accept them "as inevitable, as part and parcel of the universal 'nature of things.'" Faith as a deeply ingrained manner of perceiving reality is internalized and contributes to children's own subjective understanding of their milieu. They are socialized in such a way that the mysterious world of religious belief becomes real to them and feels chosen and valued personally rather than imposed. The process is less one of indoctrination (although that might occur) than assimilation, participant observation, and gentle coaching that nurtures a child's appreciation of religious sentiment. The perceptive parent who observes a child's emerging faith might help the child to recognize and enhance it, thereby serving as an amplifier of subtle and nuanced feelings that have not yet acquired clear meaning, that are felt but not understood. Patterns of thought, conditioned perceptions and expectations, the muscle memory of gesture, the home images and altars, and daily thanks for miracles received all convey a sense of what to do and how to feel and how to know when your prayers are getting through. Children are inducted by quotas that are imperceptible—family shrine visits, tactile devotion, commended care—because these practices are so natural a part of everyday life. They discover what it feels like to put their hands together in prayer, to be cleansed with votive candles rubbed on their bodies, to press into the swell of a crowd converging on sacred power, and to sense their singing voices flowing away from them and returning aurally as choral, almost othered, not theirs specifically but theirs as part of a group, and they can hear resonating through their heads the part that is theirs and how it mixes with the collective choral voice coming in their ears. These experiences nurture a child's sense of the sacred and awareness of supernatural resources, while also providing the opportunity for peaceful resignation to an inherited worldview.[7]

For children and adults alike, beliefs and feelings are transmitted at shrines explicitly by instruction and conversation and implicitly by contagion or osmosis of the messages emitted by faces, laments, tears, gratitude, devotional surrender, and the suffering and saved exemplars on the walls. The mood, behavior, and emotions of others are emulated in a sympathetic, interactive expression of shared experience, a sense of solidarity and empathy that coheres community and one's sense of integration and belonging. Devotees participate in a collective effervescence that they implement to their own petitionary ends, and by doing so—by participating, enacting—they add faith to their credentials and become a member of the group.[8]

Much of the social transmission occurs subliminally and unintentionally, without rote imitation, as one transitions from observer to participant. Adults, like acculturated children, must experience the devotion emotionally and assimilate it to their "own inner need to believe." Emotions are cultural productions, are learned through social interaction, and are instrumental in the transmission of cultural knowledge. "This cultural shaping of the emotions gives certain cultural representations emotional *force*, in that individuals experience the truth and rightness of certain ideas as emotions *within* themselves—as something internal to themselves." Emotions and acculturation are interactive. Emotion validates the devotion and its object, makes them real for each devotee, but only if one has a disposition to faith. In my experience at the Señor del Rayo chapel, for example, deep emotion did not bridge to devotional validation. Feeling the sacred power is contingent on feeling the faith, and ultimately, for some, the two might be one and the same feeling.[9]

A complex of related theories pertaining to causal attribution, appraisal, positive framing, cognitive bias, confirmation bias, implemental thinking, motivated reasoning, interpretive control, locus of control, perceived control, cognitive adaptation, and narrative construction (surely among others) have in common the notion that people invest their world with meanings favorable to affirmation of their beliefs and to ontological security, particularly after trauma or crises. With a base in causal-attribution theory I pursue this thematic cluster in three regards: "1) a need or desire to perceive events in the world as meaningful, 2) a need or desire to predict and/or control events, and 3) a need or desire to protect, maintain, and enhance one's self-concept and self-esteem." These three dimensions are divisible for expository convenience, but in practice fold into and roll over and act upon one another. A sense of restored control retroactively revises the meaning of a traumatic event, for example, and control itself includes interpretive control, which can modify meanings and self-concept. Petitionary devotion provides a sense of meaning, control, and self-esteem, but also, around these, hope, confidence, solace, fortitude, security, solidarity, emotional release, access to sacred resources, and agency in relation to problem solving.[10]

Meaning

The question *Why?* often emerges when people confront unexpected crises and try to make sense of unpredictability and the seeming injustice of misfortune. Why did this happen, and to me? The question itself and then the responses signal how people interpret a tragedy or misfortune, affect how they will deal with it, and provide insight into their beliefs and state of mind. One person might see an accident as a meaningless, random event; another person, perhaps one carrying a burden of guilt for some past transgression (as is common among devotees who have broken their promises of reciprocation), might view the accident as retribution; and a third person, inclined to assigning blame, might see the accident as the result of incompetence, carelessness, distraction, or malice. When something terrible happens, one searches for a solution but also for an explanation.[11]

Traumatic experiences threaten the viability of our basic assumptions. Our fundamental security is undermined and we are terrified by the event itself but also by the vulnerability that it reveals so blatantly. We can no longer assume that prudence and precaution will protect us, because randomness and arbitrariness have demonstrated that we, too, can be victims. "Trauma survivors see the world as it really is, stripped of the meaning and order we all too readily assume to exist," and "the horror of a meaningless universe and shattered assumptions creates a state of disequilibrium, dread and hyperarousal for survivors." When life-threatening illness is involved, the misery and suffering, forced withdrawal from activities and roles that give life meaning and contribute to self-esteem, and the threat of imminent death all generate anxiety and despair, and consequently "illness often creates a vicious cycle by evoking emotions that aggravate it." In these situations positive illusions, both religious and secular, ameliorate the terror of a meaningless word, moderate negative emotions, and restore a sense of control.[12]

The same ideas obtain in threats to ontological security (a sense that the order and meaning of the world are stable). Crises disrupt the "natural attitude" of everyday life, meaning what is given or taken for granted. "On the other side of what might appear to be quite trivial aspects of day-to-day action and discourse, chaos lurks. And this chaos is not just disorganization, but the loss of a sense of the very reality of things and of other persons." The natural attitude is fragile, and when it breaks down anxiety floods in because our beliefs are founded on little more than consensus and "wither away under the skeptical gaze." Our existential parameters are sustained but not guaranteed by conventions, and when our truths are exposed as façades or our routines are disrupted by crisis we experience ontological insecurity.[13]

Whether the crisis is a terminal disease, a crop killed by drought, or a broken heart, petitions to miraculous images are attempts to reassemble one's shattered world, even in the absence of a miracle. "Survivors engage in a search for meaning," and "being able to comprehend tragedy—to make it meaningful—probably constitutes the core of successful coping and adjustment." An initial response to crises is a need to validate and preserve one's fundamental assumptions, including faith, and to assimilate adverse experiences to those assumptions. Validation and assimilation often occur through such religious coping cognitions as God has reasons for the hardships that he sends to us, even though we may not understand; that pain and suffering are meaningful as a lesson, a test, a warning, a punishment, or a means of redemption; and that if all else fails the peace and just rewards of heaven will bring consolation. In petitionary devotion specifically, these are complemented by the belief that a miraculous image will remedy the problem or, that failing, will provide the strength and courage to cope with it; and that the crisis, which could have been much worse, was moderated by a sacred intervention. Through these "benevolent religious appraisals of negative events," devotion becomes an affirmative interpretation, "a framing of life problems in more positive, constructive terms." Faith as a cognitive filter is conducive to positive appraisals, better coping, a sense of optimism, and a tendency to view life gratefully. Rather than undermining faith, crises often strengthen it and catalyze a religious quest to achieve or script a happy ending to the story.[14]

Faith as a cognitive filter also operates at lower intensity to interpret and negotiate the hardships of everyday life, particularly when they are aggravated by poverty. Faith is like a theory, a theory of life that makes sense of the world and one's experiences. A degree of creative manipulation is required, as evidenced so clearly in the interpretive ingenuity of miracle attributions. Through faith, like any cognitive filter, "we are particularly likely to access those beliefs and rules that support our desired conclusions." Faith sees the world in ways that affirm faith. Experience is consistent with expectations. Consensus facilitates "seeing God in the world and making him visible to each other." Meanings are deeply embedded into social reality and then interpreted back to the surface. We are selective in our attention, interaction, encoding, and retrieval; we perceive and interpret within a self-confirming system that screens out dissonance, particularly when we have an emotional commitment to a belief; we are biased toward confirmation of our beliefs and achieving our goals; and we "arrange the evidence to support a belief that goes beyond the evidence." The last point might be reiterated in these words: "We bend our data to fit our theories far more than we bend our theories to fit the data"; or these, "people tend to persevere in their beliefs well beyond the point at which logical and evidential considerations can sustain them."[15]

I stress the point with a catalog of quotations, and clarify that I refer not to religious beliefs exclusively but rather to cognition generally. People "tend to seek out, recall, and interpret evidence in a manner that sustains beliefs"; "readily invent causal explanations of initial evidence in which they then place too much confidence"; and "act upon their beliefs in a way that makes them self-confirming." "The mind imposes upon the material of experience its own forms of cognition. This gives us confidence that what we find in reality will conform to a manageable pattern—precisely because it is we who have imposed the pattern." "People do not realize that the process is biased by their goals, that they are accessing only a subset of their relevant knowledge, that they would probably access different beliefs and rules in the presence of different directional goals, and that they might even be capable of justifying opposite conclusions on different occasions." "We maintain that a series of social and cognitive filters make information disproportionately positive and that the negative information that escapes these filters is represented in as unthreatening a manner as possible." And finally, "This is powerful evidence that humans have a need for meaning and that if a clear meaning is not present on grounds of logic or evidence, people will invent one."[16]

People do not make inaccurate associations randomly, irrationally, or because they are intentionally self-deceiving, but rather "because these conclusions seemed more plausible, given their prior beliefs and expectancies." The face of Jesus on the comal is again a good example. Faith-based cognitions, together with their secular counterparts, maintain an "illusion of objectivity" and often an unshakable certainty. There is nothing maladaptive about such cognitions; on the contrary, "regulating reality to fit existing personal and cognitive frameworks is essential for continued mental health" and "religious beliefs are an adaptive means of regulating reality." "Intrinsically religious individuals are more likely to be adept at handling traumatically induced stress; they are more likely to find meaning in traumatic crises and are more likely to experience growth following trauma than are less religious persons." Both religious and nonreligious reality negotiations are coping strategies that enable people to sustain positive illusions about themselves and their world, particularly when confronted by disconfirming events and information. Unless they become delusional, "positive illusions promote psychological well-being by fostering a biased, distorted, self-serving view of self and others which may help an individual achieve his/her basic goals." They are creative confrontations that mend and defend the realities and identities that we construct.[17]

All of these ideas are critical to petitionary devotion, where the world seen through faith affords not only meaning and solace but also resources—miraculous images—that activate interpretations for practical purposes. Devotion answers *why* questions after crises, restores equilibrium, alleviates vulnerability and ontological insecurity, provides interpretive tools for assimilation of anomalies, buffers dissonance, and engenders positive illusions. The pursuit of miracles also generates new meanings—of what constitutes illness and cure, for example—so that causes and effects engage dialectically and the meaning-making self-perpetuates.

Control

When someone is diagnosed with cancer, friends and relatives often speculate to identify a specific cause. It was the bug spray, one will conjecture, and others indict the artificial sweetener, an over-the-counter medication, the carcinogenic insulation in a building. These arguments are generally dismissive of multiple causation and impervious to the counterevidence that disconfirms them, such as a surviving spouse who used the same sweetener or lived in the same building. Their unrecognized intent is to deny the random nature of the disease and thereby maintain a degree of predictability and security. They are efforts to regain control by restoring an illusion of invulnerability. If a simple causal attribution can be made—bug spray, sweetener—then the disease can be avoided by right behavior. As expressed by a female patient in remission, doctors have complicated, compound reasons for what might have caused cancer; "the one I focused on very strongly was diet. I know now why I focused on it. It was the only one that was simple enough for me to understand and change. You eat something that's bad for you, you get sick."[18]

Similar dynamics are at play in self-blaming attributions (*I should have changed that lock, I shouldn't have worn that dress*) that clearly exemplify how we infer causality even at the expense of falsely accusing ourselves as victims. "The self-blame of survivors does not reflect a need for accuracy in evaluating the victimization, but rather a need for making sense of the event." Assuming responsibility, however unpleasant, "provides a means of modulating the terror of the traumatic event, of minimizing the panic and paralysis produced by the sudden realization of a meaningless universe and invalid internal guides and assumptions." It was my fault, one reckons, but at least it was not random, I understand what happened, and with right behavior I can prevent it in the future. Self-esteem is often protected by attributing blame to an isolated incident of one's behavior—driving after a party—rather than to an attribute more critical to identity, such as irresponsibility or incompetence. When someone else is blamed one enjoys a sense of cognitive closure—*it was his fault*—through an attributed cause, a refreshing exoneration of oneself, a cathartic validation of one's suspicions, and a recuperation of control through avoidance of the guilty party.[19]

As suggested by these examples, "people's motivation to maintain control has a pervasive influence on their attributions of causality." I lost my job and cannot find another, this is happening because I did not fulfill my promise of reciprocation to the Señor de la Misericordia, and I will go to the shrine and make amends. My daughter's illness has recurred and the prognosis is poor, but with a new petition to the Virgen de Tonatico I know that God, who sent this trial, will have mercy on us. "When stressful situations severely threaten the ability to control the substance and course of life, people strive to reestablish a sense of mastery and self-determination." A temporary loss of control arouses anxiety and a practical or interpretational pursuit of resolution, but a chronic sense of control loss can result in passivity, giving up, and succumbing to learned helplessness. Devotion prevents a slide into a chronic state of hopelessness and despair because it checks the loss of control in increments as crises are managed through shrine visits and petitions. Interpretive control is another means of mastery; I cannot control an adverse event, but I can control its meaning. One of the twins died at birth, and I thank Niño del Cacahuatito for sending two so that one could survive. Uncontrollable adverse events are interpreted through faith and neutralized, in effect, by deriving from them a positive meaning. Devotion provides a means—something to do when there is nothing to do—to confront and overcome challenges to stability and security. Next time I get pregnant I will visit Niño del Cacahuatito early, and often, so he will protect the next delivery too. "Feelings of control, however illusory, may ultimately yield greater psychological benefits than would logically impeccable inferences."[20]

The illusion of control is among the principal benefits of petitionary devotion. Learned helplessness is a defeated surrender, but the illusion of control is an enhanced sense—"higher than the objective probability would warrant"—of one's ability to influence positive outcomes. Such illusions are particularly attractive in situations—such as necessity, marginalization, or, in subjective terms, beleaguered self-esteem—in which true control is minimal or precarious. Often the illusion is enacted through ritual behavior. At a craps table, for example, blowing on dice, throwing soft for low numbers and hard for high numbers, and concentrating on a desired number all contribute to a sense that the results are not random. Illusory control is enhanced because a chance situation is approached as a skill situation, in which proper actions yield desired results. If I hold burning candles in my hands while I make my petition, it is more likely that the Cristo Negro will grant the miracle. Rather than petitioning this image, I will petition that one; rather than requesting a mass I will make a pilgrimage; rather than offering flowers I will inscribe a photograph, because if I do it the right way my son will survive his disease. Freedom of devotion gives votaries choices, and the exercise of these choices affords an illusion of control. If I make the right choices my miracle will be granted.[21]

The chances of a miracle may not be objectively improved, but making a choice and taking a considered course of action contribute to an illusion of control that in turn contributes to miracle attribution. A sense of efficacy and the corresponding optimism "can be associated with higher motivation, greater persistence, more effective performance, and ultimately, greater success. A chief value of these illusions may be that they can create self-fulfilling prophecies." Once I have petitioned a miracle to find a job and know with deep faith and certainty that the Virgen de Tonatico will not let me down, my optimism motivates my search, fuels my perseverance, improves my presence during interviews, contributes to my resilience after rejection, and, if all else fails, gives the concept "job" a certain flexibility, so that even improvised work as a street vendor can be perceived as a miracle granted.[22]

The greatest ingenuity of petitionary devotion, however, is that petitioning itself can be sufficient to resume control, even in the absence of a miracle. María is terribly worried because her son, Mario, is migrating to the United States undocumented and will have to cross the desert on foot. María's anxiety is compounded by a sense of helplessness and desperation, first because she cannot protect her son but also because she cannot control her own fear for his safety. She must cope with the dangerous migration itself and with her anxiety in relation to the migration. In this dilemma she turns to a resource provided by her culture: the Virgen de San Juan de los Lagos. María visits the shrine and with faith and sincere devotional pleading she asks the Virgin to protect Mario on the journey. She also posts a photograph of Mario in the room of offerings and writes a textual petition in a book provided there for that purpose. As María leaves the church she knows with an intuitive certainty that her prayer has been heard and that Mario will be safe. Her certainty may not benefit Mario, but it has alleviated her anxiety. Her active motherhood has protected her son. She feels a sense of peace and solace—a great weight has been lifted—and the out-of-control sense of desperate helplessness is gone. When Mario calls from the United States to announce his arrival, María returns to the Virgen de San Juan de los Lagos to give thanks for the miracle that she knew would occur.[23]

Devotion is a form of efficacy, a way of doing something rather than surrendering to helplessness or defeat. It contributes to an identity shift from passive victim to empowered agent. It also offers interim gains. A petition may result in the success of a scheduled surgery, but beforehand it reduces the patient's anticipatory anxiety and afterward it strengthens convalescence. Many petitions, like María's, are motivated by emotions, often negative emotions that a votary attempts to manage or reduce. But petitions are also driven by an optimism derived from the faith that a miraculous image will resolve one's problem. The petition itself offers allevi-ation because it interprets a present problem retrospectively from an anticipated future resolution. Hope, as goal-directed thinking, "frees you from the bleakness of beliefs that would reduce you to numbed inaction and from the burden of beliefs that wax and wane unpredictably in level of confidence. It gives you firm and friendly coordinates in an uncertain and uncompanionable world. To have hope is to have something we might described as cognitive resolve." The support of miraculous images, among other benefits, provides votaries the "confidence to act on their freedom and planfully pursue their hopes."[24]

Self-Esteem

The primary benefit of successful petitions are the miracles themselves, but there are many secondary benefits. Miracles validate one's cause (health, employment, pregnancy) as worthy of support, and once a cause becomes "saturated with religious meaning" it gains value and importance beyond those of secular endeavors. Miracles also confer status upon their recipi-ents, because miraculous images act favorably on requests in recogni-tion of a votary's worthiness. Precisely at a moment when self-esteem is wounded by a crisis (arrest, disease, unemployment), and when "access to alternative sources of self-validation" may be lacking, the miracle gives an ego-enhancing boost that strengthens resilience, motivation, self-efficacy, and the ability to tolerate or overcome adversity. The emotional gains also include the pride of having been chosen, the glow of feeling loved and bestowed with grace. By virtue of the petitioned and granted miracle the votary has established an intimate relation with a sacred figure, and consequently he or she has a story to tell that increases prestige within a devotional community. If the miracle is denied, conversely, the problem remains unresolved and the votary questions his or her worthiness: Why was I rejected when so many others are not?[25]

Self-esteem as it relates to petitionary devotion is particularly evident in medical crises, during which the most fundamental control—of one's body—is undermined or jeopardized. "The fidelity of our bodies is so basic that we never think of it—it is the certain grounds of our daily experience. Chronic illness is a betrayal of that fundamental trust. We feel under siege: untrusting, resentful of uncertainty, lost. Life becomes a working out of sentiments that follow closely from this corporeal betrayal: confusion, shock, anger, jealousy, despair," and the aloneness of being the one who is sick. One's sense of invulnerability is also devastated: such things happen to other people, not to me, and yet this happened to me. Many Mexicans have little or no access to professional health care, so the onset of a disease or an otherwise easily treatable problem—a toothache, a broken bone, an infection—escalate in severity and to increasing pain and debilitation. The person who suffers also loses themselves to the haze of discomfort, pain, fatigue, and the forfeiture of routines (work, relations, social roles) that imbue life and self with meanings. One struggles to recuperate the self lost to the disease.[26]

A votary with anemia and a kidney disorder petitioned the Virgen de Soriano to "go back to being" who she was before the diseases, and on behalf of her daughter a mother wrote to Niño del Cacahuatito, "I ask you to restore my daughter's health" and "make her able to walk again, to be a normal girl again, to recuperate everything she has lost." In 2011 a young woman crossing the street near the Zaragoza metro station in Mexico City was hit by a truck. The initial surgery on her leg was unsuccessful, so she went to the Señor de Chalma and, she wrote, "with a lot faith and devotion I asked you to give me a second chance so I could continue with my normal life and make it as though nothing had happened."

Even those who are fortunate enough to have health care can experience, as a result of the care itself, a remarkable assault to dignity, autonomy, privacy, freedom, identity, and self-reliance. A stranger says, "Strip to your underwear and put this on," and there you are sick and frightened in a ridiculous patient gown open at the back while a steady stream of doctors, nurses, and assistants enter at will to discover you in the indecorous postures of diseased sleep and they touch you, poke you, attach you to contraptions, and ask you a thousand intimate questions about your life and body until finally whoever you are is reduced to "patient" and you surrender to this benevolent, incarcerated identity. You have not lost ontological security, exactly, but more identity security and self-control. You lose yourself first to the disease and then to the treatment.

But then your wife arrives with an image of the Virgen de Zapopan and you put it on the table beside the IV rack so you can see it from your bed and with words and your distant, beseeching, somnambulant gaze you petition the miracle constantly. Your children arrive and they love you and the priest visits with friends from church and you pray together to God and the Virgen de Zapopan because they love you and are with you and want to redeem you from "patient" and give you back to José or Sarita or Alejandro. Gradually the disease assumes religious meanings and now instead of moribund inaction your devotion contributes to the cure with a higher-order efficacy that you access through faith. The ordeal begins to seem more manageable as you recuperate measures of confidence, fortitude, self-trust, self-esteem, and even such identity enhancements as a sense of being chosen. As a cancer patient in remission expressed it to the Señor de la Misericordia, "God gives the worst battles to his best warriors, and he chose me."

Miracle Attribution

In 1974 a Mixe woman left a note for her priest: "Dear Father, please do me a favor. Give me a blessing. I'm asking God on behalf of my animal. I'm asking God that my animal recover from its sickness. Father, how much will it cost? Thank you." The woman wanted the priest to say a mass for the dead, so that the sick animal would get well. The priest replied that the mass would not cure her animal and offered instead to help her get medicine. The woman insisted, however, because she and her family believed "that some dead family members caused the animal's sickness and only a mass for the dead could console their spirits."[27]

More recently, a seventy-five-year-old Mexican American woman was contacted by her dead parents after she returned from intensive care to her hospital room. "The whole time I was in my room, one of the blinds kept moving and making a small noise. I am sure it was my parents telling me I was going to be O.K. Why did it move if there was no air? But it kept tapping...I am sure it was them. They were transparent in the room."[28]

In both of these experiences one notes that the natural and supernatural worlds interact for better or worse, but also that causal attributions restrict the meanings of ambiguous phenomena. Both women perceive an effect and infer a cause that is consonant with their beliefs. The Mixe woman begins with the sick animal, discards natural causes, identifies a supernatural cause, and then takes action to neutralize that cause. The Mexican American woman begins with a meaningless sign (the rattling blinds), discards natural causes (heat rising from a radiator, a vent), and invests the sign with supernatural meanings conducive to positive emotions and recovery.

Similar attributions are apparent after *juramentos* (vows) are broken. A man leaves a party, drives drunk, and crashes into a tree. An objective secular observer would likely attribute the accident to alcohol impairment and might moralize that one should not drive after drinking, but interpretation within a community of devotees might be quite different. People often drive drunk and arrive home without crashing, so why not in this case? It is then revealed that the driver had broken a vow to the Señor de Chalma, a vow made precisely to stop drinking. Obviously, therefore, the accident was punishment for breaking the vow. The moral derived from this interpretation is not that one should not drink and drive, but rather that one should not break vows.[29]

Votaries bring to shrines their faith, needs that motivate petitions, and usually a personal or familial tradition of devotion; and at the shrine they encounter a sympathetic community, an ambience conducive to faith affirmation, and evidence (votive offerings, conversation) that supports their expectation of a miracle. Even when a miraculous image has no agency, when it cannot respond to petitions, miracles occur in attributions consistent with expectations. Miracles are not events; they are interpretations. A miracle cannot be observed, it can only be inferred, because nothing is seen but the results (successful surgery, a visa) that are attributed to miraculous images but may have other causes. The relation between an occurrence and its perceived cause is often made intuitively and then ratified by a support community and documented by votive offerings. Such attributions become explicit when offerings include variations of the phrase "everyone regarded it as a miracle."[30]

The perception of miracles evidences, precisely, an inclination to perceive miracles. Lourdes related that "A boy had cancer of the eyes. They took out his eyes. The boy says that he sees through his blind vision."

However sorrowful the infliction seems objectively, as a failure of medicine and a failure of miracles, Lourdes ultimately discerns God's plan in blindness reconceived at the nexus where seeing yields to having a vision. The transition is made through a characteristic interpretive inversion—"whoever seeks to preserve his life will lose it, but whoever loses it will save it"—that salvages rhetorically what is otherwise lost.[31]

When it began to drizzle during a colonial procession of the Virgen de los Remedios, Francisco de Florencia did not perceive an insignificant coincidence or lament rain on the parade but rather marveled at a miracle, in just the right measure, to facilitate the passage of thousands of devotees. The drizzle "dampened the dust that would be bothersome to so many people, without making mud that would hinder their walking."[32]

In other colonial cases the miracle seems not as much perceived as constructed in narrative. One text relates that priests heard loud noises in a church and thought an animal had gotten behind the altar. The vicar went to have a look and the liquid that fell on his right ear was attributed to "the many Rats in the Church" that "cast their filth at us." But then the priests discovered that the crucified Christ on the wall above was sweating—"he sweat so copiously and there was so much water that the whole floor was wet and covered with it"— and that from its deteriorated state the image had miraculously self-renovated.[33]

In another narrative from the late seventeenth century the circumstances are similar but the verdict is different. A Franciscan friar, Francisco Navarro, discovered that the images in his church were sweating, some water and some blood, "both the painted and the sculpted Images of Christ Our Lord, and his Mothers, and the other saints that there are in the said Church." Fray Francisco enthusiastically related these marvels at the monastery and distributed cotton balls soaked with the miraculous liquids, but his fellow friars were skeptical and many threw the relics in the trash and advised Fray Francisco not to believe "such nonsense." The dissenters attributed the events to nonmiraculous causes, including "the urine of Bats" and the high humidity of the region, which also caused the red paint to run and seem like blood. Others thought that Fray Francisco was crazy and attributed the madness to his advanced age and decrepit state; to asthma and its consequences, including insomnia ("every night he seemed to be dying, and so spent most sleepless"); and to difficulties with eating ("he eats very little, and easily brings up the food, from which much frailty results"). Many friars ridiculed Fray Francisco openly as a fool; others were kinder and described him as a "simple man, and extremely innocent" and a "religious man, devout, God-fearing, very humble, and so simple that he believes anything." In all cases, analysis of the evidence and judgment of the source led to natural attributions that could not support the miracle.[34]

At the St. Toribio Romo shrine in Jalisco there is an offering made by a family from Los Angeles, California, who visited after the death of an adult brother. The attending doctor had reported brain damage and that the comatose brother would never resume a normal life. After consulting among themselves regarding life support, the family members put a Toribio medal on the brother's chest, asking that Toribio intercede and that God's will be done. The brother died shortly after.

Later, following the visit to Toribio's shrine to give thanks, the family went to have breakfast. "On the tortilla of one member of the family the name CHILO appeared"—"Chilo" is the nickname of the deceased brother—"and with that we understood that saint Toribio heard us, that CHILO is with God resting in peace." That sign from Toribio, which was photographed and included in the offering, "was a comfort for all of us, and it gave us strength and tranquility to get through this difficult moment." The name burned on the tortilla was evidence that the prayer had been heard, that Toribio had interceded on behalf of the brother, that God had chosen death as the best option (sparing the family that decision), and that Chilo had been received in heaven. The tragedy was softened and the anxiety relieved. The family's faithful perception provided evidence that appended a happy ending to an otherwise tragic story.

In other cases miracle attributions are made by "refraining from classifying events too sharply into successes and failures." A miracle aspires to the ideal, but reinterpretation can assimilate disappointments by downgrading from absolute to relative relief. "I was supposed to lose my whole foot," an older votary told me in Chalma, "but only lost my toes." The man had come with his adult son and together they were carefully taping a homemade offering to the wall. "I lost my toes," he repeated, pointing with his cane, and then with a slicing motion of his hand showed where he was supposed to lose the foot. His offering, which concludes with "Testimony of his foot!" and then his name, is written in verse. One of the stanzas reads: "Today Lord I feel sad/Very tired of struggling/But I know that with your help/All of this will pass."[35]

The interpretation of lesser evils as miracles is common. Parents gave thanks because the knife that stabbed their son stopped an inch before his heart; the intensity of an earthquake was moderated by the Virgin de los

Remedios; and a girl fell off a horse, was missing for five days, and was finally found dead, but the silver-studded saddle was recovered. A photographic offering to the Virgen de Juquila expresses a votary's thanks for the miracle "of selling my land in order to pay my debts." In 2008 a migrant was grateful to the Señor de la Misericordia because, he wrote, "Upon entering the United States through the Arizona desert I fell behind because I got a cramp in my leg and I was abandoned by the group, after 9 days lost I was rescued almost dead by border patrol." Another man gave thanks to the Virgin de San Juan de los Lagos "for having performed the miracle of letting me live" after being shot twice, once in the liver: "I have an opening in my stomach, my recuperation is slow and painful, but I am alive, and so I can thank the Virgencita and God for letting me live." Some votaries who petition curative miracles are successful and others, perhaps most, settle for miracles that grant them the fortitude to persevere.[36]

Some deaths are regarded as miracles because the remains of the deceased are located. A 2007 offering gave thanks to St. Toribio Romo "for having performed the miracle of returning to us the body of our daughter Maribel," who died on the desert while migrating to the United States; and a 1937 retablo to the Virgin of San Juan de los Lagos depicts a dead man, face down and caught in a branch in the river, while his mother prays on shore to the Virgin hovering in the distance. The text reads, "I fulfill my promise to the Most Holy Virgen de San Juan for having granted the finding of the cadaver of my son who for four days had been carried by the rapids."[37]

In a colonial example, a pregnant woman "commended herself most sincerely to Our Lady of Pueblito, and in the company of her husband went personally to visit her at her shrine." In the fourth month of pregnancy the woman no longer felt fetal motion, and as time passed she realized that the fetus had stopped growing. The woman returned to the Virgen for help. Her petition was heard, she went home, and "gave birth to a daughter perfectly formed, but dead and dry." The stillbirth was without "any decay or foul odor" which "everyone took as a great miracle, because it seemed to exceed the forces of nature that a child dead for so many months had not decomposed nor caused the death of the mother."[38]

In each of these cases, votaries interpret through gratitude and count their blessings rather than their burdens. The miraculous image does not engage in preventative intervention, but rather in reactive management to minimize damage or salvage a loss. Votaries begin with an implicit premise (miracles happen), confront adverse events that threaten the premise, and then lower the bar and reinterpret the adverse events in positive, miracle-affirming terms. I asked Miguel how we know that a miracle has occurred when someone survives a car crash, and he explained that devotees commend themselves to miraculous images before leaving home and are protected throughout the day. If there is an accident and no injury, or if the injuries are less severe than expected, it is because of this miraculous protection. Commended care also provides that what does not happen can be miraculous. A campesino asks that his crops not be ruined by drought, they are not, and he gives thanks to the Virgen de Guadalupe. A woman walking home on a dark street fears she might be attacked, she is not, and she gives thanks to the Virgen de Ocotlán.

Most devotees persevere in faith and gratitude even when a petitioned miracle is not granted. The leader of a dance group explained that "the majority of people who come to dance do so because they have made a promise to San José. They promise San José to make a sacrifice by dancing if he cures them or their family members. They think that if they dance for him they will receive the favor from San José. They have faith. Some get better, but some don't, but in any case they keep dancing because faith is what counts." A similar idea is expressed in an offering to the Señor de Chalma: "The compensation is not in the result, but rather in the effort made under the eyes of God." Faith remains insulated when the results of petitions are disappointing, because ultimately it is the faith, and not the miracle, that is essential. The faith is protected by interpretation and attribution. When people have a theory (faith) and are exposed to genuinely probative evidence, whether it supports or challenges theory, or is ambiguous, the evidence "will tend to result in more belief in the correctness of the original theory." "I believe in God," an older man told me in Querétaro. "If he exists, if he doesn't exist, I believe in God."[39]

Thus miracle attributions can be made despite negative outcomes, like Chilo's death. An offering to Santiago Apóstol in Coroneo consists of a photocopied image of a teenaged girl with "rest in peace" written beside her name. The text reads: "Lord I give thanks for your infinite mercy, today that my dear friend has left to be with you and to enjoy your gifts." Rather than venting resentment for a failed medical miracle, this votary interprets the death as an expression of mercy and shifts to gratitude. The failed miracle yields to the greater miracle of eternity in heaven. The same is apparent in a 1777 retablo that represents breast-cancer surgery. "Although the wound closed perfectly on the 25th of July 1777," the text relates, "other accidents befell her from which she died on Friday, the 5th of September, at 3 p.m., with clear signs of the patronage of the Holy Image [Christ of Encino, venerated in the Church of Triana] and of her salvation." A "monument of her gratitude" was posthumously offered on behalf of the votary, not for successful cure, because the surgery failed, but rather for her presumed reception in heaven.[40]

Some votaries struggle with anger after failed commended care before finding their way back to faith and gratitude. They seem motivated to resolve the contradiction between unjust misfortune and their belief in a benevolent God. A framed petition to the Señor de la Misericordia includes a photograph of a votary and a typed text written in verse. "Lord you knocked at the door of my life/visiting suffering upon me/and now I am here/in this hospital bed/among the white ghosts of robes./A bitter experience Lord/a reality difficult to accept./Nevertheless I thank you because in this way/you broke the glass of my dreams/and I saw such beautiful and fragile life/with different eyes.//What I have and what I am/is a gift of your immense kindness./You humbled my stupid pride." The votary moves from bitterness and difficulty in accepting a harsh reality to perception of the disease as a gift of significant personal benefit. She never quite surrenders completely, however, and after rhetorical strugglings asks finally in her text's last passage to be cured if the Señor de la Misericordia so wills it.

The interpretation of hardships as blessings significantly broadens the range of gratitude and miracle attributions, often by "storying negative experiences into narratives of personal growth." "We give you thanks for all of the favors received and for the trials you have put to us," a votary wrote to the Señor de Villaseca. Another gave thanks to the Virgen de la Paz for the blessings received by her family, then added: "Thank you also for the pain, which has permitted us to feel you close to us. Give us strength, solace, joy, patience, prudence: above all to change and be better people." Thanks are given for the trials that test faith, the suffering conducive to consolation, the powerful emotions that enrich experience, and the hardships that motivate self-improvement. Sufferings are gifts because they strengthen us, correct our course, and reveal to us God's vigilance and love and our share in Christ's ubiquitous, purposeful agony. Antonio said that God sends suffering to "awaken faith" because "people forget God when things go well." Mayuela applied that same idea to nonbelievers: "God touches them with something terrible to awaken their faith," just as God had his own son crucified for salvation. "Who has ever heard of death being worshipped," John of Damascus wrote, "or suffering honored? Yet we truly worship our God's physical death and His saving sufferings."[41]

A votive text to the Señor de Villaseca expresses thanks "for everything you gave me this year, thank you for everything...good and bad," and then continues: "For my job, for getting fired which you well know was unjustified, thank you for the break-up with my partner (who I still love)...thank you Lord for ending this year without work, without money, without the love of my life, but full of health, full of hope and because despite everything I am happy and I am alive thank you Lord for everything." In another context this litany of hardships might seem bitterly ironic, but here the votary struggles—one can almost feel it—to integrate his privations and misfortunes, to make them congruent with his beliefs, and to weigh them against his blessings. A collage offered to the Señor de Villaseca includes a picture of a lantern and a text that explains, "this light is like our life it is extinguishing every day that goes by so live prepared and accepting the tests that God sends us." People who are highly grateful often view everything they have as a gift, even life itself, despite its disappointments and troubles and sufferings. "This level of appreciation for the good things in one's life may lead grateful people to avoid taking benefits for granted. As a result, they may be less prone to habituate to positive life circumstances, which might also help sustain their happiness and subjective well-being over time."[42]

The breadth of miracle attributions is also indebted to temporal extensions. The Vatican investigation of medical miracles during canonization processes has three requisites: "the healing must be complete, durable, and instantaneous." Most miracles performed by miraculous images would not qualify, in the present context because the time period of their performance is often protracted across months, years, and even decades. Patience is a virtue that makes miracles visible where others overlook them. Characteristic are pregnancies that occur several years after they are petitioned and long-term cures that require multiple surgeries and medical procedures. "Things happen little by little," Pedro said, "sometimes you don't even realize it, because sometimes the advance is so slow. The point is not to lose faith. Not to despair between the moment of asking for things with your faith and when it's over because the miracle is granted." Incremental advances sustain positive emotions and the faith that eventually the miracle will be completed.[43]

Usually the process of getting well—however long it takes and however incomplete the cure—constitutes the miracle, but on occasion the ideal of a timely and absolute cure is realized. In an early eighteenth-century miracle narrative, Father Juan Bautista's cure was complete, durable, and instantaneous, as the Congregation of Rites would have it, because "the works of God are perfect." "The kidneys that were almost completely worn out, and rotten, became healthy, and restored in an instant by the virtue of the Almighty."[44]

Far more common are slow, incomplete miracles, like one described in a collage offered to the Señor de la Misericordia. The offering includes a list of the many serious injuries to limbs, ribs, the brain, and an eye that resulted from a car crash; photographs of the wreck, the injured votary in a hospital bed, and the same votary afterward (or before); and a text that includes, "after two operations I've been getting better, although I'm still limping you could say that I'm better and all thanks to you." In another offering a construction worker fell from a roof and "an iron rod pierced his chest and went through his back." He implored the help of the Virgen de San Juan de los Lagos, and "they removed the rebar with a blowtorch, and with time he got better." Another votary offered the Señor de la Misericordia her braid and a photograph of her child in leg braces, after petitioning that the surgeries on her son Ramón would be successful: "And with your help he has managed to walk with his devices and walker." Then she asked that this incremental miracle continue until "my son is able to walk by himself."[45]

The idea of incremental or cumulative miracles was also suggested when a group of migrants asked a priest for a blessing before a journey to the United States. The priest blessed the migrants, which they understood as a form of protection, but nevertheless they were detained by immigration authorities and repatriated to Mexico. The migrants returned to the priest requesting another blessing and the priest was puzzled: if the first blessing did not work, why would they want another one? One of the migrants responded, "With that blessing we arrived as far as Houston. If we had not had your blessing, who knows how far we might have gone. Probably not even to the border." For its original purpose of successful migration the blessing was inefficacious, but the failure was reinterpreted (by the migrants, not the priest) as a partial success and the reinterpretation returned the migrants to the priest for another dose, a recharge that might take them further. The sacred power and the validity of the blessing as a protector are not questioned, and the events fall into order around those certainties.[46]

Medical Miracles

Miracle attributions are perhaps nowhere as prominent and complex as they are in health-related petitions and offerings. As suggested by a note that the elderly Félix left for the Señor de las Tres Caídas in San Andrés Teotilalpam, miraculous images compensate for unavailable or unaffordable health care. "Give me the solution to my sickness that I have," Félix wrote "I can't breathe, I'm suffocating, I can't eat tortillas, my stomach fills, and I can't walk well either." Alejandra, a young girl who petitioned the Virgen de la Paz in Querétaro, stressed unaffordability and a lack of options: "I ask you to heal my eyes please...because I don't have the resources and my parents can't fix them for me that's why I'm asking you to heal my eyes." At the Virgen de los Remedios basilica I met a young woman named María Elena, who in a common appeal to combined resources visited the Virgin and the adjacent medical clinic because the fetus in her womb had stopped moving. The clinic advised ultrasound imaging and made a referral, but María Elena had no money for the procedure. The friend who accompanied her, Juana, had a son with a deformed leg scheduled for a surgery that Juana likewise could scarcely afford.

When miracles are attributed in such cases, it is generally not for an absolute remedy—Alejandra's vision is not suddenly restored—but rather for a lesser and related felicitous occurrence. Alejandra's parents might unexpectedly acquire money for the procedure, or Félix might give thanks for forbearance or a daughter who returns home to care for him. In other cases medical procedures become unnecessary or less dreadful than expected and the averted crisis is interpreted as a miracle. Often this occurs in the context of symptoms and treatments for diabetes, which has been the primary cause of death in Mexico since 2000. The contributing causes include diet and obesity, sedentary lifestyle, genetic predisposition, and inadequate health care, and the consequences include amputations, kidney failure and dialysis, and blindness. When a doctor suggests that treatment might ultimately require foot amputation, the patient petitions a miraculous image, subsequently learns that the amputation is not necessary, and in gratitude for the miracle makes an offering at the shrine.[47]

Similar are situations in which symptoms disappear between one test and the next. Votaries see miracles where doctors see false positives. A boy named Luis offered an inscribed drawing to the Virgen de los Dolores in Soriano after, he wrote, "the doctor diagnosed a murmur in my heart my parents and everyone who loves me implored God and the Virgen de los

Dolores to help me get well and on February 24, 2010 my test results were negative." A first test had been done two weeks prior.

Inexplicable disappearances of symptoms are epitomized by the spontaneous remission of cancer. (The term is inaccurate—the remission is rarely spontaneous—but its usage is maintained by convention.) As defined in one study, spontaneous remission is "a partial or complete disappearance of a tumor in the absence of treatment capable of producing a regression." In secular scholarly perspective the attributed miracle "might be the working of an as yet undiscovered natural law," and as research progresses "what is now called 'spontaneous remission' may be explicable according to principles which medical science has yet to uncover." In the perspective of votaries redeemed from cancer, however, the miracles are indisputable, and when medical professionals marvel at unexpected outcomes—"We have no explanation for the processes involved in this tumour regression"—the miracle seems all the more authentic.[48]

In votive offerings as in canonization processes, miracles are verified by the bafflement of medical doctors. Symptoms disappear and votive offerings repeat versions of the phrase, "the doctors were surprised by the miracle." A framed collage to Niño del Cacahuatito includes baby clothes, a photograph, and text that relates that a medically predicted miscarriage resulted in a healthy baby, "breaking all the negative expectations of the doctors."[49]

The great majority of medical miracle attributions result precisely from this discrepancy between votary belief and scientific knowledge. Votaries perceive their sickness and health differently than medical professions, and they attribute miracles according to their own perceptions rather than to an external standard of scientific accuracy. This disparity of subjective perception and medical diagnosis is suggested when the seemingly synonymous "illness" and "disease" are sorted to their discrete meanings. "*Disease* refers to a malfunctioning of biological and/or psychological processes, while the term *illness* refers to the psychological experience and meaning of perceived disease." Diseases are named pathologies—diabetes, cancer—and illness is the patient's subjective understanding of disease, including the experience of being sick, the meaning given to the experience, and the attributions made regarding cause. Miracles happen in the realm of illness, not disease. Miracles are petitioned in response to diagnosed biomedical and psychological pathologies, but diseases "are accompanied by illness, that is by a psychological, social and cultural reaction to the disease process." Votaries translate or transpose the disease into an illness register where it makes sense to them and where its cause and cure can be negotiated.⁵⁰

Reynaldo illustrated that translation precisely. One might get the folk illness *susto*, he said, after being robbed at gunpoint or falling into a river. The susto causes diseases—Reynaldo gave diabetes as an example—and *limpias* (ritual cleansing) before the Señor de Otatitlán are a means of cure. When Reynaldo's sequence is viewed retrospectively, one might imagine a medical diagnosis of diabetes (disease); a patient subsequently searching for meaning, cause, and remedy (illness); and pursuit of a comprehensive intervention that treats disease at the doctor's office and illness at the shrine. A curandero (folk healer) might also be included, particularly given the belief that medical doctors cannot treat susto.⁵¹

At the same time, a translation is made in the other direction when patients relate maladies according to their nonscientific understanding of illness, and a doctor assimilates these reports to the signs and symptoms of disease. "Diagnosis is a thoroughly semiotic activity: an analysis of one symbol system followed by its translation into another." While the patient's cognitions are filtered by faith and traditional knowledge, the doctor's cognitions are filtered by training and medical knowledge. The religious components critical to the patient's concept of cure are lost in the doctor's translation. "The priorities of the practitioner lead to the selective attention to the patient's account, so that some aspects are carefully listened for and heard (sometimes when they are not spoken), while other things that are said—and even repeated—are literally not heard." Disease, like illness, derives its meaning from the context in which it is interpreted.⁵²

Given such miscommunication between patients and medical doctors, many devotees, particularly indigenous devotees, prefer to visit curanderos for their health care. The aversion to scientific medicine is also supported by the inadequacy of public health care and the unaffordable expense of private doctors, hospitals, and the medications that they prescribe. Medical doctors have alien and unintelligible ideas regarding etiology, diagnosis, and treatment, but curanderos' interpretations—which integrate body, mind, and soul, as well as social and spiritual components—are consonant with those of their patients. Devotees capture something of this integrated approach when they refer to petitions and limpias as ways to "heal body and soul" or recuperate "the health of body and soul." Curanderos' holisitic, salutogenic, religious approach to healing addresses the patient's primary concern, illness, rather than the biophysical disease that the patient often interprets as a symptom of a more critical imbalance. Holistic medicine relates disease symptoms to stress- and anxiety-inducing situations, such as conflict in family, love, employment, and social situations. Consequently votaries petition the restoration of harmony for its intrinsic worth but also for its curative efficacy. Problems like domestic violence and interpersonal conflict are intuitively interrelated with health, so that a petitioned miracle for one problem or another has cross-category benefits in biological, psychological, and social spheres.[53]

There is a decidedly psychological contribution to medical miracles, from etiology and self-diagnosis to cure. Consider for example Reynaldo's susto example as it relates to attributed causes and expected outcomes. Response expectancies (anticipation of one's reactions to situations and behaviors) can become automatic or habitual, particularly when reinforced culturally. I know that certain adverse circumstances cause susto, and therefore susto will surely, even necessarily, result if I fall victim to such circumstances. Response expectancies are self-confirming, and the outcomes are attributable less to the stimulus (robbery, falling in the river) than to the anticipation. I think I will get sick, so I get sick. This nocebo effect, by which negative expectations lead to negative results, is active in folk illnesses generally, in death and bad-luck curses, in reactions to guilt, and in expectation of punishment for breaking a promise to a miraculous image. "A society's ethnomedicine tells societal members what sicknesses there are, how they are acquired, how manifested, how treated. The nocebo phenomenon suggests that the categories of ethnomedicine may not only describe conditions of sickness, but may also foster those conditions by establishing expectations that they may occur."[54]

The prognosis is promising, however, because just as one expectation fosters the illness, another can foster the cure. The placebo effect provides that a condition can improve in the absence of any medically active substance or procedure simply because the patient has a strong expectation of improvement. Positive expectations are conducive to positive outcomes. These expectations might not be sufficient to heal a broken leg, but they can effectively alleviate psychosomatic disorders, particularly when there is a personal or cultural tendency to somatize ("to express psychological distress through physical symptoms"). Typical psychosomatic symptoms include headaches, dizziness, gastro-intestinal problems, nausea, palpitations, rashes, weakness, respiratory problems, and general malaise, as well as other symptoms that have no biological cause. When votaries petition miracles to cure such illnesses, their positive expectations—their faith—is often sufficient to result in a miraculous outcome.[55]

Social interactions contribute to a "subtle transmission of expectations" that affects both the illness and the cure. Miraculous-image shrines
are devotional but also therapeutic sites. Sick people converge there, as at
hospitals, with the expectant trust that the resources (doctor, miraculous
image) are competent and empowered to restore their health. They are
comforted and strengthened by encouragement, relief, reassurance, a
sense of safety or security, an optimistic confidence that the problem will
be resolved, and positive emotions that foster well-being. All of these are
significant psychological reinforcements that the therapeutic site and
community contribute to the anticipated cure. The context is critical to
restored well-being. A sugar-tablet placebo prescribed at a hospital can
cure an ailment but a teaspoon of sugar from a home jar cannot. A cure is
miraculous even if attributable only to the placebo effect or a response expectancy, insofar as that effect and that expectancy occurred because faith
engaged with a miraculous image in a sacred therapeutic context. The
miracle is real because it is efficacious. I was sick, I asked the Virgen de
Juquila to cure me, and now I am well.[56]

Illnesses are attributed to natural, supernatural, and combined causes,
and consequently God, miraculous images, curative rituals, scientific medicine, traditional or folk medicine, and home remedies together constitute
an arsenal of compatible resources deployable for recuperating wellness.
Rather than a hierarchy of resort, these practices indicate a lateral seriality
or simultaneity of resort. One sick person might first go to a miraculous
image, another to a curandero, and a third to a medical doctor, depending
on combinations of access and personal preference, but if the desired goal
(cure) is not achieved through one resource they will proceed to another,
even while continuing with the first. Miraculous, medical, and traditional
resources are contributing factors to one and the same integrated and essentially religious effort. A 1941 retablo shows a surgeon at work and relates
that a woman had "cancer of the face that was thought to be incurable," but
after pleading to the Virgen de Zapopan the woman "was completely cured
through the intervention of the Holy Virgin and the doctor Edmundo
Aviña." Another votary made a petition and promise with the hope of a cure
for his wife's knee problem and his granddaughter's asthma. Both were
undergoing medical treatment, but the votary hedged the bet with sacred
reinforcements: "I don't think it would hurt to bring a little faith to this,
since people rightly say that faith moves mountains."[57]

When a baby daughter got gravely sick as the result of an evil eye, her
mother took her to a curandera, a pharmacy, a doctor, and finally to a priest

for baptism in the event of anticipated death. The mother then petitioned a miracle from the Señor de Carácuaro, promising to visit the shrine if the daughter was cured, and the miracle was granted. In this case the petition to the miraculous image is a last resort; in other cases the order varies in multiple configurations, and the simultaneity of resort can cause ambiguity regarding which resource specifically—or all of them together?—effected the cure. After repeated surgeries on an infant son, a votary petitioned San José that a scheduled surgery would be the last. "It seemed like the boy was getting better little by little, so I had to fulfill my promise. I don't know if it was an act of faith, I don't know if it was the medicine that they gave him, or the surgery, or all of the treatment he had because in addition to allopathic medicine we were giving him homeopathic medicine and we were also giving him natural medicine, so I don't know which made him start to get better, but he's getting better now so we're fulfilling our promise."[58]

The miracle is never decidedly attributed, and consequently the reciprocation seems more an obligation than a genuine expression of gratitude. In other cases, quite to the contrary, the cure is attributed to a miraculous image and the medical contribution is devalued despite significant intervention. Votive texts such as this one are characteristic: "I thank the Most Holy Virgen del Pueblito for having restored my sight with surgery." A message on a cast-iron cross offering to the Virgen de Juquila gives thanks for accompaniment during cancer treatments, "because you were my doctor and my nurse." Some medical procedures are effective and others are not; votaries attribute successes to miraculous intervention. "Please allow that this fertility treatment that you have allowed us to try has good results thanks to your blessing," a woman wrote to the Virgen del Pueblito. Another petition to the same Virgin includes, "Guide the surgeon with your holy hands so that everything turns out all right." The surgeon and the scalpel are instruments of the sacred power that effects the cure. The miraculous image guides the surgeon's hand, provides the "the genuine effectiveness" that refines the action, that purifies and perfects it. The idea is illustrated precisely in a homemade retablo that shows Christ in the operating room, with his hand on the surgeon's shoulder, guiding the surgery to its successful outcome. More common are votive paintings that depict rays of grace emanating like cones of light from miraculous images to operations in progress. The outcomes are successful because the image envelops the surgeon and patient in its sacred power.[59]

When God and miraculous images themselves are represented as medical doctors, the natural and supernatural contributions fuse into one

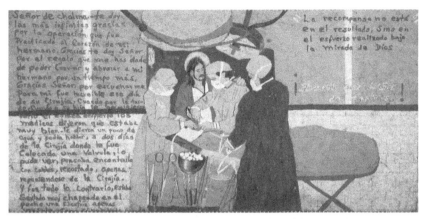

Christ overseeing surgery, from a homemade retablo offered to the Señor de Chalma.

and the same. The concept of a Christian medical deity dates back at least to the third century, when Origin referred to Christ as "the Great Physician." John of Damascus regarded a church as a "spiritual hospital," and the Church today adheres to these ideas and interprets Matthew 10:8—"Heal the sick"—as a mandate to continue Christ's mission. In a similar construction, medicine is described as God's creation, instrument, and gift to humanity. Consequently, as it is worded in an eighteenth-century English tract, "Physicians have the honor to be followers of Our Savior in the practice of the medicinal art." These ideas extend into Mexican devotion today when votaries conceive of a miraculous image as a "heavenly doctor" or "divine doctor." In a shrine booklet the Virgen del Pueblito is described as "medicine from heaven for all diseases." Others opt for a hybrid: "Faith in God is as much a help for medicine as a medicine in itself." The many Niño Doctor images, such as the roadside Niño Doctorcito de los Enfermos in León, Guanajuato, represent the Christ child as a medical doctor and are thanked for health miracles with offerings that range from toy cars to hospital bracelets. Children are often the beneficiaries. In another devotion a young girl with a kidney problem petitioned the Virgen de la Paz to cure her. "You are going to be my doctor.... I don't want that operation it's very painful I want you to cure me."[60]

As suggested in this last example, miracles are occasionally performed directly by miraculous images, without human intermediaries. One might expect that omnipotent miraculous images would routinely perform their miracles directly, "with no medicine but divine medicine," but such miracles are relatively rare. After falling off a horse a husband and wife were cured "without consulting any doctor except this divine one, the Señor de la Misericordia." An offering to the Virgen de San Juan de los Lagos gives thanks for cancer disappearing without treatment and another at the same site relates, "I was on the verge of losing my sight my vision was already blurry and you cured me a lump formed between my legs and you made it disappear." Another miracle, performed directly by the Virgin de la Soledad in Oaxaca, was recorded in a 1952 retablo: "I give you thanks My Mother of Soledad, for having cured me of a serious disease without medical treatment, only with your divine grace." In many cases a cure is effected by direct physical contact with reproductions of a miraculous image. As related in 2013 by a votary from Jalisco, "I went into shock after taking flu medicine, because of which I died for a few seconds in the hospital. There was an image of Niño del Cacahuatito that a nurse had and she put it on my chest and I began to revive."[61]

Resort to miraculous images becomes urgent, and even exclusive, when the prognoses of medical professionals are disturbing. Antonio remarked that in grave cases doctors say "let's hope for a miracle," and what I presume to be a figurative rhetorical deflection is taken quite literally by Antonio and motivates him to action. After medicine has failed, at this critical moment of helplessness, many votaries appeal to miraculous images with desperate, all-or-nothing, last-chance faith in pursuit of a positive outcome. "I brought my son so that we can ask you together that you grant us the miracle of curing him for me of an incurable disease that is diabetes," a woman wrote to the Señor de Otatitlán. Zoila, a Zapoteca in rural Oaxaca, was repeatedly diagnosed as sterile by doctors and curanderos and was advised to accept this fate, but after "earthly resources were exhausted, the woman appealed to the image of the Preciosa Sangre de Cristo," a painting in the church of the Virgen de Navidad in Teotitlán, and got pregnant at last. Another votary, "not finding human remedies," finally "beseeched the Señor de la Misericordia who miraculously cured him."[62]

In some cases medicine had seemed the better bet but then weak faith was awakened when treatment failed. "We were exhausting all medical possibilities and saw that my boy wasn't getting better, so we had to appeal to the supreme being so that he would lend us a hand." Another votary said, "I asked San José to help my brother who had already been in a coma for two months. I was desperate and in such moments you relinquish yourself to any belief or tradition that might restore the health of your family member."[63]

In other cases, the resort to miracle petitions after the failure of medical treatments serves to dramatize the unrivaled power of God and the saints. Father Juan Bautista suffered "a strange Flow of blood that at the same time came out of seven arteries of the body, these being the nostrils, eyes, ears, and mouth." This mysterious occurrence was a marvel to everyone, including the medical doctors who treated Juan Bautista without success, using medications and bleedings. Juan Bautista suffered high fever and severe pain, and with "the Art of Medicine having exhausted all of its efforts, and not knowing how to at least mitigate the sick man's sufferings," the doctors decided to send the priest "to breathe the airs of a foreign country." Before approving that exiled convalescence, however, the provincial suggested "that he invoke the assistance of Heaven" and "encouraged Father Juan Bautista to put all of his confidence in the powerful protection of his Patron Saint, Father San Francisco Xavier, from whom he had received a most exceptional favor a few years earlier." Accordingly, "abandoned of all human relief, he turned his eyes toward Heaven," prayed to "Xavier his Saint, and powerful Doctor," and Juan Bautista's blood flow ceased at last.[64]

Marco

God sends us love in the form of understanding.

On December 8, 2009 a garbage collector named Marco left his home in the Nuevo Amanecer neighborhood of Almealco, Querétaro, together with his wife and infant daughter. He left the wife and daughter at his in-laws' residence and continued walking toward the plaza, where he paused in the atrium of the church of Santa María Amealco, as he did daily, to commend himself to the Virgin of the Immaculate Conception and request her protection during the workday. Marco then joined his coworker, Adrián, at 7:00 a.m., and the two swept the walkways of the plaza's gardens while awaiting the arrival of the garbage truck, driven by Cruz. The truck began its rounds, with Adrián and Marco standing outside, and they collected trash at a school, a hospital, and some principal thoroughfares before heading toward the Las Américas neighborhood.

When they reached the house of one Alfredo, Marco jumped down, grabbed the garbage pail, and handed it to Adrián to empty; the two then climbed back up and the truck continued on its way. It was almost 9:00. Marco was conversing with Adrián when, he wrote, "suddenly I felt that the strength went out of my hands and my feet slipped falling to the mercy of the truck." The dual rear tires of the truck passed over Marco's body. The truck stopped and the coworkers rushed to Marco's aid; Alfredo cut medicinal herbs and told Marco to swallow them; Adrián, kneeling, lifted Marco's head and put it on his knee; another man brought a sweater so Marco wouldn't get a chill; and, when more police arrived, Alfredo started yelling, "We don't need another patrol car—we need an ambulance!" Marco himself was praying: "I began to commend myself to the Virgen de los Dolores and asked her not to leave me invalid because I wanted to serve my family and be useful to them to keep moving forward and to be closer to God so I could help however I can."

The ambulance paramedics gave Marco an injection for pain and took him to the Oriente clinic in San Juan del Río. Tests and x-rays revealed that Marco was bleeding internally and needed emergency surgery. A surgeon and Marco's wife were called; both arrived shortly after. The procedure began at 1:00 and ended at 4:00. At 8:00, when the anesthesia wore off, Marco's pain was complicated by an inability to urinate, due to a lesioned urethra, which required another surgery that would take place a few days later. In the interim, surgical remedies were reinforced by celestial ones when some friends visited Marco. "They gave me the best medicine that a patient could receive which is God our lord through the host and I felt as though it fortified my whole body as though it had charged my batteries and lifting my gaze upward I gave thanks for that beautiful sensation that coursed through my whole body." The second surgery occurred on December 12 and was successful. Marco had watched a mass on television beforehand.

On December 14 Marco was discharged from the hospital and was "immobilized without being able to move neither to one side nor the other I could only be on my back and like that they moved me to my in-law's house to convalesce there." He was confined to bed, and about a month later the doctor ordered new x-rays and then informed Marco and his family that another surgery was necessary. This one, scheduled for January 14, would remove the external fixator that were installed during the emergency surgery. The procedure was complicated and scheduled to last between five and six hours; Marco's family, especially his wife, was nervous. "When we left my mother-in-law's house my wife gave me a picture of the Virgen de los Dolores so that it would take care of me during the operation and they let me take it with me and into the operating room and it was under my pillow during the whole surgery." The surgery was successful and two days later, with "the doctors surprised by my recuperation," Marco went home. He was confined to bed rest for three and a half months.

The day arrived finally for Marco to get out of bed and the doctor situated a walker nearby for support. "I couldn't do it on the first try the bed pulled me back because after so much time on top of the bed it didn't want to let me go but on the second try I said help me my God and I managed to stand up although my feet hurt a lot, mostly the one that was more damaged, I managed to stand up and the doctor joking with me told me to walk and I took a few steps as though nothing had happened to me... I don't know if it was the desire I had to walk or the faith I had in god who gave me so many proofs of his love, but I began to walk my wife cried with joy because I was able to walk again."

Eventually Marco could walk with just a cane, but he was still dependent on the catheter and subsequently had two additional urethra operations. In late January 2011 he had recuperated sufficiently to remove the catheter, but the doctors advised that additional surgery might become necessary. Marco's testimony, dated August 16, 2011, concludes with these words: "I give thanks to you my god for having granted this miracle of faith and of life." Unlike others in similar situations, Marco did not perceive the accident as a punishment or test of faith.

In one of the letters solicited by Marco in support of his testimony, the principal surgeon notes some felicitous, inexplicable events, such as having in his car, which was unusual, the materials needed for Marco's first surgery. "If I had not brought it with me Marco would have died since there would not have been time to get an external fixator." In the concluding paragraph of the letter he wrote, "Unfortunately Marco has not recovered 100% from his pelvic lesions because he continues with pain, discomfort, and difficulty with walking," as well as with his urethral lesion. Amealco government personnel records for 2014 show Marco still employed in the sanitation department.

Marco's miracle narrative, a six-page testimony supplemented by letters from two surgeons, was presented to the rector of the Virgen de los Dolores de Soriano basilica, who later gave a copy to me. The testimony well illustrates many of the themes that are prominent in petitionary devotion. These include miracles as a collaborative interaction of sacred power and human agency, previous miracles as prototypes and catalysts of subsequent petitions, the transfer of sacred power by proximity and contact, and causal attribution as it relates to the meaning of tragedies, to perceived control, and to maintenance or restoration of self-esteem and self-image.

When Marco was leaving home for his most complicated surgery, his concerned wife gave him an image of Soriano's Virgen de los Dolores to accompany him in the operating room. Marco is an informed Catholic who understands the transcendental nature of divinity and explicitly states his belief that God was with him always. Nevertheless he and his wife perceived tangible accompaniment by the image as highly relevant to successful surgery. The medical staff condoned or at least tolerated the presence of the image, because it too participates in a culture in which miraculous images and the tactile transfer of sacred power are normative. From its strategic position under the pillow the image radiates power into Marco and into the operating room, thereby motivating an interactive circulation—of

Marco's fortitude, the surgeon's aptitude, and sacred protection and guidance—that result in a successful outcome.[1]

The collaborative nature of the miracle depends on the surgeon as a secondary cause but also on Marco in his ongoing efforts at recovery. From above God and the Virgin act through medical professionals, and from below Marco's independent efforts are sustained and strengthened by the sacred power he solicits in prayer. The collaboration begins with the mysterious appearance of a fixator in the surgeon's car, extends through Marco's request for strength (which on one occasion gives him the ability to stand and walk), and includes a divine message—*I will never leave you*—and even reassuring apparitions of the Virgin. "I sensed that the virgin came to visit me on two occasions," Marco wrote. While he was confined to bed rest the Virgin sat on the right side of the bed, near his head, "and I wanted to talk to her but I couldn't, on both occasions I saw only a very beautiful brilliance and a very special peace that I will never be able to describe." Marco is not a passive, helpless victim who receives a miracle that instantaneously restores his health, but rather is the protagonist of an ongoing process in which activated faith collaborates with God, the Virgin, and her representations to effect a miraculous cure.

Marco's testimony is also an outstanding example of how one miracle becomes the prototype and catalyst of others. We recall that Marco's primary devotion is to the Virgin of the Immaculate Conception at his local church, and on the morning of the accident, as was his daily custom, he commended himself to her protection prior to beginning the workday. The accident occurred despite that precaution, however, and when Marco was lying in the street and fearing that he would be permanently disabled, he petitioned the miracle not from this local Virgin but rather from the Virgen de los Dolores in Soriano. He did so because, as Marco explained, "I remembered the miracle granted to the girl María José from Colón," who had drowned and was resuscitated by the Virgen de Soriano. News of that miracle was widely disseminated, and in his moment of crisis Marco broke away from his customary devotion and turned instead to the Virgin with a strong precedent. Later Marco's own miracle story was made public through his written testimony, thereby contributing to the Virgen de Soriano's growing reputation and establishing another precedent—a multiple, accumulating precedent—that inspires new petitions.[2]

A detail from the 2007 retablo giving thanks for the resuscitation of María José. In this church-commissioned retablo, the rays of grace initiate in heaven.

Marco initially made no attribution regarding the cause of the accident and avoided blaming himself or others. After he fell and was crushed by the wheels, Adrián and Cruz rushed to help him, asking what had happened. "They asked me a thousand questions," Marco said, but he answered none of them and diverted to another matter. Later, in the clinic, he was concerned not with the cause of the accident but rather with what was not the cause, which is to say he wanted to exonerate Cruz as driver of accusations and responsibility. (After accidents in Mexico the involved parties are detained by police to clarify what happened.) In Marco's words, "I was starting to fall asleep when I had the sensation in my mind that there was something I forgot to do and I remembered my coworkers Cruz and Adrián and I began to feel very worried and told my wife to talk to Cruz and to tell him that I was all right and I wanted to make sure he wasn't arrested because it had not been his fault that what happened happened because only god knew why he did things." That last point is reinforced later in the document when the January 14 surgery is imminent. "God gave me another proof that he exists," Marco wrote, because his mother-in-law had given him a prayer that included a phrase attributed to God—"don't worry because I will never leave you alone." That phrase, Marco wrote, "said exactly what I felt and was living." Marco's response was, "thy will be done."

For Marco the accident was not an accident, but rather a manifestation of God's will, beyond our comprehension. His certainty is grounded in intuition, in Catholic common sense. God has a plan for humanity and there is meaning and peace in that, even if the immediate effects are disturbing. The mysterious loosening of Marco's grip prior to the fall quietly implies supernatural causation while at once exculpating Marco and his coworkers. The cause of the fall is of less interest to Marco than the cause of his survival, which is to say the Virgin's rapid intervention that saved him while under the truck and the ongoing support that saw him through the surgeries and contributed thereafter to his convalescence. Rather than having his belief systems crash because the accident was anomalous and unassimilable (*I didn't deserve this punishment, God is cruel, the Virgin didn't protect me*), Marco's cosmovision remains intact—his faith is even strengthened—by assimilating the accident (*Thy will be done, the Virgin saved my life, God loves me and is with me and is helping me through this crisis*). The accident itself becomes a religious event as it is divested of meaningless randomness and integrated into the everyday beliefs that Marco shares with his family. The intuition of miraculous intervention is as unquestioned as it is unsubstantiated. Miracles are interpretations, and devotees find miracles where they need them and assign them to the sacred beings to whom they entrust their care. The accident is perceived as indisputable evidence that God and the Virgin intervene to redeem us from crises. Marco's close call has a happy ending. The course of his destiny has been altered.[3]

Marco's interpretation of his accident suggests not so much that events are controllable as that they are remediable. A sense of powerlessness yields gradually to a sense of resumed control as Marco defines the crisis, knows God and the Virgin are helping him through it, and becomes certain that he will prevail and be a better person as a result of the ordeal. His devotion is a means of mastery, a manner of convalescence, and an inadvertent strategy to restore the status quo of established meanings. His subordination to divine will consequently has nothing to do with fatalism. God and Soriano's Virgen de los Dolores save Marco's life, they give him strength, they give him a sense of vicarious control, and they give his crisis meaning, but the rest is up to him and his interpretive control.

Marco's interpretations evidence his cognition at work to shape the crisis along the contours of his beliefs. They also contribute to his resilience and the restoration of his damaged dignity and self-image after his decline from a healthy supporter of his family to a bedridden invalid. Rather than being the unfortunate victim of a meaningless accident that disabled him, Marco is the beneficiary of a miracle. He has been chosen by God and the Virgin. His Christian merits have been recognized in heaven, and this attests to his worthiness.

Such extraordinary boosts to self-image are complemented by the outpouring of loving attention bestowed on Marco by family and friends, which likewise contributes to his sense of worthiness. Marco's self-image is affirmed because important others value him and demonstrate their love. After leaving the hospital to convalesce at his in-laws' house, Marco wrote, "I felt very loved because a lot of acquaintances came to receive me," and "all of my relatives, parents, in-laws, siblings, friends got to work like ants . . . and I felt a great joy because of how much they loved me." Despite all of the pain and hardship, the accident brings Marco closer to family and closer to God, while at once reaffirming—even redefining—his self-image as it dialectically interacts with these supporters.[4]

In addition, Marco's attribution of the accident to an external cause (God acting in mysterious ways) frees him of self-incrimination and self-recrimination. The external cause is established through ambiguous attribution to divine will that exculpates the driver, Cruz, but also Marco himself. Marco's sense of responsibility is reaffirmed—it's not his fault—and that assessment, together with supernatural and social support, affords a stronger will to go forward, a more stable psychological base to convalesce.

All of these themes—the investment of the accident with religious meaning, the affirmation of self-image and self-worth, the therapeutic value of positive framing—are represented by Marco's narrative but are also constructed there. The act of writing the narrative gave Marco a means of gaining perspective, of thinking through the accident, of defining it and investing it with meaning. The written narrative culminates the cognitive process of transforming the accident into a miracle and integrating it into Marco's life story. It objectifies the story by making it textual and public, fixing the nature of the accident as a miracle and establishing Marco as the protagonist—completely sympathetic—who overcomes adversity by the grace of God. The principle of sacred intervention pulls the narrated events into its orbit and gives them their place, their weight, and their allegiance to the premise that coheres them.

This is particularly evident in description of the garbage-truck tires as they passed over Marco's body. Where one would anticipate pain (Marco later says "I felt like I was cut in half"), Marco described the moment as a protective embrace: "a very beautiful hug a lovely warmth as though someone had hugged me tightly so that nothing would happen to me." This perception initiates the sacred interventions that continue throughout the surgeries and the recovery. The narrative as a whole shifts perception of the accident from doom and gloom to collaboration with God and the Virgin in a long-term process of healing. Adverse events become more acceptable, more assimilable, and more useful to convalescence through positive religious appraisal. Rather than a defeatist discourse of despair—*I can hardly walk, my life is ruined, I urinate through a catheter, I withdraw*—the narrative redirects the crisis toward affirmations: *God and the Virgin saved me, I'm alive, I'm grateful, I share my gratitude with others.* By recontextualizing the incident from a meaningless accident to a miracle, the negative emotions and cognitions that impede adjustment—self-pity, depression, fatalistic defeat—are replaced by positive, constructive, life-affirming, faith-affirming emotions and cognitions that are conducive to recuperation.

This conceptual shift evolved through a period of incubation between the occurrence of the accident on December 8, 2009 and the completion of the testimony on August 16, 2011. Marco's attentiveness to detail, his subtle reflections on his thoughts and feelings, and his faithful allegiance to the premises he lives by all contribute to the miracle that saved him.[5]

Collaborations

Sacred Power and Human Agency

All miracles performed by images are essentially collaborative, because an image's power is dependent on devotees' faith. The interdependence is more explicit when images perform miracles through guided human action. In many cases—surgeries, for example—images act through secondary causes and miracles happen when sacred power collaborates with human agency. The miraculous image (or God) is the primary cause, and a purposeful, independently causal agent (the surgeon) is secondary. As Thomas Aquinas developed the idea, "Divine Providence works through intermediaries. For God governs the lower through the higher, not from any impotence on his part, but from the abundance of his goodness imparting to creatures the dignity of causing."[1]

The Virgen de la Soledad saves a blazing building from destruction, but the retablo offered in gratitude represents firemen extinguishing the flames. A policeman arrives in time to prevent a robbery and miners dig out their coworker from a collapsed shaft, but miracles are attributed to images of Christ. Such cases could be multiplied by the thousands—the kidnap victim recovered, the lost livestock found, the visa application successful. Human contributions to happy ends are regarded as instrumental to sacred interventions, and consequently the efficacy of a mother, a student, a farmer, an ex-addict are often devalued or dismissed as votaries' interpretations gravitate toward miracles. "The doctor received no credit for her recovery," as it was worded in one instance, because the treatment and recovery followed a miracle petition. Others view human agents more generously as the angelic expediters of sacred will, but nevertheless as subordinate and instrumental.[2]

Every year Pedro makes a three-day walking pilgrimage from Puebla to the Virgen de Guadalupe because she saved him and his father through secondary causes. Some cattle had been stolen from the family's ranch, and when Pedro and his father went in pursuit the thieves overpowered them, tied them up, beat them, and tortured the father by, among other cruelties, cutting the tendons on the back of his hands. Pedro was eighteen at the time. He commended himself and his father to the Virgen de Guadalupe, and about five minutes later the police arrived and rescued them. The father was hospitalized for fifteen days.

Miraculous images also act through nonhuman secondary causes, be they animals, forces of nature, or human inventions like seat belts, chemotherapy, and fertilizer. While en route from Mexico to Spain a ship was caught in a storm, and "a wave crossed the Ship and threw a woman overboard; she invoked the Most Holy Virgen de San Juan, and shortly after another wave came and returned the woman to the Ship." When a rider's foot was caught in a stirrup and his body was dragged by a frantic horse, the rider implored an intervention and the Virgen de los Remedios responded "by means of a dog" that appeared out of nowhere, grabbed the reins in its teeth, and stopped the running horse. In 1938 a border dispute resulted in a feud, and when Rigoberto was out riding the neighbor, Indalesio, confronted him and drew a pistol. Rigoberto thought he was finished, but, as he related in a retablo text, "I commended myself to the Virgen de Zapopan so that she would protect my life and it was she who riled up my dogs so that they would distract Indalesio and give me time to get out my pistol and gallop home."[3]

The reliance of miraculous images on humans is the flipside, the inverse complement, of human reliance on miraculous images. At one pole of this human reliance is an independent agent petitioning miraculous reinforcements at times of need (collaborative control), and at the other is

Pedro was rescued by the police after commending himself to the Virgen de Guadalupe.

a dependent or depleted petitioner imploring an image to take control (deferred control). "Defer" is used here in the sense of entrusting oneself to another, pursuant to devotee's frequent use of the Spanish *encomendar* (to commend, as in "into your hands I commend my spirit"). Collaborative control is registered textually in phrases like "help me to…," "show me the way to…," "give me the strength to…"; and deferred control in phrases like "cure me," "give me," and "protect me." The same is illustrated by contrasting inmate petitions ranging from collaborative formulations like "change my character in order to be a good man with all of my loved ones" to deferent formulations like "soften the hearts of these authorities. Grant me that things go well in this court." More nuanced and complex combinations of sacred resources and human agency are evident in such phrases as "I would like to thank God for letting me arrive home safe, and giving me the knowledge not to drink and drive," in which God provides guidance that is internalized and supplements independent agency; as opposed to "God watched over me and kept me from any really serious consequences of my behavior," in which the (irresponsible) action is independent but the outcomes are dependent on God's will.[4]

Collaborative and deferred control are two of many related concepts that include God control, God-mediated control, vicarious control, and a "sense of divine control," meaning "the extent to which an individual perceives that God controls the directions and outcomes of daily life and, more broadly, life course trajectories." The benefits of perceived control are most apparent when miraculous images intervene at moments of crisis, but less dramatic and more constant benefits in everyday life include strength, fortitude, guidance, optimism, meaning, and a sense of protection and security. Miraculous images contribute to devotees' motivation, resilience, and perseverance, particularly when challenges are aggravated by poverty. Faith in miracles, even in the absence of miracles themselves, increases one's options, broadens one's range, builds confidence, facilitates risk-taking, reduces anxiety and fear of failure, and deters helpless passivity. "Faith is what gives you strength and freedom," Marta explained. "It frees you from danger; you're not afraid of anything."[5]

A collaborative or deferred style depends largely on the degree to which outcomes are perceived as results of one's own agency (internal locus) as opposed to one's reliance on other sources (external locus). "The locus of control imposes a perspective on the conceptualization of all one's experiences: from a strong internal locus of control perspective I view failures and successes as largely my own doing, whereas from an external locus perspective

Marta. "Faith is what gives you strength and freedom."

even my most effective efforts are seen as events that were outside my control," in the present case because they are attributed to miracles. The locus of control also contributes to how devotees respond to hardship and crisis. One devotee takes decisive action (which might include a petition), another surrenders helplessly and pleads for a miraculous solution, and a third strikes a balance, using sacred resources to reinforce independent initiative. In these ways locus of control moderates self-efficacy, or "people's assessments of their effectiveness, competence, and causal agency."[6]

Often votaries oscillate between collaborative and deferred control as perceived self-efficacy negotiates with the severity of crises. There are also many overlaps and hybrid combinations. In collaborative control, for example, votaries gain internal control through deferral to miraculous images responsive to their petitions. The votary maintains the locus of control, but with resources provided externally. A measure of dependence, in effect, strengthens independence. "Simply to believe that God controls the world does not insure a sense of meaning and purpose in life. To a large extent, meaningfulness and purpose result from a sense of personal effectiveness in achieving one's personal goals." Consequently, through "active religious surrender," "enacted destiny," and "positive association between the sense of divine control and personal feelings of mastery," sacred power is used as a resource for self-efficacy and independent action. From another angle, however, petitioned miracles test the malleable boundaries between individual initiative and responsibility as they relate to fatalism. If one tends toward deferral, what is one's role in bringing a crisis to its happy resolution? To what degree does belief in miraculous-image protection and intervention affect one's efficacious and preventative actions, one's motivation to excel after deferral to external control, and one's sense of invulnerability?[7]

Collaborative Control

I can do all things through Christ who strengthens me.
PHILIPPIANS 4:13

The saying "God helps those who helps themselves" dates back at least to the fifteenth century, and is echoed in other such sayings as, "If we leave it to God, it is already half lost." Equivalent expressions in Spanish include *"ayúdate, para que Dios te ayude"* ("help yourself, so that God will help you") and *"a Dios rogando y con el mazo dando,"* which conveys the idea that hard work and prayer together get the job done. Such sayings advocate independent effort and regard God as a supplement, a reinforcement, a collaborator "ready to help when difficulties and challenges arise and when people strive to attain positive goals."[8]

According to self-expansion theory, people derive attributes and resources from others who are close to them. "The perceived boundaries between the self and other can be blurred in one's cognitive and affective systems," and consequently people "incorporate aspects of others into their own identities." In a romantic relationship, for example, one's own sense of self acquires select qualities and characteristics of the partner. When votaries petition strength and forbearance, they maintain their own self-concept while at once deriving and assimilating attributes from miraculous images. The locus of control remains more or less internal but is permeable and infuses external attributes that strengthen self-efficacy. "It is as if, to some extent, the other's resources are one's own," and these resources include "assets that can facilitate the achievement of goals." After a petition the power of a miraculous image is internalized as one's own strength, even when devotees perceive the power as exclusively external.[9]

The transferal of resources from miraculous images to votaries is also suggested in selfobject theory, as illustrated by analogy in the following passage. "When our self-esteem is low after we have suffered a defeat and a friend puts his arm around our shoulder and thus symbolically allows us to merge with him—to be suffused by his calmness and security—we do not develop the delusion that we have become part of his body or mind or that he has become part of us. What we experience—and that is why he is our selfobject at such a moment—is that, on the one hand, he participates (via empathy with us) in our dismay, in our despair, in our sense of failure and defeat, while, on the other hand, we feel calmed by his calmness and strengthened by his strength because (via our empathy with him) we sense his calmness and strength and are able to participate in it." A compassionate miraculous image empathizes with a devotee's problems, while at once infusing the devotee with its accessible, inexhaustible resources.[10]

"When I have problems," Marta said, "the first thing I do is say, 'God, help me, so that I will also help myself.'" Marta inverts the common expression and seemingly the priority—God helps first, then she goes into action—in a reordering that conforms to devotional practice: first the petition (and faith in a positive outcome), then the self-efficacy and motivation. Miraculous images rarely deliver a windfall or fully realized solution; they rather facilitate and enable so that votaries can make accomplishments on their own. "If I ask for the miracle of having money and I don't work," Juana said, "I'm not going to get the miracle." If someone petitions a house, Pedro said, "God gives you the tools so that you can work. A house isn't going to come down from heaven." Carlos, referring to Christ, made a similar observation: If you ask for a car, "He doesn't give you a car, he gives you work." The practical stoicism of José Luis, who had made the pilgrimage to Chalma annually for forty years, delivered the same point unembellished: "God gives me health, so that I can take care of the work myself." In Los Angeles, California, votaries advocating immigration reform and better jobs for their families in Mexico organized a procession of the Virgen de Juquila. Miriam, the organizer of the event, explained that "we have to make the miracle happen with actions," in this case through politico-religious protest.[11]

As is evident in all of these examples, votaries inclined to collaborative control petition sacred supplements to make their own initiatives efficacious. The same is registered in textual petitions and offerings. "Help me so that the coffee I plant...takes root and grows and is harvested," a votary wrote to the Cristo Negro de Otatitlán. Others gave thanks to the Virgen de San Juan de los Lagos "for having granted us the miracle and given us the means to have finished the construction of our house." In different ways collaboration is represented when a retablo offered to the Virgen de San Juan de los Lagos shows people in a tree above flooding waters, and the text explains, "On hearing the prayer, our Divine Lady intervened and they were miraculously saved by climbing a tree"; when a sixty-five-year old woman facing a difficult pilgrimage says, "Faith moves mountains and my Lord is going to allow me to make it to Chalma; with my Nike sneakers I will make it"; and when a retablo text states that the Virgen de Guadalupe saved a man from a firing squad, while the accompanying painting shows his wife (who offered the retablo) punching and knocking down one of the soldiers.[12]

An exemplary 1880 votive painting on canvas depicts men and women pulling ropes with the aid of three yokes of oxen to remove a giant boulder from a well. In the background a prayerful man and woman, both holding flower and candles, petition the three miraculous images hovering above. The text explains that on January 3, 1879, the residents of two villages began to dig a well and in the process removed several boulders to access the water below. The painting represents the events on March 18, when after months of labor the residents and oxen teams managed to remove the largest boulder and finally reached the aquifer. "Seeing the difficulty of the enterprise" they invoked their miraculous images and "very beautiful water appeared," but months of human and ox effort were also involved.[13]

In all of these examples, votaries take responsibility for overcoming the challenges that confront them and miraculous images provide, or are attributed, the extra boost that assures successful outcomes. The sacred contribution also mitigates contingency and renders a specific effort—this harvest, this surgery, this job or visa or university application—successful among many that fail. Collaborative-control petitions have a confident, competent tone, and unlike the pleading that is characteristic of deferred control these petitions tend toward happy acknowledgment or positive persuasion. The votaries' own motivation and exertion inspire the support of a God who helps those who help themselves.

Devotees who commend themselves to miraculous images feel *acompañado*, which is to say supernaturally accompanied and protected in everyday life. This caring oversight of each individual devotee repeats in miniature the role of patron saints for a social collective. The image's paradoxical omnipresence through absence affords the security and tranquility of having a vigilant custodian, like a guardian angel, empowered and prepared to intervene at moments of need. As it is worded in a prayer to the Virgen de Tonatico, "Sweet Mother, don't avert your gaze from me don't go away. Come with me everywhere and never leave me alone." After complications resulting from a botched surgery—"a complete martyrdom and failure"—a family gave thanks to the same Virgin because "she never abandoned us she was with us she accompanied us night and day in those moments of anguish." Lourdes, who is devoted to the Señor del Rayo, said "When I'm at home, or at our store, I know that he is with me." When business is slow, "I say 'Lord, help us,' and people arrive, keep arriving;

there are no customers and I say, 'Papi, help us, we have a son to support,' and people begin to arrive, to buy."[14]

The relation between devotees and the images to which they are commended is "open to the nuances of known human relations between patron and client," but it is also loving and intimate. "I am holding your hand and know that you will never let me go," a female votary wrote to the Señor de Chalma. Others wrote, "I love you divine Niño Cachuatito for so many miracles you have done for us"; and "Señor de la Misericordia, may I lack everything but YOU. We love you a lot." The miraculous image is also a soothing presence as votaries confront the aloneness of being human among humans. Religious community might alleviate loneliness through a sense of solidarity and common purpose, but in votive offerings loneliness entails more a longing for intimacy than a lack of social contact. A photographic offering to the Virgen del Pueblito shows a woman holding her newborn baby, and on the back the woman wrote: "I come to thank you for having helped me to get through my cesarean I only had you there with me I will never forget you." When seasoned loneliness yields to depression—"I feel very sad and at times even defeated"—some votaries petition relief and others petition support in their quests to find romantic and life partners, or to reconciliate with a spouse after separation.[15]

Migrants commend themselves to miraculous images for protection during the journey, for success in border crossing, and for employment on arrival. A devotee of the Niño de la Cruzada, known in Guanajuato state as a protector of migrants, was also grateful for homecoming: "I came to give thanks to the Niño because he granted me returning to my family since I commended myself to him when I went to the United States and he guided me and kept me on the right track." Pilgrims are likewise protected en route. As Adolfo explained, pilgrims to Chalma know that "the Lord comes with us, and nothing is going to happen to us. That is the faith we have. He accompanies us, we feel him beside us. We have faith that we are going to arrive without problems, that we are going to be all right. Look, the proof is that we're all here. Nothing happened to us." Pilgrims extend this sense of protection en route to their journey through life as a whole.[16]

In other petitions the control remains collaborative and the sacred contribution remains supplemental, but the votaries' self-efficacy is weaker and more dependent on miracles. In a note left at the Augustinian church in Malinalco, a single mother petitioned Christ on behalf of herself and her children, "to have our own home so that we no longer have to be freeloaders.

Adolfo, standing at the center, led this group of pilgrims in a twenty-eight-hour walk from Mexico City to Chalma.

Lord you know I work every day in order to afford a home but it isn't possible." The mother is not seeking a magical solution but at the same time recognizes that her income is insufficient and that acquisition of a home will require external support. She knows both the limits of her agency and where to get help. A share of the internal locus is apportioned externally in order to achieve her goal. As expressed in a CELAM document, a sincere petition "is the best expression of a heart that has renounced self-sufficiency, recognizing that one can do nothing alone." A participant in a psychological study also captured the idea succinctly: "Took control over what I could and gave the rest up to God."[17]

A very different approach is apparent in the defiant, negotiating tone of a votive offering to the Virgen de San Juan de Los Lagos. Three drawings depict Juan in prison, hitchhiking outside the prison, and hugging a happy woman. The accompanying text repeats the phrase "my mother" and addresses the image almost as though it were the votary's real mother. "I want you to know in your heart and soul that you dearest mother of San Juan are very important to me despite the road I may take I will always respect your opinion although I won't always accept it as my own." Juan adds that "the pride you feel for me is one of my most valuable treasures and when I disappoint you I suffer too." He nevertheless declares his independence—"I do not always follow the road that you would chose"—and then elaborates: "You have shown me the capacity that I possess to realize the potential that we all have. Maybe I don't always chose the easiest road, maybe sometimes I make mistakes, but I have learned to make my own decisions based on what I believe to be correct in the moment...although you will not always understand my actions and decisions." Collaborative control as Juan experiences it is grounded not in petition of assistance at specific moments of need, but rather in the resources—strength, confidence, defiance—that he derives from the miraculous image in support of his independent self-efficacy, for better or worse.

Quite common among collaborative-control petitions are requests for fortitude. Particularly in Otatitlán and some churches in the nearby highlands of Oaxaca, written texts often include variations of a formulaic "give me strength and fortitude." A handwritten note in San Andrés Teotilalpam includes, "keep giving me strength and health to keep on working"; and at the same site an elderly man in a shaky hand wrote "give me strength to live more years." Votaries elsewhere likewise petition fortitude, often "the strength necessary to bear my operations" or even to bear the bad news: "tomorrow I'm going to the doctor and I'm a little afraid of what he might tell me I ask you to give us strength and courage to calmly accept whatever might happen." Reinforcements are also petitioned for stamina, courage, forbearance, patience, and a range of other attributes that contribute to coping and to success. "Give me a little intelligence," a university student wrote to the Cristo Negro de Otatitlán, "and I promise that if you give me a little intelligence I will take advantage of it." A framed collage offered to the Virgen de San Juan de los Lagos has photographs of a man and a pickup truck, together with a text that gives thanks for "the great favor that you gave me of having learned how to drive because you gave me the courage and never left me alone." In another offering, to the Niño del Arenal, a kidney donor and recipient ask for the postoperation willpower to abide by the prescribed diet. Resistance to another temptation was requested of the Niño de Atocha when a woman asked "to be a good wife" and "never permit me to be unfaithful, not with my thought nor with my body."[18]

In exceptional cases, votaries request strength to submit to God's will and to tolerate God-sent hardships. Parents of a stillborn child petitioned the Señor de la Misericordia "that you help us and give us the strength that we need to accept your will." The narrative voice then switches to the deceased child's: "Mami y Papi at this time God didn't want me to be born and grow up beside you, but remember that he knows what he is doing and is never wrong and I want you to know that from heaven I am taking care of you and bless you every day, and I ask that you don't renounce his will." These parents defer to God's will and incorporate their reason's into the child's discourse, but at once the control remains collaborative insofar as they seek strength to suffer but also overcome the loss.

Guidance is especially petitioned at moments of stress, uncertainty, and weakened self-control. Characteristic of these collaborative requests are "guide and help me in my work and orient me in my love life"; "wipe from my mind those ugly thoughts that I have and guide me on the right path"; and "remove the pain I am feeling in my soul, give me a sign to know what decision to make." Guidance is often petitioned in its most self-reliant form, enlightenment, so that votaries might acquire the insight, wisdom, and understanding to act independently and effectively. Many pilgrims visit the Señor de Chalma, Adolfo explained, "so that he will orient us if we're lost. We say to him, 'Enlighten me.'" Written petitions often include phrasing like "protect us and enlighten us to continue on the right path and with good health," as it is worded in a note to the Cristo Negro de Otatitlán. A collage at the church of San Felipe Torres Mochas includes a wedding photograph, thanks for the birth of a baby, a request for protection, and, among other text, "I ask that you enlighten us and give us the gift of being good parents."[19]

Petitions that are deeply devotional sometimes evidence a "commitment to partnership in God's good works." In these cases the collaboration is pursuant as much to the will of God or a miraculous image as it is to a votary's needs. "Partnership entails the petitioner's genuine desire in obeying, loving, and sharing the ways of God," because "without an implicit pledge of partnership a prayer is actually a request for God to *serve* us in some way, rather than to give His *assistance*." In contrast with self-interested requests that would exploit a resource, these petitions humbly, devoutly, present an urgent need, often health- or income-related, and include an allusion to or plan for partnership. Rather than requesting material gains or even "that I be saved, that my child be saved, that my husband change," explained Father Paco in Oaxaca, a proper petition should ask "that we be good, that we obey God's will, obey his commandments, because what we do here is precisely to deserve the reward of eternity." Collaboration in this perspective is with Christ's mission of salvation. The idea is captured in a petition written to the Virgen de Tonatico by a father anticipating the birth of twins: "I'm sure of one thing: as a father my priority is to baptize my babies and I promise that we are going to get married in order to be with you and be able to participate in the heavenly banquet of communion."[20]

A petition to the Virgen del Pueblito evidences partnership when it requests relief from debt but at once binds the votary to a related commitment: "I promise you that Juan and I are going to help poor people like us." Another text to the same image asks for resolution of problems and promises in exchange to spread "your faith and devotion among those around me." The family of the resuscitated drowned girl, María José, are committed to partnership in another form by volunteering at the Soriano basilica. In some votive texts the partnership is less evident but seems implicit in the tone, the expectations, and the devotional manner of the votary. A petition to the Señor de Ojo Zarco requests restored health and happiness with an allusion to partnership—"in order to be able to help others"—and then concludes: "Most loved father you who are Refuge in tribulation help in weakness solace in crying have compassion for my suffering, forgive my sins alleviate my pain and increase my faith so that I always have faith in your love and can live in your mercy." Health is also petitioned in another text, but only in sufficient measure to get right with God: "Grant me the health I need so you give me time to repent."

Deferred Control

Thy will be done.
MATTHEW 6:10

Irresolvable problems, mounting and even crippling desperation, a sense of nowhere to turn, emotional depletion and exhaustion, and the angst of inefficacy all foster pleading surrender to miraculous images. "Help me please I can't go on like this. Have compassion and pity on me," a man wrote on a scrap of paper posted in Talpa. In a similar petition to the Virgen del Pueblito a woman wrote, "I feel like I can't take any more, I don't want to collapse but I can't take any more. I only ask you for strength to bear it, some help from you soon whatever you choose but do it soon because I'm already waiting fill me with your love so I can bear it."

In these petitions the problem is not specified, but others frequently mention injury, disease, and medical interventions; or crises in families and love relationships, including conflict, separation, and problems with children. In moderate deferral, the votary remains a participant in control but trusts that the miraculous image will resolve the problem. "My Ramiro is a gift from you," a woman wrote to the Señor de Chalma, thereby establishing the deferential tone at the start. "I ask you lord for him for Ramiro so that he's cured of the disturbance in his head and keeps being that guy with a good heart who I fell in love with." She asks that no one come between them, that they be happy, and that they have a family, and then concludes: "I have faith that you're going to give me a hand because who but you Father you can do anything and you know us both what we want in life. Protect us and take care of us and don't let us go, I wish and long to be very happy and have a beautiful family. We are lord in your holy hands and you will know and will decide when it will be." The votary's tone is subordinate, she takes omniscience ("you know us both") and omnipotence for granted, and she relinquishes control of the outcome to the Señor de Chalma's disposition. At the same time, however, she maintains a measure of control by assuming ownership of her love, desire, and goals, and by asking for collaboration ("give me a hand") in her own efforts to save the relationship.

Such moderated deferral contrasts with the complete surrender expressed in a petition that Mario wrote to the Virgen de San Juan de Los Lagos. "Mother: I put myself in your hands, do whatever you want with me." The text is accompanied by a photograph of the votary and a milagrito of a kneeling devotee at prayer. Deferred control is also explicit in a petition to Soriano's Virgen de los Dolores: "I ask you with all my heart for the health of my mom [name] and for my health in your holy hands I commend the health of us both make the tumor that she has in her neck not serious, you know that she is everything to me heal her Virgencita you know how much I need her and more now that I too have a tumor make the diagnosis of the doctors change make it not cancerous please, come with me to the operation and accompany me in it, holy mother, heal me please." In this tragic situation, with mother and daughter both facing cancer, the votary feels so devastated and powerless that she has nothing to contribute to a collaboration. She narrates through her fear and anxiety, on the edge of hopelessness, and delivers herself to the image's (and doctors') care. "It is an encounter of God's power with human weakness," as Father Juan Manuel explained such situations. "Faith is the connection. If there's no faith, there's not that encounter."

Even the most surrendering deferred control is goal-oriented action, at least symbolic action, because a petition is an exertion of agency, a way of doing something to manage an adverse situation. This decisive and, in votary perspective, efficacious action counterbalances the distress and sense of impotence that undermine motivation and can ultimately result in learned helplessness ("a chronic sense of inefficacy resulting from learning that one's actions have no effect on one's environment"). Learned helplessness is particularly probable in contexts of poverty and marginalization, in which personal inefficacy is compounded by a sense of collective powerlessness.[21]

Middle-class Americans appeal to hospitals, psychologists, lawyers, and insurance companies; poor Mexicans appeal to miraculous images (among other resources to which they might have access) as sacred cultural resources provided precisely for crisis intervention. The efficacy, the doing something, is the appeal itself, because the doctor, the insurance adjuster, and the miraculous image take charge to resolve the problem. We defer to them, hand over ourselves, our bodies, and our interests to their control, but through that deference we gain vicarious control in knowing that an empowered and competent agent is intervening on our behalf. All of this constitutes agency, enacted through deference. A sense of control is recuperated or maintained by degrees of deference to a powerful—an omnipotent—miraculous image.[22]

In deferred control the balance would appear to tip toward external agency—"I am in your hands, Lord"—because the votary's contribution is undervalued or minimized by attributing successful outcomes to the miraculous image. If the paintings and statues actually have nothing to offer, however, if they have no agency of their own, then the votary plays both roles of the collaboration and attributes one role to the image. People "underestimate the power of psychological processes—and overestimate the power of external stimuli—to generate experience." "Our ability to synthesize satisfaction—to reconstrue outcomes so that they give rise to positive experience—is nothing short of remarkable. But it also tends to be invisible, and the fact that we do not know our own strength leaves us susceptible to the mistaken belief that an insightful and benevolent external agent arranged the experience for us." In devotional perspective, the votary defers control to the powerful miraculous image; in this psychological perspective, however, votaries "generate experience"—gain or maintain perceived control indirectly—by attributing power to paintings and statues. Debilitated self-efficacy is rerouted through faith to an external locus of control, but ultimately that detour leads back to its source.[23]

Disclosure

"I don't tell my problems to anyone," Juana said at the Remedios basilica, "only to the Virgin." In that wording the exclusivity seems perhaps preferential—I choose to confide only to the Virgin—but many devotees lack other options. Miguel explained that people relate their problems and concerns to miraculous images because "we don't have enough trust to tell anyone else." Another man, who turned to alcohol rather than religion, said, "Sometimes I end up thinking that only drunk or asleep can I forget how fucked up everything is. Because sometimes I don't have anyone to tell about all the experiences I have, my worries, my traumas, my complexes. Because in my family I feel... no one understand me in my family." Others who lack trusted confidants converse with and seek guidance from the dead. "Every time I find myself in trouble and I don't know what to do, I talk to her," an older woman said in reference to her deceased mother. These contacts with dead relatives or miraculous images are comforting even when—or perhaps because—the interlocutor gives no explicit response.[24]

Marta explained that venting to miraculous images is more fulfilling than venting to relatives or friends. "It's a better release," she said, "you feel more satisfied talking to him," meaning the Señor de Chalma, because "it alleviates your troubles, the pain you have inside." Carlos commented along these same lines when I asked if he preferred confiding in family members or in the Virgen de Guadalupe, to whom he is devoted. "They're for different things," he replied. "Family members help you economically," for example, but the Virgin serves to "heal your soul" and foster "peace with myself."

Confiding, or sharing private thoughts, feelings, and experiences with a trusted person, affords emotional release, "a meaningful sense of reduced aloneness," and sometimes reassurance or guidance. Disclosure can also encompass validation through feedback and the presentation of a sympathetic self-image (how one would like to be perceived by the confidant) that might inspire a positive response. Catharsis—the venting of emotions—is also a primary benefit of devotional disclosure. "Unresolved emotional distress" that has no outlet for expression can result in mental and physical health problems, and perhaps for this reason sacramental confession is represented in medical tropes like "medicine for the soul" and "the healing of souls," with the priest as "a physician of souls." Informal confession of transgressions to miraculous images similarly affords a sense of forgiveness and alleviation, but votary disclosure is more comprehensive. "I write to You to unload my afflictions, the problems that disturb me so much," a man wrote to the Niño de Atocha, and then described a roster of problems including nineteen arrests for drunk driving and his daughter's diabetes and heart problems.[25]

Devotees may simply unload on a miraculous image, finding a measure of relief by expressing emotionally charged knowledge (problems, secrets, bad news), but more common is perception of images as fully interactive confidants. Miraculous images guide, comfort, and reassure; they validate devotees' worthiness and needs, especially through miracles; and they serve as sympathetic sounding boards for self-image construction. Most importantly, after hearing one's problems they act. A suffering votary seeks a concerned listener, but also an end to the suffering. When I asked Karina if faith helped her to cope with hardships, she responded, in reference to the Señor de las Tres Caídas, "Oh, yes. Because he resolves everything. If you have a problem, if you have a disease, if you feel sad, God is there and you can talk to him" with comfortable familiarity. Reynaldo made similar points, then added that family members and friends can only listen, but the miraculous image can solve the problem.[26]

Miraculous images are ideal confidants because they are quasi-human social persons with emotions that make them empathetic and responsive to pleading, but are also mute and, consequently, discreet and not explicitly judgmental. Their unflinching, vaguely aloof, undistractable attention also spares one the discomfort of face-to-face interpersonal disclosure of matters that are difficult to share. Sacred confidants are internal representations of an ideal and as such satisfy, ideally, the desire for recognition of one's worthy subjectivity and for validation of one's emotional turmoil. The image's mysterious silence is accommodating, emits a sense of "idealized strength and calmness," and guarantees the discretion and confidentiality that are critical to disclosure. If one relates sensitive information to a friend or relative, Reynaldo said, "they're going to tell it to someone else," but with a miraculous image, "the secret stays there." The muteness protects one's privacy from gossip. Karina was unambiguous: "They are images and don't talk."[27]

Privacy is also a concern when offering votive texts, because the intimate matters related to miraculous images are posted publicly and accessible to other readers. Some votaries do not reveal their identities ("my name is not important") and others tightly fold their textual petitions, staple or tape them closed, push them into crevices, or deposit them into inaccessible confines, such as the glass cases in which many images are housed. Other votaries exclude sensitive information—withhold it from the public—because the omniscient image is already informed: "I ask you to help me to not do those things that you already know and I can't say here," a male votary wrote to the Virgen de Tonatico. Another wrote simply, "you know my problem." These votaries resolves their incompatible needs—for textual expression and for privacy—by leaving the sensitive part of messages accessible only to omniscient inference.[28]

Miraculous images are also preferred confidants because self-disclosure among humans can have relation-damaging consequences. It is partially for this reason that people reveal secrets to "safe but anonymous" strangers—airline passengers, bartenders, hairdressers—rather than to friends or relatives who might prefer not to know. The disclosure of an addiction, a sexual attraction, a transgression, a fatal disease, a desperate need, or a family crisis might be traumatic for the confidant and might jeopardize a relationship. Many people do not reveal feelings or experiences to their spouses because they fear that the material is too private, sensitive, taboo, or burdensome to unload within a marriage. Self-disclosure is a risk. A need to disclose negotiates with the doubt of appropriateness and the fear of consequences. One's pursuit of understanding, empathy, validation, and acceptance can easily result in judgment, ridicule, rejection, and a breach of confidentiality.[29]

All of these negative consequences are avoided by confiding to a miraculous image. The image is always available, is a good listener, can take the load, judges only insofar as one judges oneself, is completely trustworthy, and considers disclosures empathetically. Votaries can disclose fully and openly: "I ask your forgiveness for being so selfish, lazy, lustful, banal, vain, and such a liar and thief," a young woman wrote to the Virgen del Pueblito. "I regret everything I have done."

Contrition in votive texts is doubly advantageous, once as expiation and again because it predisposes a fair hearing. The image's miraculous power is recruited to reinforce the votary's self-control so that the problem, God willing, can be overcome. A mea culpa lament is the preface to a pledge to change, and judgment seems misapplied when votaries present their transgressions with remorseful petitions for self-improvement. The confession *I'm a bad person* comes together with a commitment, *Please help me to improve.* "I know that I haven't been able to be a good father or the best example for my children," a man wrote to the Virgen de los Remedios, "but you as the mother that you are will understand what I am saying. I ask you to guide me to treat them well and give them the love they deserve." In the process judgment is deferred and the votary reaps the secondary benefits of transient guilt alleviation, and, perhaps, while awaiting the miracle, temporary license to continue the transgression (*I'll let myself go tonight, because I'm starting my diet tomorrow*). "Grant me chastity and continence" in Augustine's notorious formula, "but not yet."

Votary disclosure is selective, and even self-deprecating disclosure entails image management—making a good impression—and manipulation of the miraculous image in support of one's petition. Votaries represent themselves as worthy or repentantly unworthy but deserving of another chance. Self-disclosure is a means of self-validation, or anticipated self-validation, when a promised version of oneself constructed for an image and an audience works reflexively on the votary from an unrealized future—*this is who I could be*—to reinforce a sense of worthiness, which in turn heightens the probability of a miracle.[30]

Votaries work through alienation and unhappiness by humbly disclosing to a trusted confidant who strengthens self-efficacy with solidarity. Wounds, confusion, disorientation, and helplessness are prominent in these petitions—*I'm alone, I'm suffering, I don't understand.* "I feel like a sailor without his boat in the middle of the ocean, in the middle of so much water, without knowing how to swim," a votary wrote to the Señor de Villaseca. In a petition to the Virgen de Tonatico a woman wrote, "I'm tired of everyone abusing and making fun of me," and she asked for help "so that someday I can manage to be happy" and "I ask you to help me form a family since I don't want to be alone in this life that is so hard for those of us who don't know how to live." A similar petition was made to the same Virgin, but now the votary links the requested miracle directly to her worthiness and to recuperation of her self-esteem. "There are many moms who have children and don't know how to take care of them but I ask you for the opportunity, that you give me the gift of a baby, I promise to take care of it and love it and adore it above everything else. Sometimes people make fun of me because I can't get pregnant but I am going to show them that I can."

Proximity and Contact

As an alternative to collaborative and deferred control through petitions, or as a concurrent resource, devotees absorb sacred power through physical contact. In biblical precedents, Jesus cured a leper (Mark 1:41–42), a deaf man (Mark 7:33–35), a blind man (Mark 8:22–24), and Peter's mother-in-law (Mark 1:31) with his touch, and by the same means resuscitated a dead girl (Mark 5:41–42.) The woman who had hemorrhaged for twelve years "heard about Jesus and came up behind him in the crowd and touched his cloak," and as she was immediately cured Jesus felt the power leaving his body (Mark 5:25–30).[31]

The transmission of sacred power through physical contact is also evident in early Christianity and extends through the medieval and early-modern periods, particularly in the cult of relics. Relics on earth were imbued with the sacred power of a saint in heaven, and this power was transferrable to devotees. Eventually two types of relics evolved: body parts—usually bones—that were corporally integral to the saints themselves and therefore empowered inherently; and contact relics, which had absorbed power through contact with or proximity to a saint or his or her remains. The proliferation of contact relics was motivated by utility, because it made power portable, but also by compensatory need, because the bodies of Jesus Christ and the Virgin Mary ascended into heaven and left behind no corporal relics. In the fourth-century Holy Land pilgrims lined up to kiss Christ's cross, because the sacred power that saturated the wood during crucifixion was transferred by contact to devotees.[32]

The idea of contact is perhaps epitomized by the thirteenth-century St. Candida's shrine, which has three oval openings beneath a stone coffin holding the saint's remains. Pilgrims inserted their diseased, wounded, or crippled limps into these openings to make contact with the power that they trusted would heal them. Similar access is shown in an illustrated, thirteenth-century Anglo-Norman verse *Life of St. Edward the Confessor*, which includes St. Edward's tomb with apertures large enough for devotees seeking cures to actually crawl inside a space beneath the relics.[33]

A fourth-century statue commemorated the hemorrhaging woman who was healed by touching Christ's cloak, an image of Christ was situated beside it, and at Christ's feet a plant grew. "When this plant has blossomed, it usually extends to the fringe of the bronze robe that clothes the statue. Once this growing plant has touched the robe with its top shoot, it absorbs powers from the robe that can drive away all diseases and illnesses . . . But if the plant is cut down before it grows and touches the hem of the bronze fringe, it acquires no powers at all." This legend perfectly illustrates transmission and absorption of sacred power through physical contact, and further how imagery—not Christ himself, but the statue of Christ—transmits power associated with the sacred figure that it represents. In another narrative Gregory of Tours pursues this idea of absorption by stressing the necessity of faith and the materiality of transferred power. At the tomb of St. Peter one takes a piece of cloth, weighs it, and lower it to the relics. After a period of vigils, fasting, and prayer, the results are sought: "If the man's faith is strong, when the piece of cloth is raised from the tomb it will be so soaked with divine power that it will weigh much more than it weighed previously." Three principal points of Gregory's narratives—the presence of sacred power in matter (bones, images), absorption through contact, and the necessity of faith—are all critical to Mexican devotion today.[34]

In many cases direct contact with relics was not possible, so devotees sought objects that had been in touch with a saint, image, or relic and were imbued with its sacred charge. A shoot from the plant that touched the statue of Christ or the cloth that touched St. Peter's tomb are good examples. Such contact relics considerably broaden the range and scope of access to sacred power. One might not be able to make the pilgrimage to John the Evangelist's tomb, but it "produces manna with the appearance of flour" and "relics of this manna are sent throughout the entire world and perform cures for ill people." Contact relics also have the capacity to transfer power to other objects, thereby redoubling the proliferation through secondary contact relics. Sacred power disseminates in chains of contact. In reference to St. Thomas of Canterbury (Thomas Beckett), Jacobus de Voragine wrote that "the water in which cloths stained by his blood were washed brought healing to many." The blood is the relic, the cloth is a contact relic, and the water is a secondary contact relic.[35]

Another simple example of a contact relic is found in a testimony published in Madrid in 1763. An archbishop had problems with his gums and could not eat or sleep due to the pain. He had his eyeteeth removed as a possible solution but the problem persisted, and when the dentist was called again he found nothing wrong except a few teeth that were loose. "Seeing, then, that I had no human recourse," the archbishop wrote, "I appealed to Heaven; and I do not know by what impulse the Venerable Juan de Palafox came to memory." Palafox was the bishop of Puebla from 1640 to 1648, and at the time of the events a candidate for beatification. The archbishop was given a letter signed in Palafox's hand, applied it to his cheek, and, he wrote, "suddenly the pain stopped, the swelling of my gums was reduced, they recuperated their color, my teeth were strengthened, and my mouth was completely free of any sign of the scurvy humor." Palafox had touched the paper, the paper touched the archbishop's cheek, and the miraculous power radiated inward to cure the problem with the gums.[36]

Such effects occur by the law of contagion, which holds that "a material medium of some sort"—the plant, cloth, and letter—"is assumed to unite distant objects and to convey impressions from one to the other." People and objects that come into contact "may influence each other through the transfer of some or all of their properties. The influence continues after the physical contact has ended and may be permanent." In the case of miraculous images there is also a lingering emotive quality that prolongs association of an image with its once human, now heavenly prototype and power source (Christ, the Virgin). In the general law of contagion the transfer of sacred power is often permanent, but in Mexico the potency of contact relics, including images, tends to diminish over time or with use and consequently requires a recharge by renewed contact. The same diminishing returns obtain in chains of contact as relics are distanced from the power source.[37]

The transmission of sacred power through contact is prominent in Mexico, even to the degree that touching, kissing, and otherwise putting oneself in physical contact with miraculous power are predominant features of devotion. In reference to the Señor de Chalma, Marta explained that devotees "are not satisfied to just see him. They want to get close, to get closer, to touch him," because "by touching the image the vibes pass to them." Devotees absorb sacred power as a general cleansing infusion conducive to well-being, or as a remedy for a specific disease, ailment, or injury. Contact with a miraculous image also strengthens the force of a petition, and objects or documents related to an occupation are sometimes touched to images to give a sacred boost to a particular enterprise.[38]

In petitions and offerings the tactility of power transfer is often represented figuratively. A votive text thanking Niño del Arenal says, "you cured me with your holy hand"; a petition to the Virgen del Pueblito includes "protect me with your mantle and your protective hand. Heal me"; and another petition to the same Virgen asks "with tears in my eyes that you who are very miraculous take away the spots that appeared on my son's hands wipe them away with your mantle my mother as you did for me with the miracle for my other son's eyes."

Retablos represent power transfer visually with rays of grace that emanate from miraculous images. The rays make contact with votaries in need or with human agents implementing sacred designs. When Christ is the source, the rays generally emanate from his wounds. A 1966 retablo illustrates a votary protected from an accidental gunshot by rays of grace from the Señor de Chalma's side wound. In a retablo offered to Soriano's Virgen de los Dolores, the text explains that Silverio was saved twice from imminent execution, once in 1937 and again in 1938. The painting illustrates both of these close calls bathed in rays emanating from the Virgin hovering above. On occasion the radiance is interpreted literally and put to practical use by a retablo painter. In one retablo a Virgin's rays guarantee a successful operation by uniting with the cone of light from a surgical lamp. After an airplane crash into the ocean, the Virgen de Talpa and the Virgen de Guadalupe cast rays that seem searchlight beams illuminating a life raft. A 1649 narrative pushed practical application to the extreme when rays of grace compensated for a slack sacristan's unfulfilled duties. The time for mass was approaching and the candles were not lit, when suddenly the priest "saw coming out of the radiance of Our Lady of heaven something like two flames or lightning bolts, which came to light the candles on both sides of the altar."[39]

The transfer of sacred power is also visually explicit in ritual cleansings (*limpias*), particularly in the form known as *rameadas*. In rameadas devotees transfer power with a sweeping or brushing motion done with a bundle of herbs, leaves, or flowers, first on a miraculous image (or the glass that encases it) and then on themselves or a friend or family member. The power transfers from the image to the devotee, but in other limpias the transfer is reversed as negative attributes, illness for example, transfer to the object used for the cleansing. The use of an egg is common ("but from a chicken on a farm, not the eggs that they sell in the shopping center," Manuela advised) and as it is rubbed on the body it absorbs impurities.

Silverio's close calls are bathed in rays of grace by Soriano's Virgen de los Dolores.

In some regions, the cleansing is done with a votive candle that is then offered in the church.[40]

Direct Contact and Proximity

Placing one's hands and lips directly on the body, clothing, or canvas of a miraculous image is the ideal, but most images are protected behind glass or situated high above altars and out of range of devotees' touch. Devotees consequently default to proximity (stairways are often provided behind altars for this purpose), to touching replicas of the image (such as those used in processions outside of the church), to touching reproductions, and to touching the glass around images. Power radiates through the glass to the hands and lips of devotees making contact. Many touch the glass and then rub their hair, their bodies, or their children, or they touch and then make the sign of the cross. Kissing and touching the glass are also affectionate forms of greeting. Some devotees put their tears on the glass coffins of dead Christs.

The quest for proximity is motivated by the idea that an image's power radiates, with diminishing concentration as one is distanced from the epicenter. (This effect is similar to the derivative glory of seating arrangements at, for example, a White House state dinner.) Devotees get as close as they can to the image, to the altar, or, if the church is closed, to the door. There are benefits even for those who live in the vicinity. When a daughter of the Virgen de Juquila—actually a modern reproduction of the image— appeared miraculously in San Felipe Tejalapam near Oaxaca city in 1995, "some migrant families decided to return to the village in order to be 'close to the miracle.'" A similar migration occurred when the Virgen de Tonatico left her altar in the church for a preferred site elsewhere and the villagers moved to remain beside her. Pilgrims are drawn almost magnetically to a shrine that is saturated, to greater and lesser intensities, with the power that emanates from the miraculous image. They are infused with grace just by being there.[41]

Francisco de Florencia tells the story of a boy who fell off a cart and was gravely injured when the cartwheel rolled over his head. The boy had no pulse and the father was unsure whether to keep the body at home or to bring it to the Virgen de Zapopan to petition a miracle. A priest advised keeping the boy at home, because the Virgin could perform the miracle from the church without the body being present, if she chose to save the boy. The father, who placed greater value on proximity and presence,

Getting as close as possible in Chalma, even when the church is closed.

thought otherwise: "If I don't bring him there to the Virgin, she won't per-form the miracle." The body was placed on the altar, the parents petitioned the miracle in prayer, and the Virgin resuscitated the boy.[42]

In ancient Greece and then in early Christianity, pilgrims absorbed sacred power by sleeping inside sanctuaries. This rite of incubation in devo-tion to the god Asklepios entailed an overnight stay during which pilgrims were visited in their dreams by the gods and often awakened cured of their ailments. In medieval Europe something of the same practice continued, now beside tombs with relics, because "it was believed that their therapeutic power acted most effectively during sleep." Sleep and dreams are less prev-alent in current devotions, but the importance of presence, of extended con-tact with the shrine, is still a principal motivator of pilgrimage. Pilgrims arrive, say their prayers, make their petitions, and present their offerings, but afterward there is great satisfaction in simply being a guest at the home of a miraculous image, and some shrines, such as Chalma and Juquila, pro-vide free dormitories so that the pilgrims can spend the night.[43]

Mediated Contact

Among early Christians, the word "blessings" (*eulogia* in Greek) originally had no material referent but "gradually came to be applied to blessed objects, such as bread." In addition, the same Greek word referred "to the blessing received by contact with a holy person, holy place, or holy object," thereby affording an ambiguity that kept the power circulating to where it was most needed, and between spiritual and material entities. In addition to direct contact of hands and lips while at the sanctuaries, Byzantine pilgrims took away souvenirs, such as tokens made from earth around a shrine and impressed with intaglio stamps and flasks that contained tomb dust, pollen shaken from tomb flowers, sacred ashes, oil, and water. "These ampullae extended the reach of the divine presence and ensured a continuous connection." In pilgrimages of the early middle ages, similarly, devotees sought physical contact but also a lasting, portable contact with sacred power, which included locus sanctus objects like "dirt, water, or oil that had come into contact with the holy site." "These objects were thought to possess a certain prophylactic or medicinal value, and the combination of image and relic would help to re-create at a distance the sanctity or spiritual validity of the original site."[44]

In Mexico today, a primary purpose of pilgrimage is to acquire objects (many pilgrims call them "relics") that transport miraculous power and make it available at a distance from the shrine. Major shrines are surrounded with huge markets catering to this demand. Pilgrims generally make purchases for their homes, for friends or family members unable to make the pilgrimage, for their villages or communities, and for maintenance of devotion after internal or international migration. The items include images and religious articles of all kinds, from wallet-sized prayer cards carried for protection and luck to ornately framed portraits of the Virgin and huge, mass-produced sculptures of the crucified Christ. Pilgrims also acquire substances that are power infused through prolonged contact with a shrine, such as sacred dirt (known as *tierra santa*), water, flowers, and, in previous centuries, lamp oil. At some churches contact relics, such as wads of cotton dipped in the wound of a Christ statue, are distributed on special occasions. At the Virgen de Talpa shrine in the nineteenth century, pilgrims took home "relics of the Virgin" that included altar flowers, the stubs of candles that had burned on the altar, and sacred dirt.

Devotees distinguish between holy water and sacred water. Holy water is blessed by priests and used primarily for the subsequent blessing of people, religious objects, cars, and livestock; and sacred water is from springs, wells, and rivers that are endowed with spiritual and curative properties, sometimes by association with an apparition. Niño del Cacahuatito was discovered while digging a well, and consequently that well's water is sacred. In Astata on the Oaxaca coast, the Señor de la Piedad appeared in a spring more than a hundred years ago and offerings are still made at the site. The Virgen of Octolán's origin is also related to sacred waters. In 1541 an indigenous Tlaxcalan named Juan Diego, a convert to Catholicism and *topil* (altar server) at the Franciscan monastery, was on his way to a river to draw water that had curative properties. There was an epidemic in the region and his family members were sick. En route Juan Diego encountered a mysterious woman who instructed him to follow her to a spring that would save the Indians from the epidemic. The site is part of the Virgen de Octolán complex today, about a quarter mile below the basilica and connected by a walkway, and its chapel has a font and murals that illustrate the apparition. Women outside sell containers so devotees can carry the water home.[45]

Dirt is also empowered by contact, proximity, and association, and the power is often accessed through ingestion. Devotees drink the sacred dirt from Otatitlán in an infusion, or apply it to a wounded or ailing body part. The dirt is also used for other purposes: "You put a little of this dirt next to cross in center of field when you plant to assure a good harvest." The tierra santa at Chalma is a soft stone, whitish gray and chalky, like compressed talc but with a grit. I once saw a mother buy a piece and hand it to her son, who walked along eating it like a piece of candy. In colonial Mexico, relic-seeking pilgrims broke chunks of adobe off the altar and walls at San Juan de los Lagos. (A uniformed guard is now stationed in the Virgen de Ocotlán basilica, in part because visitors are breaking off pieces of ornate gold-leaf woodwork). To prevent the vandalism in San Juan de Los Lagos the shrine began to fabricate "loaves of earth and to seal them with the Image of the Most Holy Virgin, and touched to her." Pilgrims took these relics home, "and the miracles done by them are countless." One man made his votive promise "before an Image of Our Lady, stamped in a loaf of earth" and to regain his health "began to eat the earth of Our Lady, even against the advice of the Doctor, who tried to persuade him not to eat it, because it could do him harm." In another colonial narrative a poisoned dog is cured by ingesting earth from San Juan de los Lagos, and the following day, on its own, "the dog went to the church and stayed there all day, not wanting to leave even to look for necessary sustenance."[46]

The sacred power of images purchased at shrines is activated by blessing, usually with holy water, and the images acquire a supplemental charge through absorption as they move through a shrine and especially when they are placed on the altar during mass. Contact with the original image would also transfer power but in most shrines access is prohibited. Devotees say that blessed images perform miracles at home, or that the miraculous image performs the miracle through these home reproductions, but votive offerings do not register the distinction between the one image and the other. Credit for the miracle is given simply to a named miraculous image, without disambiguating the original from the reproduction. The distinction is clearer in colonial miracle narratives. A blind man gained sight when he touched an image of the Virgen de Zapopan to his eyes; and another man was cured "when they put the Holy Image on his head, they had hardly put it there when the sick man felt instantly healthy." Often the reproduction is combined with an empowered substance: a sick woman was cured when an attendant "applied a painting of the Most Holy Lady of Ocotlán, rubbing her chest with oil from her Lamp." Image reproductions are also capable of other feats, such as bringing rain during a drought.[47]

The first miracle of the Virgen de San Juan de los Lagos occurred when the image—the original—was passed over and resuscitated the body of a dead girl. That motif is repeated in a later miracle, when a reproduction of the same Virgin resuscitated a drowned boy. Isidro, who was four or five years old, fell into a river and was pulled out and laid on the bank, "drowned in everyone's opinion." A slave brought a small statue "that was in the house, a copy of the image of San Juan, and they started to call her; and this witness and the Mother of the drowned boy promised to visit the Image of San Juan and have a Mass said." They placed the image on top of the boy, "and saw that a vein in his neck started to move, after which he gave signs of life." The boy was wrapped and taken home, and the witness and the mother "persevered in petitioning the mercy of the Virgen de San Juan that whole afternoon (the misfortune had occurred around mid-day) and when night was near he began to sweat, and shortly after to speak, and within a few days he was well, and got up."[48]

Despite the proliferation of empowered reproductions, the original miraculous image maintains its unique, numinous intrigue. One may have seen a thousand reproductions in churches and homes, but being in the presence of the genuine article inspires awe. Some devotees burst into tears upon approaching the miraculous images to which they are devoted. The reverence is generated by being in the presence of something sacred, but something sacred in which devotees participate as miracle recipients and as investors of emotion and faith. The intensity of the experience is relative to the emotions and ideas that devotees invest; a nonbeliever does not have the same response.[49]

The relation between devotee investment and image numinousness might be clarified by analogy if one considers, for example, the baseball from a homerun that won a World Series. The ball may have been donated to a thrift store by someone unaware of its history and remained there dusty and discarded for decades, but once rediscovered and displayed in a museum its numinousness is revived. Fans travel to look at it through glass not because it looks different than other baseballs, but rather because being in its presence releases a deep feeling bound to memories, aspirations, musings, and participation as a witness in grandeur. Like a miraculous image, the ball in context relays back to visitors the emotions and cognitions projected onto it. The ball could be replaced by a replica and nevertheless would inspire awe, insofar as the viewers remained unaware of the change.[50]

Juramentos

A *juramento*, or vow, is technically "a deliberate and free promise made to God about a possible and better good," although most *jurados* (people who make vows) feel bound in obligation more to a specific miraculous image than to God as an abstract deity. Traditional vows are made to overcome habits and addictions, such as alcohol and drug abuse or smoking, but vows also encompass abstinence from a range of other behaviors. These include crime, gambling, fighting, prostitution, spousal abuse, infidelity, suicide attempts, and casual sex. Many vows have dual purpose; abstinence from alcohol and drugs is a common combination. Some vows are more preventative than corrective, particularly when they are renewed one after the other to avert relapse into an addiction. Carlos vowed abstinence to alcohol before migrating to the United States, so that he would not squander his earnings in bars. Vows are also made for affirmative self-improvements: to take better care of one's health or to be a better son, daughter, or student, for example.[51]

A juramento is a form of petitionary devotion, but its votive contract is unique. The petition, which remains more or less implicit, requests fortitude to realize the vowed improvement; and the offering entails fulfillment of the vow itself—a sacrifice—followed by a shrine visit for closure. The vow is made formally during a priest-officiated ritual and requires a document signed by the jurado. The votive contract is consequently far more formal and binding than the improvised arrangements in everyday devotion.

Jurados begin the process by acquiring a vow card, known as an *estampita*; in most cases these are sold for a modest fee in the church store. At some sites, like Otatitlán, jurados get the card directly from a priest. One side of the card shows the miraculous image to whom the vow is made (the Guadalupe *estampita* shows San Juan Diego, with the Virgin on his tilma), and the other side has a boilerplate text with blank spaces for one's name, the behavior one wishes to change, and the duration of the vow. There is also space for a signature and date, and for the signature of the officiating priest. In Chalma, purchase of the estampita includes an illustrated booklet that offers guidance, encouragement, and, especially, information on the personal and familial consequence of alcoholism. A cartoon-like illustration on the first page conveys the common belief that jurados are supernaturally strengthened by making vows. An indecisive man—"I'm afraid"—decides finally to make a vow because "God will help me."[52]

The votive text on estampitas is relatively consistent in content from shrine to shrine but varies significantly in tone. The estampita distributed at the Virgen de los Dolores basilica in Soriano reads, "Aware by my own experience of my offense to God and the harm I cause to myself, today I want to make a vowed promise to:"—and here the jurado writes the purpose and duration of the vow. "I am confident that through the mercy of God, the prayers of my family, and my personal responsibility I will be able to faithfully fulfill this juramento that now with all awareness and with all my will I make before God and the Virgen de los Dolores de Soriano." In Chalma, by contrast, the tone is more severe. The prayer begins, "Lord, I repent having behaved badly. I want to change my life, no longer doing evil and learning to do good, but I am pure frailty and weakness."

Some jurados make the vow on their own, outside of the formal process, and sometimes use the standard wording from estampitas. A votive text at the Virgen del Pueblito shrine is headed, "Juramento not to steal" and reads, "I, [name], making use of my free will and with the firm desire to change my life promise before the Crucified Christ not to steal again ever during my whole life assisted by the grace and power of God the mediation of Our Lord Jesus Christ the intercession of Our Most Holy Mother of Pueblito and of Our Father San Francisco de Asís I confirm that I will firmly fulfill this promise under juramento not to steal again." In many cases wives petition abstinence on a husband's behalf and then give thanks, as one wife worded it, "for the great miracle you did for me of distancing my husband from alcoholism, for giving him another chance to get ahead." At the Virgen de Juquila pedimento, a bottle-shaped milagrito is sold for petitioning help with alcoholism.

Jurados complete the blank estampita together with a priest or lay assistant. The chosen periods of abstinence vary widely—from a week to several years—but periods between six months and a year are common. Shorter periods generally suggest external motivation to make the vow. Serious jurados are self-motivated; others make weak-willed commitments—a month, three months—due to pressure usually from wives, mothers, and employers. The purpose of these vows is not to control an addiction, but rather to control an intervention. They silence, at least temporarily, expressions of contempt and disapproval. Generally these jurados lapse back into their habit as soon as the vowed period concludes. When Mrs. Sánchez can no longer tolerate her husband's drinking, she threatens to leave him unless he makes a vow. The husband does so at Chalma, choses a short time period, and begins to drink as soon as the vow expires. Mrs. Sánchez again tolerates the drinking until eventually she threatens to leave, and the husband again makes a short-term vow. This cycle has been repeating for fifteen years.[53]

In view of such situations, priests stress that jurados must be self-motivated. "My juramento is only valid if I make the vow voluntarily," as it is worded in the Chama booklet. Long-term success is far more probable when abstinence is freely chosen, valued, and internalized as a personal goal by jurados (identification) than when it its accepted, sometimes reluctantly, in appeasement to avoid loss of love and esteem (introjection). "Behaviors that are regulated by introjection feel less volitional and create greater conflict. Introjected goals are only partially assimilated, and the behaviors they motivate do not feel self-determined." When they are made in response to medical diagnoses, exceptional events (the birth of a baby, an addiction-related death), and financial problems, vows have compound motivation, because external factors motivate internal commitment.[54]

During the juramento ritual vows are made orally, and sometimes collectively, and are followed by a blessing. In the juramento chapel at the Virgen de Guadalupe basilica vows are made in large groups, and at other shrines on slow days a priest might officiate with each jurado individually. Jurados then return to their lives and do the best they can. If they complete the term of abstinence successfully, many return the estampita to the shrine as an offering. Theoretically a priest receives the estampita and gives a blessing, but in practice most jurados simply drop the estampita in a receptacle provided for that purpose or post it on a wall of offerings. Jurados who live far from the shrine might offer the estampita in their local church instead. One man gave it to his mother-in-law as evidence that he had fulfilled his vow. Others keep the card for its symbolic value, as a material token of an accomplishment, almost like an Alcoholics Anonymous sobriety chip.[55]

I met Martín, his mother, and a couple of brothers at the votive wall in Chalma. Martín was offering an estampita, together with a braid he had grown and cut, upon completion of his vow to stop drinking. Generally the estampita itself constitutes the offering, but some grateful votaries supplement the card with other offerings, including pilgrimages. In Martín's experience the votive process began with the vow, continued through the months of fulfilling it (not drinking) and growing the hair, and ended with a shrine visit with family members to offer the braid and the estampita.

Success is relative even among self-motivated jurados, because many—perhaps most—relapse into their habit upon completion of the abstinence period. "I've done it several times," jurados often said in reference to their vows. Others break their vows despite their best efforts. The protocol in these cases is to confess the breach to a priest. The vow is not pardoned—the contract with God and the miraculous image remains in force—so priests advise that jurados renew or resume the vow period. At the Remedios basilica the time invested is lost: if one vowed a year and made it to six months, the full year must be completed from the beginning. At Chalma, conversely, and surprisingly, the time invested is not lost, but jurados are advised that they have broken the second commandment and must confess this sin together with any others.

Fray David, who wrote Chalma's juramento booklet, explained that jurados "appeal to the grace of God's help to reinforce their own will." When they break their vows they return to the shrine feeling guilty, "as though they had committed the worst of sins. But I tell them you didn't break (*no rompiste*) the juramento, you interrupted it (*interrumpiste*)." As far as Fray David is concerned, the jurados should resume where they left off, but often the jurados themselves want to start again from the beginning for fear of punishment. "I tell them, 'No, God is pure love. God knew that you were not going to fulfill the vow,'" but they are not easily dissuaded.

Roberto made a vow to stop drinking, broke it, and had a car accident, which he and his family interpreted as punishment. He subsequently renewed the vow, broke it again, had another accident, and again made a causal attribution. If you break a vow, you crash; drunk driving is not a contributing factor. Recently Roberto made the vow for a third time, has not broken it, or not yet, and he and the car remain intact. Other jurados avoid breaking vows and suffering the consequences by asking priests in advance for permission to drink, usually on holidays or other special occasions. Such reprieves are not granted. "It's like being in prison and saying, 'Can I get a weekend pass for my son's birthday,'" Carlos said. Another strategy is to resist temptation by carefully timing vow periods. A jurado at the Remedios basilica was asked the duration of his vow and replied, "A year, but can I begin tomorrow?" Vows at the Virgen de Guadalupe basilica drop significantly in anticipation of the so-called Guadalupe-Reyes marathon, which is an extended, well-libated holiday period from December 12 (fiesta of the Virgen de Guadalupe) to January 6 (Epiphany or Three Kings' Day).[56]

When I asked jurados why they quit drinking through vows rather than on their own, many first responded that the vow gave them the strength to persevere. José works in construction, gets paid on Fridays, wastes his money drinking on Saturdays, and needs help to break the cycle. "You can't do it alone," he said before making his vow, and others used similar wording, like "I can't do it with my own willpower." Monseñor Francisco at the Remedios basilica explained that "they make the juramento here, where the image is, but in their lives they know that the Virgin will be helping them." This sense of accompaniment and collaborative control is also captured in the prayer on the Remedios estampita: "I hope to faithfully fulfill this promise with the power of God, the intercession of the Most Holy Virgen de Remedios, and with my willpower." Similar reinforcement is apparent in an informal juramento made to the Virgen del Pueblito: "I ask you please to help me forget Luis because I love him a lot but know that I should not get back together with him and I made you the juramento not to get back together with him and I don't want to fail you that's why I'm asking that you please help me to fulfill this juramento." Secular goals—to stop drinking, to leave Luis—are infused with religious values once a juramento is made, and these "sanctified goals appear to generate more commitment, self-efficacy, and persistence than do nonsanctified goals."[57]

Other jurados appreciate the gains in fortitude but, like Roberto, keep their vows primarily for fear that a breach would result in punishment. The vow is viewed as an absolute, nonnegotiable obligation that simply eliminates the possibility of drinking. The jurado perseveres not so much through resolute self-control as through submission to the inevitable. An analogous secular situation might be a wine lover who is diagnosed with a disease and prescribed medication that is highly incompatible with alcohol. Drinking wine suddenly becomes out of the question. Abstinence is externally enforced to avoid harmful alcohol/drug interactions or, for the jurado, to avoid supernatural punishment. Arturo said he could not stop drinking on his own but after making the vow was "obligated, I can't drink," because otherwise "bad things happen to you." Javier also spoke for many when he said that jurados keep their vows "above all because of fear." He then suggested how shared beliefs contribute to self-control through fear: "When something bad happens to you, people will say 'That happened to you for breaking your vow.' " Antonio expressed a more complex and nuanced understanding when he said that "the faith you have in the Virgin gives you the strength to stop doing something," but also that after a broken vow "your soul won't rest" and "you're going to think" that all hardships are a consequence of the breach. "You won't be at peace until you fulfill the vow." Antonio's brother manages a former drug problem by making one vow immediately after another, and he perseveres in sobriety through "respect and fear for what he is doing."

Fear also controls peers who might enable or coerce a jurado to drink. When friends offer him a drink, José said, he will be able to say "I don't want it" ("I do want it, but I'll say I don't want it") because he has made a vow, and that should end the matter. In these situations the estampita serves as a credential, a form of proof. "Friends pressure you, you show them your estampita, and they stop pressuring," Marta said. If someone continues to pressure the jurado, another peer often intervenes for fear that the punishment will befall the group as a whole. "Leave him alone, he's a jurado, don't make him break his juramento, because something bad can happen to us." Adriana explained that punishment for a broken vow can also extend to a jurado's family.[58]

Guilt also makes a contribution. A broken vow disrespects the miraculous image to whom one's care is commended, disappoints loved ones, fosters shame (*my mother doesn't deserve a son like this*), and forces confrontation with one's weak inability to self-improve. All of this anticipated negative fallout, already experienced in most cases after previously broken vows, works backward from an imagined future to moderate behavior, particularly during struggles with craving or temptation. One envisions oneself as reflected in the condemnation of others. "Anticipatory capacities enable humans to be motivated by prospective consequences" and "by representing foreseeable outcomes symbolically, people can convert future consequences into current motivators of behavior." Consequently, "people sometimes base their choices and actions on the emotional outcomes they anticipate," be these negative—guilt, regret—or the anticipated positive-emotion rewards of competence and accomplishment: well-being, pride, satisfaction, recognition and esteem, faith affirmation, and sanctified success upon return to the shrine after fulfillment of the vow.[59]

Once a juramento has been made, a miraculous image assumes a role analogous to the presiding member of a support group. The vow establishes a bond of solidarity forged by commitment, and that bond reinforces resolve and fortitude as would a promise to a loved one or the oversight of a therapist. But a miraculous image also provides seemingly external and omniscient surveillance, something like a spiritual panopticon that from its empty tower monitors behavior and threatens punishment for transgressions. The illusion of surveillance, when it is successful, assists the jurado in eventually automating the desired behavior (not drinking) and consequently reducing the need for constant vigilance and self-monitoring.[60]

Vows are made publicly within a sacred and supportive community that motivates jurados in ways that private commitments cannot. "People prefer achievements that are validated, recognized, and valued by other people over solitary achievements, so there may be a substantial interpersonal component behind the need for achievement." Public vows also require public confession of failure. One's reputation is at stake, even if only among family and friends, as is one's trustworthiness within close relationships. The social aspects of self-control include the moral obligation to subordinate one's indulgences to one's commitments, which might include, for example, paying the rent or feeding one's children instead of squandering income in bars.[61]

Many critics question the effectiveness of sobriety juramentos given the current perception of alcoholism as a progressive disease. Even Fray David, who wrote the Chalma juramento booklet, described alcoholism as a disease and said that "the alcoholic has no remedy, cannot be cured." In response to a news article regarding juramentos at the Virgen de Guadalupe basilica, one critic described juramentos as "the industry of forgiveness." (In addition to purchase of the estampita, there is a more or less obligatory voluntary donation made following the juramento ceremony.) The critic argued that if the church's "mission were something other than making money, they would tell them plainly that they are sick, incurably, and the only thing they can do is bottom out." Otherwise, even if they manage to fulfill their vow, they will start drinking immediately after. Most jurados perceive their vows not as permanent commitments to abstinence—that is explicit in the time-period designation—but rather as a control mechanism, a time out, a stop gap to prevent progression into incapacitating, life-destroying alcoholism. Often vows are made at the edge of the abyss; jurados look down and pull back. They struggle alone, fail, and then seek help, as suggested by the high-volume of Monday-morning vows made by hungover jurados who recognize that they cannot abstain alone. They also recognize, however, that the abstinence is a temporary measure to regain control, so that moderated drinking can then resume.[62]

Alcoholics Anonymous (AA) is an alternative to and sometimes complement of drinking-related juramentos. AA shares with juramentos an explicit use of religious language and appeal to God or another higher power. The third step in the twelve-step program advocates surrender, "a decision to turn our will and our lives over to the care of God, *as we understood Him*." The higher power may be anything an alcoholic wishes to designate, even the AA group itself, but nevertheless alcoholism is regarded as a spiritual disorder requiring a "spiritual awakening" (step 12) and the mentioned surrender. A critical moment in the quest for sobriety occurs when the AA member realizes "that God is doing for us what we could not do for ourselves."[63]

Apparent in these ideas is a principal difference between vows to miraculous images, which are successful through collaborative control, and the AA program, which is successful through deferred control. (I refer to supernatural control. AA has a strongly collaborative therapeutic community, including sponsors, that makes use of "social support, new relationships, and identity transformation strategies.") The deference is clear in the AA dictum "thy will be done, not mine," and is echoed in countless other statements of relinquished subjective control to God: "we put ourselves in God's hands"; "god had done for him what he could not do for himself"; "all the credit belongs to God. On my own I could not have quit. I know, I tried it." "The thing I do is to say, 'God, here I am and here are all my troubles. I've made a mess of things and can't do anything about it. You take me, and all my troubles, and do anything you want with me.'" Because alcoholism is an incurable disease that has taken control of one's life, "admission of powerlessness is the first step in liberation."[64]

Such surrender contrasts sharply with the collaborative approach to abstinence through juramentos. The jurado has complete responsibility for sobriety, and failure likewise is the jurado's shame. Jurados do not defer to God or miraculous images, but quite to the contrary draw from reserves of sacred power to reinforce their willpower and renew their weakened self-control. Juramentos are paradigms of intermingling internal and external resources, of sacred power engaging with human agency.

If the power is drawn from faith in miraculous images rather than from the images themselves, however, then the locus is internal and only perceived as external and the power is ultimately proper to jurados themselves. In this view faith is a mechanism of cognitive restructuring that strengthens self-control with an illusion of external surveillance and support. Abstinence is facilitated even when a miraculous image has nothing to offer, because jurados believe in the efficacy and validity of vows and participate in a devotional culture that shares this belief.[65]

Remedios

Father's Day at the Virgen de los Remedios basilica in Naucalpan, just out-side Mexico City. The weekday calm is disrupted by an influx of devotees, religious tourists, families out for the day. Security guards are stationed at the doors, the gift shop is busy, a lifesize bronze Christ is wheeled out to the atrium, and the perimeter is active with restaurants and vendors and bars. Voladores, perched on a pole top, unwind downward suspended by their feet, arms stretched for flight, backdropped by the sky, and no one really seems to notice. Their imminent descent is announced by flutes.

On weekdays the tranquility is almost palpable, as though the chaotic city that surrounds the basilica had pushed its stillness into the complex, concentrated it there to a kind of density. The basilica is on a hilltop, insu-lated by an ecological reserve from the koyaanisqatsi visible when the smog thins. "It's like an island," Antonio said. "On an island I feel different." People come to absorb some silence, to participate in it, to activate it with prayer. The noises are predictable: song from the church, the gentle rasp of brooms on stone, footsteps that carry voices down a corridor. In the courtyard whitish wallstones are chinked with black rocks, potted gerani-ums flank the walkway to a rough sculpture of the Virgin, and the interior walls are covered with retablos. At noon one of the guards, almost a sil-houette, steps against that backdrop in uniform. His wife would not be-lieve the magnificence of his movement. He pulls a long yellow rope, leaning backward, using his weight to initiate momentum, and the church bells begin to ring. His body then rocks to the rhythm of the bells, of his pulls, and you can't see the biceps under the uniform but can image them contracting and expanding.

From the kitchen at one end of the courtyard you hear the voices and laughter of happy women cooking. The women aren't sure what to make of me but then I greet them and they adopt me with their smiles. A secu-rity guard carries in a giant bag of bread and a moment later another man follows behind, side-bent and shaky under a load more awkward than

heavy. Occasionally a wooden spoon bangs against a pot to shake off something stubborn, and at intervals a blender interrupts and overwhelms the
stillness with a violent grind that makes the silence seems deeper, more
intentional, when finally the blender is turned off. The ambient sound
shifts momentarily to the moving water of a fountain until the voices from
the kitchen resume. Cooking smells somehow get mixed up with the
voices, maybe because they waft together from the kitchen, and for a moment you sort through synesthetic confusion. Long banquet tables, check-
ered in red and white, are set across from Christ's mystical body built face
by face with the fading mugshots of devotees. Whoever is hungry and has
twenty pesos can sit for a meal with other visitors.

Elsewhere in the complex there are confession booths across the corridor from a room with a baptismal font. Behind the font, in modern
stained glass, John the Baptist pours water on the head of an effeminate,
heavyset Jesus, and a door leads to a closet with holy oil. The floor is paved
in terra cotta and the walls are tiled in ceramic, with blue and white alter-
nating in a diamond pattern. The furnishings are spare: a few wooden,

Juramentos are made on the kneeler beneath this crucifix. On the right is the glass
box where successful jurados deposit their vow cards; holy oil is stored behind the
door to the left.

penitential chairs painted brown, an old desk in a corner, a metal coin box standing against a wall, and a glass case for depositing juramento cards. One wall has a kneeler beneath a crucified Christ.

Juramentos are done in this room, together with the blessing of people and objects (images, rosaries, scapulars, estampitas) with holy water from the font. Devotees arrive in steady streams to have the priest sprinkle water over them with the drumbeat shakes of an aspergillum. The priest offering these blessings and attending to juramentos also works across the hall to take confessions. When he is on one side of the hall a few people, and sometimes a crowd, gather on the other side. There is a sense of mounting anticipation together with the restlessness of happy kids, puzzled kids, lots of kids fidgeting around the knees of men, mostly, who await the priest to make their vows. On Sundays a lay assistant sits at the desk and retired priests help out by taking shifts. The assistant has bad teeth, talks too much, and looks like an owl. His attitude is remarkably unchristian, as though he had chosen this life of service to Christ so he could exercise an arrogant condescension.

During a lull, while the priest was taking confessions, a jurado came in and sheepishly asked the assistant for permission to drink on his son's birthday. The assistant denied the request, as is customary, but did so with an endless harangue that included insights like God, not the man's son, "is the most important person in this life," and a juramento, because it's not a CD player, "doesn't have a pause button." Later a woman arrived with a similar request, one beer for Father's Day, and was also denied unkindly. During their chastisements both jurados stood before the desk—the assistant was sitting—and tried to maintain the pained smiles on their faces. The woman had a tic or twitch that threatened her overdone mascara.

Jurados are mostly young men; occasionally there are middle-aged and older men and sometimes there are women, mostly younger. Many men come with wives, girlfriends, or—particularly when fathers are making vows—whole families. When I first approached the juramento room a young man was kneeling to make his vow (to stop drinking) while his wife cried just outside the door. Often two friends or groups of friends make their vows together. There is no shame in making a vow; everyone seems familiar with the procedure, and, like most acts involving institutions, vows are made before others awaiting their turn.

The demographics are variable, but on Sundays poor votaries are less present. The basilica is close to wealthy suburbs of Mexico City, and the residents of these neighborhoods—so different in dress and demeanor from most shrine devotees—stand out conspicuously. On one occasion, while the priest was across the hall taking confessions, a crowd had accumulated. One man was wearing a color-coordinated jogging ensemble—an orange shirt with brown ticking and brown pants with orange ticking, all accented with orange sneakers. He exuded a smarminess somewhere between velvet and teflon. The three young jurados he was accompanying were vowing abstinence from drugs and were cocky in attitude and posture. One stood leaning by an elbow on the font, with his legs crossed at the ankle, laughing loudly and conversing with others in a manner so unlike most jurados' reverent solemnity within an ambience they regard as sacred and face now of necessity and sometimes with dread. Another of these three handed an iPod earpiece to the one leaning on the font and together they bobbed their heads to the rhythm of music that I was glad I couldn't imagine. Behind them you could hear the distant church bells that now sounded somehow wobbly.

Another man came in wearing an Adidas sport outfit and slick sneakers, as though out for a jog (vow to stop drinking); and behind him was a man in a pink shirt with an out-for-the-day demeanor and a point-and-shoot camera over his shoulder (vow to stop smoking). Later, when the room happened to be empty, a father arrived with his two sons who were vowing not to take drugs. The father had dishonest eyes and a cigarette behind his ear. The assistant noticed the cigarette, signaled it to me with his head, and said, "That's what I'm talking about. He brings his sons for a juramento and comes with a cigarette behind his ear." This was delivered in a voice soft enough for the man not to hear but loud enough to make me fear that he might, which would have recruited me unwillingly to complicity in the assistant's judgment.

By contrast a man of less affluent status looked serious, almost sad, before the gravity of the commitment he was making. Two older campesinos were likewise humble and contrite as they made a vow together to stop drinking. One young man with a stylish modified Mohegan haircut and a long chin-strip beard came in alone and was nervous, tentative, and apprehensive in a way that juxtaposed with the black leather he was wearing; and another—he looked like a boy—sat on one of the wooden chairs with his leg in red pants shaking nonstop until the priest called him up to make the vow. No drinks, no drugs, no excuses. Not even on weekends. Forever until the six months are over.

An older man came in accompanied by a daughter who led him by the arm; I had the sense that she helped him navigate through the world.

With a brief interview—your name, what vow, how long—the assistant completed the man's estampita and then asked him to sign. The man was illiterate, however, and said he could not, and the assistant got the same answer when he asked the man to sign instead with a cross. Pause. Then the assistant and the daughter put the pen in the man's hand, closed the hand around it, and together the three hands moved to draw the cross. I was surprised by the assistant's gentle act of kindness and regretted that maybe I had judged him too harshly.

The experience jurados have depends largely on which priest is officiating, because the room is attended in shifts. One of the priests had something of an assembly-line approach, processing each jurado without much personal contact or caring investment. It was common for him—and sometimes the others, as the demand required—to have several jurados make their vow at once. On one occasion he did six, with one of the jurados standing because the kneeler was full.

The other two priests were both retired; Father Daniel was particularly conscientious. He would greet the jurados, talk with them, and help them through the steps of making their vows. When a wife was present, he would situate her behind the kneeling jurado and place her hand on his shoulder. Father Daniel was also particularly astute at soliciting donations. There is no charge to make a vow, with the exception of the modest fee charged for the estampita, but jurados are invited to make a donation. This generally consists of a few coins dropped into a metal box behind the font. After vows Father Daniel directed jurados to the box—fair enough—but he had placed a basket over the coin slot. Periodically, when the room was empty, he would pour the donations from the basket into his hand and then into his pocket under the alb. Some jurados were aware of this informal retirement subvention and reached under the basket to put their coins directly into the box slot.

The other retired priest, Father Juan, was older and frailer. With his white robe, black hair, heavy black glasses, curved shoulders, and head facing almost downward he gave the impression of a studious vulture. At one moment, when the room was empty, Father Juan took advantage of a lull in the action to mop up the holy water that spills during blessings. A jurado arrived with his wife while the priest was mopping—it took him a while—and on instinct I reached out for the mop, Father Juan handed it to me, and I put it back in its corner. It seemed somehow too indecorous—you come to get your life together and the priest is mopping the floor?—but that worry was only mine. By your instincts you know that you're outside of your culture and have not assimilated yet to local commonsense.

At other moments the priest was across the hall taking confessions and the assistant was on an errand, so I sat alone on one of the brown chairs. My out-of-place appearance endowed me with an undue illusion of authority. Jurados arrived and handed me their vow cars, devotees asked questions, and one woman requested permission to fill a plastic detergent container with holy water from the font. Then a man with a seriously injured eye and in apparent pain requested holy oil as a remedy. The accident had occurred four days earlier. I told him that the priest and assistant would be back soon and asked if had gone to the basilica's clinic, located just outside, but that option was of no interest to him.

A medical doctor who volunteers at the clinic later described his participation in anointment rituals, which have a biblical basis in Mark 6:13. We were sitting in the atrium with the voladores' flutes behind us, and a nurse in uniform came to join us. The doctor explained that crosses are made on a sick devotee's forehead and hands using blessed oil, while the officiating priest recites a liturgical script and the devotee and others pray for alleviation of the disease. The doctor related that a man who had cancer but no faith in anointment—his wife made him attend—was cured miraculously and later gave oral testimony.[1]

The devotee with the injured eye had a simpler plan; he would apply the oil himself as a remedy. During the colonial period devotees frequently requested oil from the "miraculous lamp" burning beside the Virgen de los Remedios. They applied this oil to diseased or wounded body parts and their ailments were healed by the sacred power that the oil had absorbed. The lamp received its name from a miracle that occurred while a woman was praying. The woman noticed that the lamp oil was low, requested that the lamp be filled, and was told that the church was out of oil. She prayed to the Virgin for a solution and "had hardly said these words when the lamp glass filled with oil" that overflowed until "the entire floor of the chancel was covered."[2]

Votive Offerings

Taxonomy

Votive practice in Mexico has indigenous, Christian, and syncretic origins that contribute to the diversity of offerings, as do social class, gender, age, and location. An indigenous campesino might offer seeds or a livestock milagrito; an urban adolescent a bead necklace; a return migrant dollar bills; a village mother the hair of a newborn. Collages are a popular offering and combine the texts, images, and objects that best represent a votary's gratitude but also his or her understanding of a miracle. Many collages are framed and others are wrapped in plastic. Collages might include a drawing, photograph, and narrative text; an object associated with the miracle or its recipient (baby clothes are common) together with photographs and a text; or a text accompanied by an illustration (photograph, artwork, news clipping) and a hair cutting or braid. In simpler offerings a photograph or textual message might be pinned to an article of clothing, or diverse offerings might be enclosed together in a plastic bag. Some collages illustrate the success of a miraculous intervention with before-and-after photographs accompanied by explanatory text. The before picture shows a man in a hospital bed with disturbing wounds and tubes, and the after shows the same man as good as new. The same motif obtains in images of children before and after surgeries, and of car wrecks juxtaposed with happy votaries who walked away alive.

Unaccompanied photographs are also very common. Some are inscribed on the back with a message, a petition, or an expression of gratitude. Simple snapshots show couples, families, mothers with babies, and people at work in various occupations. Headshots and document photographs suggest commended care, as do more clearly photographs of soldiers, migrants, and children. Votaries also post photographs to commemorate special occasions like weddings, first communions, quinceañeras, childbirths, baptisms, and family reunions. The happy moment is frozen and shared

with others, especially the miraculous image that made it possible. Some
photographs illustrate not the votaries but the cars, trucks, houses, businesses, animals, and other material gains realized through petitions, or
sometimes these gains with the proud votaries standing beside them.
Such photographs are offered to give thanks for what is represented, to
place it under a miraculous image's care, and to publicize the image's efficacy and the votaries' good fortune. Other photographs, quite to the contrary, intend to arouse pity and shock the miraculous image into action, or
to evidence the tribulations suffered en route to a happy ending. Prominent
in these images are wounds, skin disorders, postsurgery stitches and scars,
medical procedures in progress, and seemingly moribund patients in hospital beds.

A variety of original or copied documents are offered, and many are
inscribed with handwritten expressions of gratitude. Common are official
documents (visas, job appointments, admission letters, licenses), educational documents (diplomas, transcripts, grade reports), and medical documents (test results, x-rays, ultrasound images). Other documents include
those pertinent to payroll, civil disputes, criminal trials, prison release,
and missing persons. At some sites wedding invitations are offered.

Textual offerings range from graffiti, inscriptions on objects, and improvised notes on scraps of paper to typed, framed narratives and carefully

Being present: Votary photographs at the Virgen de los Remedios basilica.

crafted miracle testimonies. Newspapers and church bulletins provide other opportunities for textual announcement of miracles. Votive texts are also occasionally written on lengths of ribbons known as *listones*. This practice is used primarily in widespread Mexican devotion to Saint Charbel Makhluf, whose outstretched or bent arms gradually become covered with the ribbon petitions hanging over them. In miraculous-image devotion, votaries use ribbons for petitions and offerings at Chalma, including the caves and trees above the shrine; at the Remedios basilica; and at the Sacromonte shrine in Amecameca, among other sites.

Some votaries are impressive stylists; others are barely literate and do the best they can. Some are succinct; others want to tell the story. In narratives such as the following, police-report detail brings others inside the event and attests to the authenticity of a miracle. The votary gives thanks and then relates that "while we were sleeping in our home at 5:00 in the morning on May 3, 1952 we heard suspicious noises so my son Joaquín went out to see what was happening and found three individuals." Joaquín asked what they wanted, and they replied with obscenities and attacked him. Joaquín's brother came to his aid, but "my son Joaquín received a mortal blow on the left side of the forehead with a brick his eye bled profusely believing my son would die I commended him to the Señor de Chalma. Saving him miraculously from an instant death."[1]

Objects are offered in a wide range and for multiple purposes. Crutches, hospital wristbands, casts, and vow estampitas represent a hardship that the votary overcame with miraculous assistance. The same is true of the shackles and manacles offered in previous centuries. Other objects represent an accomplishment: wedding gowns, recorded CDs, sports jerseys from the winning team. All of these objects are tangible proof and narrative testimony; each tells a story about a votary and the miracle that he or she received. *I used to need these crutches but thanks to you I don't any more, so I offer them as a token of my gratitude.* The medium is the message, and the message is often expressed again textually in notes written on or attached to an object. On a breathing apparatus a mother wrote, "Thank you for the miracle granted to my son Christian and here I bring you his tube as proof of the miracle received."

Inscribed objects communicate a message with two voices, one implicit and the other explicit, a dual narration with one voice echoing off the other. The meaning of the objects and the meaning of the words engage dialectically, and the composite signifies differently and more forcefully than would the same message written on paper. "Thank you" on paper is a weak formality compared to "thank you" on a cast removed from an infant's leg. Collage texts likewise derive a charge from their media and context. An offering to the Señor de Chalma gives only a few words of thanks for childbirth, but this brief text resonates against a pencil drawing, inscribed baby socks, and a tuft of the baby's hair, all wrapped together in plastic and bound to a mat with wire.

Milagritos also narrate an implicit story—my arm hurts—and at once are metonymies that represent not merely an arm but an arm in pain, or

A collage offered to the Señor de Chalma. "We came to give thanks for having granted us a baby."

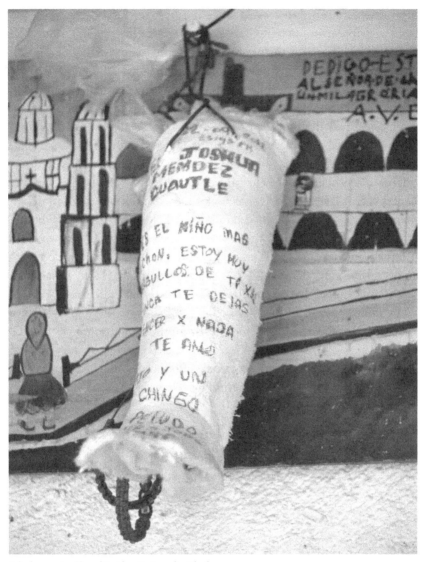

A baby cast offered to the Señor de Chalma.

a healed arm no longer in pain. A votive body part is not a static reproduction in miniature, but rather is the material vehicle of an abstraction (pain) and an intention (petition, cure). This investment is similar to the votive purpose that makes a baby shoe more than a shoe and the sacred presence that makes a miraculous image more than an inert work of art. In colonial Mexico milagritos were primarily anatomical and made of cast or stamped precious metal crafted with a degree of artistry. Votive body-parts have been offered elsewhere at least since the fifth century B.C.E., when they became popular in ancient Greece. Throughout history and around the world they are found at shrines to diverse deities, some of them long dead, and consequently are "a striking instance of the greater longevity of ritual than of gods." The gods change, the needs and protocols of petition change, but many offerings (body parts, hair, food, prayer) adapt culturally and remain essentially the same.[2]

In Spain and elsewhere in Europe, anatomical offerings were life-sized and molded in eerily flesh-like wax. A 1598 Spanish text alludes to Roman origins and explains votive customs as practiced in Catholic Europe: "And here it seems that the Christians took the custom of offering certain wax images in the temples, and certain dolls, when some part of the body is sick, such as the hand, or the foot, or a breast, we make our vows and promises to God, and to his saints, to bring them the form made in wax; and when we get well, we offer in wax that hand, or that foot, or that breast that was sick. And this custom has so prevailed that these same dolls and figures have passed from men to other animals, and these too are put in the temple for the ox, or for the sheep, or for the horse, or for a sick part of them."[3]

In Mexico today milagritos are mass-produced from cheap metals and are used both as petitions and offerings. They are available in a range of

Milagritos at the Niño del Arenal chapel.

representations beyond the more traditional body parts, sacred hearts, and kneeling votaries. Current offerings include couples, pregnant women, livestock and poultry, crops, houses, scorpions, and vehicles, among others. Ideally milagritos are pinned to the vestments of a miraculous image, but access is impossible at most shrines so votaries content themselves with votive walls, bulletin boards provided for offerings, and altar cloths. The situation varies from shrine to shrine. The Cristo Negro de Otatitlán is accessible; the Virgen de Octolán is not, but milagritos can be left at her feet; and the Virgen de Guadalupe receives milagritos in a metal box, like a coin drop, situated beside the automated people mover. At many shrines milagritos are arranged in ornamental patterns or to spell an image's name.

Also in miniature are models, such as those molded at the pedimentos in Oaxaca, that represent desired acquisitions. Models are usually petitionary, but some are used as offerings and the purpose of others is unidentified. Common forms include houses, vehicles, and children. Like milagritos, models have a long history. In the second half of the twelfth century pilgrims to the shrine of Our Lady of Rocamadour in France offered model ships, mills, farm animals, and entire villages. In a few cases actual buildings, rather than miniatures, were offered. The most notorious example is perhaps the Escorial in Spain, built by King Philip II in fulfillment of his vow made during a (victorious) battle against the French in 1527. In Mexico, the Latin inscription on a late sixteenth-century painting made for the Remedios basilica relates that the people of Mexico "for the innumerable benefits that they receive from her and for the most present protection that they have in her intercession experienced in so many miracles, as a sign of gratitude and to honor her, dedicate this temple."[4]

Food offerings have multiple meanings and purposes. Among Otomíes, offerings in general are regarded as symbolic nourishment: "People say that the tortilla is the food and essence of man and that candles, music, incense, and flowers are the food and essence of the zidahmu [saints]." These noncomestibles are the principal offerings, but literal food, like bread, is offered as well. Some of the traditional offerings to the Cristo Negro de Otatitlán are similar to those made to a precolumbian deity worshipped in the area prior to conquest. These include black and yellow corn, pumpkin seeds, eggs, and chile ancho. Indigenous devotees in Juquila gave wheat, corn, and seeds. At San Juan de Los Lagos, an annual October pilgrimage of fruit growers from Puebla brings truckloads of apples that are mounded on the altar in thanks for a bountiful harvest, and similar offerings are made at other shrines.[5]

Apple offerings on the altar at San Juan de los Lagos.

Food offering takes another form at the Templo De San Hipólito and Santuario de San Judas Tadeo in Mexico City. Every twenty minutes a priest offers a blessing with holy water, and while congregated around the altar for the blessing some devotees hand the priest bags of food—in a Wal-Mart bag, in a Kentucky Fried Chicken bag—that gather on the altar and eventually are delivered to shelters for street children. In nineteenth-century Talpa, charitable food redistribution had a different structure. Each guild offered to the Virgin a sample of what it cultivated or fabricated, and afterward the offering was given to the poor. A ranchers' guild, for example, offered beef cattle that were brought to the church door for ritual presentation and then to the main plaza for slaughter and distribution.[6]

In addition to their other functions, such as gratitude and reciprocation, many offerings that are metonymies (closely associated with the votary) or synecdoches (a part of the votary that represents the whole) perpetuate one's presence at the shrine. Clothing, particularly children's clothing, is a common offering in this regard, as are necklaces, bracelets, and headbands. Hair offerings are highly overdetermined, because their basic votive functions are compounded once by presence (the offering is part of one's body) and again, particularly when braids are offered, by sacrifice: "I am here offering you with affection that which I so much love." Hair is a most personal and intimate offering, a piece of one's self cut from the body at a cost to beauty and self-image. Hair is also free. In some cases, as Agustín in

A braid offered to the Cristo Negro de Otatitlán.

Talpa pointed out, votaries "are cutting it anyway, so they bring some here instead of throwing it out." In Otatitlán, one votary offered hair cut from his beard and sideburns.[7]

Some braid offerings follow quinceañeras, which suggest commending one's adulthood to a particular image. Other hair and braid offerings are made after regrowth following successful chemotherapy. In special cases, which are particularly honorific, hair is donated for the wigs of miraculous images. A few votaries used their hair to adorn images of the Virgen de Juquila that they made as offerings. As evidenced in votive texts, hair offerings are also made in gratitude for a variety of miracles, notably those related to health. Many braid offerings have no accompanying message and others have only the votary's name and short texts (*bless her, take care of her*) or nonspecific messages: "In gratitude to the Señor de la Misericordia for hearing my prayers."[8]

For men and women alike, and for parents, a hair offering is the culmination of a long-term process of growing and grooming. A retablo at the Soriano basilica relates the story of Osvaldo, who "had great difficulties in his marriage due to his bad conduct" and "promised not to fall again into temptation and to let his hair grow. Today he comes to the shrine together with his wife, because thanks to the Most Holy Virgen de los Dolores, God our Lord gave him the willpower to persevere in his purpose, he brings you his braid and confesses." The painting shows Osvaldo kneeling at the altar praying with his wife; the cut-off is braid beside him. Osvaldo's votive process included the informal juramento, the months of remaining faithful to his wife and to his vow, growing and caring for the hair, cutting the braid, and visiting the shrine with his wife (and eleven other family members, according to the retablo text) to formally make the offering and gain closure. The retablo, which was likely commissioned afterward, adds another dimension to the process and offering.

Many parents give thanks for safe childbirth or for resolved medical problems by offering the child's hair. The same is true of umbilical offerings. Sometimes the first hair cutting is offered, in a manner similar to first-fruit harvest offerings. One couple was married for eight years and could not have a child until the Cristo Negro de Otatitlán granted the miracle, "and that is why we come to give you our thanks and leave for you my son's first hairs." Others say that a child's hair should be offered when he or she turns three years old. An offering to the Virgen de San Juan de los Lagos is written by a mother in the voice of a child: "In gratitude for allowing me to reach my third birthday I leave you my hair." Another offering to the same Virgin is also written in the voice of a child, in this case a four-year-old girl who was cured of an eye orbit deformity: "I will enter your shrine in my blue dress, which I will give to you with my hair that for four years I took care of for you." The ancient Greeks referred to this process as "growing hair for the god." Some parents offer their own hair rather than the child's. In gratitude for curing an infant daughter's respiratory problems, a mother offered to the Virgen de Talpa a collage with a hospital photograph, a substantial braid, and a text that included, "I thank you and I'm bringing my daughter to you as I promised ... and also a piece of my hair."[9]

The many other forms of material offerings include the flowers and votive candles that are prominent at most shrines. At Chalma and Sacromonte the flower garlands worn by pilgrims are in some respect an offering. Chalma pilgrims simply deposit the garlands on poles outside the church or leave them in trees along pilgrim routes; in Sacromonte the garlands are offered on a rock face behind the church. Votive candles have the multiple and sometimes overlapping purposes of offering, petitioning, and ritual cleansing. At Chalma the crosses situated and maintained on the hills around the shrines are a form of giving thanks, and at Juquila crosses are offered on trees. Some votaries offer peso and dollar bills in gratitude for earnings at home and abroad, and others, with greater means, repay miracles with jewels and jewelry, ritual items (clerical vestments, altar vessels and cloths, waistcloths for Christ images), and cash donations in support of church operations. "I had promised 1000 pesos for the maintenance of the chamber of the image of Our Lady of Pueblito," a votary wrote, "and today I can come to deliver them."[10]

Nonmaterial offerings include shrine visits, pilgrimage, masses, ritual dance, fiesta sponsorship, and penitential sacrifices, such as walking a distance on one's knees to a shrine. Less frequently votaries repay miracles with personal or social improvements (be a better husband, abstain from an undesirable behavior, reconcile with an enemy) and charitable deeds to help others in need. The cost of fiesta sponsorship as an offering are incurred primarily by a *mayordomo* (the host responsible for the fiesta). Such sponsorship is a great honor but also a great expense and consequently unafford-able to the majority of devotees. A partial sponsor might provide fireworks, food, music, dance, adornments, or transportation. One wealthy rancher and businessman, pursuant to a promise after recovery from a nearly fatal illness, used his three trucks and rented three more to transport a troupe of one hundred twenty dancers to San Juan de Los Lagos for a fiesta. He also fed them and bought some new costumes.[11]

Dances of pre-Hispanic and colonial origin are integral to most miracu-lous-image devotions. Dancing in reciprocation for a miracle requires sacri-fice in terms of expense for travel and costumes, time commitment (there are frequent rehearsals, in addition to many votaries' long work days), and physical exertion. "The fulfillment of this commitment implies a great sac-rifice on the part of the devotee, since the majority are not in adequate phys-ical condition to begin a regimen of exercise as intense as those required by dance rehearsals." The same is true of pilgrimage, which often requires days of walking by devotees unaccustomed to physical challenge.[12]

A collection of votive offerings relates a history of misfortunes, but the suffering, despair, vulnerability, and tragedy are ultimately redirected to-ward the happy endings afforded by miraculous intervention. Unlike the iconography of Christ, which fosters toleration of suffering through empa-thetic identification, petitionary devotion subordinates suffering to the miracle of alleviation. Votive offerings transforms a community's trials into success stories conducive to perseverance through faith. They bear witness to how a miraculous image "acts on a chaotic reality and reorders it, recre-ates it and remakes it, until it becomes newly bearable and habitable."[13]

As Befits a House of God

Unlike folk-saint shrines, where votive offerings accumulate in disorderly piles viewed positively as evidence of miracles, Catholic churches must maintain order. Votive clutter is regarded as an unsightly distraction and impediment to proper devotion. The Code of Canon Law mandates "the cultivation of approved forms of popular piety" and that "votive offerings of popular art and piety are to be kept on display in the shrines or nearby places and guarded securely." At the same time, however, sacred images must be displayed "in suitable order so that the Christian people are not confused nor occasion given for inappropriate devotion." In addition, "All those responsible are to take care that in churches such cleanliness and beauty are preserved as befit a house of God and that whatever is inappropriate to the holiness of the place is excluded." In reference to popular piety the Congregation for Divine Worship and the Discipline of the Sacraments advises similarly that the Church must be "rigorous in regard to the interior conditions and the ambient requisites for a dignified celebration of the divine mysteries."[14]

The incompatibility of votive offerings and orderly shrines was already evident in ancient Greece, where the accumulation was so great at some sanctuaries that the cult image could hardly be seen. In early modern Europe, similarly, Catholic churches were overwhelmed by offerings, and, as in Mexico today, older offerings were cleared out periodically to maintain order and make room for new arrivals. At the beginning of the sixteenth century the Annunziata basilica in Florence was so full of life-sized votive statues "that space ran out; the figures had to be suspended from the entablature on cords, and the walls had to be reinforced with chains. It was not until worshipers had several times been disturbed by falling voti that the whole waxworks was banished to a side courtyard."[15]

In Mexico, particularly at pilgrimage sites, the offerings amass at such a rapid pace and of such diverse types—from retablos to umbilical cuttings—that church authorities intervene regularly, sometimes daily, to remove offerings. There was greater leniency in the past (a 1668 account describes the main altar at Remedios covered with milagritos) and even in the recent past, but today "suitable order," and "cleanliness and beauty" are carefully guarded. These measures support the more fundamental need to protect fragile sacred images from damage, and they are also intrinsic to a broader aesthetic shift illustrated so dramatically by the transition from the colonial Guadalupe church to the polished new church in modern design. Nevertheless the absence of offerings has altered—subdued—the ambiance of churches and displaced the popular aesthetic of chaotic, probative accumulation with an antiseptic neatness so alien to traditional devotion. The contrast is clear at the shrine to Niño del Cacahuatito, which on one side has votive offerings in rooms that are maintained but nevertheless exude an aesthetic of popular devotion (abundance, variety, votive graffiti) and on the other side has a church that is characteristically immaculate. The Virgen de Juquila pedimento likewise has a feel decidedly different from that of the shrine church itself. A similar contrast is evident when a confused array of homemade offerings at Chalma is compared to the orderly display of commissioned retablos in the votive museum at Soriano.[16]

The Chalma array is both permanent and transient, which is to say that one Sunday's accumulation is removed to make room for the next week's influx, so that the specific offerings change but the overall effect remains the same. Retablos and other offerings that are suitable in format and content have a longer and sometimes permanent place on the wall; more informal offerings—the majority—have a shorter shelf life. Votaries are quite aware that most new arrivals are removed and some craft their offerings accordingly or situate them strategically to have a greater chance at longevity. A sign posted on a votive wall in the Remedios courtyard provides guidance: "Let's keep writing the history of salvation. Keep making retablos. If you want them to remain exhibited here, make them with durable materials." Shrines with lesser volume, like Pueblito and Tonatico, often archive or display offerings, including votive texts. At other sites the offerings are discarded or burned, and some say that the ashes are used for the rite on Ash Wednesday (in lieu of blessed palms from the preceding Palm Sunday). In previous centuries and other regions, offerings had greater value and were recycled for practical use. Gold and silver offerings, including anatomical votives, were melted down and sold or recast into ritual vessels. At the shrine to Sainte Foy, so many chains and fetters were offered in gratitude for liberation from prison that the monks receiving them hired blacksmiths to recast the iron into grillwork and doors.[17]

Each votive offering represents a miracle and accordingly one would imagine each being cherished by churches dedicated to miraculous images. The miracles are so voluminous, however, and so dubious in clerical perspective, and the offerings are so improvised and regarded as unbefitting a sacred ambiance, that clearing them out and disposing of them occurs routinely without a thought. (Many priests "don't understand popular culture," Father Juan Manuel said, and in this context he mentioned a sacristan using a retablo as a dustpan.) Once removed from a church an offering no longer performs its votive functions (gratitude, reciprocation) and especially not its long-term functions like publicity, commemoration, and surrogate presence.[18]

If one needed a justification for removal of offerings, one might regard a votive object's ritual functions as a short-term performance realized

3333333

simply by posting, or by posting and a brief period afterward to assure that the miraculous image recognizes the reciprocation. While discussing the removal and disposal of petitionary miniatures in Juquila, Pedro said, "I see it as more spiritual. Why? Because I know that I made the little house as a petition," and the act of making it is more important than the object itself. Making the miniature object is a way of enacting the petitionary prayer. In this view longevity is unnecessary, because shortly after they are created or posted, or in the very act, offerings have already performed their votive functions and subsequently are exhausted ritual objects—junk—that can be discarded to make room for fulfillment of other reciprocations. It is not the object itself that is valuable, but rather the object invested with purpose, the performative object, and once the object has performed it can be discarded. Offered baby pajamas so heavily charged with votive functions are afterward just pajamas. And unlike many other things at a shrine—water, flowers, people, image reproductions—object offerings do not absorb sacred power and therefore are of no interest as relics.[19]

Votive practice in Mexico would ideally entail visiting a Christ or Virgin image at its home; expressing gratitude for miracles personally, as one would with another human; making physical contact to express affection and absorb power; and leaving an offering on the image's vestments, at its feet, or on an altar or wall in close proximity. Much of this is impossible in petitionary devotion today, in part because most churches have intentionally eliminated spaces designated for votive offerings. Pueblito, which once had a retablo wall in the atrium, has no place for material offerings. Retablos were removed when the church was repainted, but no one explains why they were not returned to display, or why the space was not designated for new offerings. The same occurred at Zapopan during the colonial period: "When the church was renovated all of the paintings were taken down." Available to votaries at the ornately renovated Soriano basilica are only two small, uncovered bulletin boards at stair landings. Votaries at many shrines are told to leave their offerings in the church offices, but that unsatisfactory alternative hardly fulfills the votary's needs and the object's functions. It is something like asking a dinner guest to leave a gift for the hosts in the garage. The worthy offerings are transferred from the office to storage or, at some sites, to the church museum.[20]

Many of the larger pilgrimage sites like Chalma and San Juan de los Lagos have reached a compromise solution by providing a votive space adjacent to the church. At Remedios offerings are posted in the courtyard, at Otatitlán in a room behind the altar, and at Señor de la Misericordia in

Tepatitlán in a wide walkway that flanks the church on one side. Talpa and Zapopan have small votive spaces in side rooms, from which offerings are removed to a gallery opened on special occasions. These solutions are not ideal because they distance the offerings from miraculous images and separate popular from liturgical devotion, but nevertheless the mandate for church orderliness is satisfied (by virtue of the adjacent sites and periodic clearing) while at once providing a close-enough and unmediated space for votive expression.

The lack of a designated space and rapid removal when a space is provided have decidedly dissuasive effects on material offerings. Many votaries question the relevance of making an offering that will soon be removed. When no space is provided votaries improvise by putting folded texts in coin boxes, wedging photographs wherever they will fit, and leaving offerings in unapproved places (from which they are removed), but all of these remedies are inadequate. The inhospitality to traditional votive practices is steering votaries away from material offerings and toward forms of gratitude, including masses of rogation and thanksgiving, which are more amenable to institutional religion. The current tendency to establish shrine museums is well-intentioned and beneficial in a historical sense, but nevertheless similarly detrimental to material offerings. Display predicated on a qualitative sorting—a curation—undermines the discretionary freedom of votive practice. The worthy offerings are delivered not to the miraculous image intended as the recipient, but rather to a glass case where the focus shifts from devotional functions to aesthetic contemplation and historical fascination. The nature of viewers also changes.

The Strange Life of Objects

A pair of baby socks, a braid of hair, and a turkey feather have no inherent agency. When the socks are in a store, the braid is on its head, and the feather is on its turkey these objects do nothing except quietly suggest their humanly attributed purposes as clothing, adornment, and food. When the same objects are posted on the votive wall of a shrine, however, they are activated by devotional use, assume new purposes, and become performative. This is not to say that at night, after all the priests have gone to bed, the socks, braid, and feather get mischievous and dance to the tune of Alfred Gell, but rather that agency happens in human minds and is attributed to artifacts that play assigned roles by doing nothing.

Votive objects are invested with human intention within a cultural context that makes performance viable. They perform interrelated functions relative to a votary's reciprocal obligations, including giving thanks, repaying a debt, closing a cycle, maintaining relations, witnessing and commemorating, publicizing, and relieving the anxiety of an unfulfilled promise. Offerings also perpetuate a votary's surrogate presence at a shrine (the socks and braid) and represent the tangible gains of petitions (the feather representing turkeys and fecundity). All of these functions are enriched by the implicit discourse of votive objects individually as testaments to a votary's worthiness, and collectively as evidence that sacred power is a community resource, that miracles happen, and that crises have happy endings. When a retablo is offered to a miraculous statue or painting, two works of art engage in symbolic relations. On both sides of the exchange an artwork carries out an action. One artwork (the statue or painting) performs the miracle and another (the painted offering) performs the reciprocation.

Votive objects also have public functions. They mediate between the intimate personal experience of receiving a miracle and the reception of that experience by other votaries who view posted offerings empathetically. The offerings reflect the viewers' own life stories by emphasizing the common perils through which a community struggles and prevails with assistance of the miraculous image to which all are devoted. By extension sacred presence and commended care are reaffirmed, because offerings depict miracles concerning family, love, employment, travel, and other aspects of everyday life. A community coheres around the need for miracles, the receipt of miracles, and the votive documentation that ratifies miracles. Solidarity, reassurance, belief confirmation, a sense of protection, and the emotional bonds of shared fate and shared faith are among the benefits. In the viewers' perspective, votive offerings are social mirrors that reflect plausible expectation—even anticipation—of relief at times of need. The offerings are integral to the miracles that they report but also to the future miracles that they inspire and that conform to expectations. In this perspective votive offerings are something like placeholders for votaries who observe them now and might replace them later with offerings of their own.[21]

A miraculous image is the centerpiece that coheres a religious community, and around it votive offerings provide a multiplicity of related imagery and objects that connect the community's history to miracles. It is almost as though the miraculous image were emitting a silent but certain discourse of otherworldly presence, and the votive images, like echoes returning from distance hills, provided corroborating discourse in multiple voices. The message is reinforced with each repetition. One offering guarantees the other and all attest to the continuity of miraculous intervention, and this interactive enhancement compounds across the centuries until eventually an accumulation of offerings reaches critical mass and the collective becomes self-perpetuating. The volume also demonstrates that the sacred power is undepletable.[22]

A wall of votive offerings suggest a resource and a protocol or, more specifically, an availability of sacred power and an implicit guide for managing crises. The offerings communicate implicitly that a given image is responsive to miracle petitions and that a sequence of proper action resolves problems. Votive offerings are a form of cultural transmission; they convey collective knowledge and provide a cognitive directive for negotiating challenges and perils. Some viewers are indifferent, some are casual, and others take their time, but all know that the offerings are posted, are probative of miracles, and are useful precedents. The didactic messages are not communicated to tourists who view the same offerings at a shrine, nor to nonbelievers who view retablos in a museum. These viewers will make difference inferences upon considering the same evidence, or no inference at all. Receipt of the message is contingent on faith and cultural predisposition.[23]

A devotee's gains in interpretive and practical tools are complemented by gains in identity formation and affirmation. "Seeing behavior succeed for others increases the tendency to behave in similar ways," but people are also selective and "determine which external events will be observed, how they will be perceived, whether they leave any lasting effects, what valence and efficacy they have, and how the information they convey will be organized for future use." Much of that information is provided contextually, within the votive culture of shrines and basilicas where miraculous images and pilgrimages are prominent. A particular way of being Catholic—as a votary—is chosen because it suits one's disposition and needs better than other options, like going to confession, studying the bible, or becoming a nun. One learns about oneself by appraising others' behavior, particularly as it relates to one's own identity and aspirations. Through "vicarious self-perception" the attributes and practices observed in others' devotion stimulate inferences about one's own beliefs, which might result in doing what was witnessed—a process of becoming through rehearsal—and ultimately in incorporating the observed attributes and practices into one's own repertoire or self-concept. In this view, devotees learn not only about sacred resources and votive protocols, but also that they have faith.[24]

On occasion a critical mass of votive offerings provides impetus and context but a specific, well-publicized miracle is the catalyst of new petitions. This occurs particularly when a miracle is recognized by church authorities and promoted outside the devotional community. At the Soriano basilica a large votive painting narrates the miraculous resuscitation of a three-year-old girl, María José, who in 2004 fell into a bog beside the Colón River. She was found twenty minutes later, as the text explains, "floating in the water, drowned, swollen, purple and covered with mud, almost unrecognizable." Her mother and others tried to revive her unsuccessfully for fifteen minutes and then pleaded to the Virgin, after which Maria José miraculously returned to life. News of the miracle was widely disseminated orally, by the media, and through the basilica's website.

The audience included María Teresita, who had terminal AIDS and learned of the miracle while watching television from her deathbed. Her husband transported her the one hundred and fifty miles from their home to the basilica and carried her inside because she was too frail to walk. "Beginning at that moment," the retablo text relates, María Teresita "rapidly recuperated her health." She was "living a normal life" and working again at the time the votive painting was offered in 2007. The retablo hangs beneath María José's in the basilica museum.

Later Marco, a garbage collector in his mid-twenties, fell off the truck and was run over by the dual rear tires. The ambulance was slow in arriving and in the interim Marco remembered María José's miraculous resuscitation and commended himself to Soriano's Virgen de los Dolores. Marco wrote a six-page narrative and presented it to the rector of the Soriano basilica to document the miracle, but also to witness among other devotees who might be inspired, as Marco was, by noteworthy and accumulating precedents.

Insofar as material offerings are concerned, petitionary devotion has ample free play. When votaries are asked how miracles should be reciprocated, their responses almost always include the phrase *a su manera* (in one's own way). Votive offering is an exact science of whatever works. Everyone agrees that miracles must be repaid, but also that the repayment is at individual discretion. Even a glance at a wall of offerings is sufficient to notice that the offerings are diverse, but the diversity is restricted by implicit parameters, by budget, and by purpose. "Function is the constant against which stylistic variables play." One becomes the new protagonist of an old plot that is endlessly customized. The same redundancy occurs when votaries attach their identities to mass-produced milagritos, and when their miracle narratives (like hagiographical narratives) conform to standardized precedents.[25]

Many votaries strive for individuation, so that their offering might stand out and be noticed by the miraculous image, the public, and, in some cases, by the custodians who decide which offerings merit longevity on the wall. Creative innovation first produces anomalies that are recognized as such and often rejected, but that can also modify a norm if repeated in significant numbers. As anomalies are assimilated a tradition reestablishes itself "without the perception of its own deviation" but "with all the characteristics of pressuring and binding" that contribute to slow transformation and perpetual evolution. This process is clearly evident in the transition from traditional use of commissioned retablos to current use of homemade collages. It may also eventually be revealed in a transition of unknown destination that might result from the prohibition of material offerings in shrine interiors.[26]

The evidentiary function of votive objects is critical because miracles are invisible. The driver saved when the car crashed into the tree saw nothing supernatural but inferred a miracle by virtue of survival. Even when a miracle is petitioned, such as during a long illness, votaries ultimately give thanks for an unseen, presumed intervention. These inferred miracles become visual and historical when they are objectified in votive offerings and ratified by a sacred context. The process is similar to the veracity and authority that even specious news assumes when related by media. News creates the reality that it purports to report, in part because "we cannot refer to events as such, but only to events *under a description*," and a description that is mistaken for the events. The miracle as an inference becomes a material offering regarded as validation and even as the miracle itself when devotees point to a votive wall and say, "Those are all the Virgin's miracles." A similar desymbolization is captured in anatomical votive offerings referred to as "miracles" (milagros, milagritos). Once on the wall of a shrine, a votive offering is "used as proof but cannot itself be proven." It brings into being the miracle that it represents. Each miracle is constructed by interpretation and representation, and the construct is regarded as historical truth. The compound effect of the votive wall as a whole is overwhelming and irrefutable proof.[27]

Votive offerings are consequently interactive with sacred context, oral tradition, and projective animation in endowing miraculous images with power. Devotion animates the image and miracles occur subjectively within interpretations, but the maintenance of an image's power is dependent on the visible proof, the public documentation, provided by material and textual offerings. Votaries' faith, needs, interpretations, and emotions interact with images, objects, tradition, ritual, ambiance, and community in a circulation that generates something that feels like sacred power, that is implemented as sacred power, and that is perpetuated by documented use.

Presence

Just as a miraculous image lends material presence to sacred power and, in some sense, to an absent prototype (Christ, Virgin), so photographs posted at shrines lend material presence to petitions, gratitude, and absent votaries. Petitionary devotion is negotiated in the encounter of these surrogate presences. A votary's photograph, like graffiti, is a calling card; I was here and record my visit. As a surrogate the photograph also prolongs the visit. The intent is to situate a votary in the constant presence of a miraculous image, to commend oneself or a family member, "to be in sight and put oneself under the care of the Virgin," as Monseñor Francisco put it at the Remedios basilica. An offering at the Niño del Arenal chapel includes photographs of children and a handwritten text that reads, "I am leaving my grandchildren I commend them to you take care of them and protect them from all dangers and diseases." A mother makes a similar request of the Virgen del Pueblito: "I brought photos of my children and me so that you will please take care of us and never abandon us." A material presence at home reminds votaries of the image, and a material presence at the shrine reminds the image of votaries. The shrine is the image's home, and votaries are there in surrogate presence like the framed pictures of loved ones on a wall. Before departing on their journeys migrants and soldiers often leave photographs to commend themselves—"take care of me wherever I might be"—and family members post photographs to protect missing, kidnapped, and incarcerated relatives, and, on occasion, to commend deceased family members to care in the afterlife.[28]

Votaries' presence is also individualized by names and signatures. Some petitions and offerings consist of nothing other than a name. Full names, with paternal and maternal surnames, are sometimes used, and on rare occasions votaries include document numbers. The names accomplish textually what the photographs accomplish visually: Here I am. These identifiers help the image to locate the beneficiary of the miracle or to credit the reciprocation to the right account. A retablo offered during a measles epidemic in 1937 illustrates how specificity is also used in expressions of gratitude: "Mr. Guadalupe Flores and his wife María Batalla dedicate this retablo in thanksgiving to the Señor de la Santa Veracruz for curing their four children, whose names are Carmelita, María Guadalupe, Alberta, and Benito Agustín; the four have last names corresponding to their father's." Esmeralda listed names of family members to petition their protection by the Virgen of Tonatico and then, as an afterthought, added identifying labels: mother, father, brother.... Specified identity is particularly precise when votaries name enemies or desired romantic partners, and in petitions concerning custody disputes, visa applications, professional certification, university admission, and other legal and bureaucratic matters.

Among its other purposes, votive graffiti also perpetuates presence at a shrine. In previous centuries and in other regions, votive inscriptions were sometimes scratched or etched into walls. Crosses were scratched into European church walls, pilgrims made gouge marks on exterior temple walls in Roman Egypt, and at Byzantine pilgrim shrines "many inscriptional votives took the form of an invocation, making permanent the supplicant's prayer for help." Etching continues as it can in Mexico today, notably in wood and melted candle wax. The value of votive etchings and graffiti is not in the elegance of the petition or offering but rather in its longevity. Other petitions and offerings are removed periodically, but graffiti remains until a wall is repainted. It also requires no investment or forethought. At sites where it is permitted, such as the Juquila pedimento and the votive rooms at the Niño del Cacahuatito shrine, graffiti is extensive and consists primarily of brief messages seeking commended care. Typical are phrases like "please take care of us," "bless my family," and "protect me." A visiting migrant wrote to Niño del Cacahuatito, "take good care of my family and especially of my parents give them strength to accept that I am far from them." Graffiti is also written or scratched in wall soot from rising candle smoke, and in these places is accompanied by another identifier: handprints.[29]

Personal items, such as clothing, represent specific votaries through contact and contiguity, almost as though the clothing absorbed something of the votary who offered it. An article of clothing—especially the favorite shirt or dress—is by association an extension of the person who wears it, in part because that person derived identity from how the clothing made him or her feel and some of that identity and feeling infuse by contagious transfer back into the cloth. Such relations between the person and the clothing are apparent in the creepy sadness of a dead loved one's clothing hanging empty in a closet. "The feelings inspired in us by a person or a thing are extended contagiously from the idea of that person or this thing to the representations with which they are associated." The same transfer is suggested by the active market for objects that belong to celebrities—a movie star's blouse, a rock star's guitar—because something of the celebrity seems to stick to the object, imbue it with a special quality, "some nonmaterial essence of the source being embodied in the object." John of Damascus pursued these ideas by analogy into devotion to sacred images: "I have often seen lovers gazing at the garments of their beloved, embracing the garments with their eyes and their lips as if the garment were the beloved one." In addition to clothes and especially baby clothes, votaries offer a range of metonymic items: headbands, berets, bracelets, caps, sneakers. Some votaries repeat the offering to maintain and renew a presence. One grandmother offers another of her grandson's baby hats annually at the apparition cave in Chalma. Reynaldo thought that such repeat offerings of children's clothing was a form of update, "to identify how old and how big the child is." The repeated offerings keep the miraculous image apprised of the child's progress and the success of commended care.[30]

The offering of hair and braids is more directly representational. The same is true of the umbilical cuttings left at the Chalma cave and other sites. Presence in these cases is by synecdoche, a part-object standing in for the person as a whole. In ancient Egypt drops of menstrual blood or semen were incorporated into fertility figurines and hair and fingernail clippings were used in offerings, because "the Egyptians believed that the spiritual and physical entity of a person resided in every part of the body." That belief anticipates the current understanding of DNA and suggests hair offering as a signature.[31]

It also suggests body-part milagritos as figurative people presences. The milagritos of kneeling devotees more clearly—more comprehensively—extend votary presence at shrines and redouble the benefits by representing prayer. The static *I am here* yields to the active *I am here praying to you always*. These milagritos freeze the moment (like a photograph) and offer perpetual prayer in return for perpetual protection. The same is suggested by rosary offerings. In European shrines, life-sized wax limbs suspended from walls and ceilings dramatically evoked their referents, because "wax in its texture, translucence, and dull tone can uncannily resemble flesh." "To behold a display of wax hands and feet and organs is something like coming across a box of unlabeled nineteenth-century photographs." The medium changes; the intent remains the same.[32]

In historical periods prior to the invention of photography, votaries were also represented by indexical surrogates—measured offerings—that corresponded to body height and weight. The ritual, which was done in many parts of medieval Europe, involved measuring a child's body from head to foot, and sometimes widthwise from the fingertips of outstretched arms, and then using the measuring thread to make a candle, often coiled, that would be offered at a shrine. The child was thus "measured to the saint." Weighed offerings similarly corresponded with the body or afflicted body part of a votary. The offerings were usually made in wax; a wealthy votary might use silver or silverplate. Votaries also aspired to fabricate offerings that matched an afflicted limb, for example, in both length and weight. Other offerings—grains, bread, vegetables—were made in coun-terweight to a sick child placed on a scale.[33]

Metonymical presence was more theatrical when life-size wax figures, some silverplated, were made in the same weight or height as votaries. After a boy was healed in 1497, his father kept his vow "to make him in wax as he was and the size he was at the time I made the vow with 10 pounds of new wax and all covered in fine silver." The practice was most conspicuous in the Annunziata basilica in Florence, where Florentines, popes, and prominent foreigners "left their own life-size effigies in wax by way of visiting cards." Some of these—especially those with hair, beards, and clothes—"generated the powerful illusion of the embodied presence of the votary."[34]

This progressive drama of presence achieves its maximal expression in offerings that reenact a miracle. In modern Brazil, a toddler choking on a coin coughed it out finally when the father pleaded to St. Francis. In grat-itude the father carved a votive statue the same height as his daughter and with her facial features, dressed it in the clothes that she was wearing at the time of the miracle, wedged the coin that she had choked on into a carved opening in the replica's mouth, and glued cuttings from the daughter's hair onto the statue. This restaging is reminiscent of eighteenth-century European executions that reenacted a crime prior to the punishment: "There were even some cases of an almost theatrical reproduction of the crime in the execution of the guilty man—with the same instruments, the same ges-tures." In the cases of both the miracle and the execution, the restaging serves as a ritual undoing, a restoration of the equilibrium disrupted by the accident or crime.[35]

These manners of substitution or metonymical presence were not as common in Mexico and are not used in current devotion. At the Virgen de Talpa shrine in the nineteenth century, however, ribbons measured to the length of the Virgen (called *medidas*) were taken home by pilgrims as relics. In a mid-seventeenth-century votive painting on cloth from Texcoco, a variation of counterweighing is illustrated. The text explains that Pedro's daughter, María, was sick with no hope of cure, so Pedro "weighed candles" and commended María to the Virgin with successful results. The image shows a nun praying on one side of a double-balance scale and large candles piled on the other side, illustrating the colonial practice of weighing a nun and offering her weight in candles to give thanks for or to petition a miracle. Pedro's son is shown approaching, carrying more candles for the balance.[36]

All of these offerings—photographs, names, clothes, hair, graffiti, counterweights, effigies—are surrogates that prolong votaries' presence before miraculous images. The same is true of license plates, hospital bracelets, medical reports, original or photocopied identification documents and visas, acceptance letters, and other offerings that link to a specific person and miracle. Such objects are at once representative, because they stand in for the votary; and performative, because they carry out actions like petitioning, commending, and thanksgiving. Representational relations circulate between the object (votive offering), the action (petitioning, commending, thanksgiving), the votary (in surrogate presence), and the miracle (specified by the offering). In the context of presence, each offering—the motorcycle jacket, the lock of black hair, the eye milagrito, the inscribed ultrasound report—is a kind of self-portrait. The resemblance may be minimal or lacking, the referential relation may be cloudy, and the votive object may be a photograph or a mass-produced milagrito, but nevertheless the offering intends to be "strongly evocative of the subject's presence."[37]

Votive Texts

Jacobus de Voragine tells the story of a woman who committed a sin so terrible that she could not confide it to anyone. St. John the Almsgiver advised her to write down the sin, seal the paper, and bring it to him; he would pray for her. She did so, and a few days later John died. "When the woman heard that he was dead, she feared that she would now be shamed and disgraced, thinking that he would have entrusted her paper to someone and that it would fall into the hands of some stranger." In a flood of tears at John's tomb the woman begged John to reveal the paper's location. Finally John appeared and returned the paper, still closed with her seal, and told her to read it. "She opened the paper and saw that her sin had been completely erased."[38]

Among other interpretations, this tale might be understood allegorically as an unloading of burdens (including sins) by externalizing them and objectifying them textually. As in sacramental confession to a priest, the sins are erased by expressing them, but now they also pass into an object, the text on paper, that severs and distances them from the sinner's subjectivity. A similar structure obtains in limpias when negative attributes (illnesses, sins, impurities) are drawn from the body and objectified in eggs, votive candles, and bundles of herbs that in their respective ways then dispatch what they have absorbed. Milagritos also suggest detachment, objectification, and distancing when a diabetic's nerve-damaged leg, for example, is symbolically concentrated into an incorruptible, leg-shaped miniature cut out along "the fault lines of the symptom itself" and offered in anticipation of a cure.[39]

The writing and the text as object are performative because they do not merely describe a petition but rather constitute and enact it. The same occurs to a certain degree when texts are offered following a miracle, but in these cases a text represents more than it performs an action because the textual offering usually commemorates a more comprehensive reciprocation that might include, for example, a pilgrimage. The adverse experiences unloaded on paper nevertheless seem to assume an objectivity independent of votaries. A votive text is a representative fragment of ongoing votary discourse—a life story, the history of a crisis—that is made extractable and decontextualizable, so that it serves to lift a crisis out of one's life and lay it at the feet of a miraculous image. One can leave the objectified problem in the church, relinquished to history, done with that now, because an empowered agent took care of the problem. The votive offering, as the last act in a sequence, provides a sense of closure.[40]

The urge to write is itself suggestive. Votaries attribute omniscience to God and miraculous images, communicate with them frequently in prayer, and sense that omniscient sacred figures are familiar with and involved in their everyday lives. When the moment comes to make a petition or an offering, however, many votaries opt to write and to post their texts at a shrine. This occurs for several reasons in addition to externalization and objectification. In petitionary devotion the abstract, heavenly Christ and Virgin recede into a distant background as devotion occurs in a material world to material images that require petitions and offerings in kind. The written petitions must be present so the miraculous image can read them and not forget the votary's needs, and votive texts must be offered as a testament—as evidence—of the miracle and the votary's reciprocation.

The material presence guarantees, or at least enhances, the efficacy of the petition and offering.

Writing also enhances the catharsis that devotees experience through disclosure. Written petitions provide the opportunity for redirection or addressee substitution, so that open disclosure to a miraculous image can vent emotions, thoughts, needs, and desires that the votary cannot express to another, perhaps inaccessible interlocutor. In a petition at the Virgen del Pueblito shrine, a devastated mother lamented the lost custody of her child and asked Christ to intervene. "Soften the heart of my husband so he will let me see my daughter I haven't seen her for 5 months. He took her when she was a year and five months old." "I know that I hurt him," the woman continued, but "I ask you for another chance so we can unite with you God and that you let me God show you how much and how far I still love my husband and daughter." The votary anticipates that a reunion with the husband and daughter is improbable, so later in the petition she downgrades to a more viable alternative. "But if it is no longer possibly my God soften his heart so I can see my daughter this weekend. Permit me it Lord Jesus Christ. And forgive me God. Forgive my husband. I can't take any more my Lord help me and give me more strength to bear this suffering I can't live any more without my daughter."

The request for forgiveness and for a visit is not made to the estranged husband—he will not listen—but rather to Christ through the Virgen del Pueblito. In such redirection votive texts are similar to psychotherapeutic letters that are not intended for delivery to their addressees but rather are media for confronting, working through, and venting highly emotional and unresolvable situations. Such letters are written, for example, to an ex-husband or ex-wife, a child given up for adoption, or a deceased love one. The addressees, like miraculous images, are from one angle external interlocutors and from another subjective constructs inseparable from the need to be heard. They are implied readers who influence the content and tone of the letters but who also, despite the antagonism felt by the letter writers, provide an illusion of empathy and understanding. Some therapeutic letters are written to oneself in order to vent emotions and think through an illness, addiction, or commitment to recovery. In statements that apply as well to votive texts, cancer patients participating in a therapeutic writing program explained that "writing is a way of saying things I can't say" and gives "some sort of order" to a "mass of jumbled thoughts and feelings." It is also, again, a means of objectifying: "what's within me is externalised, is deposited outside myself," and "things which swirl around my head" are externalized "instead of just keeping them like bottled up."[41]

The writing of votive texts and particularly miracle narratives, such as Marco's, is a cognitive tool to order adverse experiences, give them meaning, and integrate them into one's life story. The catharsis and the interpretation are not separate functions but rather are interacting—interconfusing—aspects of one and the same effort to process crises and to construct a narrative conducive to their miraculous resolution. As suggested by Marco's narrative, "people give meaning to their experiences by using a storytelling structure," and these "stories are not necessarily anchored in an external truth, but instead represent distinctly human constructions that reflect the social and personal perspectives of the communities and individuals who tell them." Each new votive text is influenced by audience expectation and genre tradition established by centuries of precedents. Narrative turns back on memory and restructures it, and this retrospective revision becomes indistinguishable from the experience itself. "The ways of telling and the ways of conceptualizing that go with them become so habitual that they finally become recipes for structuring experience itself, for laying down routes into memory, for not only guiding the life narrative up to the present but directing it into the future," until "narrative imitates life, life imitates narrative." Votaries also enjoy the textual reliving inherent to narrative composition, especially when the reported miracle is shared with others. "Writing about a positive experience is, itself, a positive experience."[42]

One of the principal functions of votive narrative is to construct and make public an identity of oneself as a worthy recipient of miracles. This might include combinations of representing oneself as faithfully devoted to the petitioned image, as in desperate need of help and without other recourse, as grateful for previous miracles, and as remorseful for transgressions. The miraculous image as implied reader silently but decisively contributes to narrative composition because at some level of consciousness the votary ponders, *What does the image expect of me? What version of myself would be most persuasive?* Stress of one's worthiness is complemented by stress of image attributes conducive to miracles, such as presence and power, reliability, and the maternal responsibility of the Virgins. Votive texts thus serve, among their other purposes, to define and position votaries as protagonists within a narrative sequence that concludes with a miracle.[43]

Retablos

The votive offerings known as retablos were originally painted on cloth or sometimes wood by professional artists and, given the expense, were offered by wealthier votaries. Retablos became affordable for popular use around 1825, when Mexican folk artists began painting on inexpensive tinplate. Retablo painters worked by commission and shared the votaries' religious culture. The intent of the paintings was more devotional than artistic, and the works were generally unsigned. For centuries commissioned retablos were a predominant form of votive offering in Mexico, but today their use is infrequent. Some votaries follow the traditional retablo format—a painted scene over a textual narration—in homemade offerings of varying styles and qualities, but far more common are free-form votive artworks created in paint, colored pencils, markers, pastels, and crayons. Occasionally images are computer generated or made by techniques like woodburning, embossing, and crochet.[44]

Painted votive offerings date back at least to ancient Greece, where at Epidaurus, for example, votive tablets known as *pinakes* (*pinax* in the singular) were offered to Asclepius. The tablets were made of wood and, like Mexican retablos, generally included a painting and an inscription. The first extant Christian votive painting, known as *The Virgin with Three Hands*, was offered following a miracle received by John of Damascus. As the story goes, a forged letter advocating treason against an iconoclast emperor was attributed to John, and John's hand was amputated as punishment. John prayed all night before an icon of the Virgin, his hand was restored, he hung a silver hand (a metonymy of the votary, like milagritos today) on the icon as an offering, and the hand was later painted into the Virgin's portrait. In the medieval and early modern periods, votaries offered saints "little pictures depicting the miracles obtained through their intercession." A late sixteenth-century Spanish book makes the connection to the earlier Greek practice of "hanging certain tablets in the temple of the god who favored them." The Spaniards "also usually put and nailed certain tablets in the temple, on which they paint and write some miracles to give testimony to their descendents." By the mid-seventeenth century, "making an image as a mark of thanks had become habitual."[45]

In Mexico today, the disuse of commissioned retablos as votive offerings has occurred for several reasons, including obsolescence. Access to cameras, photocopiers, computers, and art supplies has made dependence on painters unnecessary. Votary-made offerings are also attractive because they afford freedom of expression. The decline in demand for commissioned retablos has resulted in a decline of supply, and a vicious cycle has accelerated the tradition's demise. Retablo painting is a cottage industry passed from fathers to sons, and the sons are no longer interested because, among other reasons, the trade is unprofitable. Juan Rivera García, from Cadereyta de Montes in Querétaro, was born in 1926, learned the trade from his father, and painted retablos throughout his life. His own sons, however, have other jobs, one in the mayor's office, and Juan approves because their income is regular and, as he puts it, they get vacations and Christmas bonuses. When retablo painters can be found, their fees are dissuasive because votaries can fulfill reciprocal obligations inexpensively or without expense. One retablo text mentions that the votary had to beg to raise the painting fee. Other votaries reduced costs by using a single retablo to thank two or multiple miracles, or by opting for a standardized format rather than a personalized narrative painting.[46]

The removal of retablos from shrines and their display in church museums also contributes to the demise of the tradition. Votaries are left without a site for posting, and museum display conveys the impression that retablos are an outdated or historic form of offering. It further suggests that retablos should be reserved for exceptional, museum-worthy miracles rather than the everyday miracles received by most votaries. Museum display accentuates retablos' aesthetic value as folk art rather than their ritual value as reciprocation and their evidentiary value as miracle testimonies. The retablo's performative functions are dependent on a devotional context; elsewhere the functions are inactive. The votive painting's ambiguity—at once ritual object and folk art—is restricted by context. The same obtains in regard to the miraculous statues and paintings to which retablos are offered. In a church, the images' presence and power are predominant and the aesthetic qualities are insignificant, or at least subordinate; and in a museum, the sacred presence and power are lost and the image's aesthetic qualities are emphasized.[47]

While retablos as votive offerings have declined and been replaced by more informal media at shrines, retablos as works of art have gained value and prominence in secular commercial markets. Online dealers of Mexican folk art and antiques sell retablos at prices that range between about $400 and $3,000, depending on age, quality, and condition. Local devotional painters have been replaced by internationally renowned painters who market their outsider folksiness, exhibit in art galleries, and paint retablos on news stories, wrestling, prostitution, marital infidelity, and a range of commissioned topics that are displayed as art in homes rather than as votive offerings in churches. Retablos have consequently made a transition from religious to artistic predominance.

Some priests are trying to "rescue the tradition," as Father Juan Manuel put it, by reviving retablos as votive offerings. When he was rector of the Soriano basilica, Father Juan Manuel began a program in which miracle recipients reported to the church office and gave testimonies that were entered into a database (a book of narratives was intended but never published). When the miracles seemed authentic the recipient was paired with an artist, who at basilica expense painted a retablo for display in the basilica museum. The Soriano program is creative, deeply well-intentioned, and contributes to maintenance of retablo tradition, but it precludes the purposes most important to votaries. These include fulfilling votive functions in proximity to a miraculous image, making offerings in one's own way, and doing so without clerical mediation. The church-commissioned retablos also seem tonally synthetic, with a contrive naiveté, because they are produced by trained artist imitating folk art.

Priests are conspicuously absent in retablos, as befits a genre representing unmediated relations between votaries and miraculous images. The clerical absence and the institutional bypass evidence a quiet insubordination, an evasion of the impediments that filter and regulate access to sacred power. Retablos also register an understated and noncontentious protest against secular authorities, including soldiers and police. Votive offerings are narrated primarily in the perspective of poor and often marginalized Mexicans who are easy targets of abuse and whose precarious social station is aggravated and perpetuated by corruption. On occasion political protest is explicit. A 1995 votive text to San Cristóbal Magallanes Jara, who was executed in 1927 during government repression of Catholicism, includes the following: "You know that we are suffering because of bad government we have never had a good president they all rob the nation and more than forty million Mexicans are in vile poverty they tell us nothing but lies. In the community where I live we spent more than twenty years asking for electricity and they never gave it to us...the Institutional Revolutionary Party maintained us with nothing but lies, and in addition it's not Catholic that's why there have been assassinations they killed the Cardinal such an important person. And even you...were a victim of bad government."[48]

Retablos express distrust of authorities by illustrating such injustices as false accusation, wrongful imprisonment, execution attempts, and forced

Saved from certain death by Soriano's Virgen de los Dolores.

conscription. A 1932 retablo shows soldiers leading a man to his execution by firing squad "for a crime falsely accused," but he commended himself to Soriano's Virgen de los Dolores and was saved. Another retablo offered to the same Virgin depicts soldiers' rifles aimed at a blindfolded, kneeling man facing certain death until likewise "a very great miracle" saved him. In a 1937 retablo to the Señor de la Misericordia an armed soldier stands beside a man hanging by the neck from a tree branch, and a 1944 retablo to the Virgen de Talpa has much the same scene together with a text giving thanks for miraculous survival of "being hanged by the Federales." All of these offerings and many others like them illustrate narrow escapes and, implicitly, the restoration of justice, but thanks are given only for the escape. The miracles occur and the retablos are produced within a context characterized by judicial inequity, arbitrary abuse by local officials, weak state control, clientalism, corruption, and votaries' political impotence. The recourse is to miracles, and "this is an entirely pragmatic approach, a practical resort to supernatural assistance when human agencies have failed."[49]

Word and Image

After smashing church images to prevent devotees from adoring them, a bishop received an admonishing letter from Pope Gregory. "You ought not to have broken these images. For pictorial representation is made use of in Churches for this reason; that such as are ignorant of letters may at least read by looking at the walls what they cannot read in books." "Images are books of the illiterate," John of Damascus wrote pursuant to these ideas. "What a book is to the literate, that an image is to the illiterate. The image speaks to the sight as words to the ear; it brings us understanding." The Church adopted this doctrine during the Synod of Arras in 1025—"illiterate men can contemplate in the lines of a picture what they cannot learn by means of the written word"—but the idea was expressed more eloquently in a pronouncement of the Synod of Constantinople in 869: "We prescribe that the icons of our Lord...are to be venerated and shown the same honor as is accorded to the Books of the Gospels. For just as all attain salvation through the letters of the Gospel, so likewise do all—the knowing and the ignorant—draw benefit from the pictorial effects of paint."[50]

Catholic churches later benefitted doubly by incorporating texts into narrative paintings. The paintings were often in series that related a chronological sequence of events. Those who could read enjoyed the mutual enrichment of the painting and text; those who could not read, or did not want to, nevertheless acquired a sense of the story through the paintings. At the Chalma and Remedios shrines, for example, such paintings made major contributions to the identity development of their respective miraculous images.[51]

The idea that "images are silent sermons" was developed in other ways during the evangelization of indigenous populations in colonial Mexico. The Franciscan Jacobo de Testera, who arrived in 1529, instructed the catechism by using paintings that an indigenous interpreter explained to neophytes. An engraving known as the "Allegorical Atrium" in Fray Diego de Valadés's *Rhetorica Christiana* (1579) shows a friar preaching to indigenous Mexicans while pointing to paintings that illustrate biblical scenes. In a passage accompanying the engraving, Valadés wrote: "Because the Indians lack letters, it was necessary to teach them by means of some illustrations; for this the preacher demonstrates the mysteries of our redemption with a pointer." In this audiovisual technique a lesson delivered verbally is illustrated and reinforced visually.[52]

Words and images were integrated more creatively in a pictographic writing system that was based on indigenous precedents and developed by converts. José de Acosta explains: "To signify the phrase, 'I, sinner, do confess,' they paint an Indian kneeling at the feet of a priest, as though confessing; and then for the phrase 'to God almighty' they paint three faces with crowns, to represent the Trinity; and for the glorious Virgin Mary they paint the face of Our Lady and a child at half length; and for St. Peter and St. Paul, two heads with crowns, and some keys and a sword, and in this way the whole confessional is written in pictures, and where images are lacking they put in words." Friars and indigenous converts also developed a rebus writing system that used pictures to represent Amerindian words or parts of words that resembled words in Catholic prayers. Through a double substitution, from word to word and then to image, Amerindian words were paired with Latin words and then visually represented. In learning the "Our Father" prayer, for example, the Latin *pater* was paired with *pautli*, which denotes a small flag. The next word in the prayer, *noster*, was paired with *nochtli*, which denotes a cactus fruit. "Pater Noster" (Our Father) was thus represented by drawings or paintings of a small flag followed by the catus fruit.[53]

All of these antecedents are suggestive in relation to the integration of text and image in retablos. Most immediately apparent is the double narration that retablos share with church paintings that combine visual and textual narrative. In their standard format retablos include a painted scene pertinent to a miracle, a representation of the miraculous image that intervened, and a subscript text. The double narration by text and image makes the story accessible to both literate and illiterate observers, but also provides for resonance and mutual reinforcement as the two media interact. The text generally expands and clarifies the visual narration, and often reveals the date and place (of the miracle or of the offering) and the identity of an otherwise anonymous votary. The text also adds a chronological orientation to the simultaneity of the visual representation. Some retablos accomplish this sense of temporal progression by representing two or more scenes that relate a story in installments. Before-and-after compositions often show the tragedy on one side—a train crash, a fall—and the kneeling survivor-votary giving thanks on the other.[54]

An 1884 split-scene retablo shows a miraculous image on the left and on the right two standing women, one holding a baby and the other holding a candle. The first sentence of the subscript clarifies the visual image by explaining that a mother had petitioned her daughter's safety after childbirth. The text then continues, however, to add information not represented visually: that the husband thought the child was not his, that the votary feared that her daughter and the child would be severely punished by the husband, and that St. Francis of Paola intervened so that the husband would accept the child as his own. The painted image gives the viewer a vague, nonnarrative suggestion, and the text relates the drama. Other retablo paintings give more information by depicting a car crash, assault, or sick person in bed, and then the text fills in the details. An 1862 retablo offered to the Señor del Convento shows the end of a story, and the subscript relates the events leading to this frozen moment. We see three men, one kneeling, in a forest setting, and beside them other men with guns. The text relates that two boys had been abducted from their homes by ten men. After leaving town the group divided, and four men took the boys into the forest. One of the boys was forced to his knees and was going to be shot, but when he commended himself to the Señor del Convento a leader of the gang had mercy and the boys were released.

Retablo texts, like the labels beside paintings in museums, offer information that can orient or clarify what we see in a painting. The visual imagery alone is often ambiguous and "a somewhat clumsy medium for telling stories," but the label explains and provides context that helps a viewer work through the ambiguity. The same is true of captions that orient our reading of a photograph, an advertisement, or a retablo. There is a chronology to the perception: we first look at the image and then enhance our understanding by appeal to the caption. Captions focus our attention and guide our perception, and they bias our reading when our original understanding of a picture does not conform to the caption's interpretation. In this respect the caption is similar to the friar who points with a stick and speaks for a mute painting. One might have thought something else looking at Adam and Eve eating apples, but the friar is an external narrator who guides interpretation to a restricted meaning. We tend to lend the caption more credit than it deserves and sometimes align our own view with the privileged and seemingly authoritative view published together with the picture. Some captions are enigmatic and disorient our reading or generate confusion because the text and image seem misaligned. These captions disturb an understanding rather than clarifying it, and they force the eye back and forth between text and image in an attempt to resolve the discrepancy.[55]

Dependence on captions is most conspicuous in interpreting "droodles," which are abstract line drawings that seem indecipherable until the caption offers an interpretation. Many retablos are likewise dependent on their subscripts for meaning. Votaries who commissioned retablos had the option of a customized painted scene relative to the miracle or a less expensive, standardized painting of a kneeling votary or votaries praying to a particular image. When the painting represents nothing but the votary at prayer, the viewer must resort to the text for an explanation. Many of these texts briefly convey health-related miracles, such as one granted to Feliciana in 1865. Feliciana was gravely ill with a fever and "finding no recourse in medicine invoked from the bottom of her heart the Señor de la Misericordia"; that is why we see her kneeling in gratitude.[56]

A retablo at the Soriano basilica shows only a woman and a girl praying to the Virgin de los Dolores, and the text relates a story that could not be inferred from the image alone. On October 8, 1908, the visually impaired Zeferino left home guided by his six-year-old-daughter. The two disappeared, the worried wife and mother petitioned help from the Virgin, and the retablo was offered in gratitude for the safe return of the husband and daughter two years after their departure. In a 1914 retablo to San Pascual, similarly, the painting shows only a woman sitting in a chair surrounded by a modest but pleasant room. The text explains that the votary, who was the cook at this residence for fifteen years, inherited the house unexpectedly when the homeowner died.

Retablos derive their meaning and even something of their beauty from an interactive relation between text and image. The effect is reminiscent of works by religious outsider artists like Sister Gertrude Morgan and Howard Finster, who integrate written messages into the tone and composition of their paintings. This is particularly apparent when retablo painters break out of the traditional format of subscript text and integrate words elsewhere in the composition. There are several of this type at the Remedios basilica. In all cases, when the text explains the picture and the picture illustrates the text, this repetition in two media generates a mutually enhancing echo effect. The redundancy clarifies and enriches, just as what we say orally is reinforced by our facial expressions and gestures. When I say "yes" and nod my head an interlocutor gets the message twice, and when I smile while doing so the verbal and visual messages gain emotive resonance and depth. Retablos are likewise enriched by a dynamic composite effect that is delivered, in this case, by an affective charge derived from sacred context, sympathetic viewers, and votive functions.

On occasion a retablo has no text, so that the content of the miracle must be inferred from the painting alone. Often the visual narrative is more or less apparent, because the painting shows a man run over by a car or a woman undergoing surgery. In other cases the ambiguity is greater, and sometimes, when a retablo without text represents nothing but a kneeling votary, the miracle remains undisclosed. Other retablos have texts that are spare and refer the viewer to the painting for details. One such self-referential retablo, offered to the Virgen de la Soledad in 1762, has text that reports a miracle and then concludes, "as is shown in this Painting." In another of the same type, dated 1901 and offered to the Señor de la Misericordia, the text refers the viewer to the painting for more information: "he was freed from the death with which he was threatened during the moments of his misfortune represented in this retablo." In a 1924 retablo offered to the Virgen de Soriano, the painting narrates the event—a near death by firing squad—and the text is limited to nonnarrative information, such as date and the votary's identity.[57]

An offering to the Señor de Villaseca alludes to a private disclosure that the votary plans as an addendum to his retablo, thereby incorporating an external discursive supplement by reference: "I come to ask your forgiveness and give you thanks verbally and tell you the reasons for this humble retablo." The retablo then advances a preview by integrating a fragment of explanatory text into the painting itself. We see miner's picks and a man sitting on a yellow block inscribed with the words "pure gold."[58]

The interaction of words and painting is also inherent to the creative process by which retablos and, ultimately, miracles are constructed. A subtle transition occurs when the miracle recipient commissions a votive painting, because a very personal experience begins its public career. The votary's oral narrative is predisposed by the shared certainty that miracles occur in everyday life, and it is structured by articulating the events to sympathetic interlocutors, including the painter. This emerging public version of the miracle is generated by the dynamic interactions of memory, miracle precedents, interlocutor expectations, and, to some degree, the votary's self-image management. The events are assimilated to the belief in miracles, and the verisimilitude of the story—its authenticity and historical truth—coalesces when the painter hears it and eventually represents it visually for offering at a shrine. The votary testifies to a miracle exempt from tests of truth, and this exemption obtains also for the painter, who shares the votary's religious culture, is accustomed to miracles, and is supported by painting them.

An oral narrative is the bridge between the experience itself and the imagination of the painter who will represent it visually. "I lost control of the car and thought for sure I was dead," the votary relates, and this story initiates the painter's creative transformation of the oral narrative into a visual narrative, composing a scene of the crash in his mind with the curve, the tree, the cliff in the near distance. The votary affirms that the miracle is attributable to a specific miraculous image, and the painter envisions the image's well-known iconography and incorporates it into the painting's composition. Everything is coming together. A crisis is transforming into a narrow escape and cause for gratitude. When the oral version is objectified in paint and displayed within the sacred confines of a shrine or basilica, the miracle happens, in effect, because it is represented.

As the oral narrative transitions to a visual narrative, the painter makes a remarkable addition by representing a miraculous image at the scene of the incident. The inclusion of the image in a retablo painting is necessary to demonstrate visually that a miracle was performed and by whom, because otherwise the painting would seem nothing more than a car crashing into a tree. By including a miraculous image in the composition, however, the painter also elevates an invisible and presumed intervention into what seems to be an apparition. There is a degree of intention to this representation, because a miraculous intervention could be explained in the text that accompanies the painting, although less dramatically. The visual narration of the on-scene miraculous image engages viewers sensuously and emotionally while reinforcing their beliefs in presence and patronage. Repetition of this motif in countless retablos reinforces the conviction that miraculous images intervene perceptibly in everyday life, that they live and act among their devotees. Apparitions are most explicit when painters depict a miraculous images looming in grand scale, rushing down from heaven, or otherwise bursting onto the scene to expedite an intervention.[59]

The creative process continues after completion and posting of a votive painting at a shrine, now in the imaginations of devotees. The painter's visual narrative and its textual subscript are translated back into verbal narratives as viewers relate the painted miracle stories mentally to themselves and orally to others. In the long view, a miracle begins with a votary's oral narration, is elaborated in a painted narrative accompanied by a textual narrative, and returns to orality as the story is disseminated within a devotional community. The miracle is consolidated in stages of elaboration that alternate between verbal and visual representations. These include the votary's perception of the event, narrative structuring of the memory, and description of the event to the painter; the painter's visual and textual representation not of an event but of an inferred miracle; the posting of the retablo in a sacred context; and the devotional community's reception of the retablo, which validates the miracle that at once validates their beliefs.

Chalma

The gray of the streets fuses with the gray of the sky and there you are on top of it, like a silhouette superimposed. Smog-grit gray, dirty pewter, the gray of sorrowful age. A dark moldish grime descending on the walls. The shrine has an inherent need for people, a crushing human presence to enliven its austerity, its bloody Christ suffering so silently. Stone stairways saturated with gravity, sculpted by heavy feet. Mute pews arrogantly solemn. You sense it from a distance and then, as you approach, a sourceless choral hymn draws you closer, exerts a pull into the church where dense human air is the backdrop for prayer, for the song of countless devotees along the walls and in the pews and crowded at the doors, some engaged, some sleeping, some coming and going or juggling crying babies or moving up the aisle on their knees past sleeping dogs, stretched out on the marble, not even twitching, while the priest drones on—*What is truth? God is truth. What is the source of truth? God is the source of truth.*

I liked hanging out in the atrium. It could make you feel as though your loneliness were populated. On quiet days you hear voices from the candle room; sometimes the organ resonates from the church; and the little waterfall in the river makes a peaceful white noise that bends off the walls and surrounds you. Pilgrims arrive in tired, excited groups behind standards and later lie down with their heads on their backpacks and drift into effortless sleep. It takes Fray David a while to pass them as he comes from the church hunched over, almost doubled, shrunken and walking with a cane. He is carrying a plastic bag and when he reaches the sun line on the stone pavers he pauses on the shadowed side, reaches into the bag, and in slow motion, patiently, crumbles a roll for converging doves. When someone passes the doves flutter enough for a reasonable pretense of self-preservation before returning to concentrated eating. Finally the bag is empty and Fray David pivots in an eternity of deliberate side steps and makes his way back toward the enormous doors where the shadow is deeper. Crowds yield for his passage like parting seas and at the threshold he disappears into a hymn that's just ending.

This must be what it feels like to be sitting here. People on benches who have a lot of time, who are not going anywhere, who are in the middle of their lives and their place, rooted, at home, firmly grounded in tradition, with the church—massive, impressive—as backdrop but somehow completely out of place. Business is slow and the photographers look at my camera and express approval reiterated with a pursed lip gesture and a nod. A pilgrim beside me catches a giant ant in a cup and releases it beside the core of a chewed apple—to see if it will eat? Eventually the ant walks away so he catches it again and puts it back beside the core, its proper place, then checks on it a few minutes later. The cup, abandoned, rolled a few feet for a breeze, retreated a half turn to recover equilibrium, and rolled again when the breeze resumed. Then it got crushed by a boy leaning into a run, steering himself with hands on an invisible wheel and making motor sounds and tire squeals on curves. That happened near the plastic, carousel-like horses that the photographers use for props. Sitting here could make you feel as though your loneliness were populated. Between one curve and the next the boy suddenly stopped, paused to process some momentary confusion, a fleeting uncertainty, and then leaned forward to resume his course past a short wide mother in braids.

The boyish puzzlement on his face linked in my mind to a similar expression that I had seen at the Zapopan basilica. It took me a moment to consolidate the association and I must have looked withdrawn while the visual data bridged a synapse to connect one boy with the other. It was a Sunday evening in the basilica's atrium. A crippled man was working his way breadthwise toward distant rest. The mass was filling, the bells were tolling, and people were crowding in and then around the main and lateral doors. Humid, human odors, dense, intermingled with deep, dirge-like singing for a composite, synesthetic suffocation. A lot of fanning with the Sunday bulletin. Outside the backlit clouds refracted sunlight into heavenly rays, like a bad painting of God the Father. Vendors were hawking, kids were running, pigeons were flying, kids were chasing pigeons flying, and some couples were looking at religious gifts at tables staffed by Franciscan brothers. Beggars were begging and people were ignoring, an instructor with a head mic was giving dance lessons—one, two, three—to girls in tight pants, and the still-man human statue surprised everyone suddenly with motion of inhuman liquidity. Then a storm blew in and everyone ran to the arcade for cover. There was a spectacular flash of polished color as vendors selling balloons and plastic things were caught in light rain before the downpour and converged at a trot toward the arches. A man with an official vest, "Basilica de la Virgen de Zapopan," directed the foot traffic.

That's when I saw the boy, confused, standing alone in the rain, like an image from a grainy and sorrowful film. Then, inexplicably, as though the idea had just occurred to him, he bolted and ran with something of the lanky awkwardness, the jerky starts and stops, of a calf on a farm somewhere.

Chalma has its own emporium that begins at the gates of the atrium and covers the hillside between the shrine and the town above. In Chalma, as at shrines throughout Mexico, a core of deeply pious devotees is ringed by bands of votaries motivated by tradition, occasion, or need; by religious tourists and locals on day outings; by faithless and slack Catholics who show up for fiestas; and, around all of that, in its own concentric circles, commerce. Stores, stands, and hawkers offer products at once widely varied and numbingly redundant. From the bus stop visitors descend through this labyrinthine, cavernous underworld covered with blue and yellow tarps that hold down an overload of sounds and colors and odors.

A fat guy with hair moosed up drinking a giant Michelada; a lady with purple stretch pants carrying a purple votive candle; a fallen rose crushed by shoes. People talking, babies crying, fish frying, pots boiling, and musics competing until one or the other finally capitulates and engages instead with the music on its other side. Carnitas, cajita, fruit, candy, plastic jewelry, religious paraphernalia in generous assortment, and most of all bodies, bodies of all ages and sizes pressed in and locking you into the exitless, anonymous swell of collective volition that carries you. Sometimes in the distance you hear trucks with loudspeakers selling everything from torti-llas to candidates, and the vowels are stretched—*riiiicas tortiiiiillas*—by voices seemingly born for that purpose.

I often repaired to the peaceful room beside the river where votaries display their offerings. You pass through the sacristy to get there and can feel the cold, Augustinian inhospitality that the room exudes despite the woodwork. There is an encased image of the infant Christ there, called Santo Niño del Consuelo, and mothers leave toy offerings in thanks for miracles or to commend their children to the image. Many of these toys are eventually distributed to children who attend catechism in the class-room across the river. Fray David said the Santo Niño is believed to cure rheumatism. "They can't touch the image, so they touch the glass."[1]

Once outside you cross a stone bridge beside huge trees and can see devotees wading among the rocks. Beyond them, like a storybook illustration too intentionally beautiful, are massive stone walls, white-trimmed windows, and red cupolas against mountains and the sky. The view is spectacular; a world apart from the grimy confusion in the atrium and emporium. Just down the hill, not far from the site where priests bless cars, votive offerings are displayed in a covered patio walled on three sides and enclosed at the front by a metal grate. A bench tiled in saltillo pavers runs along the length. Once I interviewed Fray David there and after a question he looked skyward with something like mystical confusion, as though God might give him the answer, and then said finally, "We have to respect the simple faith of the poor, because if we take that away they are left with almost nothing." Grounds workers sometimes lean a wheelbarrow against a wall and hang out in the shade with a stillness that contributes to the calm. They tell you stories and have cousins in North Carolina and want to know why you're here and what you're doing.

The offerings are cleared often, but nevertheless always illustrate in miniature the norms of votive practice nationally. Everything from old retablos to tiny document photos. A conglomeration, a palimpsested history of misfortunes with happy endings. There are milagritos, artworks, braids, casts, documents, rosaries, vow cards, votive texts, clothes, and crucified Christs against a more or less permanent backdrop of painted retablos, the oldest of which dates to 1895. On top of that antique retablo two votaries have handwritten in pen their respective (but not respectful) petitions. Some offerings are improvised on scraps of paper and others are thoughtfully conceived in content and composition. One can imagine a conscientious votary deciding on an

Fray David.

offering, acquiring the materials, creating a collage in loving gratitude, and protecting the glass frame on a bus or in pilgrimage over a mountain until finally mounting the offering on this wall, at a site carefully selected, because all of that matters. One mother hangs a framed photograph of her son four times before she is content with its placement. A blind woman offers a mila-grito of eyes; a young family prays before baby pajamas that the mother has inscribed; and feeble fingers struggle with the tiny pin that attaches a lock of hair to a wallcloth.

Votive offerings are also made in the caves on a hillside above the pil-grim dormitories. The principal cave, known as the Cave of the Apparition, was originally a site of devotion to an indigenous god. The Señor de Chalma appeared there miraculously in 1539, after the arrival of the Augustinians. As worded in an account written in 1810 by the prior of the Chalma mon-astery, "they found the sacred image of our sovereign redeemer Jesus Christ crucified, placed on the same altar where the detestable idol had been be-fore, now knocked down to the floor, reduced to fragments." The altar and floor of the cave were "carpeted in varied and exquisite flowers."[2]

Similar stories are told of other miraculous images that inspired instanta-neous conversion. In colonial Querétaro indigenous neophytes went to church by day and to their idols by night, until a priest placed the image of the Virgen del Pueblito at the entrance to the idols' shrine. "They encoun-tered the image of the Mother of God and upon seeing her were immobilized and stunned, and she worked in them, and then in all the others, a radical change: they abandoned idolatry and embraced the Christian religion."[3]

Devotion to the Señor de Chalma continued in the cave for over a cen-tury, until the last days of 1682, when the image was transferred to a chapel that gradually developed into the current shrine. The cave was rededicated to St. Michael the Archangel, and today his image presides behind a small granite altar. A chapel façade was added to the cave and Michael is repre-sented there too between the bell towers above the door. Statues of two as-cetic hermits, Bartolomé de Jesús María and St. Mary of Egypt, flank the altar inside. They seem at home among the dead and broken gods around them. The room feels something like an open wound petrified for pos-terity, with a faint dank chill, and you might expect more of an echo.[4]

Bartolomé was a mestizo curandero and eventually Augustinian lay brother who lived and died in the cave. His penitential identification with the Señor de Chalma, together with his miracles, levitations, control of nature, and charitable generosity, attracted indigenous pilgrims seeking remedies for their hardships and illnesses. By the time of Bartolomé's death in 1658 his fame for miracles—attributed to him, but associated with the Señor de Chalma—made the cave a principal pilgrimage site in New Spain. An early eighteenth-century work described Bartolomé as a "'Christian shaman' who had become a friar" and as such could "supplant the Indian witchcraft with his own form of 'magic.'" Devotion to the original, indigenous deity in the cave was transferred to the Señor de Chalma in part through Bartolomé's miracles and mediation.⁵

Mary of Egypt was born around 344 and was a popular saint in Europe throughout the middle ages. She left home at the age of twelve and was a prostitute for decades. On one occasion she joined a pilgrimage with the hope of seducing new customers, but when the group arrived at the door of the church a mysterious force repelled Mary and impeded her entry. Mary understood the message. She begged an image of the Virgin for forgiveness and made a petitionary promise: if her sins were forgiven and she were allowed to worship in the church, then she would live in chastity and renounce the world. The prayer was granted. Mary lived an ascetic life alone in the desert for forty-seven years.

Votive offerings in the apparition cave have a jarring, almost creepy effect, perhaps because they contrast so sharply with the rough brown walls behind them. One encounters suddenly a pink baby bonnet, a red necklace, an armless doll, a scapular beside a house milagrito. Photographs are propped on rocks or wedged face-out into crevices—a wedding couple, a cook in a restaurant kitchen, a blank stare for a document mugshot. The inhospitable background makes the faces seem islands of desperation and solitude, as though only a miracle could save them. There are bracelets, hair bands, straw crosses, candles, rosaries, graffiti, and many offerings representing commended children—baby shoes, bibs, bottles, pacifiers. Mothers also leave umbilical cord cuttings that they wrap in tissue and wedge into cracks in the walls. The boys who tend the cave pulled them out in remarkable quantities.

There are other, smaller caves along the same escarpment. One is used for storage of maintenance supplies (but has a small altar with votive graffiti) and others have offerings similar to those in the apparition cave. On a few rock faces votaries have drawn primitive outline sketches of houses, probably to represent petitions. Nearby a lime-green gown, perhaps from a wedding party, is tied to the giant exposed roots of a tree growing on the cliff above. Broken images are positioned in strange repose, lying among rocks and weeds or under niche-like overhangs blackened by smoke. A mangerless infant with a cracked head; a Man of Sorrows split lengthwise toward the beard. Such images are left in the caves, and in the principal votary room near the river too, to avoid the sacrilege of throwing them in the trash. Your priest-blessed ceramic Jesus fell on the floor—now what are you going to do? Devotees bring the broken images home, in effect, back to the shrine, where the images rest in peace.

Among Nahuas in preconquest Mexico trees were associated with femininity and birth, and some trees were represented as goddesses giving birth. Montezuma bald cypress trees (*ahuehuetes* in Mexican Spanish) were sacred and epitomized these maternal associations. Similar motifs are suggested in colonial Mexico (and in other world areas through separate traditions) by the many Virgins, such as the Virgen de Ocotlán in Tlaxcala, who appeared in or are associated with trees.[6]

Offerings are still made to a massive bald cypress on a pilgrim route to Chalma, in the town of Ahuehuete about five kilometers from the shrine. Originally the offerings were attached to the trunk; now, since the tree has been fenced to protect it, branches or the fence itself are used. Umbilical cuttings, protected in fabric or plastic bags and tied to branches, are a common offering. Sometimes a baby's hair is used instead. These offerings are means of commending a child to protective care but also of giving thanks for childbirth and petitioning continued procreation. The offerings are made to the tree, but there is a deep ambiguity—even a continuity—between the sacredness of the tree and of the Señor de Chalma connected to it by a river and pilgrim route.[7]

The ahuehuete near Chalma is especially sacred because a spring emerges among its roots, as though the tree itself were the source of the water. Pilgrims stop en route to Chalma to bathe or soak their feet; there are pools below the tree for this purpose. Pilgrims say that the water alleviates fatigue, and more generally that its curative properties wash away spiritual and corporal impurities, including illness. The water, like the tree, is also associated with fertility, which likewise motivates bathing.

The Chalma shrine itself, like many other devotional sites in Mexico (the Ocotlán basilica is again a good example), is closely associated with sacred water. Spring water from Ahuehuete flows with the river to and through the Chalma grounds, or at least people believe it does, and consequently bathing occurs in the river at Chalma for the same reasons that it does in the pools at Ahuehuete. One pilgrim said the purpose of bathing was to "wash away sins," and another said "it is important to bathe in this cold water to leave here all of my *males*," with that ambiguous word accommodating forms of negativity ranging from sin to disease. Parents visiting

Chalma with infants dip the children feet-first into the river. Some people fear that a dipping in the cold water will make the child sick, and others respond that on the contrary it makes the sick child well. Carlos was one of these dipped infants, lowered into the cold, heavy water with his fat little infant legs kicking, and his knowledge of that experience now as an adult underscores the impact and importance of the ritual.[8]

I met Sandy together with her son, daughter, and a group of about twenty-five pilgrims who had just arrived from Mexico City. The children have amazingly beautiful faces with warm eyes that exude something like serenity and kindness. Sandy is a US citizen, born in California to Mexican immigrant parents, and has the chronic autoimmune disease known as lupus. "It could get bad," she said in English, and it has no cure. "I came here for a miracle, because I have two small children, I want to see them grow up and everything so we came all the way from Mexico City, all the way walking." The trip lasted twenty-eight hours and "there's no food up there, there's no water, there's no restrooms. There's only mountains, and it's raining, up there it's so cold, we were wet, and in the night so we were like freezing to death up there." Freezing to death under plastic on a rocky barren slope ungodly and moonless but the suffering a prelude to hope. Sandy focused on the miracle she would request upon arrival but the pilgrimage itself was already a miracle. "I can't really walk, I can't do a lot of things, and since I came from over there with a lot of faith, I made it. Twenty-eight hours! I still can't believe it, you know? I have to drink medications so I can move, and then with the faith, I made it. All these people— with the faith, we made it."

Research Sites

Iglesia de Santiago Astata, Oaxaca
Iglesia Arcángel San Miguel, Jerécuaro, Guanajuato
Iglesia de San Andrés Teotilalpam, Oaxaca
Iglesia de San Pedro Teutila, Oaxaca
Parroquia del Divino Salvador y el ex-Convento Agustino de la Transfiguración, México
Parroquia Mayor de Santiago, Querétaro
San Miguel Arcángel, San Felipe Torres Mocha, Guanajuato
Santuari d'el Miracle, Cataluña, Spain
Santuari de Sant Ramon Nonat, Cataluña, Spain
Santuario della Madonna dei Bagni, Umbria, Italy
Santuario de Santiago Apóstol, Coroneo, Guanajuato
Santuario del Señor del Sacromonte, México
Santuario del Santo Toribio Romo, Jalisco
Santuario del Señor de Villaseca, Guanajuato
Santuario de la Virgen de Lourdes, Querétaro
Santuario de la Virgen de Schoenstatt, Querétaro
Templo de San Agustín, Querétaro
Templo de San Felipe Neri (aka La Profesa), México
Templo de San Hipólito y Santuario de San Judas Tadeo, México
Templo del Señor de Ojo Zarco, Morelos
Templo de San Francisco, Querétaro

MUSEUMS AND SPECIAL COLLECTIONS

Museu Frederic Marès, Barcelona
Museo Nacional de Arte, Mexico City
Museo del Virreinato, Tepozotlán
Museo Frida Kahlo, Mexico City
Museum of International Folk Art, Santa Fe
Museum of Spanish Colonial Art, Santa Fe
National Library of Medicine, Washington, DC
New Mexico State Records Center and Archives, Santa Fe
San Antonio Museum of Art, San Antonio
University of New Mexico Center for Southwest Research, Albuquerque
University Art Gallery, New Mexico State University, Las Cruces
Wellcome Collection, London

Notes

PREFACE

1. The first quoted passage is from Hans Belting, *Likeness and Presence: A History of the Image before the Era of Art*, tr. Edmund Jephcott (Chicago: University of Chicago Press, 1994) 416. The second quoted passage is from Don DeLillo, *Point Omega* (New York: Scribner, 2010) 9. See 8, "to be alive to what is happening in the smallest registers of motion," and emotion. I also learned what I could about tempo and texture from Damien Rice and the Tallis Scholars.

2. The first quoted passage is from David Gary Shaw, "Modernity Between Us and Them: The Place of Religion within History," *History and Theory* 45/4 (2006): 3. The second quoted passage is from Heinz Kohut, *The Search for the Self: Selected Writings of Heinz Kohut: 1978–1981*, vol. 4, ed. Paul H. Ornstein (Madison, CT: International Universities Press, 1991) 663 ("Letter to Senator J. W. Fulbright," April 16, 1980). See Brad S. Gregory, "The Other Confessional History: On Secular Bias in the Study of Religion," *History and Theory* 45/4 (2006): 136, where the foundational beliefs of modern scholarship "are by now so pervasive and so taken for granted that they are not even self-consciously regarded as beliefs at all. Rather, they are implicitly considered in academic discourse as true, neutral descriptions of the nature of reality." See also Tor Egil Førland "Acts Of God? Miracles and Scientific Explanation," *History and Theory* 47/4 (2008): 491.

3. The quoted passage is from Donald Tuzin, "Miraculous Voices: The Auditory Experience of Numinous Objects," *Current Anthropology* 25/5 (1984): 580.

4. See Caterina Pizzigoni, *The Life Within: Local Indigenous Society in Mexico's Toluca Valley, 1650–1800* (Redwood City, CA: Stanford University Press, 2012) 40, where colonial Nahuas adopt the Spanish term *santo* in reference to images.

5. Catholic Church, Code of Canon Law, Canon 1230: www.vatican.va/archive/ ENG1104/__P4J.HTM. See Congregación para el Culto Divino y la Disciplina de los Sacramentos, *Actas y documentos pontificios: directorio sobre la piedad popular y la liturgia* (Mexico City: San Pablo, 2002) 212.

SEÑOR DEL RAYO

1. Luz's reference to expense in relation to medical miracles is common in Mexico today and has a long history. The hemorrhaging woman in Mark 25–34 "had suffered greatly at the hands of many doctors and had spent all that she had" before she was cured by touching Jesus's cloak (Mark 5:26).

2. The quoted phrase is from Luis Castañeda Guzmán, "Breve historia de la imagen del 'Señor del Rayo' que se venera en la Santa Iglesia Catedral de Oaxaca," a photocopied pamphlet written in 1992 and acquired at the cathedral office.

3. See Gerald L. Clore, "Psychology and the Rationality of Emotion," *Modern Theology* 27/2 (2011): 331, where "actions are motivated by anticipated affect."

MIRACULOUS IMAGES

1. The Martin inscription is quoted in Sabine MacCormack, "Loca Sancta: The Organization of Sacred Topography in Late Antiquity," *The Blessings of Pilgrimage*, ed. Robert Ousterhout (Urbana: University of Illinois Press, 1990) 17. See Ernst Kitzinger, "The Cult of Images in the Age before Iconoclasm," *Dumbarton Oaks Papers* 8 (1954): 116, where "one can discern something of the roots of future image worship" in relic devotion; and Charles Barber, *Figure and Likeness: On the Limits of Representation in Byzantine Iconoclasm* (Princeton, NJ: Princeton University Press, 2002) 37, where "the icon was understood in terms prescribed by the cult of relics." See also Richard C. Trexler, "Florentine Religious Experience: The Sacred Image," *Studies in the Renaissance* 19 (1972): 9–10.

2. The quoted passage is from Patrick J. Geary, *Furta Sacra: Thefts of Relics in the Central Middle Ages* (Princeton, NJ: Princeton University Press, 1990) 118; see 34. See also MacCormack, "Loca Sancta," 7, where "The relic did not just represent the saint, to the faithful of the Middle Ages it *was* the saint"; Peter Brown, *The Cult of the Saints: Its Rise and Function in Latin Christianity* (Chicago: University of Chicago Press, 1981) 3, where "the saint in Heaven was believed to be 'present' at his tomb on earth"; and Hugo van der Velden, *The Donor's Image: Gerard Loyet and the Votive Portraits of Charles the Bold*, tr. Beverley Jackson (Turnhout, Belgium: Brepols, 2000) 199.

3. See Ralph Merrifield, *The Archaeology of Ritual and Magic* (New York: New Amsterdam, 1987) 93; van der Velden, *Donor's Image*, 199; Valerie I. J. Flint, *The Rise of Magic in Early Medieval Europe* (Oxford: Clarendon Press, 2001) 254; Amanda Porterfield, *Healing in the History of Christianity* (New York: Oxford University Press, 2005) 69; and R. W. Southern, *The Making of the Middle Ages* (New Haven, CT: Yale University Press, 1976) 254. By "syncretism" I refer not to a hierarchical arrangement in which an authentic original is bastardized by improper use, but rather to a process by which religion—like culture and language—is always evolving.

4. See Pamela Sheingorn, *The Book of Sainte Foy* (Philadelphia: University of Pennsylvania Press, 1995) 17 and 77–79; and Benedicta Ward, *Miracles and the Medieval Mind: Theory, Record and Event, 1000–1215* (Philadelphia: University of Pennsylvania Press, 1982) 37.

5. The quoted phrase is from Hans Belting, *Likeness and Presence: A History of the Image Before the Era of Art*, tr. Edmund Jephcott (Chicago: University of Chicago Press, 1994) 59. On "living painting" see 261 and Bissera V. Pentcheva, "The Performative Icon," *Art Bulletin* 88/4 (2006): 632. See also Kitzinger, "Cult," 101, 104, and 119; Moshe Halbertal and Avishai Margalit, *Idolatry*, tr. Naomi Goldblum (Cambridge, MA: Harvard University Press, 1992) 41–42; and van der Velden, "Donor's Image," 203.

6. The quoted passage is from Peter Brown, *Society and the Holy in Late Antiquity* (Berkeley: University of California Press, 1982) 279. See Peter Brown, "A Dark-Age Crisis: Aspects of the Iconoclastic Controversy," *English Historical Review* 88/346 (1973): 7; and Seventh Ecumenical Council, "Excursus on the Present Teaching of the Latin and Greek Churches on the Subject," *A Select Library of Nicene and Post-Nicene Fathers of the Christian Church*, Second Series, Volume 14, ed. Philip Schaff and Henry Wace (New York: Christian Literature Company, 1898) 553. See also Gary Vikan, *Sacred Images and Sacred Power in Byzantium* (Aldershot: Ashgate Publishing, 2003) 1; Pentcheva, "Performative Icon," 634–636; van der Velden, *Donor's Image*, 203; Bissera V. Pentcheva, *The Sensual Icon: Space, Ritual, and the Senses in Byzantium* (University Park: Pennsylvania State University Press, 2010) 43; and Joanna Tokarska-Bakir, "Why Is the Holy Image 'True'? The Ontological Concept of Truth as a Principle of Self-Authentication of Folk Devotional Effigies in the 18th and 19th Century," *Numen* 49/3 (2002): 262.

7. The first quoted passage is from a report in the *Libri Carolini* (circa 790) appended to Belting, *Likeness*, 534. The second quoted passage is from the thirteenth-century William of Auvergne, bishop of Paris, in Michael Camille, *The Gothic Idol: Ideology and Image-Making in Medieval Art* (Cambridge: Cambridge University Press, 1989) 207–208. The third quoted passage is from Epiphanius, a fourth-century Greek bishop, in Kitzinger, "Cult," 93; see 149. See also W. W. Meissner, *Psychoanalysis and Religious Experience* (New Haven, CT: Yale University Press, 1984) 181, where we are "incapable of maintaining a commitment to something so abstract as a religious belief system without some means of real—sensory, visual, or auditory—concretization."

8. The quoted passage is from the *Libri Carolini* appended to Belting, *Likeness*, 534. See Pentcheva, *Sensual Icon*, 44 and, regarding Byzantine iconoclasm, 55–65.

9. The first quoted passage is from St. John of Damascus, *On the Divine Images: Three Apologies Against Those Who Attack the Divine Images*, tr. David Anderson (Crestwood, NY: St. Vladimir's Seminary Press, 1980) 23; and the second is from St. John Damascene, *On Holy Images*, tr. Mary H. Allies (London: Thomas Baker, 1898) 23–24. See Alain Besançon, *The Forbidden Image: An Intellectual*

History of Iconoclasm, tr. Jane Marie Todd (Chicago: University of Chicago Press, 2000) 115; Pentcheva, *Sensual Icon*, 66–71; Jaroslav Pelikan, *Imago Dei: The Byzantine Apologia for Icons* (Princeton, NJ: Princeton University Press, 1990) 81; and Herbert L. Kessler, *Spiritual Seeing: Picturing God's Invisibility in Medieval Art* (Philadelphia: University of Pennsylvania Press, 2000) 35, where the Second Council of Nicea describes iconoclasm as "the worst of all heresies, the worst of all evils, because it subverts the incarnation of the Lord."

10. The first longer quoted passage is from Pelikan, *Imago Dei*, 82; see 81–83 and 176. See also Kessler, *Spiritual Seeing*, 196–197. The second is from St. John of Damascus, *On the Divine Images*, 80. In Hebrews 1:3, Christ is "the stamp of God's very being." See also Kitzinger, "Cult," 121 and 140–143; Andrew Louth, *St. John Damascene: Tradition and Originality in Byzantine Theology* (New York: Oxford University Press, 2002) 193–222; and Bissera V. Pentcheva, *Icons and Power: The Mother of God in Byzantium* (University Park: Pennsylvania University Press, 2006) 153.

11. The quoted passage is from St. John Damascene, *On Holy Images*, 92. See Belting, *Likeness*, 145.

12. The first quoted passage is from the resolutions of the Second Council of Nicea appended to Belting, *Likeness*, 506. The second quoted passage is from Norman P. Tanner, ed., *Decrees of the Ecumenical Councils*, volume 2 (London: Sheed and Ward and Washington, DC: Georgetown University Press, 1990) 775. For overviews of the councils, see Daniel J. Sahas, *Icon and Logos: Sources in Eighth-Century Iconoclasm* (Toronto: University of Toronto Press, 1986), 32–35 (Hiereia) and 36–44 (Nicea). The third quoted passage is from Congregación para el Culto Divino y la Disciplina de los Sacramentos, *Actas y documentos pontificios: directorio sobre la piedad popular y la liturgia* (Mexico City: San Pablo, 2002) 193. Lesson 15, paragraph 233 of the Baltimore Catechism similarly states, "We do not pray to the crucifix or to the images and relics of the saints, but to the persons they represent." See also Catholic Church, *Catechism of the Catholic Church* (New York: Doubleday, 1995), page 337, paragraph 1192.

13. Regarding survival as opposed to salvation, see Anna M. Fernández Poncela, "De la salvación a la sobrevivencia: la relgiosidad popular, devotos y comerciantes," *Dimensión antropológica* 13/36 (2006): 134, 136, 167, and 168; and Isabel Lagarriga Attias, "Participación religiosa: viejas y nuevas formas de reivindicación femenina en México," *Alteridades* 9/18 (1999): 72.

14. The first quoted passage is from St. John Damascene, *On Holy Images*, 92. See Belting, *Likeness*, 145, where John of Damascus is quoted and makes a distinction more explicit: "The image is a likeness that expresses the archetype in such a way that there is always a difference between the two." The second quoted passage is from St. John of Damascus, *On the Divine Images*, 36. The third quoted passages is from Congregación para el Culto Divino, *Actas y documentos*, 193. The other quoted passages are from Tanner, *Decrees*, 136. The text is also

appended to Belting, *Likeness*, 506. There is an alternate translation in "The Decree of the Holy, Great, Ecumenical Synod, The Second of Nice," Schaff and Wace, *A Select Library*, 550: "For the honour which is paid to the image passes on to that which the image represents, and he who reveres the image reveres in it the subject represented." In Besançon, *Forbidden Image*, 123, "For the honor shown to the icon reaches the prototype, and he who bows before the icon bows before the hypostasis of the one inscribed within it." See 132 for a related text from 843: "The honor and veneration directed toward the image rise to the prototype." Tokarska-Bakir, "Why," 261 notes that elsewhere in the decrees the council's argument carries a lingering implication that "sanctity amasses in images in its own mysterious ways."

15. See Congregación para el Culto Divino, *Actas y documentos*, 51–54 and 193. Thomas More (1478–1535), canonized in 1935, made an argument similar to Fray Hugo's; see van der Velden, *Donor's Image*, 208. See also David Morgan, "Aura and the Inversion of Marian Pilgrimage: Fatima and Her Statues," *Moved by Mary: The Power of Pilgrimage in the Modern World*, ed. Anna-Karina Hermkens, Willy Jansen, and Catrien Notermans (Farnham, U K: Ashgate, 2009) 57; David Freedberg, *The Power of Images: Studies in the History and Theory of Response* (Chicago: University of Chicago Press, 1989) 159–160; and Matthew of Janov, *Rules of the Old and New Testaments* (circa 1390), excerpt appended to Belting, *Likeness*, 539: "If all images are equal yet one is venerated more than others and attracts the people on the grounds of fanciful, unproven events," then "it should be removed as a vexation."

16. Regarding the stolen crown, see Everardo Ramírez Bohórquez, *Oaxaca en la Soledad* (Oaxaca: Carteles Editores, 2000) 18 and 35–38. See also Edward N. Wright-Rios, "Envisioning Mexico's Catholic Resurgence: The Virgin of Solitude and the Talking Christ of Tlacoxcalco 1908–1924," *Past & Present* 195 (207): 209–221.

17. Regarding Bustamante, see Alonso de Montúfar, *Información que el arzobispo de México Don Fray Alonso de Montúfar mandó practicar con motivo de un sermón: que en la fiesta de la Natividad de Nuestra Señora (8 de setiembre de 1556) predicó en la capilla de San José de Naturales del Convento de San Francisco de Méjico, el Provincial Fray Francisco de Bustamante acera de la devoción y culto de Nuestra Señora de Guadalupe* (Mexico City: Ireneo Paz, 1891) 1–3; and Robert Ricard, *The Spiritual Conquest of Mexico: An Essay on the Apostolate and the Evangelizing Methods of the Mendicant Orders in New Spain, 1523–1572*, tr. Lesley Byrd Simpson (Berkeley: University of California Press, 1974) 189–191. Bustamante also said that the Virgen de Guadalupe was painted by an Indian, whom he named, rather than having appeared miraculously on Juan Diego's tilma.

18. The quoted phrase is in Anna María Fernández Poncela, "El santo Niño de Atocha: origen, función y actualidad," *Cuicuilco* 10/27 (2003): 14. Regarding human attributes, see Alicia M. Barabas Reyna, "Los santuarios de vírgenes y

santos aparecidos en Oaxaca," *Cuicuilco* 13/36 (2006): 236; Alicia M. Barabas, "Etnoterritorios y rituales terapéuticos en Oaxaca," *Scripta Ethnologica* 24 (2002): 14; Alicia M. Barabas, *Dones, duenos y santos: ensayo sobre religiones en Oaxaca* (Mexico City: Instituto Nacional de Antropología e Historia, 2006) 228; William B. Taylor, *Shrines and Miraculous Images: Religious Life in Mexico before the Reform* (Albuquerque: University of New Mexico Press, 2010) 22, 29, and 31; and Ramiro Alfonso Gómez Arzapalo Dorantes, *Los santos, mudos predicadores de otra historia: la religiosidad popular en los pueblos de la región de Chalma* (Veracruz, Mexico: Editora de Gobierno del Estado de Veracruz, 2009) 205, 207, and 255. For human attributes in other regions and periods, see for example H.S. Versnel, "Religious Mentality in Ancient Prayer," *Faith, Hope, and Worship: Aspects of Religious Mentality in the Ancient World,"* ed. H. S. Versnel (Leiden: E. J. Brill, 1981) 38; Sylvia M. Schomburg-Scherff, "The Power of Images: New Approaches to the Anthropological Study of Images," *Anthropos* 95/1 (2000): 189–199; Fredrika H. Jacobs, *Votive Panels and Popular Piety in Early Modern Italy* (New York: Cambridge University Press, 2013) 116–117; Graham Harvey, *Animism: Respecting the Living World* (New York: Columbia University Press, 2006) 110 ("the agency and intentionality of human persons affects objects that are utilised culturally so that these objects become, in some sense, subjects") and 205; María Cruz de Carlos Varona "'Imágenes rescatadas' en la Europa moderna: el caso de Jesús de Medinaceli," *Journal of Spanish Cultural Studies* 12/3 (2011): 329; and Aron Gurevich, *Medieval Popular Culture: Problems of Belief and Perception*, tr. Jájnos M. Bak and Paula A. Hollingsworth (New York: Cambridge University Press, 1988) 49, where the saint "was clearly modelled on a human image and likeness, endowed with human emotions, passions, interests, and reactions."

19. Regarding guilt, see Peter Berger, *The Sacred Canopy: Elements of a Sociological Theory of Religion* (Garden City, NY: Doubleday and Company, 1967) 9.

20. See Nina P. Azari and Dieter Birnbacher, "The Role of Cognition and Feeling in Religious Experience," *Zygon* 39/4 (2004): 906–907, where "the perception of the inner and outer world is changed by emotion, so that the world is seen to mirror the emotional state of the subject even without his or her being aware of the emotion itself."

21. The first quoted passage is from James R. Averill, "Emotional Creativity: Toward 'Spiritualizing the Passions,'" *Handbook of Positive Psychology*, ed. C. R. Snyder and Shane J. Lopez (New York: Oxford University Press, 2002) 180. The other three quoted passages are from Fray Luis de Cisneros in Francisco de Florencia, *La milagrosa invención de un tesoro escondido en un campo que halló un venturoso cacique, y escondió en su casa, para gozarlo a sus solas : patente ya en el santuario de los remedios en su admirable imagen de ntra. señora; señalada en milagros; invoca por patrona de las lluvias, y temporales; defensora de los españoles, abogada de los indios, conquistadora de México, erario universal de las misericordias de Dios, ciudad de refugio para todos los que a ella se acogen. Noticias de su origen, y venidas a*

México; maravillas que ha obrado con los que la invocan; descripción de su casa, y meditaciones para sus novenas, ed. Teresa Matabuena Peláez and Marisela Rodríguez Lobato (Mexico City: Universidad Iberoamericana, 2008) 235, 235, and 236, respectively.

22. The quoted passages are from Francisco de Florencia, *Zodiaco mariano*, ed. Juan A. Oviedo, intro. Antonio Rubial García (Mexico City: Consejo Nacional para la Cultura y las Artes, 1995) 194–195. Prayers to the Virgen del Pueblito make reference to her vitality; see Eulalio Hernández Rivera, *Catecismo de la advocación mariana Nuestra Señora del Pueblito* (El Pueblito, Querétaro: Impresos Azteca, 2009) 36. See also 19 regarding veneration of images.

23. The quoted passage is from Gómez Arzapalo Dorantes, *Los Santos*, 181; see 179–181.

24. María del Pilar Iracheta Cenecorta, "El Santuario de Tonatico," *Estudios Del Hombre* 25 (2006): 20–21.

25. Regarding candlelight in other regions and periods, see for example Pentcheva, "Performative Icon," 631 and 639–40; and Paul Davies, "The Lighting of Pilgrimage Shrines in Renaissance Italy," *The Miraculous Image in the Late Middle Ages and Renaissance*, ed. Erik Thunø and Gerhard Wolf (Rome: "L'erma" di Bretschneider, 2004) 79.

26. Mario Alberto Nájera Espinoza, *La Virgen de Talpa* (Zamora, Michoacán: El Colegio de Michoacán and Colotlán, Jalisco: Universidad de Guadalajara, Centro Universitario del Norte, 2003) 46–47 and 170; Ricardo Avila and Martín Tena, "Morir peregrinando a Talpa," *Estudios Del Hombre* 25 (2006): 232; Manuel Carrillo Dueñas, *Historia de Nuestra Señora del Rosario de Talpa* (Talpa de Allende: [n. p.], 1962) 80–85; Andrés Estrada Jasso, *Imagenes en caña de maíz: estudio, catálogo y bibliografía* (San Luis Potosí, Mexico: Universidad Autónoma de San Luis Potosí, 1996) 110 and the catalog entries on 95–138; Anna María Fernández Poncela, "La Virgen de Talpa: religiosidad, turismo y sociedad," *Política y Cultura* 38 (2012): 35; and Roberto G. Cruz Floriano, "Cornstalk Paste: Pasta de Caña de Maíz," *Saints and Sinners: Mexican Devotional Art*, ed. James Caswell and Jenise Amanda Ramos (Atglen, PA: Schiffer Publishing, 2006) 191–192.

27. The quoted passages are from Alonso A. Velasco, *Exaltación de la divina misericordia en la milagrosa renovación de la soberana imagen de Christo Señor Nuestro Crucificado* (Mexico City: Oficina de Don Mariano de Zuñiga y Ontiveros, 1807) 3–4, 7–8, 11, and 14.

28. Regarding images that chose their sites, see Barabas, *Dones*, 206; Barabas Reyna, "Los santuarios," 234–236, 244–245, 248, 251; Gómez Arzapalo Dorantes, "Imágenes," 287; María J. Rodríguez–Shadow and Robert D. Shadow, *El pueblo del Señor: las fiestas y peregrinaciones de Chalma* (Toluca: Universidad Autonoma del Estado de Mexico, 2000) 177; Edward W. Osowski, *Indigenous Miracles: Nahua Authority in Colonial Mexico* (Tucson: University of Arizona Press, 2010)

52–53; and José Luis Noria Sánchez, "El Santuario de Juquila y los usos ideológi-
cos," *Caminos terrestres al cielo: contribución al estudio del fenómeno romero*, ed.
Beatriz Barba de Piña Chan (Mexico City: Instituto Nacional de Antropología e
Historia, 1998) 105. Regarding the Virgen de la Soledad see Ramírez Bohórquez,
Oaxaca, 7–8. For other examples of images becoming too heavy to move, see
Barabas, *Dones*, 86 and 196; and Gilberto Giménez, *Cultural popular y religión en
el Anahuac* (Mexico City: Centro de Estudios Ecuménicos, 1978) 148, where local
patron-saint images taken in pilgrimage to Chalma become heavy because they
do not want to return home. For relics that become too heavy to move in medi-
eval devotions, see Jacobus de Voragine, *The Golden Legend: Readings on the
Saints*, tr. William Granger Ryan (Princeton, NJ: Princeton University Press,
1993) 1/242 and 2/138; Patrick J. Geary, *Living with the Dead in the Middle Ages*
(Ithaca, NY: Cornell University Press, 1994) 172–173; and Gregory of Tours,
Glory of the Martyrs, tr. Raymond Van Dam (Liverpool: Liverpool University
Press, 1988) 79.

29. See Iracheta Cenecorta, "El Santuario de Tonatico," 18, n. 4.

30. See Gonzalo Aguirre Beltrán, *Pobladores del Papaloapan: biografía de una hoya*
(Mexico City: Centro de Investigaciones y Estudios Superiores en Antropología
Social, 1992) 161–162; and Genny M. Negroe Sierra, "Iglesia y control social en
Yucatán. Culto al Cristo de las Ampollas," *Temas Antropológicos*, 21/1 (1999):
5–35.

31. Regarding the Otomíes, see James W. Dow, *Santos y supervivencias: funciones de
la religión en una comunidad otomí* (Mexico City: Instituto Nacional Indigenista
and Secretaría de Educación Pública, 1974) 95. For a similar example from another period and region, see Gary Vikan, *Early Byzantine Pilgrimage Art, Revised
Edition* (Washington, DC: Dumbarton Oaks Byzantine Collection Publications,
2010) 76, where a saint tells a devotee to "come to his house." The Señor de
Carácuaro passage is quoted in Susana Carro-Ripalda, "El Señor de Carácuaro:
una etnografía fenomenológica de una peregrinación en México," *Guaraguao*
5/13 (2001): 31. See also Leila Scannell and Robert Gifford, "Comparing the
Theories of Interpersonal and Place Attachment," *Place Attachment: Advances in
Theory, Methods and Applications*, ed. Lynne C. Manzo and Patrick Devine-Wright
(New York: Routledge, 2014) 22.

32. The quoted passages regarding the colonial Nahuas are from Caterina Pizzigoni,
The Life Within: Local Indigenous Society in Mexico's Toluca Valley, 1650–1800
(Redwood City, CA: Stanford University Press, 2012) 29. See 40, 45, and 171–177.
See also Stephanie Wood, "Christian Images in Nahua Testaments of Late
Colonial Toluca," *The Americas* 47/3 (1991): 280; Rodrigo Martínez Baracs, *La
secuencia tlaxcalteca: orígenes del culto a Nuestra Señora de Ocotlán* (Mexico City:
Instituto Nacional de Antropologia e Historia, 2000) 190; and James Lockhart,
*The Nahuas after the Conquest: A Social and Cultural History of the Indians of
Central Mexico, Sixteenth through Eighteenth Centuries* (Redwood City, CA:

Stanford University Press, 1992) 237, where "saints were imagined as the parents of their people and as the true owners of the unit's land." The Chatino quoted passage is from James B. Greenberg, *Santiago's Sword: Chatino Peasant Religion and Economics* (Berkeley: University of California Press, 1981) 87. See George M. Foster, *Tzintzuntzan: Mexican Peasants in a Changing World* (New York: Elsevier-New York, 1979) 238; and Manuel M. Marzal, *Tierra encantada: tratado de antropología religiosa en América Latina* (Lima: Editorial Trotta, 2002) 375. Regarding identity as social persons, see Michael Lambek, "Spirit Possession/Spirit Succession: Aspects of Social Continuity among Malagasy Speakers in Mayotte," *American Ethnologist* 15/4 (1988): 724; and Michael Lambek, "Spirits and Spouses: Possession as a System of Communication among the Malagasy Speakers of Mayotte," *American Ethnologist* 7/2 (1980): 319. For personal relationships in Protestant devotions, see T. M. Luhrmann, "A Hyperreal God and Modern Belief: Toward an Anthropological Theory of Mind," *Current Anthropology*, 53/4 (2012): 372, where "God is undeniably real and actively involved in their daily lives. He is alive for them in a quite literal way"; and 378, where "God is deliberately presented as real like a person." See also Helen K. Black, "Poverty and Prayer: Spiritual Narratives of Elderly African-American Women," *Review of Religious Research* 40/4 (1999): 363–364, where these women's "interaction with God is personal, concrete and this-worldly. They are able to talk to God about any major or minor matter in their lives, and in some cases named God as 'the person closest to me.'"

33. Quoted in the shrine publication *Santa Maria de El Pueblito*, 12 (2007): 16.
34. See for example Barabas, *Dones*, 85, where the Señor del Rayo "is the brother of the Christ of Otatitlán." See also Barabas Reyna, "Los santuarios," 228. Other relations are in Gómez Arzapalo Dorantes, *Los Santos*, 12, 205, and 226. The Virgin sisters are from Avila and Tena, "Morir peregrinando," 233, n. 3. The Catemaco example is from Guadalupe Vargas Montero, "El santuario del Cristo Negro de Otatitlán: los peregrinos de oriente y sus líderes espirituales," *Sotavento* 2/3 (1997): 143. See also Ricardo F. Macip, "Creación de espacios y paisaje sagrado en una peregrinación campesina a Chalma," *Caminos terrestres*, 77, where pilgrims to Chalma from San Juan Tetla ask local saints for permission before departing. Regarding images visiting one another, see Gómez Arzapalo Dorantes, *Los Santos*, 11, 28, and 39–40; and Giménez, *Cultural popular*, 147.
35. The quoted passage is from Alfred Gell, *Art and Agency: An Anthropological Theory* (Oxford: Clarendon Press, 1998) 5; see 12. See also Robert Maniura, "Ex Votos, Art and Pious Performance," *Oxford Art Journal* 32/3 (2009): 411, where fifteenth-century images were "fully integrated into the practices of daily life and mobilised in strategies of social interaction" and "constitutive of social relationships"; and Kenneth I. Pargament, David S. Ensing, Kathryn Falgout, Hannah Olsen, Barbara Reilly, Kimberly Van Haitsma, Richard Warren, "God help me: (1): Religious Coping Efforts as Predictors of the Outcomes to Significant Negative

Life Events," *Spiritual Needs and Pastoral Services: Readings in Research*, ed. Larry VandeCreek (Decatur, GA: Journal of Pastoral Care Publications, 1995) 102, where "God can be viewed as another member of a social network." Related observations are in Janice Brody, "Spirit Possession Revisited: Beyond Instrumentality," *Annual Review of Anthropology* 23 (1994): 413; Ewa Domanska, "The Material Presence of the Past," *History and Theory*, 45/3 (2006): 339; Gómez Arzapalo Dorantes, *Los Santos*, 12 and 207; Fernández Poncela, "De la salvación," 135; Jorge A. González, "Exvotos y retablitos: religión popular y comunicación social en México," *Estudios sobre las culturas contemporáneas* 1/1 (1986): 39; and Ian Hodder, *Entangled: An Archaeology of the Relationships between Humans and Things* (Oxford: Wiley-Blackwell, 2012) 33–38.

36. Quoted in Carro-Ripalda, "El Señor de Carácuaro," 46.

37. See F. T. Van Straten, "Gifts for the Gods," *Faith, Hope, and Worship: Aspects of Religious Mentality in the Ancient World*, ed. H. S. Versnel (Leiden: E. J. Brill, 1981) 151, where a woman going blind begins by "offering silver eyes, then insisting with gold ones."

38. The first quoted passage is from St. John Damascene, *On Holy Images*, 35; the second is from Trexler, "Florentine," 24; and the third is from Mireille Holsbeke, "The Object as Mediator," *The Object as Mediator: On the Transcendental Meaning of Art in Traditional Cultures*, ed. Mireille Holsbeke (Antwerp: Ethnografisch Museum Antwerp, 1996) 15–16.

39. See Trexler, "Florentine,"17, where "popular devotion and divine response were not only consecutive realities, cause and effect. Both were considered effects of the power of the image."

40. The quoted passages are from Dow, *Santos*, 104. The same is true in other regions and periods: In Kitzinger, "Cult," 146: "While some writers think in terms of divine substance, force or energy flowing from prototype to image, others go further and stipulate actual residence of the former in the latter." See 148. See also David Freedberg, "The Structure of Byzantine and European Iconoclasm," *Iconoclasm*, ed. Anthony Bryer and Judith Herrin (Birmingham: University of Birmingham, 1977) 167; and Justin L. Barrett and Frank C. Keil, "Conceptualizing A Nonnatural Entity: Anthropomorphism in God Concepts," *Cognitive Psychology* 31/3 (1996): 240–244.

41. The quoted passage is from a retablo text in Carlos Monsiváis and Elin Luque Agraz, *Los relatos pintados: la otra historia, exvotos mexicanos* (Mexico City: Centro de Cultura Casa Lamm, 2010) 157; see 110 and 117. For examples and comments related to those in this paragraph, see Gell, *Art and Agency*, 5, 7, 12, and 17–19; *Congregación para el Culto Divino*, 51 and 193–194; Mireille Holsbeke, "Introduction," *Object as Mediator*, 8 and 15; and Lockhart, *Nahuas*, 238, where the spiritual being and the tangible form of home images were "fully integrated." Biblical passages related to the Colossians quotation in the text include, "the Father who dwells in me is doing his works" (John 14:9–10); and "The Father and I are one" (John 10:30).

42. The quoted passages are from Francisco de Florencia, *Origen de los dos célebres santuarios de la Nueva Galicia, obispado de Guadalaxara, en la América septentrional* (Zapopan, Mexico: Amate Editorial, 2001) 150, 4, and 150, respectively.

43. The last quoted passage is from Hebrews 9:11, Amplified Bible. Regarding images not made by hands, see for example Kitzinger, "Cult," 101 and 113; Kessler, "Spiritual Seeing," 11–15 and 70–87; and Vikan, "Early Byzantine," 79–82. For a fifteenth-century example, see Megan Holmes, "The Elusive Origins of the Cult of the Annunziata in Florence," *Miraculous Image in the Late Middle Ages and Renaissance*, 97–102. See also, in the same collection, Barbara Wisch, "Keys to Success: Propriety and Promotion of Miraculous Images by Roman Confraternities," 163.

44. The first quoted passage is from Gilbert Dagron, "Holy Images and Likeness," *Dumbarton Oaks Papers* 45 (1991): 23. See Kitzinger, "Cult," 150; and Dow, *Santos*, 104, where God guides the sculptor's hand. The second quoted passage is from Scott Atran, *In Gods We Trust: The Evolutionary Landscape of Religion* (New York: Oxford University Press, 2002) 267.

45. The quoted passage on the procession is from Voragine, *Golden Legend*, 1/174. Regarding Luke, see Belting, *Likeness*, 57–59; Pentcheva, *Icons and Power*, 124–127; Robert Maniura, *Pilgrimage to Images in the Fifteenth Century: The Origins of the Cult of Our Lady of Częstochowa* (Woodbridge, UK: Boydell Press, 2004) 56–68; Pelikan, *Imago Dei*, 124–127, and 89, where a detail from *Saint Luke with Scenes from His Life*, circa 1672, depicts Luke the painter at work. The Spanish Virgen de Guadalupe, among other images, is said to have been made by Luke.

46. The quoted passage is from Joaquín Sardo, *Relación histórica y moral de la portentosa imagen de N. Sr. Jesucristo Crucificado aprecido en una de las cuevas de S. Miguel de Chalma*, facsimile of the 1810 edition (Mexico City: Biblioteca Enciclopédica del Estado de México, 1979) 46–47. Regarding the Virgen de Guadalupe not made by hands, see Víctor Campa Mendoza, *Santuarios y milagros* (Mexico City: Consejo Nacional de Ciencia y Technología, 2002) 170–206. The painting *El padre eterno pintando a la Virgen de Guadalupe* is reproduced in Jaime Cuadriello, Carmen M. R. Galván, and Beatriz B. L. Mariscal, *La Reina de las Américas: Works of Art from the Museum of the Basílica de Guadalupe* (Chicago: Mexican Fine Arts Center Museum, 1996) figure 41. There is a similar painting in Granada, Spain: *El padre eterno pintando a la Inmaculada Concepción*. For discussion see José María Torres-Pérez, "El padre eterno pintando a la Inmaculada Concepción. Una iconografía poco difundida," *V Simposio Bíblico Español, La Biblia en el arte y en la literatura*, vol. 2 (Valencia-Pamplona: Fundación Bíblica Española: Universidad de Navarra, 1999) 539–551; the image is reproduced on 550. For seventeenth-century texts regarding God painting the Virgin Mary, see 541–545. See also Victor I. Stoichita, "Image and Apparition: Spanish Painting of the Golden Age and New World Popular Devotion," *Res: Anthropology and*

Aesthetics 26 (1994): 33, where God is again the painter of the Virgin of the Immaculate Conception.

Supernatural origin enhances perceptions of miraculous power, but human-made, mass-produced, plastic, and plaster imagery also rise to the occasion.

47. The first quoted passage is from St. John of Damascus, *On the Divine Images*, 67. See Dow, *Santos*, 114, where images are "the focal point of the vital forces" of a figure in heaven. Regarding Teofilio, see the video *Señor de Otatitlán*, posted by Juan Francisco Urrusti, from the series "Los caminos de lo sagrado," produced by the Consejo Nacional para la Cultura y las Artes (Conaculta): https://vimeo .com/79940049.

48. The last quoted passage is in Ward, *Miracles*, 104. See St. Thomas Aquinas, *Summa Theologica*, First Part, Question 8, part 3, where "God is everywhere by essence, presence and power." See also Kenneth I. Pargament, Gina M. Magyar-Russell, and Nichole A. Murray-Swank, "The Sacred and the Search for Significance: Religion as a Unique Process," *Journal of Social Issues* 61/4 (2005): 671, where "virtually any object can be perceived as sacred"; and Richard C. Trexler, "Being and Non-Being: Parameters of the Miraculous in the Traditional Religious Image," *The Miraculous Image in the Late Middle Ages and Renaissance* 15, where "the miraculous resides only in the temporally and spatially limited imaginations and manipulations of certain persons, societies and cultures" and "these images return just as quickly to a profane or non-active state."

49. The first quoted passage is from Francisco Miranda, *La Virgen de los Remedios: origen y desarrollo de un culto, 1521–1684* (Zamorra, Michoacán: Morevallado Editores, 2009) 222.

50. I am adapting a more general observation from Richard A. Shweder, "Cultural Psychology—What is it?" *Cultural Psychology: Essays on Comparative Human Development*, ed. James W. Stigler, Richard A. Shweder, and Gilbert Herdt (Cambridge: Cambridge University Press, 1990) 2.

51. See Berger, *Sacred Canopy*, 3–4, where the three stages are called externalization, objectivation, and internalization. See also Gell, *Art and Agency*, 7; and Jerome S. Bruner, *On Knowing: Essays for the Left Hand* (Cambridge: The Belknap Press of Harvard University Press, 1962) 25–26, where objects invested with projected thoughts act independently.

52. See Peter L. Berger and Thomas Luckmann, *The Social Construction of Reality: A Treatise in the Sociology of Knowledge* (New York: Doubleday, 1966) 21, 57, 82, 96; Berger, *Sacred Canopy*, 4, 9 and 19–29; Peter Berger and Stanley Pullberg, "Reification and the Sociological Critique of Consciousness," *History and Theory* 4/2 (1965): 200, 204, and 208.

53. In the first sentence I follow Berger, *Sacred Canopy*, 4 and the preface to Stigler, Shweder, and Herdt, *Cultural Psychology*, vii. In the rest of the paragraph I follow W. W. Meissner, *Psychoanalysis*, 181–182 (the first quoted passage is on 181); and James W. Jones, *Contemporary Psychoanalysis and Religion: Transference and*

Transcendence (New Haven, CT: Yale University Press, 1991) 44–46. On 40, a miraculous image (for our purposes) "belongs neither to the individual's private world nor to the surrounding religious environment but is rather a synthesis of the two." See also D. W. Winnicott, *Playing and Reality* (New York: Basic Books, 1971) 2; and Serge Viderman, "The Subject-Object Relation and the Problem of Desire," *Psychoanalysis in France*, ed. Serge Lebovici and Daniel Widlöcher (Madison, CT: International Universities Press, 1980) 186–187, where he discusses "two essential modalities: as a reality belonging to the world of things, and as a purely inner reality projected by the subject." On 185, the subject "has taken form in a constituent relationship with the object: the latter is part of the subject himself." The second quoted passage is from Ryan LaMothe, "Sacred Objects as Vital Objects: Transitional Objects Reconsidered," *Journal of Psychology & Theology* 26/2 (1998): 161; I am adapting his more general observation. See 162, where "transitional objects facilitate the joining of a subjective and intersubjective sense of identity, continuity, and cohesion." See also Thomas H. Ogden, "On Potential Space," *Tactics and Techniques in Psychoanalytic Therapy, Volume 3, The Implications of Winnicott's Contributions*, ed. Peter J. Giovacchini (Northvale, NJ: Jason Aronson, 1990) 90.

54. The first quoted passage is from Daniel T. Gilbert, Ryan P. Brown, Elizabeth C. Pinel, Timothy D. Wilson, "The Illusion of External Agency," *Journal of Personality and Social Psychology* 79/5 (2000): 699. The second quoted passage is from Meissner, *Psychoanalysis*, 171. See LaMothe, "Sacred Objects," 162, where for Winnicott "transitional objects are precursors of the capacity for symbolization." See also Stephen Gudeman, "Saints, Symbols, and Ceremonies," *American Ethnologist* 3/4 (1976): 709. Regarding objectified intentions, see Mihaly Csikszentmihalyi and Eugene Rochberg-Halton, *The Meaning of Things: Domestic Symbols and the Self* (New York: Cambridge University Press, 1981) 91.

55. The quoted phrase is from Megan Holmes, "Miraculous Images in Renaissance Florence," *Art History* 34/3 (2011): 438. See Csikszentmihalyi and Rochberg-Halton, *Meaning*, 91, where dolls expect to be nurtured and children respond accordingly. Augustine wrote that pagan idolatry occurs principally when "a form resembling that of a living person . . . seems to demand worship" because it is "powerfully persuasive to the emotions." Boniface Ramsey, ed., *The Works of Saint Augustine*, vol. 3/19, *Exposition on the Psalms*, tr. Maria Boulding (Hyde Park, NY: New City Press, 2003) 316. See 315–316: "Does anyone worship or pray with his eyes fixed on the image, without being persuaded that the image is hearing his petition and without hoping that it will give him what he wants? Probably not."

56. The quoted phrases is from Jones, *Contemporary Psychoanalysis*, 65. See Humberto Nagera, "The Imaginary Companion: Its Significance for Ego Development and Conflict Solution," *The Psychoanalytic Study of the Child*, volume 24, ed. Ruth S. Eissler, Anna Freud, Heinz Hartmann, Marianne Kris, and Seymour

L. Lustman (New York: International Universities Press, 1969) 195; and Sandra L. Murray, John G. Holmes, and Dale W. Griffin, "The Benefits of Positive Illusions: Idealization and the Construction of Satisfaction in Close Relationships," *Journal of Personality and Social Psychology* 70/1 (1996): 79, where "people immersed in the experience of romantic love often appear to bend reality to the will of their hopes and desires." See also 81.

57. The first two quoted phrases are from Heinz Kohut, *The Search for the Self: Selected Writings of Heinz Kohut: 1978–1981*, vol. 4, ed. Paul H. Ornstein (Madison, CT: International Universities Press 199) 455. The quoted full sentence is on 670; see 671. See also Chris R. Schlauch, "Neglected Questions at the Interface of Psychology and Religion," *Pastoral Psychology* 47/3 (1999): 221; and Charles B. Strozier, "Kohut and God," *Creative Dissent: Psychoanalysis in Evolution*, ed. Alan Roland, Barry Ulanov, and Claude Barbre (Westport, CT: Praeger, 2003) 247. The last quoted passage is from Sigmund Freud, *Civilization and its Discontents, Standard Edition of the Complete Psychological Works of Sigmund Freud*, ed. James Strachey, Vol. 21 (London: Hogarth Press and the Institute of Psycho-Analysis, 1961) 79. In *The Future of an Illusion* in the same volume, Freud's classification of religion as an illusion has little to do with truth or falsity: "An illusion is not the same thing as an error; nor is it necessarily an error" (29), but rather "what is characteristic of illusions is that they are derived from human wishes" (30). Projection as I am describing it is similar to projective identification, but without the aggression associated with that term. See Ogden, "On Potential Space," 107, where "projective identification...is a coercive enlistment of another person to perform a role in the projector's externalized unconscious fantasy." See also Thomas H. Ogden, "On Projective Identification," *International Journal of Psycho-Analysis* 60 (1979) 358: "first, there is the fantasy of projecting a part of oneself into another person and of that part taking over the person from within; then there is pressure exerted via the interpersonal interaction such that the 're-cipient' of the projection experiences pressure to think, feel, and behave in a manner congruent with the projection; finally, the projected feelings, after being 'psychologically processed' by the recipient, are reinternalized by the projector."

58. The quoted passage is from Belting, *Likeness*, 42. See Menachem Brinker, "Aesthetic Illusion," *The Journal of Aesthetics and Art Criticism*, 36/2 (1977): 194, where "the phrase 'aesthetic illusion' denotes...a situation of psychological concentration on the art-engendered imaginary object which makes the viewer behave in a manner which is reminiscent...of the behavior toward real objects." See also Eddy M. Zemach, "Emotion and Fictional Beings," *Journal of Aesthetics and Art Criticism* 54/1 (1996): 47; Juliet Koss, "On the Limits of Empathy," *Art Bulletin* 88/1 (2006): 139–141; Ludger Schwarte, "Intuition and Imagination: How to See Something that Is Not There," *Dynamics and Performativity of Imagination: The Image between the Visible and the Invisible*, ed. Bernd Huppauf and Christopher Wulf (New York: Routledge, 2009) 74; Robert L. Solso, *Cognition*

and the Visual Arts (Cambridge, MA: MIT Press, 1994) 4; David Morgan, *The Embodied Eye: Religious Visual Culture and the Social Life of Feeling* (Berkeley: University of California Press, 2012) 73, where the "reciprocal gaze" is a "two-way iconic colloquy" between devotees and images; and Jean-Paul Sartre, *The Psychology of the Imagination* (New York: Routledge, 2002) 160, where "each affective quality is so deeply incorporated in the object [miraculous image, for our purposes] that it is impossible to distinguish between what is felt and what is perceived." St. John Damascene, *On Holy Images*, 153, wrote, "Blessed are they who see with spiritual eyes."

59. With the first quoted passage I am adapting the definition of an artifact in Michael Cole, *Cultural Psychology: A Once and Future Discipline* (Cambridge, MA: Belknap Press, 2000) 117; the second quoted passage is on 118; see 120. See also Marx W. Wartofsky, *Models: Representation and the Scientific Understanding* (Dordrecht, Holland: D. Reidel, 1979) 204. In Berger, "Sacred Canopy," 4, objectivation is when products confront their producers "as a facticity external to and other than themselves." See Berger and Pullberg, "Reification," 199.

60. The first quoted passage is from Gerald L. Clore, "Psychology and the Rationality of Emotion," *Modern Theology* 27/2 (2011): 325. See 333 and 336; on the latter, emotions motivate thought and "emotions are cognitively-shaped affective reactions." The second quoted phrase is from Richard S. Lazarus, *Emotion and Adaptation* (New York: Oxford University Press, 1991) 173; see 127–129. See also Richard S. Lazarus, "Cognitive and Coping Processes in Emotion," *Stress and Coping: An Anthology*, ed. Alan Monat & Richard S. Lazarus (New York: Columbia University Press, 1977) 145. In Richard S. Lazarus, "Thoughts on the Relations Between Emotion and Cognition," *American Psychologist* 37/9 (1982): 1022, "the cognitive appraisals that shape our emotional reactions can distort reality as well as reflect it realistically."

61. The quoted passage is from Gerald L. Clore and W. Gerrod Parrott, "Moods and Their Vicissitudes: Thoughts and Feelings as Information, *Emotion and Social Judgments*, ed. Joseph P. Forgas (Oxford: Pergamon Press, 1991) 109. See Jonathan Mercer, "Emotional Beliefs," *International Organization* 64/1 (2010): 1, where "feeling is believing because people use emotion as evidence"; and 5, where "emotion and cognition co-produce beliefs." Regarding feelings as evidence, see also R. B. Zajonc, "Feeling and Thinking: Preferences Need No Inferences," *American Psychologist* 35/2 (1980): 172. For examples of feelings conducive to intuitive judgments, see Stephen Vaisey, "Motivation and Justification: A Dual-Process Model of Culture in Action," *American Journal of Sociology* 114/6 (2009): 1696. See also Nina P. Azari and Dieter Birnbacher, "The Role of Cognition and Feeling in Religious Experience," *Zygon* 39/4 (2004): 902 and 905; Joseph P. Forgas, "Feeling and Thinking: Summary and Integration," *Feeling and Thinking: The Role of Affect in Social Cognition*, ed. Joseph P. Forgas, (Cambridge: Cambridge University Press and Paris: Éditions de la Maison des

Sciences de l'Homme, 2000) 400, where "the relationship between affect and cognition is complex, context sensitive, and clearly bidirectional"; Roy F. Baumeister, Kathleen D. Vohs, C. Nathan Dewall, and Liqing Zhang, "How Emotion Shapes Behavior: Feedback, Anticipation, and Reflection, Rather Than Direct Causation," *Personality and Social Psychology Review* 11/2 (2007): 175–176; Leslie S. Greenberg and Juan Pascual-Leone, "Emotion in the Creation of Personal Meaning," *The Transformation of Meaning in Psychological Therapies: Integrating Theory and Practice*, ed. Michael J. Power and Chris Brewin (Chichester, UK: Wiley, 1997) 157; Southern, *Making*, 233, where for St. Anselm "thought and feeling are like two sides of a coin," and for St. Bernard "thought and feeling are one"; and Roy D'Andrade, "A Folk Model of the Mind," *Cultural Models in Language and Thought*, ed. Dorothy Holland and Naomi Quinn (Cambridge: Cambridge University Press, 1987) 125, where "the feedback loops in which belief affects feeling, which, in turn, affects belief, and in which perception affects belief, which then affects perception, give the portrayed machinery of the mind a complexity and flexibility it would not have if the causal chain were depicted as running solely in one direction."

Edmund T. Rolls, *The Brain and Emotion* (New York: Oxford University Press, 1999) 67–69, discusses aspects of emotion functions—autonomic responses (such as a change in heart rate) and endocrine responses (such as adrenaline release)—that can affect devotional experience.

62. The quoted passage is from Berg and Luckmann, *Social Construction*, 57. See Berger, "Sacred Canopy," 3 and 4; on the latter, internalization is described as a reappropriation. See Keith H. Basso, *Wisdom Sits in Places: Landscape and Language Among the Western Apache* (Albuquerque: University of New Mexico Press, 1996) 108, where places "yield to consciousness only what consciousness has given them to absorb." See also Howard Tennen and Glenn Affleck, "Blaming Others for Threatening Events," *Psychological Bulletin* 108/2 (1990): 224, where people "create realities to which they then respond"; Fernández Poncela, "El santo Niño de Atocha," 31, where the relation between votaries and images is circular; and Rodríguez-Shadow and Shadow, *El pueblo*, 177, where human love, worship, and commitment are retransmitted by miraculous images as divine energy in the form of consolation, grace, and miracles.

63. The quoted passage is from Joseph P. Forgas, "Affect and Person Perception," *Emotion and Social Judgments*, 269. In Baumeister, Vohs, Dewall, and Zhang, "How Emotion Shapes Behavior," 184, "emotions bias expectancies." On mirror-image dependence see Umberto Eco, *A Theory of Semiotics* (Bloomington: Indiana University Press, 1976) 202. See also Hans-Georg Gadamer, *Truth and Method* (New York: Seabury Press, 1975) 122; Bruce R. Klein, "A Child's Imaginary Companion: A Transitional Self," *Clinical Social Work Journal* 13/3 (1985): 275, where an imaginary companion is a mirror that reflects a "fading omnipotent ideal"; and Ana-Maria Rizzuto, *The Birth of the Loving God* (Chicago: University of

Chicago Press, 1979) 179, where a miraculous image (for our purposes) "will, in reflecting what we have done, affect our sense of ourselves." One is reminded of the saint statues in San Juan Chamula, Chiapas, which have mirrors on their chests.

64. The quoted passage is in Carro-Ripalda, "El Señor de Carácuaro," 43. See Marcel Mauss, *A General Theory of Magic*, tr. Robert Brain (London and New York: Routledge, 2001) 134, where a fundamental feature of magic is "the confusion between actor, rite and object"; Richard A. Shweder, "Likeness and Likelihood in Everyday Thought: Magical Thinking in Judgments About Personality," *Current Anthropology* 18/4 (1977): 641, where "the temptation to confuse one's interpretive categories with the events they describe is the basis of magical thinking"; and Gilbert, Brown, Pinel, and Wilson, "Illusion," 698. The quoted passages between the dashes are from, respectively, Jean-Paul Sartre and Anthony Wilden in Jacques Lacan and Anthony Wilden, *The Language of the Self: The Function of Language in Psychoanalysis* (Baltimore: Johns Hopkins Press, 1968) 130, n. 103. See Mikhail Bakhtin, *Problems of Dostoevsky's Poetics*, tr. R. W. Rotsel (Ann Arbor, MI: Ardis, 1973) 167, where words come to us "saturated with other people's interpretations"; one "receives the word from the voice of another, and the word is filled with that voice"; one's "own thought finds the word already inhabited"; and a word "can never wholly free itself from the dominion of the contexts of which it has been a part." See also H. Porter Abbott, "Reading Intended Meaning Where None is Intended: A Cognitivist Reappraisal of the Implied Author," *Poetics Today* 32/3 (2011): 464; and Christopher Tilley, "Interpreting Material Culture," in *The Meanings of Things: Material Culture and Symbolic Expression*, ed. Ian Hodder (London: Unwin Hyman, 1989) 189. Regarding voicelessness, see Shlomith Rimmon-Kenan, *Narrative Fiction: Contemporary Poetics* (London and New York: Methuen, 1983) 87; and Seymour Chatman, *Story and Discourse: Narrative Structure in Fiction and Film* (Ithaca, NY: Cornell University Press, 1980) 148, where an implied author "has no voice, no direct means of communicating." Regarding silence, see Muriel Saville-Troike, "The Place of Silence in an Integrated Theory of Communication," in *Perspectives on Silence*, ed. Deborah Tannen and Murile Saville-Troike (Norwood, NJ: Ablex Publishing Company, 1985) 11 and 10, respectively: Silence "is more context-embedded than speech, that is, more dependent on context for its interpretation," and in the numinous space around images, as elsewhere, "silence constitutes an active presence (not absence) in communication." See also "interactive silences," "varieties of communicative silences," and "silence as a means of exerting control" in Michal Ephratt, "Linguistic, Paralinguistic and Extralinguistic Speech and Silence," *Journal of Pragmatics* 43/9 (2011): 2286–2307, especially 2287.

65. The quoted passages are from San Juan de la Cruz, *Obra poética* (Mexico City: Editorial Porrúa, 1984) 89. As the catechism has it, Christ is "the eternal Word of the living God" and "Christianity is the religion of the 'Word' of God, which is 'not a written and mute word, but the Word which is incarnate and living.'"

Catholic Church, *Catechism*, page 37, paragraph 108. See César Izquierdo, "Palabra (y Silencio) de Dios," *Scripta Theologica* 41/3 (2009): 946.

66. The quoted passages are from Florencia, *Origen*, 129. See Gustav Sobin, *Luminous Debris: Reflecting on Vestige in Provence and Languedoc* (Berkeley: University of California Press, 1999) 3, regarding the votive offering of mirrors. Pope Boniface VIII's bull "Unam Sanctam" (1302) dogmatized the Church as "one mystical body whose head is Christ." See Ephesians 4:4–13 and Ernst H. Kantorowicz, *The King's Two Bodies: A Study in Mediaeval Political Theology* (Princeton, NJ: Princeton University Press, 1957) 96. See also Megan Holmes, "Ex-votos: Materiality, Memory, and Cult," *The Idol in the Age of Art: Objects, Devotions and the Early Modern World*, ed. Michael Cole and Rebecca Zorach (Aldershot: Ashgate, 2009) 180.

67. For other examples of images formed with milagritos, see Museo Casa Estudio Diego Rivera y Frida Kahlo and Mexic-Arte Museum, *Fe, arte y cultura: Santo Niño de Atocha, exvotos* (Mexico: Consejo Nacional para la Cultura y las Arte, Instituto Nacional de Bellas Artes, Museo Casa Estudio Diego Rivera y Frida Kahlo, Mexic-Arte Museum, Diócesis de Zacatecas, Santuario de Plateros, 2000) 116 (Niño de Atocha) and 120 (Virgen de Guadalupe). The names of miraculous images are often written in milagritos. In Tlaxcala, the star behind the Virgen de Ocotlán is made of milagritos. For an example of images made of votive offerings elsewhere, see Maniura, *Pilgrimage to Images*, 109.

68. The first quoted passage is from Samuel Taylor Coleridge, *Biographia Literaria Or, Biographical Sketches of My Literary Life and Opinions* (New York: Macmillan, 1926) 191; and the second is from Luhrmann, "A Hyperreal God," 383. See Murray Krieger, "The Anthropological Persistence of the Aesthetic: Real Shadows and Textual Shadows, Real Texts and Shadow Texts," *New Literary History*, 25/1 (1994): 31.

69. See Meissner, "Psychoanalysis," 175; and Krieger, "Anthropological Persistence," 27. Sam and belief dossiers are from Zemach, "Emotion," 41 and 45, respectively. See also a related example of "double consciousness" in John Corrigan, *Business of the Heart: Religion and Emotion in the Nineteenth Century* (Berkeley: University of California Press, 2002) 2–7. In George Orwell, *Nineteen Eighty-Four* (London: Secker and Warburg, 1949) 38–39, doublethink is the simultaneous acceptance of two mutually contradictory beliefs.

70. The quoted passage is from Adam B. Seligman, *Ritual and its Consequences: An Essay on the Limits of Sincerity* (New York: Oxford University Press, 2008) 25–26. See Elisa Galgut, "Poetic Faith and Prosaic Concerns. A Defense of 'Suspension of Disbelief,'" *South African Journal of Philosophy* 21/3 (2002): 197; Alfred R. Mele, *Irrationality: An Essay on Akrasia, Self-Deception, and Self-Control* (New York: Oxford University Press, 1987) 151 and 158; Steve Kirby, "Telling Lies? An Exploration of Self-Deception and Bad Faith," *European Journal of Psychotherapy, Counselling, and Health* 6/2 (2003): 99–104; and Luhrmann, "A Hyperreal God,"

375. Clifford Geertz, "Religion as a Cultural System," *The Interpretation of Cultures: Selected Essays* (London: Fontana Press: 1993) 120, describes people "moving more or less easily, and very frequently, between radically contrasting ways of looking at the world."

71. The first quoted passage is from Umberto Eco, *The Open Work*, tr. Anna Cancogni (Cambridge, MA: Harvard University Press, 1989) 21; the second is from Gilles Deleuze, "Plato and the Simulacrum," tr. Rosalind Krauss, *October* 27 (1983): 51; and the third is from Josef Breuer and Sigmund Freud, *Studies in Hysteria*, in Freud, *Standard Edition*, vol. 2, 164. See Winnicott, *Playing*, xvi, where a paradox is to be "accepted and tolerated and respected... and not to be resolved"; and 89, where an essential feature of transitional objects and phenomena is "paradox, and the acceptance of the paradox." See also Clore, "Psychology," 328; Meredith B. McGuire, *Lived Religion: Faith and Practice in Everyday Life* (New York: Oxford University Press, 2008) 16; and Fraser Watts and Mark Williams, *The Psychology of Religious Knowing* (Cambridge: Cambridge University Press, 1988) 36, where "the creative balance between inner and outer in the transitional world is a delicate one. If there is insufficient psychic involvement, not enough 'play', meaning drains away and religious ideas lose their significance. Equally, if the religious world becomes too autistic, too merely magical, it loses its creative power. The transitional world can fall apart into mere fantasy on the one hand, and mere external ritual on the other."

72. See Marina Warner, *Alone of All Her Sex: The Myth and the Cult of the Virgin Mary* (New York: Knopf, 1976) 3–4, 7, 14, 19–20, 236–254 (on the immaculate conception) and 252–253 (on the assumption). See also Miri Rubin, *Mother of God: A History of the Virgin Mary* (New Haven, CT: Yale University Press, 2009) 4–8; and Anne Baring and Jules Cashford, *The Myth of the Goddess: Evolution of an Image* (New York: Arkana/Penguin Books, 1991) 549–556. For in-depth discussion, see Raymond E. Brown, Karl P. Donfried, Josepha A. Fitzmyer, and John Reumann, eds., *Mary in the New Testament: A Collaborative Assessment by Protestant and Roman Catholic Scholars* (Philadelphia: Fortress Press, 1978). The title "Mother of God" was conferred by the Council of Ephesus in 431, and the title "Mother of the Church" was added in 1964.

73. The quoted passage is from Dagron, "Holy Images," 31. See Gadamer, *Truth and Method*, 125.

74. The quoted passage is from Dagron, "Holy Images," 28; see 31, and 33. For examples of visions and apparitions that resemble church images, see Frank Graziano, *Wounds of Love: The Mystical Marriage of Saint Rose of Lima* (New York: Oxford University Press, 2004) 55–58; and Voragine, *Golden Legend*, 2/87, where the Virgin appears, "looking like a painting that the boy had seen on the altar." In Paisley Livingston and Andrea Sauchelli, "Philosophical Perspectives on Fictional Characters," *New Literary History* 42/2 (2011): 348, claims about fiction are subject not to truth values or truth conditions but rather to their faithfulness to the story.

75. The quoted passages are from Kenneth Burke, "Four Master Tropes," *Kenyon Review* 3/4 (1941): 424. The essay is also appended to Burke's *A Grammar of Motives* (Berkeley: University of California Press, 1969) 503–517. The quoted phrases at the end of the paragraph are from, respectively, Trexler, "Florentine," 18; and Gadamer, *Truth and Method*, 126. See Stephen Ullmann, *Semantics. An Introduction to the Science of Meaning* (New York: Barnes and Noble, 1962) 218–220; and Halbertal and Margalit, *Idolatry*, 40–42. This subgroup of part-to-whole relations is also known as synecdoche; I use "metonymy" here following the sources. For a summary of metonymy as displacement in psychoanalysis, see for example Lacan and Wilden *Language of the Self*, 238–249; and J. LaPlanche and J. B. Pontalis, *The Language of Psycho-Analysis*, tr. Donald Nicholson-Smith (New York: Norton, 1973) 121–123. For an overview of metonymy generally, see Helena Beristáin, *Diccionario de retórica y poética* (Mexico City: Editorial Porrúa, 1998) 327–331.

76. The first quoted passage is from Fredric Jameson, *Postmodernism, Or, the Cultural Logic of Late Capitalism* (Durham, NC: Duke University Press, 1991) 18. The second quoted passage is from Jean Baudrillard, *Simulacra and Simulation*, tr. Sheila Faria Glaser (Ann Arbor: University of Michigan Press, 1997) 6. The third and fourth quoted passages are from Michael Camille, "Simulacrum," *Critical Terms for Art History*, ed. Robert S. Nelson and Richard Shiff (Chicago: University of Chicago Press, 1996) 31. The last quoted passage is from Baudrillard, *Simulacra*, 6. See Richard J. Lane, *Jean Baudrillard* (London and New York: Routledge, 2000) 86–89 and 94; Besançon, *Forbidden Image*, 135; and Deleuze, "Plato," 47–48 and 52–53. Presuming an original behind a replica, Rafael said that the image of the Virgen de Juquila is like a photograph, so that today we can "see how she looked."

77. The quoted passage is from Eduardo Viveiros de Castro, "Exchanging Perspectives: The Transformation of Objects into Subjects in Amerindian Ontologies," *Common Knowledge* 10/3 (2004): 471. See Philippe Descola, "Constructing Natures: Symbolic Ecology and Social Practice," *Nature and Society: Anthropological Perspectives*, edited by Philippe Descola and Gísli Pálsson (London and New York: Routledge, 1996) 82–84; and Nurit Bird-David "'Animism' Revisited: Personhood, Environment, and Relational Epistemology," *Current Anthropology* 40/S1 (1999): S78: "Against materialistic framing of the environment as discrete things stands relationally framing the environment as nested relatednesses." See also Hodder, *Entangled*, 34, for "cultural diversity in the ways in which humans construe things."

78. In this paragraph I am adapting insights from Amie L. Thomasson, *Fiction and Metaphysics* (Cambridge: Cambridge University Press, 1999) 148–149 (the quoted passages) and 176 (the quoted phrase at the end). Viveiros de Castro, "Exchanging Perspectives," 484, similarly calls for "richer ontologies."

OTATITLÁN

1. The shrine is formally known as the Santuario del Santísimo Cristo de Otatitlán, and the image is known as the Cristo Negro, Señor Santuario, or Señor de Otatitlán. There are many other black Christs in the region, including the Señor de Chalma, the Señor de Tila in Chiapas, the Cristo de las Ampollas in Mérida, and the Cristo Negro de Esquipulas in Guatemala. See Jasso A. Estrada, *Imágenes en caña de maíz: estudio, catálogo y bibliografía* (San Luis Potosí, Mexico: Universidad Autónoma de San Luis Potosí, 1996) 315–316. The Señor de Tilma used to be darker but miraculously changed his color to better resemble his devotees.

2. The quoted passage is in José Velasco Toro, *De la historia al mito: mentalidad y culto en el santuario de Otatitlán* (Veracruz: Instituto Veracruzano de Cultura, 2000) 101. Regarding the profanation, see Gustavo Vergara Ruiz, "Otatitlán en el perfil del tiempo," *Santuario y región: imágenes del Cristo Negro de Otatitlán*, ed. José Velasco Toro (Veracruz: Instituto de Investigaciones Históricos-Sociales, Universidad Veracruzana, 1997) 99; and Fernando Winfield Capitaine, "La Cofradía del Cristo Negro de Otatitlán en el Siglo XVIII," *La Palabra y el Hombre* 89 (1994): 49. In some versions the head is sawn off before the attempt to burn the body.

3. The events described in this paragraph are from news accounts in Velasco Toro, *De la historia*, 100; and from Winfield Capitaine, 48–49; and Vergara Ruiz, "Otatitlán," 99. Secondary devotional sites inside and outside of the church include a cross believed (erroneously) to be the image's original cross. See José Velasco Toro, "Imaginario cultural e identidad devocional en el santuario de Otatitlán," *Santuarios, peregrinaciones y religiosidad popular*, ed. María J. Rodríguez-Shadow and Ricardo Avila (Guadalajara: Universidad de Guadalajara, 2010) 193–194, n. 2. Multiple devotional sites within a shrine are common in Latin American. For a medieval example, regarding St. Thomas of Canterbury, see Benedicta Ward, *Miracles and the Medieval Mind: Theory, Record and Event, 1000–1215* (Philadelphia: University of Pennsylvania Press, 1982) 100–101. Regarding devotion to the head, in Chalhuanca, Peru, the head of a Christ image discovered during the plowing of a field in 1886 became an object of devotion and evolved into the Señor de Animas. The decapitation is also reminiscent of the Peruvian myth of Inkarrí. For a summary see Frank Graziano, *The Millennial New World* (New York: Oxford University Press, 1999) 188–198 (the Chalhuanca example is on 191). In Umán, near Mérida in Yucatán, there is devotion to a decapitated head of the Virgin. Elsewhere, in the fourth century, iconoclasts broke a statue of Christ but Christians rescued the head and enshrined it in a local church. See Ewa Kuryluk, *Veronica and Her cloth: History, Symbolism, and Structure of a "True" Image* (Cambridge, MA: Basil Blackwell, 1991) 94. After the beheading of St. John the Baptist, the head went on many journeys—to Jerusalem, to a cave in Emissa [Emesa], to Constantinople, where a church was

built for it and it performed miracles, and finally to France. See Jacobus de Voragine, *The Golden Legend: Readings on the Saints*, tr. William Granger Ryan (Princeton, NJ: Princeton University Press, 1993) 2/138. Part of the skull is currently venerated in the Amiens Cathedral north of Paris.

4. Some seventeenth-century Spanish images were rescued after being imprisoned in North African territories. Once recovered, they were "venerated by devotees who, by doing so, compensated them for their past sufferings." María Cruz de Carlos Varona, "'Imágenes Rescatadas' en la Europa moderna: el caso de Jesús de Medinaceli," *Journal of Spanish Cultural Studies* 12/3 (2011): 329; see 341. A Cuzco-school image depicts the Christ of Medinaceli being dragged and beaten by Moors. See the reproduction on 338.

5. The quoted passage is in Velasco Toro, "Imaginario," 195. See Velasco Toro, *De la historia*, 102. In John 13:21–30, Jesus arranges his own betrayal, assigning Judas to the deed and enabling him.

6. The first quoted passage is in Velasco Toro, "Imaginario," 200, n. 3. See Velasco Toro, "De la historia," 141. Regarding the miraculous dirt, see Guadalupe Vargas Montero, "Venimos a cumplir con la promesa. Las peregrinaciones corporadas de oriente," *Santuario y región*, 340–341; Francisco Rubén Córdoba Olivares, "Señor Santuario: hacedor de vida," *Santuario y región*, 396; Velasco Toro, "Imaginario," 200; and Miguel Angel Rubio, *La morada de los santos: expresiones del culto religioso en el sur de Veracruz y en Tabasco* (Mexico City: Instituto Nacional Indigenista, Secretaría de Desarrollo Social, 1995) 75.

The second quoted passage is from an indigenous woman interviewed in *Señor de Otatitlán*, posted by Juan Francisco Urrusti, from the series "Los caminos de lo sagrado," produced by Consejo Nacional para la Cultura y las Artes (Conaculta): https://vimeo.com/79940049.

7. Regarding the ethnic groups, see Velasco Toro, *De la historia*, 7 and 31; Velasco Toro, "Imaginario," 185–186; Alicia M. Barabas Reyna, "Los santuarios de vírgenes y santos aparecidos en Oaxaca," *Cuicuilco* 13/36 (2006): 247; and Galindo G. Münch, *Etnología del istmo veracruzano* (México: Universidad Nacional Autónoma de México, Instituto de Investigaciones Antropológicas, 1983) 258. Regarding the offerings, see Córdoba Olivares, "Señor Santuario," 384–85 and 387; Barabas Reyna, "Los santuarios," 247; and Rubio, *La morada*, 74.

8. Velasco Toro, *De la historia*, 144 and 156–157; the quoted passages are on 157. Regarding revenge, see Barabas Reyna, "Los santuarios," 247. Ancient Egyptian letters to deceased family members provided a means to vent and to petition supernatural intervention as a remedy for affronts and perceived injustice. See Edmund S. Meltzer, ed., *Letters from Ancient Egypt*, tr. Edward F. Wente (Atlanta, GA: Scholars Press, 1990) 210–220.

9. Regarding the events in this paragraph, see Velasco Toro, "Imaginario," 184–185; Velasco Toro, *De la historia*, 65–71 and 73–77; Velasco Toro, "'Vamos al santuario del Señor de Otatitlán.' Expresión numinosa de un ámbito regional,"

Santuario y región, 129–131; and Guadalupe Vargas Montero, "El santuario del Cristo Negro de Otatitlán: los peregrinos de oriente y sus líderes espirituales," *Sotavento* 2/3 (1997): 121.

10. The versions of the head's return are from Velasco Toro, *De la historia*, 103. The Cristo de las Tres Caídas was originally destined for Teutila, Karina said, but the image "chose his place" in San Andrés Teotilalpam. "They wanted him to stay there [in Teutila], but he didn't want to stay."

11. The quoted passages, from Joseph Villaseñor y Sanchez, 1746, are in in Gonzalo Aguirre Beltrán, *Pobladores del Papaloapan: biografía de una hoya* (Mexico City: Centro de Investigaciones y Estudios Superiores en Antropología Social, 1992) 161–162. See Vargas Montero, "El santuario," 120–121. Versions of the myth are presented and discussed in Rubio, "La morada," 49–54. See also Winfield Capitaine, "La Cofradía," 43–49.

12. Velasco Toro, "Imaginario," 193. Other images offered boat processions include the Virgen de Candelaria of Tlacotalpan, the Virgin of the Immaculate Conception on Isla Mujeres, and the Virgen de la Medalla Milagrosa in Progreso, Yucatán.

13. Regarding the pilgrim rituals, see Velasco Toro, "Imaginario," 193 and 200; James B. Greenberg, *Santiago's Sword: Chatino Peasant Religion and Economics* (Berkeley: University of California Press, 1981) 85; and Fernando Winfield Capitaine, "Otatitlán y Yacatecuhtli," *La Palabra y el Hombre* 32 (1979): 30.

14. The first quoted passage is in Carlos Bernardo González Absalón, "El camino de una fe. Etnografía de la peregrinación de Cosoleacaque al santuario de Otatitlán," *Santuario y región*, 556. The others are in Velasco Toro, *Santuario y región*, 507, with the exception of the last, which is in Vargas Montero, "Venimos," 344.

15. The quoted passage is in the video *Señor de Otatitlán*.

PETITIONARY DEVOTION

1. See, for example, Manuel M. Marzal, *Tierra encantada: tratado de antropología religiosa en América Latina* (Lima: Editorial Trotta, 2002) 375, where saints are sources of miracles rather than life models; Anna M. Fernández Poncela, "De la salvación a la sobrevivencia: la relgiosidad popular, devotos y comerciantes" *Dimensión antropológica* 13/36 (2006): 134, 136, and 167–168; María J. Rodríguez-Shadow and Robert D. Shadow, *El pueblo del Señor: las fiestas y peregrinaciones de Chalma* (Toluca: Universidad Autónoma del Estado de México, 2000) 176–177; Yolanda Lastra, Dina Sherzer, and Joel Sherzer, *Adoring the Saints: Fiestas in Central Mexico* (Austin: University of Texas Press, 2009) 28; Isabel Lagarriga Attias, "Participación religiosa: viejas y nuevas formas de reivindicación femenina en México," *Alteridades* 9/18 (1999): 72. In psychology, see for example Robert A. Emmons, "Is Spirituality an Intelligence? Motivation, Cognition, and the Psychology of Ultimate Concern," *International Journal for the Psychology of Religion* 10/1 (2000): 3, where "There is an intimate connection between

religion and goals"; and Kenneth I. Pargament and June Hahn, "God and the
Just World: Causal and Coping Attributions to God in Health Situations," *Journal
for the Scientific Study of Religion* 25/2 (1986): 203–204, where experiment sub-
jects "turn to God more as a source of support during stress than as a moral
guide or as an antidote to an unjust world," and God is "one source of reassur-
ance, support, and encouragement" to help people endure stresses. See also
Rodney Stark, "Micro Foundations of Religion: A Revised Theory," *Sociological
Theory* 17/3 (1999): 268; and Hans Belting, *Likeness and Presence: A History of the
Image before the Era of Art*, tr. Edmund Jephcott (Chicago: University of Chicago
Press, 1994) 6.

2. For deep precedents see, for example, Tony W. Cartledge, *Vows in the Hebrew
Bible and the Ancient Near East* (Sheffield: JSOT Press, 1992) 25, where in the
Old Testament the word "vow" (*neder*) is a conditional promise, made in peti-
tionary prayer, that the votary "will give to God some gift or service in return for
God's willingness to hear and answer his prayer." On conditional vows in the Old
Testament see also Anne Katrine Gudme, "Barter Deal or Friend-Making Gift?
A Reconsideration on the Conditional Vow in the Hebrew Bible," *The Gift in
Antiquity*, ed. Michael L. Satlow (Malden, MA; Oxford: Chichester, UK: Wiley-
Blackwell, 2013) 190. See also Catherine M. Keesling, *The Votive Statues of the
Athenian Acropolis* (New York: Cambridge University Press, 2003) 5, where some
votive statues on the Athenian Acropolis have contractual inscriptions. In
George M. Foster, *Tzintzuntzan: Mexican Peasants in a Changing World* (New
York: Elsevier-New York, 1979) 239, "we really lose nothing" when making
petitions.

3. See the many examples in *The Book of Saint Foy*, tr. Pamela Sheingorn
(Philadelphia: University of Pennsylvania Press, 1995) 43–56; 56–58; 112–115;
and 152–155. Similarly, God is causal in some life events (illness) but not others
(relationship problems). See Kate Miriam Loewenthal, Andrew K. MacLeod,
Vivienne Goldblatt, Guy Lubitsh, and John D. Valentine, "Comfort and Joy?
Religion, Cognition and Mood in Protestants and Jews Under Stress," *Cognition
and Emotion* 14/3 (2000): 356.

4. For some background see M. P. J. Dillon, "The Didactic Nature of the Epidaurian
Iamata," *Zeitschrift für Papyrologie und Epigraphik* 101 (1994): 249 for "incuba-
tion by proxy"; and André Vauchez, *Sainthood in the Later Middle Ages*, tr. Jean
Brill (Cambridge: Cambridge University Press, 1997) 453. Regarding the Niño
de Atocha, see Juan Javier Pescador, *Crossing Borders with the Santo Niño de
Atocha* (Albuquerque: University of New Mexico Press, 2009) 144–145; and
Anna María Fernández Poncela, "El santo Niño de Atocha: origen, función y
actualidad," *Cuicuilco* 10/27 (2003): 16–17.

5. The quoted passage is from Enriqueta Valdez Curiel, *Danza de los sonajeros de
Zapotlán el Grande: promesas religiosas para recuperar la salud* (Guadalajara:
Universidad del Guadalajara, Centro Universidad del Sur, 2006) 33. For an

example of a proxy offering, see Ricardo Avila and Martín Tena, "Morir peregrinando a Talpa," *Estudios del hombre* 25 (2006): 242.

6. I borrow the concept of votive complex from Hugo van der Velden, *The Donor's Image: Gerard Loyet and the Votive Portraits of Charles the Bold,* tr. Beverley Jackson (Turnhout, Belgium: Brepols, 2000) 212.

7. The first two quoted passages are from Fernández Poncela, "Santo Niño de Atocha," 20 and 21, respectively. The last quoted passage is from "Llegan cientos de peregrinos al santuario de Padre Jesús, en Taxco," *La Jornada guerrero,* March 14, 2011: www.lajornadaguerrero.com.mx/2011/03/14/index.php?section=sociedad& article=005n2soc. In F. T. Van Straten, "Gifts for the Gods," *Faith, Hope, and Worship: Aspects of Religious Mentality in the Ancient World,"* ed. H. S. Versnel (Leiden: E. J. Brill, 1981) 74, offerings are durable but "the Greeks also felt the need to 'recharge' their votive offerings" as though the effectiveness were gradually depleted. Daniel B. Lee, "Maria of the Oak: Society and the Problem of Divine Intervention," *Sociology of Religion* 70/3 (2009): 220, describes textual petitions amended on subsequent shrine visits to indicate the dates that miraculous help was received.

8. The quoted passages are from Jorge Ayala Q., *Chalma: su Señor, su santuario, su convento, sus ferias, sus danzas, sus leyendas, y tradiciones* (Chalma: shrine published, 2002) Book 2, 36. Greater sensitivity is apparent in Quinta Conferencia General del Episcopado Latinoamericano y del Caribe, "Documento conclusivo," Aparecida, Brazil, 2007 (Bogotá: Consejo Espiscopal Latinoamericano, 2007) 150; and CELAM, Región Cono Sur, "Piedad popular a la luz de Aparecida" (Buenos Aires, October 26–30, 2009) 9. See David Freedberg, *The Power of Images: Studies in the History and Theory of Response* (Chicago: University of Chicago Press, 1989) 138, where the votive offering "absolved one from further demonstrating one's thanks" and one's faith.

9. The first quoted passage is from Juan Castro Méndez, *La Virgen de Juquila en la historia* (Oaxaca: Imprenta Postal, 2000) 85. Father Paco describes celebration of the eucharist—the mass—as the primary prayer of thanksgiving. The word "eucharist" is derived from the Greek *eukharistia,* meaning thanksgiving or gratitude. According to Dostoyevsky's underground man, "the best definition of man is—a creature that walks on two legs and is ungrateful." Fyodor Dostoyevsky, *Notes from Underground and the Grand Inquisitor,* tr. Ralph E. Matlaw (New York: Dutton, 1960) 26.

10. I include intercessory prayer in my concept of petition, because frequently petitions are made and miracles are reciprocated by proxies. For a brief summary of prayer taxonomies in the psychology of religion, see Kevin L. Ladd and Bernard Spilka, "Inward, Outward, and Upward: Cognitive Aspects of Prayer," *Journal for the Scientific Study of Religion* 41/3 (2002): 475–476.

11. "El Señor de la columna: una fe, un solo patrono," *El piñero de la cuenca*: www .elpinerodelacuenca.com.mx/epc/index.php/oaxaca/7474-el-senor-de-la-columna-una-fe-un-solo-patrono.

12. The longer quoted passage is from Søren Kierkegaard, *The Journals of Søren Kierkegaard*, ed. and tr. Alexander Dru (Oxford: Oxford University Press, 1938) 153–154. See Immanuel Kant, *Lectures on Philosophical Theology*, tr. Allen W. Wood and Gertrude M. Clark (Ithaca, NY: Cornell University Press, 1978) 155, where "we must never regard prayer as a means to getting our own way; if a prayer concerns our corporeal advantage, we ought to say it both with a trust in God's wisdom and with a submission to this wisdom."

13. The mayordomo's passage is in José Luis Pérez Chacón, *Los choles de Tila y su mundo* (Tuxtla Gutiérrez, Mexico: Gobierno del Estado de Chiapas, Consejo Estatal de Fomento a la Investigación, y Difusión de la Cultura, Instituto Chiapaneco de Cultura, 1993) 242. See Paul Davies, "The Lighting of Pilgrimage Shrines in Renaissance Italy," *The Miraculous Image in the Late Middle Ages and Renaissance*, ed. Erik Thunø and Gerhard Wolf (Rome: "L'erma" di Bretschneider, 2004), where an image of the Virgin could "'see' the candle, and in 'seeing' it would intercede on their behalf."

14. See Jesse M. Bering and Dominic D. P. Johnson, "'O Lord...You Perceive my Thoughts from Afar': Recursiveness and the Evolution of Supernatural Agency," *Journal of Cognition and Culture* 5/1–2 (2005): 120, where "supernatural agents... have privileged epistemic access to the self's mental states."

15. For images of pedimento offerings, see Alicia M. Gonzalez, *The Edge of Enchantment: Sovereignty and Ceremony in Huatulco, Mexico* (National Museum of the American Indian, Smithsonian Institution, 2002) 41. See also Alicia M. Barabas, *Dones, dueños y santos: ensayo sobre religiones en Oaxaca* (Mexico City: Instituto Nacional de Antropología e Historia, 2006) 174, n. 119. Regarding the cochinitos, see the Extranormal video "La cruz del Pedimento," Huatulco, Oaxaca, February 7, 2010: www.youtube.com/watch?v=wHHVKS01A1M.

16. For examples of petitionary objects, see Maria J. Rodríguez-Shadow, "Peticiones y plegarias femeninas en los exvotos de Chalma," *Creatividad invisible: mujeres y arte popular en América Latina y el Caribe*, ed. Eli Bartra (Mexico City: Universidad Nacional Autónoma de México, 2004) 263–264; and Francisco Gallegos Franco, *Los retablos del Señor de la Misericordia de Tepatitlán* (Guadalajara: Conaculta, Secretaría de Cultura de Jalisco, Feca, Grupo Modelo, 2001) 44. See Daniel Wojcik, "'Polaroids from Heaven': Photography, Folk Religion, and the Miraculous Image Tradition at a Marian Apparition Site," *Journal of American Folklore* 109/432 (1996) 135, where photographs have petitionary aspects when one concentrates "on a specific subject or 'asking heaven' a specific question" while taking the photograph.

17. The example with the silver head is from a 1649 account in Luis Lasso de la Vega, "El gran acontecimiento,..." *Testimonios históricos guadalupanos*, ed. Ernesto de la Torre Villar and Ramiro Navarro de Anda (Mexico: Fondo de Cultura Económica, 1982) 303. The Porfiria example is from a retablo dated April 18, 1899 in the New Mexico State University Art Gallery retablo collection, in Las

Cruces. See Aurora Castillo Escalona and Genoveva Orvañanos Busto, *Nuestra Señora del Pueblito: su historia y culto* (Querétaro: Universidad Autónoma de Querétaro, 1987) 23–24.

18. The quoted warning is in Víctor Campa Mendoza, *Santuarios y milagros* (Mexico City: Consejo Nacional de Ciencia y Tecnología, 2002) 239. Regarding prompt payment of vows, see Cartledge, *Vows*, 135; van der Velden, *Donor's Image*, 194; and Deuteronomy 23:22, where "When you make a vow to the Lord, your God, you shall not delay in fulfilling it; for the Lord, your God, will surely require it of you and you will be held guilty." See Ryszard Kapuściński, *The Shadow of the Sun: My African Life*, tr. Klara Glowczewska (Victoria, Australia: Penguin Books, 2008) 277, where in some African cultures "The unreciprocated gift lies heavily on the head of the one who has received it, torments his conscience, and can even bring down misfortune, illness, death." It requires "a quick restoration of equilibrium."

19. The retablo example is from Elin Luque Agraz and Michele Beltrán, "Regalo para el arte: los exvotos mexicanos de los siglos XIX y XX," *Dones y promesas: 500 años de arte ofrenda (exvotos mexicanos)* (Mexico City: Centro Cultural/Arte Contemporáneo, 1996) 111 and cat. 83 on page 57. The channeling dead woman is from Neal Krause and Elena Bastida, "Exploring the Interface between Religion and Contact with the Dead among Older Mexican Americans," *Review of Religious Research* 51/1 (2009): 16. For another example of punishment for not fulfilling a vow, see Francisco de Florencia, *Origen de los dos celebres santuarios de la Nueva Galicia, obispado de Guadalaxara, en la America septentrional* (Zapopan, Mexico: Amate Editorial, 2001) 41 and 63. Regarding death as punishment, see José Velasco Toro, *De la historia al mito: mentalidad y culto en el santuario de Otatitlán* (Veracruz: Instituto Veracruzano de Cultura, 2000) 146. See also Patrick J. Geary, *Living with the Dead in the Middle Ages* (Ithaca, NY: Cornell University Press, 1994) 120; and Robert A. Emmons and Michael E. McCullough, "Counting Blessings Versus Burdens: An Experimental Investigation of Gratitude and Subjective Well-being in Daily Life," *Journal of Personality and Social Psychology* 84/2 (2003): 379, where coerced reciprocation can generate strong negative feelings toward benefactors.

20. Sandra Velázquez, "En la ciudad: un milagro paga otro milagro" hoydallas.com, October 13, 2013: www.hoydallas.com/index.php/hoy-dfw/metroplex/1094-en-la-ciudad-un-milagro-paga-otro-milagro. See Stark, "Micro Foundations," 277–278, where people seek to delay payment and minimize their religious costs.

21. The quoted passage is from Florencia, *Origen*, 63. The tortilla-machine example is from Barabas, *Dones*, 222; see 90 and 223. The San Juan de los Lagos example is from Florencia, *Origen*, 63 (sight was restored after the man begged for mercy). The bandit example is from the broadside José Guadalupe Posada, "True Portrait of Our Lord of the Sanctuary of Otatitlán" (Mexico City: Antonio Vanegas Arroyo, 1911), Library of Congress Prints and Photographs Division: http://hdl.loc.gov/loc.pnp/ppmsc.04460. For examples of punishment in Mexico,

see Gilberto Giménez, *Cultural popular y religión en el Anahuac* (Mexico City: Centro de Estudios Ecuménicos, 1978) 184; Susana Carro-Ripalda, "El Señor de Carácuaro: una etnografía fenomenológica de una peregrinación en México," *Guaraguao* 5/13 (2001): 46. Rodríguez-Shadow, "Peticiones," 256; Francisco Rubén Córdoba Olivares, "Señor Santuario: hacedor de vida," *Santuario y región: imagenes del Cristo Negro de Otatitlán*, ed. José Velasco Toro (Veracruz: Instituto de Investigaciones Históricos-Sociales, Universidad Veracruzana, 1997) 386; James Lockhart, *The Nahuas after the Conquest: A Social and Cultural History of the Indians of Central Mexico, Sixteenth through Eighteenth Centuries* (Redwood City, CA: Stanford University Press, 1992) 245; and James W. Dow, *Santos y supervivencias: funciones de la religión en una comunidad otomí* (Mexico City: Instituto Nacional Indigenista and Secretaría de Educación Pública, 1974) 105. For punishments in other regions and periods, see Lynn R. LiDonnici, *The Epidaurian Miracle Inscriptions: Text, Translation and Commentary* (Atlanta, GA: Scholars Press, 1995) 121, where fish are struck by lightning because a fishmonger did not fulfill her promise to Asklepios; Dillon, "Didactic," 252–253; Marcus Bull, *The Miracles of Our Lady of Rocamadour: Analysis and Translation* (Woodbridge, UK: Boydell Press, 1999) 102, 117, 190; Michael E. Goodich, *Violence and Miracle in the Fourteenth Century: Private Grief and Public Salvation* (Chicago: University of Chicago Press, 1995) 31; Jacalyn Duffin, *Medical Miracles: Doctors, Saints, and Healing in the Modern World* (New York: Oxford University Press, 2009) 149; Robert Maniura, *Pilgrimage to Images in the Fifteenth Century: The Origins of the Cult of Our Lady of Częstochowa* (Woodbridge, UK: Boydell Press, 2004) 105–106; *The Book of Sainte Foy*, tr. Pamela Sheingorn (Philadelphia: University of Pennsylvania Press, 1995) 58–73; Lester K. Little, *Benedictine Maledictions: Liturgical Cursing in Romanesque France* (Ithaca, NY: Cornell University Press, 1993) 198; Bering and Johnson, "O Lord," 126–128; Aron Gurevich, *Medieval Popular Culture: Problems of Belief and Perception*, tr. Jájnos M. Bak and Paula A. Hollingsworth (New York: Cambridge University Press, 1988) 46–47; and Frank Graziano. *Wounds of Love: The Mystical Marriage of Saint Rose of Lima* (Oxford: Oxford University Press, 2004) 144–148.

22. The quoted passages in the last sentence are from Ayala Q., *Chalma*, 85.

23. Regarding positive aspects of punishment, see Marzal, *Tierra*, 376–367 and 391; and Little, "Benedictine," 198, n. 30. For contrasting views from the United States, see Bernard Spilka, *The Psychology of Religion: An Empirical Approach* (New York: Guilford Press, 2003) 43, where "people rarely blame God for the bad things that happen to them"; and Pargament and Hahn, "God," 195, where "people are generally reluctant to view God in negative terms."

24. See Guillermo Tovar de Teresa, "Santuarios, imágenes milagrosas y sus prodigios en la Nueva España," *México peregrino: diez santuarios procesionales*, ed. Luis Mario Schneider and Guillermo Tovar de Teresa (Mexico City: Patronato Cultural Iberoamericano, 1990) 18.

25. The quoted passage is from St. John Damascene, *On Holy Images*, tr. Mary H. Allies (London: Thomas Baker, 1898) 201. The 1745 example is from Elin Luque Agraz, *El arte de dar gracias: los exvotos pictóricos de la Virgen de la Soledad de Oaxaca* (Mexico City: Centro de Cultura Casa Lamm, 2007) 77. For examples of publicizing miracles in another period and region, see Cartledge, *Vows*, 86, and 94–98. See also Vauchez, *Sainthood*, 457, where "people felt under an obligation to promote the reputation of their protector."

26. The first quoted phrase is from Robert Maniura, "Ex Votos, Art and Pious Performance," *Oxford Art Journal* 32/3 (2009): 425; see 422–423. See also Stark, "Micro Foundations," 269–270 and 276, where "in pursuit of rewards, humans will seek to utilize and manipulate the supernatural" and do so through exchange (269); Velasco Toro, *De la historia*, 150; Rodríguez-Shadow and Shadow, *El pueblo*, 178; Gurevich, *Medieval*, 45–46; Robert A. Scott, *Miracle Cures: Saints, Pilgrimage, and the Healing Powers of Belief* (Berkeley: University of California Press, 2010) 33; W. J. Mander, "Theism, Pantheism, and Petitionary Prayer," *Religious Studies* 43/03 (2007): 320; Keith Thomas, *Religion and the Decline of Magic* (New York: Charles Scribner's Sons, 1971) 43; Eamon Duffy, *The Stripping of the Altars: Traditional Religion in England c.1400–c.1580* (New Haven, CT: Yale University Press, 1992) 183–184; and Margaret M. Poloma and George H. Gallup, Jr., *Varieties of Prayer* (Philadelphia: Trinity Press International, 1991) 31, where devotees make the "egocentric assumption that God's control of the world is dependent on the desires of the person praying."

27. The first quoted passage is from Bull, *Miracles*, 118. The second quoted passage is from Lasso de la Vega, "El gran acontecimiento," 303. See LiDonnici, *Epidaurian*, 93 and 105; Van Straten, "Gifts," 73; Freedberg, *Power of Images*, 138; and Philip. C. Watkins, Jason Scheer, Melinda Ovnicek, and Russell Kolts, "The Debt of Gratitude: Dissociating Gratitude and Indebtedness," *Cognition and Emotion* 20/2 (2006): 236.

28. The first quoted passage is from Barabas, *Dones*, 173. Regarding other punishments, see Ramiro Alfonso Gómez Arzapalo Dorantes, *Los santos, mudos predicadores de otra historia: la religiosidad popular en los pueblos de la región de Chalma* (Veracruz, Mexico: Editora de Gobierno del Estado de Veracruz, 2009) 54 and 207. For a San Antonio example, see John M. Ingham, *Mary, Michael, and Lucifer: Folk Catholicism in Central Mexico* (Austin: University of Texas Press, 1986) 100. In folk tales spiritual helpers are held in bondage; see Lewis Hyde, *The Gift: Imagination and the Erotic Life of Property* (New York: Vintage Books, 1983) 48–49. Regarding images "punished in order to force them to carry out their duties" (111), see Patrick J. Geary, *Living with the Dead in the Middle Ages* (Ithaca, NY: Cornell University Press, 1994) 111–117. See also Duffy, "Stripping of the Altars," 185; and H. S. Versnel, "Religious Mentality in Ancient Prayer," *Faith, Hope, and Worship*, 38–40. Regarding devotees as slaves, see Avila and Tena, "Morir," 236 and 247; and Elin Luque Agraz, *El arte de dar gracias: los exvotos*

pictóricos de María del Rosario de Talpa (Mexico City: Editorial Lamm, 2014) 36–37, where the text of the slavery pledge is reproduced.

29. The first quoted passage is from a retablo in Karina Jazmín Juárez Ramírez, *Exvotos retablitos: el arte de los milagros* (Guanajuato, Mexico: Centro de las Artes de Guanajuato and Ediciones Rana, 2008) 63; and the second is from a retablo in the Museo Frida Kahlo collection. The last quoted passage is in Van Straten, "Gifts," 71. Among Nahuas, *nextlahualli* (debt payment) was a commonly used metaphor for human sacrifice.

Regarding votive offerings as receipts, see Dillon, "Didactic," 251. Regarding accounting, see R. C. Finucane, *The Rescue of the Innocents: Endangered Children in Medieval Miracles* (New York: St. Martin's, 1997) 12; and Alexia Petsalēs-Diomēdēs, *Truly Beyond Wonders: Aelius Aristides and the Cult of Asklepios* (Oxford: Oxford University Press, 2010) 254–255.

30. For examples of expressed gratitude, see Juárez Ramírez, *Exvotos*, 103 and 105; and Gloria Fraser Giffords, ed. *Artes de México* 53, *Retablos y exvotos* (2000): 52–55. The quoted passage regarding dissociation is from Watkins, Scheer, Ovnicek, and Kolts, "The Debt," 236. See Maureen A. Matthews and Jeffrey D. Green, "Looking at Me, Appreciating You: Self-Focused Attention Distinguishes between Gratitude and Indebtedness," *Cognition and Emotion* 24/4 (2010): 711. The quoted passages at the end of the paragraph are from Joel R. Davitz, *The Language of Emotion* (New York: Academic Press, 1969) 60. See Emmons and McCullough, "Counting Blessings," 377–379 and 386–388; Neal Krause, "Gratitude Toward God, Stress, and Health in Late Life," *Research on Aging* 28/2 (2006): 165–167; David Steindl-Rast, "Gratitude as Thankfulness and as Gratefulness," *The Psychology of Gratitude*, ed. Robert E. Emmons and Michael E. McCullough (New York: Oxford University Press, 2004) 283; Ross Buck, "The Gratitude of Exchange and the Gratitude of Caring," *Psychology of Gratitude*, 101; Sara B. Algoe, Jonathan Haidt, and Shelly L. Gable, "Beyond Reciprocity: Gratitude and Relationships in Everyday Life," *Emotion*, 8/3 (2008): 425 and 429; and Joseph Anthony Amato II, *Guilt and Gratitude: A Study of the Origins of Contemporary Conscience* (Westport, CT: Greenwood Press, 1982) 28.

31. See Duffin, *Medical Miracles*, 180, where votive offerings "transform the brief moment of cure into a static and enduring object that argues silently."

32. See Vauchez, *Sainthood*, 452–453, where "the act of the donor was also a piece of propaganda."

33. The quoted passage regarding Niño de Atocha is in Museo Casa Estudio Diego Rivera y Frida Kahlo and Mexic-Arte Museum, *Fe, arte y cultura: Santo Niño de Atocha, exvotos* (Mexico City: Consejo Nacional para la Cultura y las Arte, Instituto Nacional de Bellas Artes, Museo Casa Estudio Diego Rivera y Frida Kahlo, Mexic-Arte Museum, Diócesis de Zacatecas, Santuario de Plateros, 2000) 106.

34. The newsletter announcement is from *Santa María de El Pueblito* 12/12 (2007): 17. Note that the word "miracle" is not used; that the miracles are performed

through intercession, not by the image; and that published acknowledgment of miracles is in lieu of material offerings. For an example of a rapid increase of miracles as a result of promoted precedents, see Kate Wagle, "Vernacular of the Sacred: Laminae Ex Voto in Southern Italy," *Metalsmith* 18/2 (1998): 32.

35. In the first sentence I am adapting a phrase from Michel Foucault, *Discipline and Punish: The Birth of the Prison,* tr. Alan Sheridan (New York: Vintage Books, 1979) 111. The last quoted passage is in Carlos Monsiváis and Elin Luque Agraz, *Los relatos pintados: la otra historia, exvotos mexicanos* (Mexico City: Centro de Cultura Casa Lamm, 2010) 41. For other examples of offerings as publicity see 31, 79, and 157. See also Juárez Ramírez, 75, 87, 107, 109, 116, and 118.

36. The first quoted passage is from Marzal, *Tierra,* 376. Regarding ratified recipients, see Marta Dynel, "'You Talking to Me?' The Viewer as a Ratified Listener to Film Discourse," *Journal of Pragmatics* 43/6 (2011): 1629–1630. In film the characters are talking to one another, not to the viewer, but viewers are ratified recipients because the scripted discourse "is designed for them first and foremost" (1630). See Little, *Benedictine,* 20; and Christopher S. Wood, "The Votive Scenario," *Res: Anthropology and Aesthetics* 59/60 (2011): 207, where fifteenth-century pilgrims perform for miraculous saints, but also for one another.

37. The penultimate quoted passage is from a retablo in Juárez Ramírez, "Exvotos," 75; and the last quoted passage is from a retablo in the New Mexico State University Art Gallery collection.

38. The quoted passage is from Albert Bandura, *Self-Efficacy: The Exercise of Control* (New York: W. H. Freeman, 1997) 17. See Foster, *Tzintzuntzan,* 228 and 242. Regarding Gaby's remark, see Robert E. Emmons, "The Psychology of Gratitude: An Introduction," *Psychology of Gratitude,* 8, for "the perceived inferiority of the receiver relative to the giver." Regarding asymmetrical exchange, see David Morgan, *The Embodied Eye: Religious Visual Culture and the Social Life of Feeling* (Berkeley: University of California Press, 2012) 87–88.

39. The quoted passages on compadrazgo are from Robert V. Kemper, "The Compadrazgo in Urban Mexico," *Anthropological Quarterly* 55/1 (1982): 26. The phrase "affectionate dependence" is from Duffy, "Stripping of the Altars," 161. Regarding human norms as models, see Gómez Arzapalo Dorantes, *Los Santos,* 53; and Maniura, "Ex Votos," 422. Linguistic "rules of request" are summarized in William Labov and David Fanshel, *Therapeutic Discourse: Psychotherapy as Conversation* (New York: Academic Press, 1977) 78–93.

40. The last quoted passage is in Renée de la Torre and Fernando Guzmán, "Santo Toribio: De mártir de Los Altos a santo de emigrantes," *Estudios del hombre* 25 (2008): 121. See Jacobus de Voragine, *The Golden Legend: Readings on the Saints,* tr. William Granger Ryan (Princeton, NJ: Princeton University Press, 1993) 1/152, where a woman had nothing but a single pig, a wolf made off with it, and St. Blaise made the wolf give it back. In thanks the woman killed the pig and offered its head, its feet, a candle, and a loaf of bread; she kept the meat.

41. See Kapuściński, *Shadow*, 277, for similar symbolic exchange in Africa.
42. The Ramón example is from Patricia Campos Rodríguez, "Migración a través de los exvotos. El Niño de la Cruzada: El que cruza el Río Bravo. Parritas, San Diego de la Unión, Guanajuato," *Sincronía* 3 (2009): 6. The Chela example is from Carro-Ripalda, "Señor de Carácuaro," 40. The last quoted passage is from field-notes in Manuel Uribe Cruz, *Identidad étnica y mayordomías en zonas de alta concentración industrial. El caso de nos Nahuas, Popolucas y Zapotecas del Istmo Veracruzano en el siglo XX*," doctoral dissertation (Universidad Veracruzana, 2002) 243, n. 141.
43. See Congregación para el Culto Divino y la Disciplina de los Sacramentos, *Actas y documentos pontificios: directorio sobre la piedad popular y la liturgia* (Mexico City: San Pablo, 2002) 231.
44. The last quoted passage is in Neal Krause and Elena Bastida, "Religion, Suffering, and Health among Older Mexican Americans," *Journal of Aging Studies* 23/2 (2009): 117.
45. The last quoted phrases are from Avila and Tena, "Morir," 241; see 242 regarding the priests' encouragement. The Theophrastus passage is from Van Straten, "Gifts," 68. See Minucius Felix quoted in Ernst Kitzinger, "The Cult of Images in the Age before Iconoclasm," *Dumbarton Oaks Papers* 8 (1954): 89: "Shall I offer to God victims and sacrifices which He has furnished for my use, and so reject His bounties?" See also Dow, *Santos*, 118, where offerings are "more a moral commitment than a commercial relation." Friedrich Nietzsche, *On the Genealogy of Morals; Ecce Homo*, tr. Walter Kaufmann and R. J. Hollingdale (New York: Vintage Books, 1969) 65 and 66 (from *Genealogy*) questions, "to what extent can suffering balance debts or guilt?" and "how can suffering constitute a compensation?" On 92 (from *Genealogy*), "suddenly we stand before the paradoxical and horrifying expedient that afforded temporary relief for tormented humanity, that stroke of genius on the part of Christianity: God himself sacrifices himself for the guilt of mankind, God himself makes payment to himself, God as the only being who can redeem man from what has become unredeemable for man himself—the creditor sacrifices himself for the debtor, out of love (can one credit that?), out of love for his debtor!"
46. The first quoted passage is from a retablo in the Wellcome Collection exhibit "Infinitas Gracias: Mexican Miracle Paintings," London, October 6, 2011–February 26, 2012. The Guadalupe example is from a 1649 account in Lasso de la Vega, "El gran acontecimiento," 299; and the Zapopan and Talpa examples are from Francisco de Florencia, *Zodiaco mariano*, ed. Juan A. Oviedo, intro. Antonio Rubial García (Mexico City: Consejo Nacional para la Cultura y las Artes, 1995) 344 and 354–356. See other resuscitations on 360, 362, 364, 365; and in Florencia, *Origen*, 21.
47. The quoted passage is from Marzal, *Tierra*, 375. See Gómez Arzapalo Dorantes, *Los Santos*, 246. See also Mark Corner, *Signs of God: Miracles and their Interpretation*

(Burlington, VT: Ashgate, 2005) 13, where "there is no absent Deity making occasional visits; there is an ever-present Deity who varies the divine modus operandi in relation to the world." In R. W. Southern, *The Making of the Middle Ages* (New Haven, CT: Yale University Press, 1976) 254, miracles are everyday occurrences but also expand "the range of human experience."

48. The quoted passages are in Krause and Bastida, "Exploring," 8, 9, 9, and 16, respectively. See 8–10 and 13 for other examples. See also Gómez Arzapalo Dorantes, *Los Santos,* 256.

49. The quoted passage is from CELAM, "Documento conclusivo,"150. See CELAM, Región Cono Sur, "Piedad," 9, where God's care is experienced as "always present" in everyday life. See Gómez Arzapalo Dorantes, *Los Santos,* 245; Cornelio Chaparro and Jaime Enrique, "La religiosidad popular entre los matlatzincas," *Espacios públicos* 8/15 (2005): 256; and Peter L. Berger and Thomas Luckmann, *The Social Construction of Reality: A Treatise in the Sociology of Knowledge* (New York: Doubleday, 1966) 103, for "the ongoing penetration of the world of everyday experience by sacred forces."

50. Fidencio's story is from José Guadalupe Posada, "Verdadera imagen del Señor de Chalma" (Mexico City: Antonio Vanegas Arroyo 1903), Library of Congress Prints and Photographs Division: www.loc.gov/pictures/item/99615958/. The Virgen de la Bala example is from Florencia, *Zodiaco,* 130. See Nicanor Quirós y Gutiérrez, *Historia de la aparición de Nuestra Señora de Ocotlán: y de su culto en cuatro siglos (1541–1941)* (Mexico City: Taller Linotipograf de la Escuela R. Donde, 1940) 178, where a man is shot but saved because the bullet landed precisely on the medallion of the Virgen de Ocotlán that he was wearing. See also Gregory of Tours, *Glory of the Martyrs,* tr. and with an introduction by Raymond Van Dam (Liverpool: Liverpool University Press, 1988) 49, where one is "protected more by his faith than by a shield."

51. There is a photograph of the bent crucifix in Campa Mendoza, *Santuarios,* 174. See 176. For another example from a different period and region, see Peggy McCracken, "Miracles, Mimesis, and the Efficacy of Images," *Yale French Studies* 110 (2006): 55, where a wooden image of the Virgin extends a leg to take an arrow intended for an archer defending her church.

52. For an example of constant help that intensifies during crises, see Foster, *Tzintzuntzan,* 234–235.

53. The Pueblito example is in *Santa Maria de El Pueblito* 12/12 (2007): 15.

54. The tortilla example is from "Interview with María Isabel Cuellar and her son Rogelio Torres, Guanajuato," in a 2010 film by Livia Radwanski included in the exhibit "Infinitas Gracias" at the Wellcome Collection, London.

55. The first mentioned study is Vauchez, *Sainthood,* 468 (he calls the miracles "therapeutic"); and the second is Duffin, *Medical Miracles,* 72; see 73. In Elin Luque Agraz, "Ellas querían construir un idioma propio. Selección de exvotos pictóricos de México con la imagen de la mujer como protagonista de la obra,"

Espacio, tiempo y forma 7/17 (2004): 237, 60 percent of the miracles in retablos concerned health problems. See Avila and Tena, "Morir," 240; and José Luis Noria Sánchez, "El Santuario de Juquila y los usos ideológicos," *Caminos terrestres al cielo: contribución al estudio del fenómeno romero*, ed. Beatriz Barba de Piña Chán (Mexico City: Instituto Nacional de Antropología e Historia, 1998) 99.

56. The example is from *Dones y promesas*, 169, cat. 205.

57. The last example is from Luis E. Orozco, *Los Cristos de caña de maíz y otras venerables imágenes de Nuestro Señor Jesucristo* (Guadalajara [n. p.] 1970) 457. There is another similar example on the same page.

58. For horse-related accidents, see Luque Agraz, *El Arte*, 101 and 151; Florencia, *Origen*, 20 and 107; Francisco de Florencia, *La milagrosa invención de un tesoro escondido*, ed. Peláez T. Matabuena and Lobato M. Rodríguez (Mexico City: Universidad Iberoamericana, 2008) 228; Campa Mendoza, *Santuarios*, 243; and Francisco Gallegos Franco, *Los retablos del Señor de la Misericordia de Tepatitlán* (Guadalajara: Conaculta, Secretaría de Cultura de Jalisco, Feca, Grupo Modelo, 2001) 60; on 117 a woman is saved from a bear attack.

59. The Virgen de San Juan example is from a retablo in the International Museum of Folk Art, Santa Fe, New Mexico (accession number 66.77.3). For other examples of lightning strikes see *Dones y promesas*, 182, cat. 246 and cat. 248. For fires see James Caswell and Jenise Amanda Ramos, eds., *Saints and Sinners: Mexican Devotional Art* (Atglen, PA: Schiffer, 2006) 161.

60. A retablo in Luque Agraz, "Ellas," 225, shows the attempted murder of a wife due to malicious gossip. See 231.

61. Migration-related retablos are reproduced in Jorge Durand and Douglas S. Massey, *Miracles on the Border: Retablos of Mexican Migrants to the United States* (Tucson: University of Arizona Press, 1995); and Pescador, *Crossing Borders*, 141–142.

62. For examples of saints petitioned for rain and good harvest, see John M. Ingham, *Mary*, 99–100.

63. The last quoted passage is in Thomas Calvo, Marianne Bélard, and Philippe Verrier "Cotidiano familiar y milagro: el exvoto en el occidente de Mexico. 1880–1940," *Familia y vida privada en la historia de Iberoamérica*, ed. Pilar Gonzalbo Aizpuru and Cecilia Rabell Romero (Mexico City: El Colegio de Mexico and Universidad Autónoma de México, 1996) 467.

64. For examples of victims of abuse, injustice, and near execution, see Caswell and Ramos, *Saints*, 70 and 157 ("beaten by a policeman who left him almost dead without any reason"); and Roberto Montenegro, *Retablos de México* (Mexico City: Ediciones Mexicanas, 1950) 63. Several medieval examples of freedom from prison are in *The Book of Sainte Foy*, 189–197.

65. The embroidered offering is in *Dones y promesas*, 181, cat. 244, and also reproduced in Luque Agraz, "Ellas," 233. The retablo to the Virgen de San Juan is in *Dones y promesas*, 167, cat. 199.

66. The passage from San Juan de los Lagos is in Campa Mendoza, *Santuarios*, 253. See M. E. McCullough, R. A. Emmons, and J. Tsang, "The Grateful Disposition: A Conceptual and Empirical Topography," *Journal of Personality and Social Psychology* 82/1 (2002): 113, where "what might distinguish grateful people is an ability to stretch their attributions to incorporate the wide range of people who contribute to their well-being."

JUQUILA

1. Regarding the difficulty of expressing intuitive knowledge, see Scott Atran, *In Gods We Trust: The Evolutionary Landscape of Religion* (New York: Oxford University Press, 2002) 83, where commonsense beliefs "remain implicit and are rarely articulated." On 96, "a few fragmentary narrative descriptions or episodes suffice to mobilize an enormously rich network of implicit background beliefs." See also Roy D'Andrade, "A Folk Model of the Mind," *Cultural Models in Language and Thought*, ed. Dorothy Holland and Naomi Quinn (Cambridge: Cambridge University Press, 1987) 114, where "They use the model but they cannot produce a reasonable description of the model. In this sense, the model is like a well-learned set of procedures one knows how to carry out rather than a body of fact one can recount." Similar ideas are developed in C. R. Brewin, "Cognitive Change Processes in Psychotherapy," *Psychological Review* 96/3 (1989): 380 ("dissociation between verbal knowledge and task performance"); and Richard S. Lazarus, *Emotion and Adaptation* (New York: Oxford University Press, 1991) 152–153. See also Corey M. Abramson, "From 'Either-Or' to 'When and How': A Context-Dependent Model of Culture in Action," *Journal for the Theory of Social Behaviour* 42/2 (2012): 155–158 and 162.

2. Regarding the constitutive role, see Yaacov Yadgar, "Tradition," *Human Studies* 36/4 (2013): 456.

3. Regarding scripts, see Ronnie Janoff-Bulman and Christine Timko, "Coping with Traumatic Life Events: The Role of Denial in Light of People's Assumptive Worlds," *Coping with Negative Life Events: Clinical and Social Psychological Perspectives*, ed. C. R. Snyder and Carol E. Ford (New York: Plenum Press, 1987) 137–138; and Michael Cole, *Cultural Psychology: A Once and Future Discipline* (Cambridge, MA: Belknap Press, 2000) 126. In the last sentence I am adapting an insight from James R. Averill, "Emotional Creativity: Toward 'Spiritualizing the Passions,'" *Handbook of Positive Psychology*, ed. C. R. Snyder and Shane J. Lopez (New York: Oxford University Press, 2002) 175.

4. The earliest published source on the Virgen de Juquila is Joseph Manuel Ruiz y Cervantes, *Memorias de la portentosa imagen de Nuestra Señora De Xuquila* (Mexico City: Felipe de Zúñiga y Ontiveros, 1791). I am following María Concepción Amerlinck De Corsi, "Las memorias de la portentosa imagen de Nuestra Señora de Xuquila y el grabador Francisco Agüera Bustamante," *Boletín de monumentos*

históricos 3/27 (2013): 199–200. See also a booklet sold at the pedimento, Juan Castro Méndez, *La Virgen de Juquila en la historia* (Oaxaca: Imprenta Postal, 2000) 17. An 1899 source describes multitudes of pilgrims visiting Juquila in Edward Wright-Rios, *Revolutions in Mexican Catholicism: Reform and Revelation in Oaxaca, 1887–1934* (Durham, NC: Duke University Press, 2009) 88. *Santocales* in Nahua devotion are discussed in Caterina Pizzigoni, *The Life Within: Local Indigenous Society in Mexico's Toluca Valley, 1650–1800* (Redwood City, CA: Stanford University Press, 2012) 23–25, 44, and 223.

5. Fake money and miniatures of petitioned objects are used in some Andean devotions, including Qoyllur Rit'i rituals and devotion to the god of abundance known as Ekeko. In Argentina, models (primarily of houses and businesses) are used as votive offerings to the folk saint Difunta Correa. See Frank Graziano, *Cultures of Devotion: Folk Saints of Spanish America* (New York: Oxford University Press, 2007) 188–189.

SEEING THROUGH FAITH

1. See Corey M. Abramson, "From 'Either-Or' to 'When and How': A Context-Dependent Model of Culture in Action," *Journal for the Theory of Social Behaviour* 42 (2012): 172; Curtis D. Hardin and E. Tory Higgins, "Shared Reality: How Social Verification Makes the Subjective Objective," *Handbook of Motivation and Cognition*, Vol. 3, *The Interpersonal Context*, ed. Richard M. Sorrentino and E. Tory Higgins (New York: Guilford Press, 1996) 36; David R. Heise, "Delusions and the Construction of Reality," *Delusional Beliefs*, ed. Thomas F. Oltmanns and Brendan A. Maher (New York: John Wiley and Sons, 1988) 259; Paul W. Pruyser, *Between Belief and Unbelief* (New York: Harper & Row, 1974) 201; Sharon Hays, "Structure and Agency and the Sticky Problem of Culture," *Sociological Theory* 12/1 (1994): 65; Peter Berger, *The Sacred Canopy: Elements of a Sociological Theory of Religion* (Garden City: Doubleday and Company, 1967) 6 and 19; Peter Berger and Stanley Pullberg, "Reification and the Sociological Critique of Consciousness," *History and Theory* 4/2 (1965): 206; Jerome S. Bruner, *Acts of Meaning* (Cambridge, MA: Harvard University Press, 1990) 67; Ann Swindler, "Culture in Action: Symbols and Strategies," *American Sociological Review* 51/2 (1986): 280–281; Miguel A. Cabrera, Anna Fagan, and Marie McMahon, "On Language, Culture, and Social Action," *History and Theory* 40/4 (2001): 84; James W. Jones, *Contemporary Psychoanalysis and Religion: Transference and Transcendence* (New Haven, CT: Yale University Press, 1991) 85; Robert A. Orsi, "Is the Study of Lived Religion Irrelevant to the World We Live In? Special Presidential Plenary Address, Society for the Scientific Study of Religion, Salt Lake City, Utah, November 2, 2002," *Journal for the Scientific Study of Religion* 42/2 (2003): 172; and David Morgan, *The Sacred Gaze: Religious Visual Culture in Theory and Practice* (Berkeley: University of California Press, 2005) 3. The epigraph to this

chapter is from Richard S. Lazarus, "Cognitive and Coping Processes in Emotion," *Stress and Coping: An Anthology,* ed. Alan Monat and Richard S. Lazarus (New York: Columbia University Press, 1977) 149.

2. The quoted passage is from CELAM, Región Cono Sur, "Piedad popular a la luz de Aparecida: un desafío para el ver, juzgar y actuar pastoral. Encuentro sobre misión continental y conversión pastoral" (Buenos Aires, October 26 to 29, 2009) 10. See Nina P. Azari and Dieter Birnbacher, "The Role of Cognition and Feeling in Religious Experience," *Zygon* 39/4 (2004): 912; and Clifford Geertz, "Religion as a Cultural System," *The Interpretation of Cultures: Selected Essays* (London: Fontana Press: 1993) 89, where "sacred symbols function to synthesize a people's ethos—the tone, character, and quality of their life, its moral and aesthetic style and mood—and their world view—the picture they have of the way things in sheer actuality are, their most comprehensive ideas of order"; and 124, where "more than a gloss, such beliefs are also a template. They do not merely interpret social and psychological processes in cosmic terms... but they shape them."

3. The quoted passage is from Ray Paloutzian, Steven A. Rogers, Erica L. Swenson, and Deborah A. Lowe, "Miracle Attributions, Meaning, and Neuropsychology," *Miracles: God, Science, and Psychology in the Paranormal,* Vol. 2 *Medical and Therapeutic Events,* ed. J. Harold Ellens (Westport, CT: Greenwood Publishing, 2008) 53. See Orsi, "Is the Study," 172–173; Robert Orsi, "Everyday Miracles: The Study of Lived Religion," *Lived Religion in America: Toward a History of Practice,* ed. David D. Hall (Princeton, NJ: Princeton University Press, 1997) 7; Berger, *Sacred Canopy,* 42; Brad S. Gregory, "The Other Confessional History: On Secular Bias in the Study of Religion," *History and Theory* 45/4 (2006): 133 and 148; and Richard A. Shweder, "Likeness and Likelihood in Everyday Thought: Magical Thinking in Judgments About Personality," *Current Anthropology* 18/4 (1977): 641.

4. The quoted passage is from Richard S. Lazarus, "Thoughts on the Relations Between Emotion and Cognition," *American Psychologist* 37/9 (1982): 1020. See Harold G. Koenig, Michael E. McCullough, and David B. Larson, *Handbook of Religion and Health* (New York: Oxford University Press, 2001) 221; H. Porter Abbott, "Reading Intended Meaning Where None is Intended: A Cognitivist Reappraisal of the Implied Author," *Poetics Today* 32/3 (2011): 479; and Mark Currie, *Postmodern Narrative Theory* (New York: St. Martin's, 1998) 133, where a narrative is articulated by a reading with "oscillation between objectivity and subjectivity."

5. The quoted passages are from Berger, *Sacred Canopy,* 29 and 50, respectively.

6. The first two quoted phrases are from T. M. Luhrmann, "A Hyperreal God and Modern Belief: Toward an Anthropological Theory of Mind," *Current Anthropology* 53/4 (2012): 372 and 380, respectively. Regarding faith and doubt, I am adapting insights from Brendan A. Maher, "Anomalous Experience and Delusional

Thinking: The Logic of Explanations," *Delusional Beliefs*, 20–21. See also Orsi, "Everyday Miracles," 5; and Jesse M. Bering and Dominic D. P. Johnson, "'O Lord... You Perceive my Thoughts from Afar': Recursiveness and the Evolution of Supernatural Agency," *Journal of Cognition and Culture* 5/1–2 (2005): 119.

7. The quoted passage is from Berger, *Sacred Canopy*, 24; see 21 and 47. See also Michael E. McCullough and Brian L. B. Willoughby, "Religion, Self-Regulation, and Self-Control: Associations, Explanations, and Implications," *Psychological Bulletin* 135/1 (2009): 79. Regarding the parent as amplifier, I am adapting an insight from Paul S. Fiddes, *The Creative Suffering of God* (Oxford: Clarendon Press, 1988) 154. Regarding assimilation of youth to religion, see W. W. Meissner, *Psychoanalysis and Religious Experience* (New Haven, CT: Yale University Press, 1984) 178. For an example see Vicente Acosta, *Nuestra Señora del Pueblito: compendio histórico de su culto* (Querétaro: Gobierno del Estado de Querétaro, 1996) 37.

8. See Tanya L. Chartrand and John A. Bargh, "The Chameleon Effect: The Perception-Behavior Link and Social Interaction," *Journal of Personality and Social Psychology* 76/6 (1999): 897; Stephen Gudeman, "Saints, Symbols, and Ceremonies," *American Ethnologist* 3/4 (1976): 727; and Hardin and Higgins, "Shared Reality," 30.

9. The quoted phrase is from Meissner, 178. The longer quoted passage is from Roy D'Andrade, *The Development of Cognitive Anthropology* (Cambridge: Cambridge University Press, 1995) 229. See the discussion regarding identification and introjection in McCullough and Willoughby, "Religion," 79–80. Regarding social transmission, see John F. Kihlstrom, Shelagh Mulvaney, Betsy A. Tobias, and Irene P. Tobis, "The Emotional Unconscious," in Eric Eich, John F. Kihlstrom, Gordon H. Bower, Joseph P. Forgas, and Paula M. Niedenthal, *Cognition and Emotion* (New York: Oxford University Press, 2000) 33–34; Richard S Lazarus, *Emotion and Adaptation* (New York: Oxford University Press, 1991), 135 and 377–383; John F. Kihlstrom, Terrence M. Barnhardt, and Douglas J. Tataryn,"Implicit Perception," *Perception without Awareness*, ed. Robert F. Bornstein and Thane S. Pittman (New York: Guilford Press, 1992) 22; Claire Armon-Jones, "The Thesis of Constructionism," *The Social Construction of Emotions*, ed. Rom Harré (Oxford: Basil Blackwell, 1986) 33–34; and Joseph P. Forgas, "Feeling and Thinking: Summary and Integration," *Feeling and Thinking: The Role of Affect in Social Cognition*, ed. Joseph P. Forgas (Cambridge: Cambridge University Press and Paris: Éditions de la Maison des Sciences de l'Homme, 2000) 393. Regarding my experience at the Señor del Rayo chapel, see Gerald L. Clore and W. Gerrod Parrott, "Moods and Their Vicissitudes: Thoughts and Feelings as Information," *Emotion and Social Judgments*, ed. Joseph P. Forgas (Oxford: Pergamon Press, 1991) 109, where "we would insist on interposing between events and emotions a cognitive analysis wherein the personal significance of the events is appraised."

10. The quoted passage is from Bernard Spilka, Phillip Shaver and Lee A. Kirkpatrick, "A General Attribution Theory for the Psychology of Religion,"

Journal for the Scientific Study of Religion 24/1 (1985): 3; see 6–7. Regarding control, see also Shelley E. Taylor, "Adjustment to Threatening Events: A Theory of Cognitive Adaptation," *American Psychologist* 38/11 (1983): 161; Katherine L. Fiori, Judith C. Hays, and Keith G. Meador, "Spiritual Turning Points and Perceived Control Over the Life Course," *International Journal of Aging and Human Development* 59/4 (2004): 397; James E. Maddux, "Expectancies and the Social-Cognitive Perspective: Basic Principles, Processes, and Variables," *How Expectancies Shape Experience*, ed. Irving Kirsch (Washington, DC: American Psychological Association, 1999) 31; and Fred Rothbaum, John R. Weisz, and Samuel S. Snyder, "Changing the World and Changing the Self: A Two-Process Model of Perceived Control," *Journal of Personality and Social Psychology* 42/1 (1982): 11. See also Kenneth I. Pargament, David S. Ensing, Kathryn Falgout, Hannah Olsen, Barbara Reilly, Kimberly Van Haitsma, and Richard Warren "God help me: (1): Religious Coping Efforts as Predictors of the Outcomes to Significant Negative Life Events," in Larry VandeCreek, *Spiritual Needs and Pastoral Services: Readings in Research* (Decatur, GA: Journal of Pastoral Care Publications, 1995) 82. For an overview of studies regarding prayer as a coping strategy, see Michael E. McCullough and David B. Larson, "Prayer," *Integrating Spirituality Into Treatment: Resources for Practitioners*, ed. William R. Miller (Washington, DC: American Psychological Association, 2000) 85–86.

11. See Pargament "God help me: (1)," 81; and Geertz, "Religion," 100.

12. The first two quoted passages are from Ronnie Janoff-Bulman and Cynthia McPherson Frantz, "The Impact of Trauma on Meaning: From Meaningless World to Meaningful Life," *The Transformation of Meaning in Psychological Therapies: Integrating Theory and Practice*, ed. Michael J. Power and Chris Brewin (Chichester, UK: Wiley, 1997) 95. I am closely following 94–95; see 101. See also Ronnie Janoff-Bulman and Christine Timko, "Coping with Traumatic Life Events: The Role of Denial in Light of People's Assumptive Worlds," *Coping with Negative Life Events: Clinical and Social Psychological Perspectives*, ed. C. R. Snyder and Carol E. Ford (New York: Plenum Press, 1987) 142. The third quoted passage and its context are from Jerome D. Frank, *Persuasion and Healing: A Contemporary Study of Psychotherapy* (Baltimore: Johns Hopkins University Press, 1973) 47. See Roy F. Baumeister and Kathleen D. Vohs, "The Pursuit of Meaningfulness in Life," in C. R. Snyder and Shane J. Lopez, eds., *Handbook of Positive Psychology* (New York: Oxford University Press, 2002) 609.

13. The first quoted passage is from Anthony Giddens, *Modernity and Self-Identity: Self and Society in the Late Modern Age* (Redwood City, CA: Stanford University Press, 1991) 36; the later quoted phrase and its context are from 37.

14. The first quoted phrase is from Janoff-Bulman and McPherson Frantz, "Impact," 95; and the second is from Bernard Spilka, *The Psychology of Religion: An Empirical Approach* (New York: Guilford Press, 2003) 483.The third quoted passage is from Kenneth I. Pargament and Annette Mahoney, "Spirituality:

Discovering and Conserving the Sacred," *Handbook of Positive Psychology*, 653; and the fourth is from Kenneth I. Pargament, Hannah Olsen, Barbara Reilly, Kathryn Falgout, David S. Ensing, and Kimberly Van Haitsma, "God Help Me (II): The Relationship of Religious Orientations to Religious Coping with Negative Life Events," *Journal for the Scientific Study of Religion* 31/4 (1992): 509. Regarding religious coping cognitions, see Kenneth I. Pargament, *The Psychology of Religion and Coping: Theory, Research, Practice* (New York: Guilford Press, 1997); Baumeister and Vohs, "Pursuit," 613; Neal Krause, "Gratitude Toward God, Stress, and Health in Late Life," *Research on Aging* 28/2 (2006): 163 and 166; Kate Miriam Loewenthal, Andrew K. MacLeod, Vivienne Goldblatt, Guy Lubitsh, and John D. Valentine, "Comfort and Joy? Religion, Cognition and Mood in Protestants and Jews Under Stress," *Cognition and Emotion* 14/3 (2000) 357; Andrew P. Tix and Patricia A. Frazier, "The Use of Religious Coping During Stressful Life Events: Main Effects, Moderation, and Mediation," *Journal of Consulting and Clinical Psychology* 66/2 (1998): 411–412; Helen K. Black, "Poverty and Prayer: Spiritual Narratives of Elderly African-American Women," *Review of Religious Research* 40/4 (1999): 359 and 372; Susan Nolen-Hoeksema and Christopher G. Davis, "Positive Responses to Loss: Perceiving Benefits and Growth," *Handbook of Positive Psychology*, 604; Barbara L. Fredrickson and Thomas Joiner, "Positive Emotions Trigger Upward Spirals Toward Emotional Well-Being," *Psychological Science* 13/2 (2002): 172; Laura A. King, "Gain Without Pain? Expressive Writing and Self-Regulation," *The Writing Cure: How Expressive Writing Promotes Health and Emotional Well-Being*, ed. Stephen J. Lepore and Joshua M. Smyth (Washington, DC: American Psychological Association, 2002) 126; Taylor, "Adjustment," 1163 and 1165; Shelley E. Taylor and Jonathon D. Brown, "Illusion and Well-Being: A Social Psychological Perspective on Mental Health," *Psychological Bulletin* 103/2 (1988): 201; and Thomas Ashby Wills and James M. Sandy, "Comparing Favorably: A Cognitive Approach to Coping Through Comparison with Other Persons," *Coping with Stress: Effective People and Processes*, ed. C. R. Snyder (New York: Oxford University Press, 2001) 160–162.

15. The first quoted passage is from Ziva Kunda, *Social Cognition: Making Sense of People* (Cambridge, MA: MIT Press, 1999) 262; the second is from Henri J. M. Nouwen, *Gracias!: A Latin American Journal* (San Francisco: Harper & Row, 1983) 21; and the third is from Jonathan Mercer, "Emotional Beliefs," *International Organization* 64/1 (2010): 6. See William B. Swann and Brett W. Pelham, "The Truth About Illusions: Authenticity and Positivity in Social Relationships," *Handbook of Positive Psychology*, 369–373; and John A. Robinson, "Perspective, Meaning, and Remembering," *Remembering Our Past: Studies in Autobiographical Memory*, ed. David C. Rubin (New York: Cambridge University Press, 1996) 210. The fourth quoted passage is from Janoff-Bulman and Timko, "Coping," 139; see 138. The fifth quoted passage is from Richard Nisbett and Lee Ross,

Human Inference: Strategies and Shortcomings of Social Judgment (Englewood Cliffs, NJ: Prentice-Hall, 1980) 192. On the same page: "Beliefs tend to sustain themselves even despite the total discrediting of the evidence that produced the beliefs initially." See also Geertz, "Religion," 98; Kenneth I. Pargament and Crystal L. Park, "Merely a Defense? The Variety of Religious Means and Ends," *Journal of Social Issues* 51/2 (1995): 16; Valerie Braithwaite, "The Hope Process and Social Inclusion," *Annals of the American Academy of Political and Social Sciences* 592 (2004): 133; Robert A. Emmons, "Is Spirituality an Intelligence? Motivation, Cognition, and the Psychology of Ultimate Concern," *International Journal for the Psychology of Religion* 10/1 (2000): 20; Steven L. Neuberg, "Social Motives and Expectancy-Tinged Social Interactions," *Handbook of Motivation and Cognition*, 233–234; and Azari and Birnbacher, "Role," 912. Regarding faith as a theory, I am adapting an insight in Maher, "Anomalous Experience," 20.

16. The first three quoted passages (grouped together) are from Nisbett and Ross, *Human Inference*, 180; see 180–183. The fourth quoted passage is from Mark Corner, *Signs of God: Miracles and their Interpretation* (Burlington, VT: Ashgate, 2005) 200. The fifth quoted passage is from Ziva Kunda, "The Case for Motivated Reasoning," *Psychological Bulletin* 108/3 (1990): 483. The sixth quoted passage is from Taylor and Brown, "Illusion," 201. The last quoted passage is from Paloutzian, Rogers, Swenson, and Lowe, "Miracle Attributions," 50. See Gregory, "Other Confessional History," 135, where the veracity of religious claims is "entirely irrelevant to the issue of whether certain people believe and are motivated by them"; and Peter L. Berger and Thomas Luckmann, *The Social Construction of Reality: A Treatise in the Sociology of Knowledge* (New York: Doubleday, 1966) 114, where once a doctrine becomes ideology "it is modified in accordance with the interests it must now legitimate." See also Fraser Watts and Mark Williams, *The Psychology of Religious Knowing* (Cambridge: Cambridge University Press, 1988) 7 and 113.

17. The first quoted passage is from Kunda, "Case," 480; and the subsequent quoted phrase and its context are on 482–483. The quoted passages on regulating reality are from Lazarus, "Cognitive," 145. The next quoted passage, on intrinsically religious people, is from Emmons, "Is Spirituality," 12. The last quoted passage is from Andrew Kinney, "Positive Illusions of Well-Being and Irrationality: Implications for Rational-Emotive Behavior Therapy," *Journal of Contemporary Psychotherapy* 30/4 (2000): 410. See Spilka, Shaver, and Kirkpatrick, "General," 8; Raymond L. Higgins, "Reality Negotiation," *Handbook of Positive Psychology*, 355; and Meredith B. McGuire, *Lived Religion: Faith and Practice in Everyday Life* (New York: Oxford University Press, 2008) 33, where "a mode of action is not irrational if a person perceives it to work." Regarding the creative and positive aspects of illusion, see D. W. Winnicott, *Playing and Reality* (New York: Basic Books, 1971) 2–3 and 51; Meissner 176–177; and Jones, *Contemporary*, 38, where "Winnicott's intention is clearly to reframe 'illusory experience' from something

suspect to something positive, as the origin of all creativity and culture." See 39–42. See also Taylor and Brown, "Illusion," 204, where "the mentally healthy person appears to have the enviable capacity to distort reality in a direction that enhances self-esteem, maintains belief in personal efficacy, and promotes an optimistic view of the future." Regarding community reinforcement of this interpretive process, see Neal Krause, "God-Mediated Control and Change in Self-Rated Health," *International Journal for the Psychology of Religion* 20 (2010): 270. For a moderating view, see Kinney, "Positive Illusions," 409, where positive illusions are adaptive to a degree, but "it can be argued that at extreme levels positive illusions are founded on an irrational belief system." For a dissenting view—"there is insufficient evidence to claim that unrealistic optimism is positively related to mental health" (12)—see C. Randall Colvin and Jack Block, "Do Positive Illusions Foster Mental Health? An Examination of the Taylor and Brown Formulation," *Psychological Bulletin* 116/1 (1994): 3–20. See also Swann and Pelham, "Truth," 366–381. Another dissenting opinion is closer to Sigmund Freud's view in *The Future of an Illusion* of religion as "a system of wishful illusions together with a disavowal of reality." See Martin J. Dorahy and Christopher Alan Lewis, "The Relationship between Dissociation and Religiosity: An Empirical Evaluation of Schumaker's Theory," *Journal for the Scientific Study of Religion* 40/2 (2001): 315.

18. The quoted passages is in Taylor, "Adjustment," 1161–1162. See 1164 and 1170–1171. See also Paul T. Wong and Bernard Weiner, "When People Ask 'Why' Questions, and the Heuristics of Attributional Search," *Journal of Personality and Social Psychology* 40/4 (1981): 661; Linda S. Perloff, "Social Comparison and Illusions of Invulnerability to Negative Life Events," *Coping with Negative Life Events*, 235; and Janoff-Bulman and McPherson Frantz, "Impact," 94, where "we maintain an illusion of invulnerability" and right behaviors protect us from misfortune.

19. The quoted passages are from Janoff-Bulman and McPherson Frantz, "Impact," 97. See Jones, *Contemporary*, 83; Arthur Kleinman, *The Illness Narratives: Suffering, Healing, and the Human Condition* (New York, Basic Books, 1988) 20; and Howard Tennen and Glenn Affleck, "Blaming Others for Threatening Events," *Psychological Bulletin* 108/2 (1990): 215 and 217. On 221, "observers are inclined to view outcomes as originating from the actor, whereas actors focus on the situational constraints on their behavior."

20. The first quoted passage is from Viktor Gecas, "The Social Psychology of Self-Efficacy," *Annual Review of Sociology* 15 (1989): 293. The second quoted passage is from Brenda S. Cole and Kenneth I. Pargament, "Spiritual Surrender: A Paradoxical Path to Control," *Integrating Spirituality into Treatment*, 181. The third quoted passage is from Daniel T. Gilbert and Patrick S. Malone, "The Correspondence Bias," *Psychological Bulletin* 117/1 (1995): 29. See Rothbaum, Weisz, and Snyder, "Changing," 11–12, 24, and 26; and Wong and Weiner, "When People

Ask," 661–662. For strategies of interpretive control, see Alfred R. Mele, *Irrationality: An Essay on Akrasia, Self-Deception, and Self-Control* (New York: Oxford University Press, 1987) 125–126 and 144–145. See also Martin E. P. Seligman and Suzanne M. Miller, "The Psychology of Power: Concluding Comments," *Choice and Perceived Control*, ed. Lawrence C. Perlmuter and Richard A. Monty (Hillsdale, NJ: Lawrence Erlbaum, 1979) 355, where in the absence of control predictability is a way to "minimize the perceived randomness of the world."

21. The quoted passage is from Ellen J. Langer, "The Illusion of Control," *Journal of Personality and Social Psychology* 32/2 (1975): 313. Throughout this paragraph I am following this source, particularly 323 and 325.

22. The quoted passage is from Taylor and Brown, "Illusion," 199.

23. The migration example is an adaptation of an insight from Pargament and Hahn, "God," 196. See Jack W. Brehm, "Control, Its Loss, and Psychological Reactance," in Gifford Weary, Faith Gleicher, and Kerry L. Marsh, *Control Motivation and Social Cognition* (New York: Springer-Verlag, 1993) 5; Susana Carro-Ripalda, "El Señor de Carácuaro: una etnografía fenomenológica de una peregrinación en México," *Guaraguao* 5/13 (2001): 42; and Helena Waddy Lepovitz, "The Religious Context of Crisis Resolution in the Votive Paintings of Catholic Europe," *Journal of Social History* 23/4 (1990): 770, where "invokers are purposeful agents acting to solve their problems in a common-sense fashion prescribed by their own cultural context."

24. The first quoted passage is from Philip Pettit, "Hope and Its Place in the Mind," *Annals of the American Academy of Political and Social Sciences* 592 (2004): 159. The second quoted passage is from Valerie Braithwaite, "Collective Hope," *Annals of the American Academy of Political and Social Sciences* 592 (2004): 10. See Braithwaite, "Hope Process," 130. For a more detailed definition of hope, see C. R. Snyder, "Hope Theory: Rainbows in the Mind," *Psychological Inquiry* 13/4 (2002): 250–251.

25. The first quoted phrase is from McCullough and Willoughby, "Religion," 78. See 79, where "goal sanctification promotes effective goal striving." See also Emmons, "Is Spirituality," 11–12; Taylor, "Adjustment," 1161; and Scott Schieman, Tetyana Pudrovska, and Melissa A. Milkie, "The Sense of Divine Control and the Self-Concept: A Study of Race Differences in Late Life," *Research on Aging* 27/2 (2005): 166. Regarding worthiness and a sense of being chosen, see Spilka, Shaver and Kirkpatrick, "General,"14; Black, "Poverty," 364; Enriqueta Valdez Curiel, *Danza de los sonajeros de Zapotlán el Grande: promesas religiosas para recuperar la salud* (Guadalajara: Universidad de Guadalajara, Centro Universidad del Sur, 2006) 8; and Carro-Ripalda, "El Señor de Carácuaro," 48.

26. The quoted passage is from Kleinman, *Illness Narratives,* 45.

27. The quoted passages are in Etsudo Kuroda, *Bajo el Zempoaltépetl: la sociedad mixe de las tierras altas y sus rituales* (Mexico City: Centro de Investigaciones y Estudios Superiores de Antropología Social, 1993) 168 and 169, respectively.

28. Neal Krause and Elena Bastida, "Exploring the Interface between Religion and Contact with the Dead among Older Mexican Americans," *Review of Religious Research* 51/1 (2009): 10.

29. For an insightful related driving analogy in another context, see Ryszard Kapuściński, *The Shadow of the Sun: My African Life*, tr. Klara Glowczewska (Victoria, Australia: Penguin Books, 2008) 186.

30. See Neuberg, "Social Motives," 228–231; Nisbett and Ross, *Human Inference*, 183–186; and Shweder, "Likeness," 640.

31. The last quoted passage is from Luke, 17:33. See John 9:2.

32. Francisco de Florencia, *La milagrosa invención de un tesoro escondido*, ed. Peláez T. Matabuena and Lobato M. Rodríguez (Mexico City: Universidad Iberoamericana, 2008) 201–202.

33. Alonso A. Velasco, *Exaltación de la divina misericordia en la milagrosa renovación de la soberana imagen de Christo Señor Nuestro Crucificado* (Mexico City: Oficina de Don Mariano de Zúñiga y Ontiveros, 1807) 14.

34. "El Señor Fiscal del Santo Oficio, contra Fray Francisco Navarro del Orden de San Francisco, por alumbrado. Guatemala," AGN, Inquisición, Vol. 682, Exp. 4 (1691–1693), consulted at Center for Southwest Research and Special Collections, University of New Mexico, Richard E. Greenleaf Papers, Box 1/Folder 36. The quoted phrases are on 2, 3, 21, 21, 21, 21, and 22, respectively.

35. The quoted passage is from Watts and Williams, *Psychology*, 120. See Daniel M. McIntosh, "Religion-as-Schema, with Implications for the Relation Between Religion and Coping," *International Journal for the Psychology of Religion* 5/1 (1995): 2–3; Boris Nieswand, "Enacted Destiny. West African Charismatic Christians in Berlin and the Immanence of God," *Journal of Religion in Africa* 40/1 (2010): 53; and Black, "Poverty," 364–367.

36. The last two quoted passages are in Víctor Campa Mendoza, *Santuarios y milagros* (Mexico City: Consejo Nacional de Ciencia y Technología, 2002) 252. The stabbing example is from Elin Luque Agraz and Michele Beltrán, "Regalo para el arte: los exvotos mexicanos de los siglos XIX y XX," *Dones y promesas: 500 años de arte ofrenda (exvotos mexicanos)* (Mexico City: Centro Cultural/Arte Contemporáneo, Fundación Cultural Televisa, 1996) 133, cat. 245. The earthquake example is from Florencia, *Milagrosa invención*, 217.

37. The 1937 example and quoted passage are in Luque Agraz and Beltrán, "Regalo," 129, cat. 203. The same is in Elin Luque Agraz, "Ellas querían construir un idioma propio. Selección de exvotos pictóricos de México con la imagen de la mujer como protagonista de la obra," *Espacio, tiempo y forma* 17 (2004): 230. See Carlos Monsiváis and Elin Luque Agraz, *Los relatos pintados: la otra historia, exvotos mexicanos* (Mexico City: Centro de Cultura Casa Lamm, 2010) 32, where thanks are given to the Virgen de Guadalupe for finding the cadaver of a missing son.

38. Francisco de Florencia, *Zodiaco mariano*, ed. Juan A. Oviedo, intro. Antonio Rubial García (Mexico City: Consejo Nacional para la Cultura y las Artes, 1995) 195–196.

39. The first quoted passage is in Valdez Curiel, *Danza*, 10. The quoted passage regarding theory correctness is from Nisbett and Ross, *Human Inference*, 169.

40. The 1777 Peres Maldonado retablo is in the collection of Davis Museum and Cultural Center, Wellesley College. See Lisa Pon and James F. Amatruda, "Breast Cancer Between Faith and Medicine: The Peres Maldonado Ex-Voto," *Medical Humanities* 36/2 (2010): 112–114.

41. The first quoted passage is from Kate C. McLean, Monisha Pasupathi, Jennifer L. Pals, "Selves Creating Stories Creating Selves: A Process Model of Self-Development," *Personal and Social Psychology Review* 11/3 (2007): 264. The last quoted passage is from St. John of Damascus, *On the Divine Images: Three Apologies Against Those Who Attack the Divine Images*, tr. David Anderson (Crestwood, NY: St. Vladimir's Seminary Press, 1980) 49. See Friedrich Nietzsche, *On the Genealogy of Morals; Ecce Homo*, tr. Walter Kaufmann and R. J. Hollingdale (New York: Vintage Books, 1969) 68. See also Neal Krause, "Gratitude," 166; Neal Krause, "Religious Involvement, Gratitude, and Change in Depressive Symptoms Over Time," *International Journal for the Psychology of Religion* 19/3 (2009): 158; and Neal Krause and Elena Bastida, "Religion, Suffering, and Health among Older Mexican Americans," *Journal of Aging Studies* 23/2 (2009): 117, where a study participant says, "If you have it all, we never need anything, nothing every hurts, we will never remember there is a God." In Neal Krause, "Assessing Coping Responses within Specific Faith Traditions: Suffering in Silence, Stress, and Depressive Symptoms among Older Catholics," *Mental Health, Religion and Culture* 13/5 (2010): 516, some older Mexican American participants "indicated that suffering made them feel more grateful to God." See Pargament and Hahn, "God," 202, where a participant says, "I would thank God for the situation although I didn't understand it, knowing that God is motivated out of Love for me, and that he allows me to experience suffering even as His son did, so that I can grow." See similar statements in Ronnie Janoff-Bulman, and Camille B. Wortman, "Attributions of Blame and Coping in the 'Real World': Severe Accident Victims React to Their Lot, *Journal of Personality and Social Psychology* 35/5 (1977): 358; and in Miles Richardson, Marta Eugenia Pardo, and Barbara Bode, "The Image of Christ in Spanish America as a Model for Suffering: An Exploratory Note," *Journal of International Studies and World Affairs* 13/2 (1971): 252. See also Jacobus de Voragine, *The Golden Legend: Readings on the Saints*, tr. William Granger Ryan (Princeton, NJ: Princeton University Press, 1993) 1/62, where a cured man reverts to his illness because health "was not in the best interest of his soul." A similar example is on 1/158.

42. The last quoted passage is from M. E. McCullough, R. A. Emmons, and J. Tsang, "The Grateful Disposition: A Conceptual And Empirical Topography," *Journal of Personality and Social Psychology* 82/1 (2002): 114. A female patient in Taylor, "Adjustment," 1163, said, "When you frame it, it becomes significant. I feel as if I were for the first time really conscious. My life is framed in a certain amount of time."

43. The first quoted phrase is from Jacalyn Duffin, *Medical Miracles: Doctors, Saints, and Healing in the Modern World* (New York: Oxford University Press, 2009) 140. Regarding the last sentence, see Amy L. Ai, Terrence N. Tice, Bu Huang, Willard Rodgers, and Steven F.Bolling, "Types of Prayer, Optimism, and Well-Being of Middle-Aged and Older Patients Undergoing Open-Heart Surgery," *Mental Health, Religion and Culture* 11/1 (2008): 144.

44. The quoted passages are from Philippe Verheyen, *Curación milagrosa de un extraordinario fluxo de sangre de los ojos, narizes, oidos, y boca....* (Spain, [n. p.], circa 1708) 15.

45. The quoted passages regarding the construction worker are in Campa Mendoza, *Santuarios,* 252.

46. The quoted passage and its context are from Jacqueline Maria Hagan, *Migration Miracle: Faith, Hope and Meaning on the Undocumented Journey* (Cambridge, MA: Harvard University Press, 2008) 38. See Nieswand, "Enacted Destiny," 49–51; and Maïté Maskens, "Mobility among Pentecostal Pastors and Migratory 'Miracles,'" *Canadian Journal of African Studies* 46/3 (2012): 400.

47. For examples of saved limbs, see Francisco Gallegos Franco, *Los retablos del Señor de la Misericordia de Tepatitlán* (Guadalajara: Conaculta, Secretaría de Cultura de Jalisco, Feca, Grupo Modelo, 2001) 27, 41, and 61.

48. The first quoted passage is from Warren H. Cole, "Opening Address: Spontaneous Regression of Cancer and the Importance of Finding its Causes," *Conference on Spontaneous Regression of Cancer, Held at the Johns Hopkins Medical Institutions, Baltimore, Maryland, May 9 and 10, 1974,* ed. Edward F. Lewison (Bethesda: US Department of Health, Education, and Welfare, 1976) 5. See 6–8 for factors contributing to spontaneous regression. The second and third quoted passages are from Corner, *Signs of God,* 13. The last quoted passage is from Gurswinder Gary Jawanda and Darrel Drachenberg, "Spontaneous Regression Of Biopsy Proven Primary Renal Cell Carcinoma: A Case Study," *Canadian Urological Association Journal* 6/5 (2012): E203. For other examples see Behzad Niakan, "Spontaneous Remission of Cancer: Steady and Aggressive Malignant Growth Faced with Hypoxia or Hypoglycemia," *Medical Hypotheses* 75/6 (2010): 505–506; Dragomir Marisavljevic, Zoran Rolovic, Milena Ludoski-Pantic, Vesna Djordjevic, and Angelina Novak, "Spontaneous Remission in Adults with Primary Myelodysplastic Syndromes; Incidence and Characteristics of Patients," *Medical Oncology* 22/4 (2005): 407; Steven W. Clay and Scott Jenkinson, "Merkel Cell Carcinoma: A Case of Complete Spontaneous Remission and Review," *Internet Journal of Family Practice* (March 20, 2008): https://ispub.com/IJFP/6/1/5176; and Tilden C. Everson and Warren H. Cole, *Spontaneous Regression of Cancer: A Study and Abstract of Reports in the World Medical Literature and of Personal Communications Concerning Spontaneous Regression of Malignant Disease* (Philadelphia: W. B. Saunders, 1966) 4–7 and 518–529.

49. Regarding doctors, see Duffin, *Medical Miracles*, 142–143; and David Gentilcore, "Contesting Illness in Early Modern Naples: Miracolati, Physicians and the Congregation of Rites," *Past & Present* 148/1 (1995): 137

50. The first quoted passage is from Arthur Kleinman, *Patients and Healers in the Context of Culture: An Exploration of the Borderland between Anthropology, Medicine, and Psychiatry* (Berkeley: University of California Press, 1980) 72. The second quoted passage is from Cecil G. Helman, "Disease Versus Illness in General Practice," *Journal of the Royal College of General Practitioners* 31 (1981): 550; see 548. See also Robert A. Orsi, *Thank You, St. Jude: Women's Devotion to the Patron Saint of Hopeless Causes* (New Haven, CT: Yale University Press, 1996) 182–184.

51. Regarding diabetes as a result of susto, see Susan C. Weller, Roberta D. Baer, Javier Garcia de Alba Garcia, Mark Glazer, Robert Trotter, Lee Pachter, and Robert E. Klein, "Regional Variation in Latino Descriptions of *Susto*," *Culture, Medicine and Psychiatry* 26/4 (2002): 463. See also Alvarado A. F. Rodríguez, *Los Tuxtlas: nombres geográficos pipil, náhuatl, taíno y popoluca* (Boca del Río, Veracruz: M Ediciones Culturales Exclusivas, 2007) 185.

52. The quoted passages are from Kleinman, *Illness Narratives*, 17 and 52, respectively. See 13 and 186 ("Illness meanings are shared and negotiated"). In Kleinman, *Patients and Healers*, 73, "disease and illness are explanatory concepts, not entities."

53. See Irwin Press, "Urban Illness: Physicians, Curers and Dual use in Bogota," *Journal of Health and Science Behavior* 10/3 (1969): 215; and Daniel E. Moerman and Wayne B. Jonas, "Deconstructing the Placebo Effect and Finding the Meaning Response," *Annals of Internal Medicine* 136/6 (2002): 475. Regarding holistic medicine and miracles, see José Velasco Toro, *De la historia al mito: mentalidad y culto en el Santuario de Otatitlán* (Veracruz: Instituto Veracruzano de Cultura, 2000) 149–150.

54. The quoted passage is from Robert A. Hahn, "The Nocebo Phenomenon: Concept, Evidence, and Implications for Public Health," *Preventive Medicine* 26/5 (1997): 610. See Irving Kirsh, "Response Expectancy: An Introduction," *How Expectancies Shape Experience*, ed. Irving Kirsh (Washington, DC: American Psychological Association, 1999) 4–5; Kate Faasse and Keith J Petrie, "The Nocebo Effect: Patient Expectations and Medication Side Effects," *Postgraduate Medical Journal* 89/1055 (2013): 5; and Amanda Porterfield, *Healing in the History of Christianity* (New York: Oxford University Press, 2005) 13–18.

55. See Ernestina Carrillo, "Assessment and Treatment of the Latino Patient," *The Latino Patient: Assessment and Treatment*, ed. Ernestina Carrillo and Alberto López (Washington, DC: American Psychiatric Publishing, 2001) 50; Faasse and Petrie, "Nocebo Effect," 2 and 4; and Alice-Mary Talbot, "Pilgrimage to Healing Shrines: The Evidence of Miracle Accounts," *Dumbarton Oaks Papers* 56 (2002): 158, where the placebo effect accounts "for such a high percentage of

reportedly successful cures." Regarding sociogenic illness, see Hahn, "Nocebo," 607–608 and 610.

56. The quoted phrase is from Faasse and Petrie, "Nocebo Effect," 2. See Frank, *Persuasion*, 72–74; and Robert L. Sevensky, "The Religious Foundations of Health Care: A Conceptual Approach," *Journal of Medical Ethics* 9/3 (1983): 166.

57. The last quoted passage is in Valdez Curiel, *Danza*, 17. See George M. Foster, "Disease Etiologies in Non-Western Medical Systems," *American Anthropologist* 78/4 (1976): 775–777, where multiple causation obtains for all types of misfortune—accidents, economic problems, family discord.

58. The quoted passage is in Valdez Curiel, *Danza*, 20. The Carácuaro example is from Carro-Ripalda, "Señor de Carácuaro," 32–34.

59. The fertility quotation is in *Santa María de El Pueblito* 12/12 (2007): 16. "Genuine effectiveness" is from a description of mana in Marcel Mauss, *A General Theory of Magic*, tr. Robert Brain (New York: Routledge, 2001) 137. On the same page mana is "what causes the net to bring in a good catch," and "it is clear that it is the mana and not the arrow point to which they attribute the actual effectiveness of the arrow." See Campa Mendoza, *Santuarios*, 253; *Dones y promesas*, 152, cat. 127; and Joseph Ziegler, "Practitioners and Saints: Medical Men in Canonization Processes in the Thirteenth to Fifteenth Centuries," *Social History of Medicine* 12/2 (1999): 200, where a doctor petitions a miracle for the patient. A nurse at the Basilica de los Remedios clinic told me that patients view medical doctors as angels doing God's work. The motto of the French surgeon Ambroise Paré (1517–1590) was, "I dressed his wounds, God cured him."

60. Regarding Origin, see Porterfield, *Healing*, 53; the St. John of Damascus passage is in *Divine Images*, 39. See *Catechism of the Catholic Church*, section 1509 (see also 1503) and Matthew 4:24, where "they brought to him all who were sick with various diseases and racked with pain, those who were possessed, lunatics, and paralytics, and he cured them." In Exodus 15:26, "I, the Lord, am your healer." The English-tract passage is from William Stukeley, *The Healing of Diseases, A Character of the Messiah* (London: C. Corbet, 1750) 19. Regarding images as divine doctors, see Campa Mendoza, *Santuarios*, 280; Calixto Aguirre, *Nueva novena dedicada al milagrosisimo Niño de Nuestra Señora de Atocha, que se venera en el Santuario de Plateros, á estramuros de la ciudad del Fresnillo, Zacatecas* (Imprenta y Litografia de N. Espinosa, 1886); and Ingrid Geist, *Comunión y disensión: prácticas rituales en una aldea cuicateca* (Oaxaca: Instituto Oaxaqueño de las Culturas and Mexico City: Instituto Nacional de Antropología e Historia, 1997) 139, where limpias are done in the San Andrés Teotilalpam church because the Señor de las Tres Caídas there is a "divine doctor." The hybrid quotation is from Benjamín Monroy Ballesteros, *El cristianismo como terapia: soteriología para principiantes* (Zapopan, Mexico: Publicaciones Franciscanas, 2008) 107. For examples of God as the origin of medicine, see Antonio Pérez de

Escobar, *Avisos medicos, populares, y domesticos....* (Madrid: D. Joachin Ibarra, 1776) 57; and Pedro León Gómez, *Dissertaciones morales, y medicas....* (Madrid: Oficina de la viuda de Manuel Fernandez, 1751) 1–2. See also Stanley J. Tambiah, *Magic, Science, Religion and the Scope of Rationality* (Cambridge: Cambridge University Press, 1991) 20, where "sickness was God's visitation" and "medicine worked with God's permission"; and JoAnn O'Reilly, "The Hospital Prayer Book: A Partner for Healing," *Literature and Medicine* 19/1 (2000) 70, where a letter to Jesus includes, "You are a great physician and healer and can do all things." In Emma J. Edelstein and Ludwig Edelstein, *Asclepius: Collection and Interpretation of the Testimonies* (Baltimore: Johns Hopkins University Press, 1998) 180, Asklepius "taught the medical art to mankind."

61. The first two quoted passages are from an 1856 retablo in Gallegos Franco, *Los retablos*, 61 and 44, respectively.

62. The diabetes quotation is in Velasco Toro, *De la historia*, 150. The Zoila example is from, "La preciosa sangre de Cristo sigue haciendo milagros en Oaxaca," *Contenido* (July, 2001): 68–69. The quoted passages in the last sentence are from Gallegos Franco, *Los retablos*, 80. For examples of miracles as a last resort, see Florencia, *Origen*, 180; Monroy Ballesteros, *El cristianismo* 106; Gallegos Franco, *Los retablos*, 26; and María Rodríguez-Shadow and Martha Monzón Flores, "La Virgen María en los exvotos mexicanos," *Tradiciones y culturas populares* 3/15 (2008): 346. For medieval last resort, see André Vauchez, *Sainthood in the Later Middle Ages*, tr. Jean Brill (Cambridge: Cambridge University Press, 1997) 466. See also Joseph Ziegler, "Practitioners and Saints: Medical Men in Canonization Processes in the Thirteenth to Fifteenth Centuries," *Social History of Medicine* 12/2 (1999): 194, where canonization processes "show that people when ill went first to the doctor (if they could afford it) or doctored themselves; recourse to alternative channels of health (i.e. miraculous) usually came as a last resort when conventional methods had failed."

63. The quoted passage are both in Valdez Curiel, *Danza*, 17.

64. Verheyen, *Curación*, 5–10. Regarding medical cures for "fluxo de sangre," see Bernardino de Obregon and Andrés Fernández, *Instrucción de Pedro José de enfermos: y modo de aplicar los remedios* (Madrid: Imprenta de Bernardo Peralta, 1728) 10–13.

MARCO

1. Marta, in Chalma, had a similar experience: "They brought me to the operating room and I was on the gurney and saw on the wall a Christ, an image of Christ hanging there, and it gave me confidence, it gave me confidence and I wasn't afraid. I felt protected." The epigraph to this chapter is from a village woman in Michael Maccoby, "Love and Authority: A Study of Mexican Villagers," *Atlantic* 213/3 (1964): 123.

2. María José's father is pictured in the retablo that illustrates the miracle but actually was not present when the accident occurred. For a medieval English example of a drowning miracle similar to María José's, see R. C. Finucane, *The Rescue of the Innocents: Endangered Children in Medieval Miracles* (New York: St. Martin's, 1997) 172–206.

3. See Neal Krause, "Gratitude Toward God, Stress, and Health in Late Life," *Research on Aging* 28/2 (2006): 166. I am also following Bernard Spilka, Phillip Shaver and Lee A. Kirkpatrick, "A General Attribution Theory for the Psychology of Religion," *Journal for the Scientific Study of Religion*, 24/1 (1985): 13; Fred Rothbaum, John R. Weisz, and Samuel S. Snyder, "Changing the World and Changing the Self: A Two-Process Model of Perceived Control," *Journal of Personality and Social Psychology* 42/1 (1982): 11 and 26 ("the increased sense of control gained by … ability to reinterpret events"); Katherine L. Fiori, Judith C. Hays, and Keith G. Meador, "Spiritual Turning Points And Perceived Control Over The Life Course," *International Journal of Aging And Human Development* 59/4 (2004): 412; and Kenneth I. Pargament, *The Psychology of Religion and Coping: Theory, Research, Practice* (New York: Guilford Press, 1997) 90.

4. See M. E. McCullough, R. A. Emmons, and J. Tsang, "The Grateful Disposition: A Conceptual And Empirical Topography," *Journal of Personality and Social Psychology* 82/1 (2002): 114, where "Seeing oneself as the beneficiary of other people's generosity may lead one to feel affirmed, esteemed, and valued, which may boost self-esteem and perceived social support." See also Raymond L. Higgins, "Reality Negotiation," *Handbook of Positive Psychology*, ed. C. R. Snyder and Shane J. Lopez (New York: Oxford University Press, 2002) 355, where finding meaning in adverse outcomes may help restore a positive self-concept; Shelley E. Taylor, "Adjustment to Threatening Events: A Theory of Cognitive Adaptation," *American Psychologist* 38/11 (1983): 1170–1171; Scott Schieman, Tetyana Pudrovska, and Melissa A. Milkie, "The Sense of Divine Control and the Self-Concept: A Study of Race Differences in Late Life," *Research on Aging* 27/2 (2005): 166, where "In the face of adversity, belief in God's care, love, and guidance may be particularly beneficial for sustaining feelings of self-worth"; and Beth Morling and Sharrilyn Evered, "Secondary Control Reviewed and Defined," *Psychological Bulletin* 132/2 (2006): 285, where an "outcome of secondary control might be a sense of closeness or interdependence with others."

5. See Joshua M. Smyth and James W. Pennebaker, "Sharing One's Story: Translating Emotional Experiences into Words as a Coping Tool," *Coping: The Psychology of What Works*, ed. C. R. Snyder (New York: Oxford University Press, 1999) 79. On decontextualization and recontextualization, see Richard Bauman and Charles L Briggs, "Poetics and Performance as Critical Perspectives on Language and Social Life," *Annual Review of Anthropology* 19 (1990): 73–74. For prayer as cognitive reframing, see J. Irene Harris, Sean W. Schoneman, and Stephanie R. Carrera, "Preferred Prayer Styles and Anxiety Control," *Journal of*

Religion and Health 44/4 (2005): 405. See also Neal Krause, "God-Mediated
Control and Change in Self-Rated Health," *International Journal for the Psychology
of Religion* 20/4 (2010): 283; Robert A. Orsi, "The Cult of the Saints and the
Reimagination of the Space and Time of Sickness in Twentieth-Century American
Catholicism," *Religion and Healing in America*, ed. Linda L. Barnes and Susan S.
Sered (New York: Oxford University Press, 2005) 30; David Gentilcore, "Contesting
Illness in Early Modern Naples: Miracolati, Physicians and the Congregation of
Rites," *Past & Present* 148/1 (1995): 123, where "In a world shattered by illness,
the construction of narrative allows the sick person to 'reconstitute' the world";
Ronnie Janoff-Bulman and Cynthia McPherson Frantz, "The Impact of Trauma
on Meaning: From Meaningless World to Meaningful Life," *The Transformation
of Meaning in Psychological Therapies: Integrating Theory and Practice*, ed. Michael
J. Power and Chris Brewin (Chichester, UK: Wiley, 1997) 100; John A. Robinson,
"Perspective, Meaning, and Remembering," *Remembering Our Past: Studies in
Autobiographical Memory*, ed. David C. Rubin (New York: Cambridge University
Press, 1996) 214, where "remembering, like perceiving, is guided by present
ways of understanding" and, on 202, "the meaning of any experience can change
over time"; and Bernard Spilka, *The Psychology of Religion: An Empirical Approach*
(New York: Guilford Press, 2003) 483, where making tragedy meaningful "prob-
ably constitutes the core of successful coping and adjustment. For most people,
religion performs this role quite well, especially in times of personal crisis."
Regarding the embrace, note that the miracle is represented as physical contact.
María José, the drowned girl, was revived when the Virgen de los Dolores
touched her head.

COLLABORATIONS

1. St. Thomas Aquinas, *The Summa Theologica* (1a.22.3). Aquinas does not attribute secondary causation to miracles in the strict sense of the term (revival of
   a dead person), but miracles as understood in votary devotion (successful surgery, finding a job) are appropriate to secondary causation as Aquinas defines it.
   See Brian Davies, *The Thought of Thomas Aquinas* (Oxford: Clarendon Press,
   1993) 170–174. See also Immanuel Kant, *Lectures on Philosophical Theology*, tr.
   Allen W. Wood and Gertrude M. Clark (Ithaca, NY: Cornell University Press,
   1978) 154, where God "can use natural causes merely as a means for bringing
   about this or that event which he has placed before himself as an end, and for
   the sake of the greater perfection of the whole"; E. Thomas Lawson and Robert
   N. McCauley, *Rethinking Religion: Connecting Cognition and Culture* (New York:
   Cambridge University Press, 1990) 8, where "religious ritual form is largely the
   product of a compromise between religions' commitments to superhuman
   agents and everyday views of human action"; Boris Nieswand, "Enacted Destiny:
   West African Charismatic Christians in Berlin and the Immanence of God,"

Journal of Religion in Africa 40/1 (2010): 55, where "human agency is considered as a central means through which the divine manifests itself in the world"; and Friar Pedro Font and Dan S. Matson, "Letters of Friar Pedro Font, 1776–1777," *Ethnohistory* 22/3 (1975): 279, where the friar writes, "I also know that God permits secondary causes to function and that we are not supposed to hope for miracles when matters can be taken care of in some other way."

2. The quoted passage is in George M. Foster, *Tzintzuntzan: Mexican Peasants in a Changing World* (New York: Elsevier, 1979) 236–237. For examples of collaborative miracles, see Carlos Monsiváis and Elin Luque Agraz, *Los relatos pintados: la otra historia, exvotos mexicanos* (Mexico City: Centro de Cultura Casa Lamm, 2010) 18, 19, 21, 33, 81, and 139. See also Katherine L. Fiori, Judith C. Hays, and Keith G. Meador, "Spiritual Turning Points And Perceived Control Over The Life Course," *International Journal of Aging And Human Development* 59/4 (2004): 407, where a doctor recommends surgery and the patient replies, "Well, my body is in God's hands, but also in your hands. I know God is going to guide you."

3. The ship example is from Francisco de Florencia, *Origen de los dos célebres santuarios de la Nueva Galicia, obispado de Guadalaxara, en la America septentrional* (Zapopan, Mexico: Amate Editorial, 2001) 125. The rider and dog example is in Francisco de Florencia, *La milagrosa invención de un tesoro escondido*, ed. Peláez T. Matabuena and Lobato M. Rodríguez (Mexico City: Universidad Iberoamericana, 2008) 228. The feud example is from a retablo in *Dones y promesas: 500 años de arte ofrenda (exvotos mexicanos)* (Mexico City: Centro Cultural/Arte Contemporáneo, 1996) 179, cat. 239. God also acts through nature in such biblical passages as Exodus 14:21.

4. The quoted passage regarding success in court is from Anna María Fernández Poncela, "El Santo Niño de Atocha: origen, función y actualidad" *Cuicuilco* 10/27 (2003): 18. The two quoted passages regarding drinking and driving are both in Kenneth I. Pargament and June Hahn, "God and the Just World: Causal and Coping Attributions to God in Health Situations," *Journal for the Scientific Study of Religion* 25/2 (1986): 201. See Nieswand, "Enacted," 40, 49, 51, and 55. A number of theorists use related terms (God-mediated control, proxy control, vicarious control) and often in three or four categories or approaches. Kenneth I. Pargament, *The Psychology of Religion and Coping: Theory, Research, Practice* (New York: Guilford Press, 1997) 180, describes self-directing, "wherein people rely on themselves in coping rather than on God"; deferring, "in which the responsibility for coping is passively deferred to God"; and collaborating, "in which the individual and God are both active partners in coping." See 180–183. Later, "control-oriented religious coping methods" include "sharing control with God (collaborative), relinquishing control to God (deferring), exerting control with God (self-directing), and seeking control from God (pleading)." Kenneth I. Pargament, Gina M. Magyar-Russell, and Nichole A. Murray-Swank, "The

Sacred and the Search for Significance: Religion as a Unique Process," *Journal of Social Issues* 61/4 (2005): 676. See also Kenneth I. Pargament, Joseph Kennell, William Hathaway, Nancy Grevengoed, Jon Newman, and Wendy Jones, "Religion and the Problem-Solving Process: Three Styles of Coping," *Journal for the Scientific Study of Religion* 27/1 (1988): 91–92 and 102–103. In another configuration, God-mediated control is "the notion that problems can be overcome, and goals in life can be reached by working together with God." Neal Krause, "God-Mediated Control and Psychological Well-Being in Late Life," *Research on Aging* 27/2 (2005): 137. In Neal Krause, "Religious Involvement, Gratitude, and Change in Depressive Symptoms Over Time," *International Journal for the Psychology of Religion* 19/3 (2009): 156, "God-mediated control is defined as the belief that God works together with people to help them overcome the difficulties and challenges that arise in their lives." For clarity of exposition and in consideration of my focus on petitionary devotion to miraculous images, I consolidate these approaches into two categories—collaborative control and deferred control—which I view on a continuum with constant slide between poles.

5. The first quoted phrase and passage are from Scott Schieman, Tetyana Pudrovska, and Melissa A. Milkie, "The Sense of Divine Control and the Self-Concept: A Study of Race Differences in Late Life," *Research on Aging* 27/2 (2005): 529. See Krause, "God-Mediated Control," 283; Pargament, *Psychology*, 289; and Neal Krause and Elena Bastida, "Exploring the Interface between Religion and Contact with the Dead among Older Mexican Americans," *Review of Religious Research* 51/1 (2009): 15. For examples of these ideas as they relate to migrant motivation, see Jacqueline Hagan and Helen Rose Ebaugh, "Calling Upon the Sacred: Migrants' Use of Religion in the Migration Process," *International Migration Review* 37/4 (2003): 1152; Jacqueline Hagan, "Faith for the Journey: Religion as a Resource for Migrants," *A Promised Land, A Perilous Journey: Theological Perspectives on Migration*, ed. Daniel G. Groody and Gioacchino Campese (Notre Dame, IN: University of Notre Dame Press, 2008) 3–19; and Jacqueline Maria Hagan, *Migration Miracle: Faith, Hope and Meaning on the Undocumented Journey* (Cambridge, MA: Harvard University Press, 2008). For an example of *promesas* or votive contracts concerning Dominican migration, see Cristina Sánchez-Carretero, "Santos y Misterios as Channels of Communication in the Diaspora: Afro-Dominican Religious Practices Abroad," *Journal of American Folklore* 118/469 (2005): 315–316. Regarding Cuban migration, see Thomas A. Tweed, *Crossing and Dwelling: A Theory of Religion* (Cambridge, MA: Harvard University Press, 2006) 2–3, 80–81, and 131–132.

6. The first quoted passage is from Bruce N. Waller, "Comparing Psychoanalytic and Cognitive-Behavioral Perspectives on Control," *Philosophy, Psychiatry, & Psychology* 11/2 (2004): 126. The second quoted passage is from Viktor Gecas, "The Social Psychology of Self-Efficacy," *Annual Review of Sociology* 15 (1989): 292. For a summary of locus of control, see Bernard Spilka, *The Psychology of*

Religion: An Empirical Approach (New York: Guilford Press, 2003) 46–47. See also Bernard Spilka, Phillip Shaver and Lee A. Kirkpatrick, "A General Attribution Theory for the Psychology of Religion," *Journal for the Scientific Study of Religion* 24/1 (1985): 10–11; Herbert M. Lefcourt, *Locus of Control: Current Trends in Theory and Research* (Hillsdale, NJ: Lawrence Erlbaum Associates, 1982) 1–18; Julian B. Rotter, "Generalized Expectancies for Internal Versus External Control of Reinforcement," *Psychological Monographs: General and Applied* 80/1 (1966): 1, where "If the person perceives that the event is contingent upon his own behavior or his own relatively permanent characteristics," then the control is internal; and Fred Rothbaum, John R. Weisz, and Samuel S. Snyder, "Changing the World and Changing the Self: A Two-Process Model of Perceived Control," *Journal of Personality and Social Psychology* 42/1 (1982): 6, where "persons with an external locus of control—those who see circumstances, chance, and powerful others as controlling outcomes—are, in general, more likely to manifest such inward behaviors as passivity, withdrawal, compliance, conformity, and depressive symptomatology than are persons with an internal locus of control—those who see their own effort or ability as controling outcomes." Regarding distinctions between locus of control and God control, see Laurence E. Jackson and Robert D. Coursey, "The Relationship of God Control and Internal Locus of Control to Intrinsic Religious Motivation, Coping and Purpose in Life," *Journal for the Scientific Study of Religion* 27/3 (1988): 407–408.

7. The first quoted passage is from Jackson and Coursey, "Relationship," 407. The subsequent quoted phrases and passage are from, respectively, Michael E. McCullough and Brian L. B. Willoughby, "Religion, Self-Regulation, and Self-Control: Associations, Explanations, and Implications," *Psychological Bulletin* 135/1 (2009): 70; Nieswand, "Enacted," 51, where "enacted destiny refers to an idea of divine empowerment, which enables believers to deal with risk and contingency. Second, it refers to a scheme of interpretation in which a correspondence between God's agency and human agency is ascribed retrospectively. The interaction of both elements, empowerment and interpretation, create the practical dynamic of the enactment of destiny"; and Schieman, Pudrovska, and Milkie, "Sense," 169. For an example of an analysand who moves from deferred control to collaborative control, see James W. Jones, *Contemporary Psychoanalysis and Religion: Transference and Transcendence* (New Haven, CT: Yale University Press, 1991) 70–71. See also Kenneth I. Pargament, David S. Ensing, Kathryn Falgout, Hannah Olsen, Barbara Reilly, Kimberly Van Haitsma, and Richard Warren, "God help me: (1): "Religious Coping Efforts as Predictors of the Outcomes to Significant Negative Life Events," in Larry VandeCreek, *Spiritual Needs and Pastoral Services: Readings in Research* (Decatur, GA: Journal of Pastoral Care Publications, 1995): 102; and Helen K. Black, "Poverty and Prayer: Spiritual Narratives of Elderly African-American Women," *Review of Religious Research* 40/4 (1999): 364, where "covenental partnership makes them co-actors with

God in surviving poverty." Regarding devotion-strengthened internal control, see Harold G. Koenig, "Religion and Hope for the Disabled Elder," *Religion in Aging and Health: Theoretical Foundations and Methodological Frontiers*, ed. Jeffrey S. Levin (Thousand Oaks, CA: Sage Publications, 1994) 42, where "Although religious elders may appear to be relying on an external locus of control...religious belief is actually associated with a greater internal locus of control." See also Jackson and Coursey, "Relationship," 406–407, where "a strong belief in God control does not preclude a belief in personal (internal) control" (406).

8. The second quoted passage is in John Shinners, ed., *Medieval Popular Religion, 1000–1500: A Reader* (Peterborough, Ontario: Broadview Press, 2007) 398. See 400. The last quoted passage is from Krause, "Religious Involvement," 156. One is reminded of the Nicaraguan slogan, "Thanks to God and the revolution."

9. The first quoted passage (in two parts) is from Noah J. Goldstein and Robert B. Cialdini, "The Spyglass Self: A Model of Vicarious Self-Perception," *Journal of Personality and Social Psychology* 92/3 (2007): 403. The second quoted passage (in two parts) is from Arthur P. Aron, Debra J. Mashek, and Elaine N. Aron, "Closeness as Including Other in the Self," *Handbook of Closeness and Intimacy*, ed. Debra J. Mashek and Arthur Aron (Mahwah, NJ: Lawrence Erlbaum Associates, 2004) 27. See Daniel J. Weidler and Eddie M. Clark, "A Distinct Association: Inclusion of Other in the Self and Self-Disclosure," *New School Psychology Bulletin* 9/1 (2011): 34; and Noah J. Goldstein and Nicholas A. Hays, "Illusory Power Transference: The Vicarious Experience of Power," *Administrative Science Quarterly* 56/4 (2011): 593 and 595.

10. The quoted passage is from Heinz Kohut, *The Search for the Self: Selected Writings of Heinz Kohut, 1978–1981*, vol. 4, ed. Paul H. Ornstein (Madison, CT: International Universities Press, 1991) 671 (letter dated July 24, 1980).

11. José Luis is quoted in Gilberto Giménez, *Cultural popular y religión en el Anahuac* (Mexico City: Centro de Estudios Ecuménicos, 1978) 158. I changed the name from José to José Luis to avoid confusion with another José in my text. Miriam is quoted in Jorge Morales Almada, "Esperan milagro de la Virgen de Juquila," (December 5, 2011): http://m.impre.com/entry/view/id/41795/pn/all/p/0/?KSID=8959ede79fbd35a18d1430c74df6b1bf.

12. The first quoted passage is in José Velasco Toro, *De la historia al mito: mentalidad y culto en el santuario de Otatitlán* (Veracruz: Instituto Veracruzano de Cultura, 2000) 153. The pilgrim with the sneakers is quoted in Lourdes Almazán, "Vamos manita, esfuerzo, por el Señor de Chalma," *El universal*, May 26, 2007: www.eluniversal.com.mx/ciudad/84475.html. See Benedicta Ward, *Miracles and the Medieval Mind: Theory, Record and Event, 1000–1215* (Philadelphia: University of Pennsylvania Press, 1982) 38, where Sainte Foy's miracles in freeing captives was done "as much by encouraging their natural ingenuity through dreams as by direct supernatural intervention."

13. This retablo is in the Museum of Spanish Colonial Art, Santa Fe.

14. See Peter Brown, *The Cult of the Saints: Its Rise and Function in Latin Christianity* (Chicago: University of Chicago Press, 1981) 50, where saints are "invisible friends" or "intimate friends" in the fifth century; Lester K. Little, *Benedictine Maledictions: Liturgical Cursing in Romanesque France* (Ithaca, NY: Cornell University Press, 1993) 197, where "The saint was an active participant in the life of the community, someone to talk with, someone to seek advice from, above all someone to call upon in times of need"; and T. M. Luhrmann, "A Hyperreal God and Modern Belief: Toward an Anthropological Theory of Mind," *Current Anthropology* 53/4 (2012): 378–379. On 379, "It was as if people overreached to make what they reached for more real" when they poured a cup of coffee for God in the morning or had a "date night with God." For a similar clinical example, see Pedro Cano, "Erotomanía y nombre del padre," in *Metáfora y delirio* (Editorial: Eolia/Dor, S.L., 1993) 123–134, especially 125.

15. The first quoted passage is from Brown, *Cult*, 61; see 51. Regarding intimacy as opposed to social contact, I am adapting an insight from Roy F. Baumeister and Mark R. Leary, "The Need to Belong: Desire for Interpersonal Attachments as a Fundamental Human Motivation," *Psychological Bulletin* 117/3 (1995): 507; see 497 and 513. See also Lee A. Kirkpatrick, Daniel J. Shillito, and Susan L. Kellas, "Loneliness, Social Support, and Perceived Relationships with God," *Journal of Social and Personal Relationships* 16/4 (1999): 514 and 520. Regarding the photograph offered to the Virgen del Pueblito, see Nichole A. Murray-Swank and Kenneth I. Pargament, "God, Where Are You? Evaluating a Spiritually-Integrated Intervention for Sexual Abuse," *Mental Health, Religion and Culture* 8/3 (2005): 191, where a childhood sexual abuse survivor says, "God was the only one who was always there for me."

16. The first quoted passage is in Patricia Campos Rodríguez, "Migración a través de los exvotos. El Niño de la Cruzada: El que cruza el Río Bravo. Parritas, San Diego de la Unión, Guanajuato": http://sincronia.cucsh.udg.mx/camposfall09 .html, 4.

17. The CELAM quoted passage is from "Documento conclusivo: discípulos y misioneros de Jesucristo para que nuestros pueblos en El tengan vida. Quinta Conferencia General del Episcopado Latinoamericano y del Caribe, Aparecida, Brazil, 2007" (Bogotá: Consejo Espiscopal Latinoamericano, 2007) 149. The last quoted passage is in Pargament, "God help me: (1)," 102. See Amy L. Ai, Terrence N. Tice, Bu Huang, Willard Rodgers, and Steven F. Bolling "Types of Prayer, Optimism, And Well-Being of Middle-Aged and Older Patients Undergoing Open-Heart Surgery," *Mental Health, Religion and Culture* 11/1 (2008): 143, where "when patients lost confidence in any personal control over surgery, trust in their God among believers would take the load."

18. The student passage is in Velasco Toro, *De la historia*, 152. The Niño de Atocha passages are in Fernández Poncela, "Santo Niño," 14.

19. The ugly thoughts passage is in Fernández Poncela, "Santo Niño," 14.

20. The quoted passages regarding partnership are from Nicholas D. Smith and Andrew C. Yip, "Partnership with God: A Partial Solution to the Problem of Petitionary Prayer," *Religious Studies* 46/03 (2010): 404–405.

21. The parenthetically quoted passage is from Gecas, Social," 294; see 310. See Ellen J. Langer, "The Illusion of Incompetence," *Choice and Perceived Control*, ed. Lawrence C. Perlmuter and Richard A. Monty (Hillsdale, NJ: Lawrence Erlbaum, 1979) 301–302 and 305; Ellen J. Langer, "The Illusion of Control" *Journal of Personality and Social Psychology* 32/2 (1975): 325; and Lyn Y. Abramson, Martin E. Seligman, and John D. Teasdale, "Learned Helplessness in Humans: Critique and Reformulation," *Journal of Abnormal Psychology* 87/1 (1978): 52.

22. See Brenda S. Cole and Kenneth I. Pargament, "Spiritual Surrender: A Paradoxical Path to Control," *Integrating Spirituality into Treatment*, ed. William R. Miller (Washington, DC: American Psychological Association, 2000) 179–180 and 185–186, where "a greater sense of control may ensue from the act of surrender"(186); Beth Morling and Sharrilyn Evered, "Secondary Control Reviewed and Defined," *Psychological Bulletin* 132/2 (2006): 270; Christopher Peterson, Steven F. Maier, and Martin E. P. Seligman, *Learned Helplessness: A Theory for the Age of Personal Control* (New York: Oxford University Press, 1993) 136, where "ostensible signs of hopelessness may reflect alternative forms of control"; Schieman, Pudrovska, and Milkie, "Sense," 532; Pargament, *Psychology*, 183 (see 295), where "the individual who pleads for divine intercession is actively, albeit indirectly, attempting to shape the outcome of the situation"; Gecas, "Social," 300, where "spiritual surrender is much more than a cognitive shift. It is an experiential shift as well, one that involves changes in motivation, affect, values, perception, thought, and behavior"; and Susan T. Fiske and Beth Morling, "Stereotyping as a Function of Personal Control Motives and Capacity Constraints," *Handbook of Motivation and Cognition*, Vol. 3, *The Interpersonal Context*, ed. Richard M. Sorrentino and E. Tory Higgins (New York: Guilford Press, 1996) 329, where "When subjects were under the control of powerful ingroup members [miraculous images], they felt more positive, less anxious, and more in control of their outcomes, even though they actually had no personal control themselves."

23. The quoted passages are from Daniel T. Gilbert, Ryan P. Brown, Elizabeth C. Pinel, and Timothy D. Wilson, "The Illusion of External Agency," *Journal of Personality and Social Psychology* 79/5 (2000): 698 and 699, respectively. See 690–692. See also Marjorie Taylor, Sara D. Hodges, and Adèle Kohányi, "The Illusion of Independent Agency: Do Adult Fiction Writers Experience their Characters as Having Minds of their Own?" *Imagination, Cognition and Personality* 22/4 (2002–2003): 366.

24. The alcoholic is quoted in Matthew C. Gutmann, *The Meanings of Macho: Being a Man in Mexico City* (Berkeley: University of California Press, 1996) 178. The older woman is quoted in Krause and Bastida, "Exploring," 13; see 11.

25. The first quoted phrase is from Stanley W. Jackson, *Care of the Psyche: A History of Psychological Healing* (New Haven, CT: Yale University Press, 1999) 143. The second quoted phrase is from Roy F. Baumeister, Kathleen D. Vohs, C. Nathan Dewall, and Liqing Zhan, "How Emotion Shapes Behavior: Feedback, Anticipation, and Reflection, Rather Than Direct Causation," *Personality and Social Psychology Review* 11/2 (2007): 186. The medical confession tropes are in Jackson, *Care*, 146. The last quoted passage is in Javier Pescador, *Crossing Borders with the Santo Niño de Atocha* (Albuquerque: University of New Mexico Press, 2009) 150. Regarding the health benefits of disclosure, see Joshua M. Smyth and James W. Pennebaker, "Sharing One's Story: Translating Emotional Experiences into Words as a Coping Tool," *Coping: The Psychology of What Works*, ed. C. R. Snyder (New York: Oxford University Press, 1999) 70, 72–74, and 77; Keith J. Petrie, Roger J. Booth, and Kathryn P. Davison, "Repression, Disclosure, and Immune Function: Recent Findings and Methodological Issues," *Emotion, Disclosure, and Health*, ed. James W. Pennebaker (Washington, DC: American Psychological Association, 2002) 223–237; and Laura A. King and Kathi N. Miner, "Writing About the Perceived Benefits of Traumatic Events: Implications for Physical Health." *Personality and Social Psychology Bulletin* 26/2 (2000): 220–222. See also Jackson, *Care*, 139, where "From its earlier meanings of purification and cleansing to the notion of purging and, eventually, to the idea of emotional release, catharsis has implied getting something out, getting rid of something, becoming freed from something through some sort of evacuative mode, whether literally or metaphorically." For a brief Pentecostal testimony of prayer as catharsis, see Thomas I. De Vol, "Ecstatic Pentecostal Prayer and Meditation," *Journal of Religion and Health* 13/4 (1974): 286. See also Valerian J. Derlega, Sandra Metts, Sandra Petronio, and Stephen T. Margulis, *Self-Disclosure* (Newbury Park: Sage Publications, 1993) 1–3, 37, and 42.

26. For comments similar to Reynaldo's, see Susana Carro-Ripalda, "El Señor de Carácuaro: una etnografía fenomenológica de una peregrinación en México," *Guaraguao* 5/13 (2001): 45.

27. The first quoted phrase is from Kohut, "Search," 674. See James W. Pennebaker, *Opening Up: The Healing Power of Expressing Emotions* (New York: Guilford Press, 1997) 104–120; Anita E. Kelly and Jennifer E. Carter, "Dealing with Secrets," in *Coping with Stress: Effective People and Processes*, ed. C. R. Snyder (New York: Oxford University Press, 2001) 212–214; Anita E. Kelly, "Revealing Personal Secrets," *Current Directions in Psychological Science* 8/4 (1999): 106–107; and Anita E. Kelly, *The Psychology of Secrets* (New York: Kluwer Academic/Plenum Publishers, 2002) 178–186. See also Jesse M. Bering and Dominic D. P. Johnson, "'O Lord... You Perceive my Thoughts from Afar': Recursiveness and the Evolution of Supernatural Agency," *Journal of Cognition and Culture* 5/1–2 (2005): 124, where the omniscience of supernatural agents "does not pose much of a threat because these agents have no direct means by which to communicate

potentially damaging social information about the self with other ingroup members."

28. See Alexia Petsalēs-Diomēdēs, *Truly Beyond Wonders: Aelius Aristides and the Cult of Asklepios* (Oxford: Oxford University Press, 2010) 24, where in a second-century A.D. inscription to Kypris a votary wrote, "you know who the dedicant is, and for what I am grateful."

29. See John P. Caughlin, Walid A. Afifi, Katy E. Carpenter-Theune, and Laura E. Miller, "Reasons for, and Consequences of, Revealing Personal Secrets in Close Relationships: A Longitudinal Study," *Personal Relationships* 12/1 (2005): 45; Pennebaker, *Opening Up*, 113 and 116; K. Greene, V. J. Derlega, and A. Mathews, "Self-Disclosure in Personal Relationships," *Cambridge Handbook of Personal Relationships*, ed. A. Vangelisti and D. Perlman (Cambridge: Cambridge University Press, 2006) 413–416 and 422; and Derlega, Metts, Petronio, and Margulis, *Self-Disclosure*, 3, 10, and 96–99.

30. See Kate C. McLean, Monisha Pasupathi, and Jennifer L. Pals, "Selves Creating Stories Creating Selves: A Process Model of Self-Development," *Personal and Social Psychology Review* 11/3 (2007): 274.

31. See Constance Classen, "Tactile Therapies," *The Book of Touch*, ed. Constance Classen (Oxford: Berg, 2005) 347–348.

32. Regarding kissing the cross, see Bissera V. Pentcheva, *The Sensual Icon: Space, Ritual, and the Senses in Byzantium* (University Park: Pennsylvania State University Press, 2010) 20. In Mexico today long lines form on Good Friday to kiss images of the dead Christ's face and wounds. For an example see María J. Rodríguez-Shadow and Robert D. Shadow, *El pueblo del Señor: las fiestas y peregrinaciones de Chalma* (Toluca: Universidad Autónoma del Estado de Mexico, 2000) 128; see also 132. For a New Testament precedent of contact relics see for example Acts 19:11, where Paul's clothes "were applied to the sick, [and] their diseases left them and the evil spirits came out of them." Acts 5:15 suggests that Paul's shadow was curative.

33. The St. Candida image is reproduced in Eamon Duffy, *The Stripping of the Altars: Traditional Religion in England C.1400–C.1580* (New Haven, CT: Yale University Press, 1992) plate 78. A manuscript copy of Matthew Paris, *Life of St. Edward the Confessor*, is at the University of Cambridge and available in its digital library. For examples regarding physical contact see Georgia Frank, *The Memory of the Eyes: Pilgrims to Living Saints in Christian Late Antiquity* (Berkeley: University of California Press, 2000) 118; and Megan Holmes, "The Elusive Origins of the Cult of the Annunziata in Florence," *The Miraculous Image in the Late Middle Ages and Renaissance*, ed. Erik Thunø and Gerhard Wolf (Rome: "L'erma" di Bretschneider, 2004) 91 and 110. For examples of placing sick, injured, or dead children on saints' tombs or shrine altars, see R. C. Finucane, *The Rescue of the Innocents: Endangered Children in Medieval Miracles* (New York: St. Martin's, 1997) 11–12. Regarding contact with relics or substances associated with relics in

the middle and late Byzantine era, see Alice-Mary Talbot, "Pilgrimage to Healing
Shrines: The Evidence of Miracle Accounts," *Dumbarton Oaks Papers* 56 (2002):
159–161.

34. The quoted passages are from Gregory of Tours, *Glory of the Martyrs*, tr.
Raymond Van Dam (Liverpool: Liverpool University Press, 1988) 39 (quoting
Eusebius) and 45–46. See Charles Barber, *Figure and Likeness: On the Limits of
Representation in Byzantine Iconoclasm* (Princeton, NJ: Princeton University
Press, 2002) 34, where Gregory distinguishes between relics and other power-
infused objects according to their degree of contact with the sacred body.

35. The first quoted passage is from Gregory of Tours, 47; see 73. St. Andrew's tomb
also exuded a "flourlike manna," together with a "sweet-smelling oil" in Jacobus
de Voragine, *The Golden Legend: Readings on the Saints*, tr. William Granger
Ryan (Princeton, NJ: Princeton University Press, 1993) 1/18. The Thomas of
Canterbury passage is from Voragine, *Golden Legend*, 1/61. For similar examples
see Finucane, *Rescue*, 11; and Ward, *Miracles*, 64, 101–102, and 135; and Ewa
Kuryluk, *Veronica and Her Cloth: History, Symbolism, and Structure of a "True"
Image* (Cambridge, MA: Basil Blackwell, 1991) 31–32. See also André Vauchez,
Sainthood in the Later Middle Ages, tr. Jean Brill (Cambridge: Cambridge University
Press, 1997) 452, where from the thirteenth century in Italy and the fourteenth
century in France and England, miracles occurred increasingly at a distance
from the shrine, using imagery; and R. W. Southern, *The Making of the Middle
Ages* (New Haven, CT: Yale University Press, 1976) 247–248.

36. The example is from Ottavio Antonio Baiardi, *Relacion de lo sucedido al illmo.
Señor Octavio Antonio Bayardi, arzobispo de Tiro, que padecía un largo y obstinado
mal escorbútico en las encías, de que sanó instantaneamente* (Madrid: En la Imprenta
Real de la Gazeta, 1763) 5–8. For other examples of healing by contact, see
Francisco de Florencia, *Zodiaco mariano*, ed. Juan A. Oviedo, intro. Antonio
Rubial García (Mexico City: Consejo Nacional para la Cultura y las Artes, 1995)
194–195, 321, 360, 362, 365; and Florencia, *Origen*, 14 and 193.

37. The first quoted passage (in two parts), is from James George Frazer, *The Golden
Bough: A Study in Magic and Religion* (1922), chapter 3/section 3. The second
quoted passage is from Carol Nemeroff and Paul Rozin, "The Contagion Concept
in Adult Thinking in the United States: Transmission of Germs and of Interpersonal Influence," *Ethos* 22/2 (1994): 159; see 172.

38. For examples of contact with images and relics in other periods and regions, see
for example Jacalyn Duffin, *Medical Miracles: Doctors, Saints, and Healing in the
Modern World* (New York: Oxford University Press, 2009) 153 and 156–62; David
Gentilcore, "Contesting Illness in Early Modern Naples: Miracolati, Physicians
and the Congregation of Rites," *Past & Present* 148/1 (1995): 121, 126–127, 130,
136–137, and 140–141; Robert Maniura, "Ex Votos, Art and Pious Performance,"
Oxford Art Journal 32/3 (2009): 412; Paul Cassar, "Medical Votive Offerings in
the Maltese Islands," *Journal of the Royal Anthropological Institute of Great Britain*

and Ireland 94/1 (1964): 23 and 25; and Ernst Kitzinger, "The Cult of Images in the Age before Iconoclasm," *Dumbarton Oaks Papers* 8 (1954): 106–107.

39. The liferaft image is in Monsiváis amd Luque Agraz, *Los relatos pintados,* 122–123. See a retablo with rays of grace in *Dones y promesas*: 202, cat 315. The quoted passage is in Luis Lasso de la Vega, "El gran acontecimiento...," *Testimonios históricos guadalupanos,* ed. Ernesto de la Torre Villar and Ramiro Navarro de Anda (Mexico City: Fondo de Cultura Económica, 1982) 302. See Jane Garnett and Gervase Rosser, *Spectacular Miracles: Transforming Images in Italy from the Renaissance to the Present* (London: Reaktion Books, 2013) 198, image 114, where an 1801 Italian painted offering shows rays of grace emanating from a Virgin to empower an image (of this same Virgin) held by a sick woman.

40. Other forms of limpias include rubbing a coin on the body before dropping it in the coin box. This was done by almost all devotees at the Señor del Rayo chapel. Contact with the coin also suggests personalizing one's donation—crediting it to one's account—and extending one's surrogate presence in the chapel.

41. The quoted passage is from Alicia M. Barabas, *Dones, duenos y santos: ensayo sobre religiones en Oaxaca* (Mexico City: Instituto Nacional de Antropología e Historia, 2006) 220. See Patrick J. Geary, *Furta Sacra: Thefts of Relics in the Central Middle Ages* (Princeton, NJ: Princeton University Press, 1990) 34.

42. Florencia, *Origen,* 42–43.

43. The quoted passage is from Vauchez, *Sainthood,* 444. Regarding incubation, see Gary Vikan, *Early Byzantine Pilgrimage Art,* Revised Edition (Washington, DC: Dumbarton Oaks Byzantine Collection Publications, 2010) 76; and Talbot, "Pilgrimage," 153. For a collection of passages on incubation and healing in dreams, see Emma J. Edelstein and Ludwig Edelstein, *Asclepius: Collection and Interpretation of the Testimonies* (Baltimore: Johns Hopkins University Press, 1998) 209–240.

44. The first two quoted passage are from Vikan, *Early,* 13; see 14–15. The third quoted passage is from Pentcheva, "Sensual Icon," 20. The last quoted passage is from Robert Ousterhout, "Loca Sancta and the Architectural Response to Pilgrimage," *The Blessings of Pilgrimage,* ed. Robert Ousterhout (Urbana: University of Illinois Press, 1990) 109. Regarding the ambiguity, see Marcel Mauss, *A General Theory of Magic,* tr. Robert Brain (London and New York: Routledge, 2001) 133, where mana is similarly ambiguous as a force, a being, an action, a quality, and a state. Regarding the souvenirs, see Vikan, *Early,*15, 32–40, 59, and 62–66. See an eighteen-century pilgrim's flask from Italy in Garnett and Rosser, *Spectacular,* 180.

45. For an example of holy water distinguished from sacred water in the middle ages, see Ward, *Miracles,* 85. In Gregory of Tours, *Glory,* 42, people drank from a sixth-century pool of sanctified water and then "each carried back home a container full of water, intending to protect their fields and vineyards by sprinkling the beneficial water."

46. The first quoted passage is in Miguel Angel Rubio, *La morada de los santos: expresiones del culto religiosos en el sur de Veracruz y en Tabasco* (Mexico City: Instituto Nacional Indigenista, Secretaría de Desarrollo Social, 1995) 75. The second quoted passage (in two parts) is from Florencia, *Origen*, 56. See 106, where dirt from San Juan de los Lagos cures a woman's wound. The passages regarding the man who ate a loaf of earth are from Florencia, *Origen*, 180. The last quoted passage is from Florencia, *Zodiaco*, 91. See a similar example in Florencia, *Origen*, 102. Religious bread stamps have a long history, beginning in antiquity and then adapting to early Christianity. See George Galavaris, *Bread and the Liturgy: The Symbolism of Early Christian and Byzantine Bread Stamps* (Madison: University of Wisconsin Press, 1970) 22–39. Images of Virgin bread stamps are on 136 and 138. See also Antonio Rubial García, "Cuerpos milagrosos; las relíquias novohispanas," *Estudios de historia novohispana* 18 (1998): 27, where dust from the tomb of Sor María de Jesus cured diseases and protected crops.

47. The first quoted passage is from Florencia, *La milagrosa*, 231; and the second is from Nicanor Quirós y Gutiérrez, *Historia de la aparición de Nuestra Señora de Ocotlán: y de su culto en cuatro siglos* (1541–1941) (Mexico City: Taller Linotipograf. de la Escuela "R. Donde," 1940) 170. See 172 and 174. See also Florencia, *Origen*, 100 and 163; and Florencia, *Zodiaco*, 342.

48. The Isidro example and quoted passages are from Florencia, *Origen*, 88. Regarding the girl resuscitated by the original image, see Víctor Campa Mendoza, *Santuarios y milagros* (Mexico City: Consejo Nacional de Ciencia y Technología, 2002) 223–226. An illustration of the miracle is reproduced on 216. See also 241 and 243.

49. See Rachel P. Maines and James J. Glynn, "Numinous Objects," *The Public Historian* 15/1 (1993): 10; and Catherine M. Cameron and John B. Gatewood, "Seeking Numinous Experiences in the Unremembered Past," *Ethnology* 42/1 (2003): 67–68, where "Places that focus on human suffering and sacrifice are most likely to foster a strong affective response" (67). The former Holocaust camps are a good example, as are, in a different way, shrines in which the crucified Christ presides. See also Rudolf Otto, *The Idea of the Holy*, tr. John W. Harvey (London: Oxford University Press, 1950) 5–7.

50. See Maines and Glynn, "Numinous Objects," 8–25. See also Catherine M. Cameron and John B. Gatewood, "Battlefield Pilgrims at Gettysburg National Military Park," *Ethnology* 43/3 (2004): 211, regarding the emotional experience of being at the very spot where something extraordinary happened.

51. The quoted passage is from Catholic Church, Code of Canon Law, Canon 1191, section 1: www.vatican.va/archive/ENG1104/__P4E.HTM. The Vatican translates *juramento* as "oath," but the English word that best corresponds to Mexican use of *juramento* is "vow," as defined in Canons 1191, 1193, and 1194.

52. The quoted passage is from David Ibarra Carrillo, *Mi juramento en el Santuario del Señor de Chalma*, (Chalma: Santuario del Señor de Chalma [no date]), 1. The vow prayer is on the back cover of this booklet rather than on the estampita.

53. The Sánchez family is from Mary Cuadrado and Louis Lieberman, "The Virgen de Guadalupe as an Ancillary Modality for Treating Hispanic Substance Abusers: Juramentos in the United States," *Journal of Religion and Health* 50/4 (2011): 925. See Gutmann, *Meanings*, 186.

54. The quoted passage is from McCullough and Willoughby, "Religion," 80. See Glen D. Walters, "Spontaneous Remission from Alcohol, Tobacco, and Other Drug Abuse: Seeking Quantitative Answers to Qualitative Questions," *American Journal of Drug and Alcohol Abuse* 26/3 (2000): 455–456.

55. The mother-in-law example is in Cuadrado and Lieberman, "Virgen," 926.

56. See Stanley Brandes, *Staying Sober in Mexico City* (Austin: University of Texas Press, 2002) 37–38, where jurados make direct appeals to a Virgin.

57. McCullough and Willoughby "Religion," 79. See 86, where religion influences the goals people choose and how they pursue them. See also Michael R. Welch, Charles R. Tittle, and Harold G. Grasmick, "Christian Religiosity, Self-Control and Social Conformity," *Social Forces* 84/3 (2006): 1605–1606; and Wayne Proudfoot, *Religious Experience* (Berkeley: University of California Press, 1985) 43, where "Religious beliefs and practices are interpretations of experience in that they are attempts to make sense of and to account for the phenomena and events with which one is confronted, including one's own behavior."

58. The last quoted passage is in Rodríguez-Shadow and Shadow, *El pueblo*, 77.

59. The first quoted passage (in two parts) is from Albert Bandura, *Social Learning Theory* (Englewood Cliffs, NJ: Prentice-Hall, 1977) 18. The second quoted passage is from Baumeister, Vohs, Dewall, and Zhang, "How," 192. See 190–194 and 173–175. See also Dianne M. Tice, "Self-Concept Change and Self-Presentation: The Looking Glass Self Is also a Magnifying Glass," *The Self in Social Psychology*, ed. Roy F. Baumeister (Philadelphia: Psychology Press, 1999) 215; and Pargament, Magyar-Russell, and Murray-Swank, "The Sacred," 670.

60. See Kenneth I. Pargament and Crystal L. Park, "Merely a Defense? The Variety of Religious Means and Ends," *Journal of Social Issues* 51/2 (1995): 25, where "the sense of partnership with God is empowering; through interaction with the divine, the individual feels a greater sense of personal power and efficacy"; and Schieman, Pudrovska, and Milkie, "Sense," 167, where "God is akin to a supportive significant other—albeit with an omnipotent status."

61. The quoted passage is from Baumeister and Leary, "Need," 498. See McCullough and Willoughby, "Religion," 82–83 and 86; Walters, "Spontaneous," 456; Krause, "God-Mediated Control," 270; Roy F. Baumeister, Ellen Bratslavsky, Mark Muraven, and Dianne M. Tice, "Ego Depletion: Is the Active Self a Limited Resource?" *Journal of Personality and Social Psychology* 74/5 (1998): 1263; Tice, "Self-Concept," 212; Robert Granfield and William Cloud, "Social Context and 'Natural Recovery': The Role of Social Capital in the Resolution of Drug-Associated Problems," *Substance Use and Misuse* 36/11 (2001): 1557; and John

Corrigan, "Introduction," *Religion and Emotion: Approaches and Interpretations,*
ed. John Corrigan (New York: Oxford University Press, 2004) 14.

62. The quoted phrase and then passage from the critic are from Fernando Iván de
la Rosa Avile, "La industria del perdón," which is a reader's response to the article Carolina Gómez Mena, "Acuden cientos de personas a la Capilla de los Juramentos para 'dejar vicios,'" *Periódico la jornada* (June 30, 2011): www.jornada.
unam.mx/2011/06/30/sociedad/044n1soc. See Granfield and Cloud, "Social,"
1544, where two surveys found that "over 77% of individuals who had overcome
an alcohol abuse problem did so without treatment"; and Walters "Spontaneous,"
454, where in one study about 71 percent of problem cocaine users quit without
treatment, and in another spontaneous remission was 26 percent by a broad
definition and 18 percent by restrictive definition. Resolution of drug and alcohol problems without treatment has many names: "natural recovery," "matur-
ing out," "autoremission," "spontaneous remission," "unassisted change," and
"spontaneous recovery."

The idea of alcoholism as a disease is sometimes explicit in votive offerings.
A retablo offered to the Virgen de San Juan de los Lagos gives thanks for being
cured "of the disease of alcoholism," and in another to the Señor de Ojo Zarco a
wife petitions "that you save my husband from the dangerous disease of alcoholism." Regarding Monday morning, see Gady Zabicky Zirot and Luis R. Solís
Rojas, "El juramento: maniobra no médica, coadyuvante en el manejo de los
sujetos con consumo patológico de etanol en México," *Salud Mental* 23/4 (2000):
25. Fridays are popular too to prevent another weekend binge.

63. The first quoted passage is from *Twelve Steps and Twelve Traditions* (New York:
Alcoholics Anonymous World Services, 2003) 5; see 34–41 and steps 11 and
12. The last quoted phrase is from *Alcoholics Anonymous* ("Big Book") (New
York: Alcoholics Anonymous World Services, 1976) 84. For testimonies of
alcoholics achieving and maintaining sobriety with divine assistance, see
*Came to Believe...: The Spiritual Adventure of A.A. as Experienced by Individual
Members* (New York: Alcoholics Anonymous World Services, 1973). In theory
juramentos and AA approaches are incompatible, but for many years the
Señor de Chalma shrine provided a room for AA meetings and encouraged
jurados to attend. See Jorge Ayala Q., *Chalma: su Señor, su santuario su convento, sus ferias, sus danzas, sus leyendas, y tradiciones.* Chalma: shrine published, 2002) Book 2, 25.

64. The first quoted passage is from Walters "Spontaneous," 455. See Sarah E.
Zemore and Lee Ann Kaskutas, "Helping, Spirituality and Alcoholics Anonymous
in Recovery," *Journal of Studies on Alcohol* 65/3 (2004): 383; and Cuadrado and
Louis, "Virgen," 926, where some alcoholics prefer juramentos to AA for the
relative privacy. Mr. Sánchez did not want to go to AA because he was concerned
that his confessed misdeeds would be related to others outside the group. For
examples of "they will be done," see *Alcoholics Anonymous: The Story of How*

Many Men and Women Have Recovered from Alcoholism (New York: Alcoholics Anonymous World Services, 2001) 207; and *Twelve Steps*, 41. The three quoted passages in the same sentence are from, respectively, *Alcoholics Anonymous: The Story*, 100 (see 120 and 199), 11; and 485. The penultimate quoted passage is on 215. For a more collaborative relation with God, see 300. The last quoted passage is from *Twelve Steps*, 5. See also Ronald E. Hopson, "The 12-Step Program," *Religion and the Clinical Practice of Psychology*, ed. Edward P. Shafranske (Washington, DC: American Psychological Association, 1996) 544, where "The first three steps place the addicted person in the midst of a paradox. There is acknowledgment of the addicted person's inability to control the self and, paradoxically, a call for the alcoholic to exercise the will to surrender control of the self to a beneficent higher power. The steps embrace this paradox by acknowledging the reality of volition in the midst of the loss of volition. Despite the lack of a sense of efficacy, the possibility of agency is assumed as the addicted person is charged to act. However, this action is not in keeping with the sense of alienation from self and others and the corresponding loss of control. Rather, the action proposed assumes relationship with a beneficent power greater than the self. This element of submission and surrender may be highly important in working with religiously committed persons."

65. See McCullough and Willoughby, "Religion," 69–93; Roy F. Baumeister and Julie Juola Exline, "Self-Control, Morality, and Human Strength," *Journal of Social and Clinical Psychology* 19/1 (2000): 33 and 37; Roy F. Baumeister, "Ego Depletion and Self-Control Failure: An Energy Model of the Self's Executive Function," *Self and Identity* 1/2 (2002): 131–134; Michael Inzlicht and Brandon J. Schmeichel, "What is Ego Depletion? Toward a Mechanistic Revision of the Resource Model of Self-Control," *Perspectives on Psychological Science* 7/5 (2012): 450–479; James E. Maddux, "Self Efficacy: The Power of Believing You Can," *Handbook of Positive Psychology*, ed. C. R. Snyder and Shane J. Lopez (New York: Oxford University Press, 2002) 279; Brandon J. Schmeichel and Roy F. Baumeister, "Self-Regulatory Strength," *Handbook of Self-Regulation: Research, Theory, and Applications*, ed. Roy F. Baumeister and Kathleen D. Vohs (New York, Guilford Press, 2004) 86–87 and 95; Joni Y. Sasaki and Heejung S. Kim, "At the Intersection of Culture and Religion: A Cultural Analysis of Religion's Implications for Secondary Control and Social Affiliation," *Journal of Personality and Social Psychology* 101/2 (2011): 402; and Kenneth I. Pargament, Hannah Olsen, Barbara Reilly, Kathryn Falgout, David S. Ensing, and Kimberly Van Haitsma, "God Help Me (II): The Relationship of Religious Orientations to Religious Coping with Negative Life Events," *Journal for the Scientific Study of Religion* 31/4 (1992): 505, where "People do not face stressful events without resources. They bring with them a system of general beliefs, practices, aspirations, and relationships which affect how they deal with difficult moments. Religion is, to a greater or lesser extent, part of this general orienting system."

REMEDIOS

1. Regarding anointment rituals, see Catholic Church, *Catechism of the Catholic Church* (New York: Doubleday, 1995) sections 1511–1523.
2. Francisco de Florencia, *La milagrosa invención de un tesoro escondido*, ed. Peláez T. Matabuena and Lobato M. Rodríguez (Mexico City: Universidad Iberoamericana, 2008) 233. Regarding cures with lamp oil, see Francisco de Florencia, *Zodiaco mariano*, ed. Juan A. Oviedo (Mexico City: Consejo Nacional para la Cultura y las Artes, 1995) 127 (general cures) and 363 (eye problems healed with lamp oil from San Juan de los Lagos).

VOTIVE OFFERINGS

1. The example and quoted passages are in María J. Rodríguez-Shadow, "Peticiones y plegarias femeninas en los exvotos de Chalma," *Creatividad invisible: mujeres y arte popular en América Latina y el Caribe*, ed. Eli Bartra (Mexico City: Universidad Nacional Autónoma de México, 2004) 261–262. For other examples of detailed narratives, see Mexican Migration Project, plate 6, 1942; plate 4, 1947; and plate 106, 1949: http://mmp.opr.princeton.edu/expressions/retablos-en.aspx. See also the Artstor collection, "Mexican Retablos (Jorge Durand and Douglas Massey)": www.artstor.org/content/mexican-retablos-jorge-durand-and-douglas-massey.
2. The quoted passage is from Ralph Merrifiled, *The Archaeology of Ritual and Magic* (New York: New Amsterdam, 1987) 88. For examples from other periods and regions, see Jessica Hughes, "Fragmentation as Metaphor in the Classical Healing Sanctuary," *Social History of Medicine* 21/2 (2008): 218–220. On 222–223, terracotta figurines point to the body part in question. See also F. T. Van Straten, "Gifts for the Gods," *Faith, Hope, and Worship: Aspects of Religious Mentality in the Ancient World,*" ed. H. S. Versnel (Leiden: E. J. Brill, 1981) figures 50–64 in the unnumbered appendix. Some second-century A.D. bronze plaques of eyes and ears are reproduced in Alexia Petsalēs-Diomēdēs, *Truly Beyond Wonders: Aelius Aristides and the Cult of Asklepios* (Oxford: Oxford University Press, 2010) 260. See also the sixth- or seventh-century Syrian "Votive Plaque with Eyes" in the Walters Art Museum, which resembles modern stamped milagritos: http://learn.columbia.edu/treasuresofheaven/relics/Votive-Plaque-with-Eyes.php. In Lester K. Little, *Benedictine Maledictions: Liturgical Cursing in Romanesque France* (Ithaca, NY: Cornell University Press, 1993) 189, a prayer "enumerated parts of the body and asked that each part be protected."
3. The quoted passage is from Juan Sánchez Valdés de la Plata, *Crónica y historia general del hombre: en que se trata del hombre en común...* (Madrid: Luis Sánchez, 1598) 171. See Benedicta Ward, *Miracles and the Medieval Mind: Theory, Record and Event, 1000–1215* (Philadelphia: University of Pennsylvania Press, 1982) 94.

4. The quoted passage is in Francisco de Florencia, *La milagrosa invención de un tesoro escondido*, ed. Peláez T. Matabuena and Lobato M. Rodríguez (Mexico City: Universidad Iberoamericana, 2008) 163. Regarding models as offerings, see Marcus Bull, *The Miracles of Our Lady of Rocamadour: Analysis and Translation* (Woodbridge. UK: Boydell, 1999) 184–185, and also 34, 175, 187, and 190. See also Ward, *Miracles*, 148; and, for an Argentine example, Frank Graziano, *Cultures of Devotion: Folk Saints of Spanish America* (New York: Oxford University Press, 2007) 188–189.

5. The quoted passage is from James W. Dow, *Santos y supervivencias: funciones de la religión en una comunidad otomí* (Mexico City: Instituto Nacional Indigenista and Secretaría de Educación Pública, 1974) 117. See 117–118. Regarding the offerings in Otatitlán, see Fernando Winfield Capitaine, "Otatitlán y Yacatecuhtli," *La Palabra y el hombre* 32 (1979): 29; and regarding the offerings in Juquila, see María Concepción Amerlinck De Corsi, "Las memorias de la portentosa imagen de Nuestra Señora de Xuquila y el grabador Francisco Agüera Bustamante," *Boletín de monumentos históricos* 3/27 (2013): 201.

6. Regarding the ranchers, see Manuel Carrillo Dueñas, *Historia de Nuestra Señora del Rosario de Talpa* (Talpa de Allende, Mexico: [n.p.], 1962) 233.

7. Regarding metonymy, see Mose Halbertal and Avishai Margalit, *Idolatry*, tr. Naomi Goldblum (Cambridge, MA: Harvard University Press, 1992) 40–42. See also Helena Beristáin, *Diccionario de retórica y poética* (Mexico City, Editorial Porrúa, 1998) 327–331. Regarding the beard and sideburns, see José Velasco Toro, *De la historia al mito: mentalidad y culto en el santuario de Otatitlán* (Veracruz: Instituto Veracruzano de Cultura, 2000) 153.

8. For other examples of hair and braid offerings, see George M. Foster, *Tzintzuntzan: Mexican Peasants in a Changing World* (New York: Elsevier, 1979) 235–236; Luis Mario Schneider, *Cristos, Santos y Vírgenes: santuarios y devociones en México* (Mexico City: Grupo Editorial Planeta, 1995) 20; and Frank S. Edwards, *A Campaign in New Mexico with Colonel Doniphan* (Albuquerque: University of New Mexico Press, 1996) 24, where a mid-nineteeth-century narrative of a military campaign notes what appear to be hair offerings in Santa Fe. For examples in other regions and periods, see G. J. Tassie, "Hair-Offerings: An Enigmatic Egyptian Custom," *Papers from the Institute of Archaeology* 7/59 (1996): 64; Lynn R. LiDonnici, *The Epidaurian Miracle Incriptions: Text, Translation and Commentary* (Atlanta, GA: Scholars Press, 1995) 41 and 44; R. C. Finucane, *The Rescue of the Innocents: Endangered Children in Medieval Miracles* (New York: St. Martin's, 1997) 14; Van Straten, "Gifts," 90, where boys' hair was dedicated to nymphs and river-gods; and 96–97, where shipwreck survivors dedicated their hair or their clothes to gods of the sea.

9. The first quoted passage is in Velasco Toro, *De la historia*, 150. Regarding first-fruit offerings in a related context, see Hugo G. Nutini, *Todos Santos in Rural Tlaxcala: A Syncretic, Expressive, and Symbolic Analysis of the Cult of the Dead*

(Princeton, NJ: Princeton University Press, 1988) 181, where first fruits are "an entreaty and a reminder to the dead to watch over the crops." The quoted Greek phrase is from David D. Leitao, "Adolescent Hair-Growing and Hair-Cutting Rituals in Ancient Greece: A Sociological Approach," *Initiation in Ancient Greek Rituals and Narratives: New Critical Perspectives*, ed. David Dodd and Christopher A. Faraone (London: Routledge, 2003) 111. Regarding umbilical cuttings, see Alicia M. Barabas, *Dones, duenos y santos: ensayo sobre religiones en Oaxac*a (Mexico City: Instituto Nacional de Antropología e Historia, 2006) 175; and Victor Turner and Edith Turner, *Image and Pilgrimage in Christian Culture: Anthropological Perspectives* (New York: Columbia University Press, 1978), where plate 5 shows strips of cloth, some with umbilical cuttings, on exposed tree roots on a pilgrim route (see page 55). See also Paul Cassar, "Medical Votive Offerings in the Maltese Islands," *Journal of the Royal Anthropological Institute of Great Britain and Ireland* 94/1 (1964): 2, where votive offerings include kidney stones, swallowed objects, and other things removed from organs.

10. In Francisco de Florencia, *Zodiaco mariano*, ed. Juan A. Oviedo (Mexico City: Consejo Nacional para la Cultura y las Artes, 1995) 360, a slave was offered following a miracle.

11. Regarding the rancher, see Soledad González Monted, "La fiesta interminable: celebraciones públicas y privadas en un pueblo campesino del estado de México," *Historia de la vida cotidiana en México; Siglo XX. Campo y ciudad* (Mexico City: El Colegio de México y Fondo de Cultura Económica, 2004) 378. The cost of requesting a mass for petition (rogation) or thanksgiving varies from shrine to shrine, but is generally around two hundred or three hundred pesos.

12. The quoted passage is in Enriqueta Valdez Curiel, *Danza de los sonajeros de Zapotlán el Grande: promesas religiosas para recuperar la salud* (Guadalajara: Universidad de Guadalajara, Centro Universidad del Sur, 2006) 25.

13. The quoted passage is from Karina Jazmín Juárez Ramírez, *Exvotos retablitos: el arte de los milagros* (Guanajuato, Mexico: Centro de las Artes de Guanajuato and Ediciones Rana, 2008) 24. See Viktor Gecas, "The Social Psychology of Self-Efficacy," *Annual Review of Sociology* 15 (1989): 310. For overviews of votive offerings in other regions and periods, see Francisco de Florencia, *Origen de los dos celebres santuarios de la Nueva Galicia, obispado de Guadalaxara, en la America septentrional* (Zapopan, Mexico: Amate Editorial, 2001) 133–137; Hugo van der Velden, *The Donor's Image: Gerard Loyet and the Votive Portraits of Charles the Bold*, tr. Beverley Jackson (Turnhout, Belgium: Brepols, 2000) 213–222; LiDonnici, *Epidaurian*, 42–44; and Mercedes Cano Herrera, "Exvotos y promesas en Castilla y León," *La religiosidad popular*, Vol. 3, *Hermandades, romerías y santuarios*, ed. Carlos Alvarez Santaló, María Jesús Buxó i Rey, and Salvador Rodríguez Becerra (Barcelona: Editorial Anthropos; Sevilla: Fundación Machado, 1989) 392–395. Cicero relates an exchange between Diagoras of Melos and a friend. The friend asked, " 'You think the gods have no care for man? Why, you can see from all

these votive pictures here how many people have escaped the fury of storms at sea by praying to the gods, who have brought them safe to harbour.' 'Yes, indeed,' said Diagoras, 'but where are the pictures of all those who suffered shipwreck and perished in the waves?' " Cicero, *The Nature of the Gods,* tr. Horace C. P. McGregor (Harmondsworth, UK: Penguin Books, 1972) 232.

14. The first quoted passage (in two parts) is from Catholic Church, Code of Canon Law, Canon 1234; the second quoted passage is from Canon 1188; and the third quoted passage is from Canon 1220: www.vatican.va/archive/ENG1104/_INDEX.HTM. The fourth quoted passage is from Congregación para el Culto divino y la Disciplina de los Sacramentos, *Actas y documentos pontificios: directorio sobre la piedad popular y la liturgia* (Mexico City: San Pablo, 2002) 31.

15. The quoted passage is from Aby Warburg, *The Renewal of Pagan Antiquity: Contributions to the Cultural History of the European Renaissance,* tr. David Britt (Los Angeles: Getty Research Institute, 1999) 190. See also Richard C. Trexler, "Florentine Religious Experience: The Sacred Image," *Studies in the Renaissance* 19 (1972): 8, where in the same church "the weight of rows of life-size wax ex-votos threatened to bring down the structure." Regarding suspended anatomical offerings, see Christopher S. Wood, "The Votive Scenario," *Res: Anthropology and Aesthetics* 59/60 (2011): 207 and 217. Regarding the Greek offerings, see Van Straten, "Gifts," 78. See also David Freedberg, *The Power of Images: Studies in the History and Theory of Response* (Chicago: University of Chicago Press, 1989) 136.

16. Regarding the Remedios milagritos, see Linda Curcio-Nagy "Native Icon to City Protectress to Royal Patroness: Ritual, Political Symbolism and the Virgin of Remedies," *The Americas* 52/3 (1996): 384.

17. For examples of melted precious-metal offerings, see Van Straten, "Gifts," 80; Cassar, "Medical," 25; and Warburg, *Renewal,* 206. Regarding the doors and ironwork, see *The Book of Sainte Foy,* tr. Pamela Sheingorn (Philadelphia: University of Pennsylvania Press, 1995) 102–103 and 17.

18. Regarding Father Juan Manuel's observations, in Museum of International Folk Art (Santa Fe) accession notes dated July 1963, a curator mentions many painted votive offerings in Spain. "When guides were asked about them, they always replied, 'No es importante.'"

19. See *Book of Sainte Foy,* 103, where frequent miracles at Conques made monks similarly indifferent or inappreciative. I am using "performative" in the sense of illocutionary speech acts, by which words themselves (or in the present case objects) perform an action. Regarding speech acts see J. L. Austin, "Performative Utterances," in *Philosophical Papers* (London: Oxford University Press, 1961); and J. L. Austin, *How To Do Things with Words* (Cambridge, MA: Harvard University Press, 1962). The theory is further developed in John R. Searle, *Speech Acts: An Essay in the Philosophy of Language* (London: Cambridge University Press, 1970) and in John R. Searle, ed., *The Philosophy of Language* (London: Oxford University Press, 1971).

20. The quoted colonial passage is from Florencia, *Origen*, 45–46. In addition to disposal, many retablos were lost to gifting and theft. The possibility of integrating votive offerings into devotional spaces is beautifully exemplified by the Italian church Madonna dei Bagni (Casalina, Perugia, Umbria) where narrative ceramic plaques, the earliest one dated 1657, cover the interior walls. There is brief discussion in Freedberg, *Power*, 138–41.

21. See Michael E. Goodich, *Miracles and Wonders: The Development of the Concept of Miracle, 1150–1350* (Aldershot: Ashgate, 2007) 13, where represented miracles create a social bond. I borrow the idea of placeholders from Wood, "Votive," 222, where "The possibility that you might find yourself suspended in the subjunctive mood of the scenario creates interest." See Pilar Gonzalbo Aizpuru, "Lo prodigioso cotidiano en los exvotos novohispanos," *Dones y promesas: 500 años de arte ofrenda (exvotos mexicanos)* (Mexico City: Centro Cultural/Arte Contemporáneo: Fundación Cultural Televisa, 1996) 47.

22. See David Morgan, "The Ecology of Images: Seeing and the Study of Religion," *Religion and Society: Advances in Research* 5/1 (2014): 92, where power is distributed through a network of relations; and Robert Klee, "Why Some Delusions Are Necessarily Inexplicable Beliefs," *Philosophy, Psychiatry, & Psychology* 11/1 (2004): 28, where beliefs are "networked together in complex relations of support and countersupport." For an overview of human/object networks and interrelations, see Ian Hodder, *Entangled: An Archaeology of the Relationships between Humans and Things* (Malden, MA: Wiley-Blackwell, 2012) 89.

23. For offerings as inspiration to votaries in other regions and periods, see M. P. J. Dillon, "The Didactic Nature of the Epidaurian Iamata," *Zeitschrift für Papyrologie und Epigraphik* 101 (1994): 240, where miracle records encouraged others to petition cures; R. A. Tomlinson, *Epidauros* (Austin: University of Texas Press, 1983) 21; David Frankfurter, "Amuletic Invocations of Christ for Health and Fortune," *Religions of Late Antiquity in Practice*, ed. Richard Valantasis (Princeton, NJ: Princeton University Press, 2000) 34; Gary Vikan, *Early Byzantine Pilgrimage Art*, Revised Edition (Washington, DC: Dumbarton Oaks Byzantine Collection Publications, 2010) 78; Finucane, *Rescue*, 15; Jerome D. Frank, *Persuasion and Healing: A Contemporary Study of Psychotherapy* (Baltimore: Johns Hopkins University Press, 1973) 68, where votive offerings are "a validation of the shrine's power"; Peter Brown, *The Cult of the Saints: Its Rise and Function in Latin Christianity* (Chicago: University of Chicago Press, 1981) 38, where miracles are private events "deliberately made public"; Paul Davies, "The Lighting of Pilgrimage Shrines in Renaissance Italy," *The Miraculous Image in the Late Middle Ages and Renaissance*, ed. Erik Thunø and Gerhard Wolf (Rome: "L'erma" di Bretschneider, 2004) 79, where "candles acted as visible index of the image's power"; and, in the same collection, Richard C. Trexler, "Being and Non-Being: Parameters of the Miraculous in the Traditional Religious Image," 27. See also William B. Taylor, *Shrines and Miraculous Images: Religious Life in Mexico before the Reform*

(Albuquerque: University of New Mexico Press, 2010) 22; and Mario Colin, *Retablos del Señor del Huerto, que se venera en Atlacomulco* (Mexico City: Biblioteca Enciclopédica de México, 1981) 25, where retablos transmit popular culture visually as corridos do musically. Regarding evidence and inferences, see Julian B. Rotter, "Generalized Expectancies for Internal Versus External Control of Reinforcement," *Psychological Monographs: General and Applied* 80/1 (1966): 4–5.

24. The first quoted passage is from Albert Bandura, *Social Learning Theory* (Englewood Cliffs, NJ: Prentice-Hall, 1977) 117; and the second (in the same sentence) is on 160. The subsequent quoted phrase is from Noah J. Goldstein and Robert B. Cialdini, "The Spyglass Self: A Model of Vicarious Self-Perception," *Journal of Personality and Social Psychology* 92/3 (2007): 413; I am following 402–404 and 414.

25. The quoted passage is from Jules David Prown, "Style as Evidence," *Winterthur Portfolio* 15/3 (1980): 198.

26. The quoted passage (in two parts) is from Pietro Caggiano, Michele Rak, and Angelo Turchini, *Sweet Mother* (Pompeii: Pontifical Sanctuary of Pompeii, 1990) 98. See 95, where "The devotee learns a compact code of values and symbols" but "introduces just enough variation to guarantee his own identity."

27. The first quoted passage is from Louis O. Mink, "Narrative Form as a Cognitive Instrument," *The Writing of History: Literary Form and Historical Understanding,* ed. Robert H. Canary and Henry Kozicki (Madison: University of Wisconsin Press, 1978) 145. See David Yamane, "Narrative and Religious Experience," *Sociology of Religion* 61/2 (2000): 174–176. The quoted passage on proof is from François Hartog, *The Mirror of Herodotus: The Representation of the Other in the Writing of History,* tr. Janet Lloyd (Berkeley: University of California Press, 2009) 128. See also Walter Burkert, *Homo Necans: The Anthropology of Ancient Greek Sacrificial Ritual and Myth,* tr. Peter Bing (Berkeley: University of California Press, 1983) xx, where a religious claim "establishes and explains, but needs no explanation"; Clifford Geertz, "Religion as a Cultural System," *The Interpretation of Cultures: Selected Essays* (London: Fontana Press: 1993) 90, where "Religious symbols formulate a basic congruence between a particular style of life and a specific (if, most often, implicit) metaphysic, and in so doing sustain each with the borrowed authority of the other"; Steven L. Neuberg, "Social Motives and Expectancy-Tinged Social Interactions," in Richard M. Sorrentino and E. Tory Higgins, *Handbook of Motivation and Cognition,* Vol. 3, *The Interpersonal Context* (New York: Guilford Press, 1996) 228–231; Adam B. Seligman, *Ritual and its Consequences: An Essay on the Limits of Sincerity* (New York: Oxford University Press, 2008) 25–26; Ray Paloutzian, Steven A. Rogers, Erica L. Swenson, and Deborah A. Lowe, "Miracle Attributions, Meaning, and Neuropsychology," *Miracles: God, Science, and Psychology in the Paranormal,* Vol. 2 *Medical and Therapeutic Events,* ed. J. Harold Ellens (Westport, CT: Greenwood Publishing, 2008)

50–59; Robert Maniura, "Ex Votos, Art and Pious Performance," *Oxford Art Journal* 32/3 (2009): 423; and Juárez Ramírez, 23–25.

28. See Gerard Rooijakkers, "Cult Circuits in the Southern Netherlands: Mediators Between Heaven and Earth," *The Object as Mediator: On the Transcendental Meaning of Art in Traditional Cultures*, ed. Mireille Holsbeke (Antwerp: Ethnografisch Museum Antwerp, 1996) 37, where photographs placed behind the altar ensure perpetual protection; Jacalyn Duffin, *Medical Miracles: Doctors, Saints, and Healing in the Modern World* (New York: Oxford University Press, 2009) 156, where "the object lingers at the holy site as a permanent invocation"; van der Velden, *Donor's Image*, 238, where "the portrait of the votary simulated his presence"; and Megan Holmes, "Ex-Votos: Materiality, Memory, and Cult," *The Idol in the Age of Art: Objects, Devotions and the Early Modern World*, ed. Michael Cole and Rebecca Zorach (Aldershot: Ashgate, 2009) 166, where votive offerings are "in the sight of the mother of God."

29. The first quoted passage is from Vikan, *Early*, 72. For an example of pilgrim gouges on an exterior wall of the temple of a local god in Roman Egypt, see David Frankfurter, *Religion in Roman Egypt: Assimilation and Resistance* (Princeton, NJ: Princeton University Press, 1998) plate 21. Regarding longevity, see Matthew Champion, "The Medium is the Message: Votive Devotional Imagery and Gift Giving amongst the Commonality in the Late Medieval Parish," *Peregrinations* 3/4 (2012): 114 and 120.

30. The first quoted passage is from Emile Durkheim, *The Elementary Forms of Religious Life*, tr. Carol Cosman (New York: Oxford University Press, 2001) 239. The second quoted passage is from Carol Nemeroff and Paul Rozin, "The Contagion Concept in Adult Thinking in the United States: Transmission of Germs and of Interpersonal Influence," *Ethos* 22/2 (1994): 172. The third quoted passage is from St. John of Damascus, *On the Divine Images: Three Apologies Against Those Who Attack the Divine Images*, tr. David Anderson (Crestwood, NY: St. Vladimir's Seminary Press, 1980) 71.

31. The quoted passage is from Tassie, "Hair-Offerings," 66. See 69.

32. The quoted passages are from Wood, "Votive," 209 and 223, respectively. See 224–225. See also Joan Breton Connelly, "Standing before One's God: Votive Sculpture and the Cypriot Religious Tradition," *The Biblical Archaeologist* 52/4 (1989): 211; and Van Straten, "Gifts," 103, where the intent of votary representation in offerings was "permanent attention of the god." Regarding anatomical offerings, see Hughes, "Fragmentation," 220–221.

33. The quoted phrase is from Finucane, *Rescue*, 11. See an example on 172. Regarding measuring, see also Eamon Duffy, *The Stripping of the Altars: Traditional Religion in England c.1400–c.1580* (New Haven, CT: Yale University Press, 1992) 184; Ward, *Miracles*, 95; Wood, "Votive," 213; Merrifield, *Archaeology*, 90; van der Velden, *Donor's Image*, 240; André Vauchez, *Sainthood in the Later Middle Ages*, tr. Jean Brill (Cambridge: Cambridge University Press, 1997) 456;

and Caggiano, Rak, and Turchini, *Sweet*, 55. Regarding weighed offerings, see Georges Didi-Huberman, "Ex-Voto: Image, Organ, Time," *L'Espirit Créateur* 47/3 (2007): 15, n. 16; Caggiano, Rak, and Turchini, *Sweet*, 76; Finucane, *Rescue*, 15; and Vauchez, *Sainthood*, 458.

34. The first quoted passage is in Robert Maniura, "The Images and Miracles of Santa Maria Delle Carceri," *Miraculous Image*, 89. The second quoted passage is from Warburg, *Renewal*, 206. The third quoted passage is from Holmes, "Ex-Votos," 177; see 173. See also Megan Holmes, "The Elusive Origins of the Cult of the Annunziata in Florence," *Miraculous Image*, 109, n. 43; Vauchez, *Sainthood*, 455–458; Connelly, "Standing," 217; van der Velden, *Donor's Image*, 253–254; Maniura, "Ex Votos," 412; and Catherine M. Keesling, *The Votive Statues of the Athenian Acropolis* (New York: Cambridge University Press, 2003) 116–117.

35. The quoted passage is from Michel Foucault, *Discipline and Punish: The Birth of the Prison*, tr. Alan Sheridan (New York: Vintage Books, 1979) 45. See Holmes, "Ex-Votos," 175, where a votive offering incorporates the noose in which the votary was almost hanged. The Brazilian example is from C. Lindsey King, "Pilgrimage, Promises, and Exvotos: Ingredients for Healing in Northeast Brazil," *Pilgrimage and Healing*, ed. Jill Dubish and Michael Winkelman (Tucson: University of Arizona Press, 2005) 65.

36. Regarding the *medidas*, see Carrillo Dueñas, *Historia*, 218. The votive painting is in Elin Luque Agraz, *El arte de dar gracias: los exvotos pictóricos de la Virgen de la Soledad de Oaxaca* (Mexico City: Centro de Cultura Casa Lamm, 2007) 12–13. See Rosario Inés Granados Salinas, "Mexico City's Symbolic Geography: The Processions of Our Lady of Remedios," *Journal of Latin American Geography* 11/2 (2012): 156, where money was raised by selling "portions of ribbon that replicated Remedio's height." See also Gary Vikan, *Sacred Images and Sacred Power in Byzantium* (Aldershot: Ashgate Publishing, 2003) 386, where the impressions of Christ's hands and chest on the column where he was scourged are so clear "that you can use them to take 'measures' for any kind of disease, and people can wear them around their neck and be cured"; Ernst Kitzinger, "The Cult of Images in the Age before Iconoclasm," *Dumbarton Oaks Papers* 8 (1954): 105; and Joanna Tokarska-Bakir, "Why Is the Holy Image 'True'? The Ontological Concept of Truth as a Principle of Self-Authentication of Folk Devotional Effigies in the 18th and 19th Century," *Numen*, 49/3 (2002): 271 and 277.

37. The quoted phrase is from van der Velden, *Donor's Image*, 235; see 227. I am following Wood, "Votive," 223. See Freedberg, *Power*, 155.

38. The example and quoted passages are from Jacobus de Voragine, *The Golden Legend: Readings on the Saints*, tr. William Granger Ryan (Princeton, NJ: Princeton University Press, 1993) 1/118. See 1/382, where the same motif appears in a petition to St. Mary Magdalene.

39. The quoted passage is from Didi-Huberman, "Ex-Voto," 13. See Caggiano, Rak, and Turchini, *Sweet*, 76.

40. I am adapting insights from Richard Bauman and Charles L Briggs, "Poetics And Performance as Critical Perspectives on Language And Social Life," *Annual Review of Anthropology* 19 (1990): 73–74. See Richard Bauman, *A World of Others' Words: Cross-Cultural Perspectives on Intertextuality* (Oxford: Blackwell, 2004) 4, where objectification serves "to render a text extractable from its context of production"; and Michael White and David Epston, *Narrative Means to Therapeutic Ends* (New York: Norton, 1990) 4, 38, and 40–41.

41. The quoted passages are in G. Bolton "'Writing is a Way of Saying Things I Can't Say'—Therapeutic Creative Writing: A Qualitative Study of its Value To People With Cancer Cared for in Cancer and Palliative Healthcare," *Medical Humanities* 34/1 (2008): 43. See Margaretta Jolly, "What I Never Wanted to Tell You: Therapeutic Letter Writing in Cultural Context," *Journal of Medical Humanities* 32/1 (2011): 47–59; Julie Juola Exline, Joshua M. Smyth, Jeffrey Gregory, Jill Hockemeyer, and Heather Tulloch, "Religious Framing by Individuals with PTSD when Writing about Traumatic Experiences," *International Journal for the Psychology of Religion* 15/1 (2005): 18–19; Anita E. Kelly, "Revealing Personal Secrets," *Current Directions in Psychological Science* 8/4 (1999): 106; Joshua M. Smyth and James W. Pennebaker, "Sharing One's Story: Translating Emotional Experiences into Words as a Coping Tool," *Coping: The Psychology of What Works*, ed. C. R. Snyder (New York: Oxford University Press, 1999) 79, where "the act of converting emotions and images into words changes the way the person organizes and thinks about the trauma"; JoAnn O'Reilly, "The Hospital Prayer Book: A Partner for Healing," *Literature and Medicine* 19/1 (2000): 81, where "they write so that they may not feel so alone"; and 68, where written prayer is "a means of coping with the chaotic emotions raised by confrontation with helplessness, with finitude, with situations beyond their limits." See also Søren Kierkegaard, *Purity of Heart Is To Will One Thing: Spiritual Preparation for the Feast of Confession*, tr. Douglas V. Steere (New York: Harper and Row, 1938) 22, where "The all-knowing One does not get to know something about the maker of the confession, rather the maker of confession gets to know about himself." On 23, "The prayer does not change God, but it changes the one who offers it"; and "Prayer is probably better described as a reinterpretation of what is in some sense already known than as an exercise in the acquisition of knowledge."

42. The first two quoted passages are from Robert A. Neimeyer and Heidi Levitt, "Coping and Coherence: A Narrative Perspective on Resilience," *Coping with Stress: Effective People and Processes*, ed. C. R. Snyder (New York: Oxford University Press, 2001) 48 and 40, respectively. The third and fourth quoted passages are from Jerome Bruner, "Life as Narrative," *Social Research* 71/3 (2004): 708 and 692, respectively. The last quoted passage is from Chad M. Burton and Laura A. King, "The Health Benefits of Writing about Positive Experiences: The Role of Broadened Cognition," *Psychological Health* 24/8 (2009): 868. See Smyth and

Pennebaker, "Sharing," 79 and 82; K. Greene, V. J. Derlega, and A. Mathews, "Self-Disclosure in Personal Relationships," *Cambridge Handbook of Personal Relationships*, ed. A. Vangelisti & D. Perlman (Cambridge: Cambridge University Press, 2006) 421; and Kate C. McLean, Monisha Pasupathi, Jennifer L. Pals, "Selves Creating Stories Creating Selves: A Process Model of Self-Development," *Personal and Social Psychology Review* 11/3 (2007): 268, where audiences prefer stories of "managing traumatic events" to stories of vulnerability.

43. Deborah Schiffrin, "Narrative as Self-Portrait: Sociolinguistic Construction of Identity," *Language in Society* 23/2 (1996): 168 and 170; McLean, Pasupathi, and Pals, "Selves," 273; Tilmann Habermas and Susan Bluck, "Getting a Life: The Emergence of the Life Story in Adolescence," *Psychological Bulletin* 126/5 (2000): 749; and Bruner, "Life," 694.

44. An elaborate eighteenth-century votive painting on cloth is reproduced in Ignacio Realino Frías Camacho, *Semblanza y realidad a través de la Santísima Virgen del Pueblito* (Querétaro [n. p.], 1997) 76.

45. The first quoted passage is from Vauchez, *Sainthood*, 452. The second and third quoted passages are from Sánchez Valdés de la Plata, *Crónica*, 127. The fourth quoted passage is from Freedberg, *Power*, 138. Regarding pinakes, see John Boardman, "Painted Votive Plaques and an Early Inscription from Aegina," *Annual of the British School at Athens* 49 (1954): 193; and LiDonnici, *Epidaurian*, 45. For votive paintings in other region and periods, see for example Hans Belting, *Likeness and Presence: A History of the Image before the Era of Art*, tr. Edmund Jephcott (Chicago: University of Chicago Press, 1994) 82–88; and Wood, "Votive," 209.

46. The painting fee is mentioned in Mercedes Iturbe, *Los favores del cielo: ex votos de Guanajuato: del 19 de octubre al 17 de Noviembre de 1991, Museo Regional Alhóndiga De Granditas...XIX Festival Internacional Cervantino* (Guanajuato, Mexico: [n. p.], 1991) 29.

47. See Jules David Prown, "Mind in Matter: An Introduction to Material Culture Theory and Method," *Winterthur Portfolio* 17/1 (1982): 6, where "the object stays relatively the same, but people change and cultural values change." Regarding the influence of context on meaning, see Yamane, "Narrative," 180; Robert Layton, "Art & Agency: A Reassessment," *Journal of the Royal Anthropological Institute* 9/3 (2003): 449; David Morgan, "Thing," *Material Religion*, 7/1 (2011): 143–146; and Edwina Taborsky, "The Discursive Object," *Objects of Knowledge*, ed. Susan Pearce (London: Athlone Press, 1990) 51, where an object has "a meaning which is not inherent in that object, but which is socially assigned to it"; and 59, where "meaning is contextual and interactive." Regarding the objectification of gratitude, see the editors' "Introduction," *Handbook of Material Culture*, ed. Christopher Tilley, Webb Keane, Susanne Kuechler-Fogden, Mike Rowlands, and Patricia Spyer (Thousand Oaks: Sage Publications, 2006) 4. See also Dr. Atl, *Las artes populares en México* (Mexico City: Librería México, 1921) 63, where the retablo

tradition's demise is dated earlier: "Shortly before 1910 the custom of eternaliz-
ing an act of kindness of a heavenly personage in a retablo had disappeared almost completely," and was "substituted by pecuniary offerings to priests."

48. The quoted passage is in Amílcar Carpio Pérez, *Exvoto y migración: secular-
    ización y religiosidad popular en torno a la devoción a San Cristóbal Magallanes
    Jara en Totatiche, Jalisco,* Master's thesis, Universidad Autónoma Metropolitana,
    Iztapalapa, 2009) 221. Priests do appear in some Spanish retablos; see Eulalia
    Castellote Herrero, *Exvotos pictóricos del Santuario de Nuestra Señora de la Salud
    de Barbatona* (Guadalajara, Spain: Ediciones AACHE, 2005) 61, 75, 83, 91, 101,
    103, 109, 113, and 137–138.

49. The 1944 example and quoted phrase are from *Dones y promesas,* 180 cat. 241.
    See the related retablos on 183–185. See also retablos in Carlos Monsiváis and
    Elin Luque Agraz, *Los relatos pintados: la otra historia, exvotos mexicanos* (Mexico
    City: Centro de Cultura Casa Lamm, 2010) 27 (unjustly imprisoned), 31 (tor-
    tured by police), 86 (saved from execution), and 91 (workers killed by troops
    during a factory strike). The last quoted passage is from Goodich, *Violence,* 68.
    See 1–3, 28, 44, 83, 149, 155, and, for examples of miraculous interventions
    during executions, 51–57.

50. The first quoted passage is from Gregory the Great, "To Serenus, Bishop of
    Massilia," *A Select Library of Nicene and Post-Nicene Fathers of the Christian
    Church, Second Series,* ed. Philip Schaff and Henry Wace (New York: Christian
    Literature Company, 1898) 13/23. The quoted passages from St. John of Damascus
    are from, respectively, *On the Divine Images* 39 (see 77–78); and St. John
    Damascene, *On Holy Images,* tr. Mary H. Allies (London: Thomas Baker, 1898)
    19. On 39, "Do you understand that both image and sermon teach one lesson?"
    The 1025 quoted passage is in Moshe Barasch, *Icon: Studies in the History of an
    Idea* (New York: New York University Press, 1992) 202; and the 869 quoted pas-
    sage is in Belting, *Likeness,* 150. For other statements related to Gregory's dictum,
    see Jeffrey F. Hamburger, "Introduction," *The Mind's Eye: Art and Theological
    Argument in the Middle Ages,* ed. Jeffrey F. Hamburger and Anne-Marie Bouché
    (Princeton, NJ: Department of Art and Archaeology in Association with
    Princeton University Press, 2006) 15; Herbert L. Kessler, "Turning a Blind Eye:
    Medieval Art and the Dynamics of Contemplation," *The Mind's Eye,* 413–415;
    Michael Camille, *The Gothic Idol: Idology and Image-Making in Medieval Art*
    (Cambridge: Cambridge University Press, 1989) 206; and Alain Besançon, *The
    Forbidden Image: An Intellectual History of Iconoclasm,* tr. Jane Marie Todd (Chicago:
    University of Chicago Press, 2000) 150, where "What telling offers the ears,
    painting reveals silently by imitation" (Basil the Great); and "The image is a book
    of language" (Gregory of Nyssa).

51. See Herbert L. Kessler, *Spiritual Seeing: Picturing God's Invisibility in Medieval Art*
    (Philadelphia: University of Pennsylvania Press, 2000) 1; and Miguel Angel
    Rubio, *La morada de los santos: expresiones del culto religiosos en el sur de Veracruz*

y en Tabasco (Mexico City: Instituto Nacional Indigenista, Secretaría de Desarrollo Social, 1995) 68. Regarding Chalma, see María J. Rodríguez-Shadow and Robert D. Shadow, *El pueblo del Señor: las fiestas y peregrinaciones de Chalma* (Toluca: Universidad Autónoma del Estado de Mexico, 2000) 84–86; and the text of the Chalma paintings in Gilberto Giménez, *Cultural popular y religión en el Anahuac* (Mexico City: Centro de Estudios Ecuménicos, 1978) 72–73. Regarding Remedios, see Francisco Miranda Godínez, *Dos cultos fundantes: los Remedios y Guadalupe. Historia documental (1521–1649)* (Zamora, Mexico: Colegio de Michoacán, 2001) 31. See also Holmes, "Ex-Votos," 172, where text and image combine in wax effigies accompanied by narratives.

52. The first quoted phrase is from Juan José de Eguiara y Eguren in Taylor, *Shrines*, 19. The quoted Valadés passage is in Samuel Y. Edgerton, *Theaters of Conversion: Religious Architecture and Indian Artisans in Colonial Mexico* (Albuquerque, University of New Mexico Press, 2001) 116. The "Allegorical Atrium" is reproduced, for example, in Kelly Donahue-Wallace, *Art & Architecture of Viceregal Latin America, 1521–1821* (Albuquerque: University of New Mexico Press, 2008) figure 2; see 34. See also Justino Cortés Castellanos, *El catecismo en pictogramas de Fray Pedro de Gante* (Madrid: Fundación Universitaria Española, 1987) 57 and 59. For a twentieth-century example of religious instruction using paintings in the Putumayo lowlands, see Michael Taussig, *Shamanism, Colonialism, and the Wild Man: A Study in Terror and Healing* (Chicago: University of Chicago Press, 1987) 384–387. Visual aids were also used in music studies. See a hand image used to teach intervals in David Wakely and Thomas A. Drain, *A Sense of Mission: Historic Churches of the Southwest* (San Francisco: Chronicle Books, 1994) 103.

53. The quoted passage is from José de Acosta, *Historia natural y moral de las Indias*, ed. Francisco Mateos (Alicante: Biblioteca Virtual Miguel de Cervantes, 1999) Book 6, Chapter 7 ("Del modo de letras y escritura que usaron los mejicanos"). On the rebus system, see Nicolas León, "A Mazahua Catechism in Testera-Amerind Hieroglypics," *American Anthropologist* 2/4 (1900): 726. *Nochtli* is also given as *nuchtli* in this source. See also Cortés Castellanos, 64; Serge Gruzinski, *The Conquest of Mexico: The Incorporation of Indian Societies into the Western World, 16th–18th Centuries*, tr. Eileen Corrigan (Cambridge: Polity Press, 1993) 30 and 33; and Gordon Brotherston, *Book of the Fourth World: Reading the Native Americas through their Literature* (Cambridge: Cambridge University Press, 1992), 51–52; see 50–73.

54. Regarding chronology and simultaneity, see Julio Ramos, "Roadside Miracles: Commemoration and Non-Synchronicity in Ecuadorian *Ex Votos*," *Journal of Latin American Cultural Studies* 19/1 (2010): 108. See also Petsalēs-Diomēdēs, "Truly," 254, for "a double thank offering—the objects themselves and the inscription"; and Freedberg, *Power*, 155, where "the inscription is essential...just in case picturing fails."

55. The first quoted phrase is from Jules Lubbock, *Storytelling in Christian Art from Giotto to Donatello* (New Haven, CT: Yale University Press, 2006) 275; see 287. See also Roland Barthes, *Image-Music-Text*, tr. Stephen Heath (New York: Hill and Wang, 1978) 39–40. Regarding captions, see Lorenzo Vilches, *La lectura de la imagen: prensa, cine, television* (Barcelona: Ediciones Paidós, 1990) 193.

56. Regarding droodles, see Robert L. Solso, *Cognition and the Visual Arts* (Cambridge, MA: MIT Press, 1994) 255.

57. The first quoted passage is in Luque Agraz, *El Arte*, 126; and the second is in Francisco Gallegos Franco, *Los retablos del Señor de la Misericordia de Tepatitlán* (Guadalajara: Conaculta, Secretaría de Cultura de Jalisco, Feca, Grupo Modelo, 2001) 126.

58. The quoted passage is from a retablo in Rosamond Purcell, "The Stories of Strangers: Mexican Ex-Voto Paintings," *Virginia Quarterly Review* 84/2 (2008): 89.

59. For examples of seeming apparitions, see *Dones y promesas*, 191, cat. 275 and 194, cat. 283; 195, cat. 286; 199, cat. 302; 204, cat. 321; 205, cat. 328; and 207, cat. 335. See also Kessler, "Turning," 431, where in the thirteenth century Lucas of Tuy wrote: "Since the aim of religious art is to arouse the emotions of the spectator...the artist needs to devise unusual motifs and to invent new ideas" even if these "contradict the literal truth and only serve to deepen the love for Christ through the emotion they arouse."

CHALMA

1. Regarding a sense of inhospitality and condescension toward popular devotion at the shrine, see Silvia A. Benuzzi, *Pilgrimage to Chalma: The Analysis of Religious Change* (Greeley: University of Northern Colorado, 1981) 106–108.

2. The quoted passages are from Joaquín Sardo, *Relación histórica y moral de la portentosa imagen de N. Sr. Jesucristo Crucificado aprecido en una de las cuevas de S. Miguel de Chalma*, facsimile of the 1810 edition (Mexico City: Biblioteca Enciclopédica del Estado de México, 1979) 19–20. On the origin and history of the image, see Luis E. Orozco, *Los Cristos de caña de maíz y otras venerables imágenes de Nuestro Señor Jesucristo*, vol. 1 (Guadalajara, Mexico: [n. p.], 1970) 176–177, where the image was placed in the cave by two priests, Nicolás de Perea and Sebastián de Tolentino; Roberto G. Cruz Floriano, "Cornstalk Paste: *Pasta de Caña de Maíz*," *Saints and Sinners: Mexican Devotional Art*, ed. James Caswell and Jenise Amanda Ramos (Atglen, PA: Schiffer Publishing, 2006) 191–192; Gilberto Giménez, *Cultural popular y religión en el Anahuac* (Mexico City: Centro de Estudios Ecuménicos, 1978) 71; María J. Rodríguez-Shadow and Robert D. Shadow, *El pueblo del Señor: las fiestas y peregrinaciones de Chalma* (Toluca: Universidad Autónoma del Estado de México, 2000) 75; and Jennifer Scheper Hughes, *Biography of a Mexican Crucifix: Lived Religion and Local Faith from the Conquest to the Present* (New York: Oxford University Press, 2010) 275, n. 35.

3. Vicente Acosta, *Nuestra Señora del Pueblito: compendio histórico de su culto* (Querétaro: Gobierno del Estado de Querétaro, 1996) 14.

4. Regarding the date, see Jorge Ayala Q., *Chalma: su Señor, su santuario su convento, sus ferias, sus danzas, sus leyendas, y tradiciones* (Chalma: shrine published, 2002) 18–19 and 64. The plaque outside the cave chapel gives 1664 as the date of transfer.

5. The quoted passages are from Matías de Escobar in Scheper Hughes, *Biography*, 115; see 114–115. See also Antonio Rubial García, "Tebaidas en el Paraíso. Los ermitaños de la Nueva España," *Historia mexicana* 44/3 (1995): 371–373; and Stephanie Wood, "Christian Images in Nahua Testaments of Late Colonial Toluca," *The Americas* 47/3 (1991): 274, where devotion to the Señor de Chalma is mentioned in late colonial Nahua testaments.

6. See Patrizia Granziera, "The Worship of Mary in Mexico: Sacred Trees, Christian Crosses, and the Body of the Goddess," *Toronto Journal of Theology* 28/1 (2012): 44–48, 51, and 54. On the indigenous origins of the Virgen de Ocotlán, see Rodrigo Martínez Baracs, *La secuencia tlaxcalteca: orígenes del culto a Nuestra Señora de Ocotlán* (Mexico City: Instituto Nacional de Antropología e Historia, 2000) 180–181.

7. Before the fence was installed, offerings—primarily clothes—were attached to the trunk and lower branches. See a photograph in Martha Egan, *Milagros: Votive Offerings from the Americas* (Santa Fe, NM: Museum of New Mexico Press, 1991). See also Victor Turner and Edith Turner, *Image and Pilgrimage in Christian Culture: Anthropological Perspectives* (New York: Columbia University Press, 1978) 55 and plate 5; Luis Mario Schneider, "La fe de los caminos," *México peregrino: diez santuarios procesionales,"* ed. Luis Mario Schneider and Guillermo Tovar de Teresa (Mexico City: Patronato Cultural Iberoamericano, 1990) 103; H. R. Harvey, "Pilgrimage and Shrine: Religious Practices among the Otomí of Huixquilcan, Mexico," *Pilgrimage in Latin America*, ed. N. Ross Crumrine and Alan Morinis (Westport, CT: Greenwood Press, 1991) 101; and Judith Francis Zeitlin, "Contesting the Sacred Landscape in Colonial Mesoamerica," (Los Angeles: Foundation for the Advancement of Mesoamerican Studies, 2008): www.famsi.org/reports/07085.

8. The quoted passages are from, respectively, Rodríguez-Shadow and Shadow, *El pueblo*, 78; and "Católicos mexicanos veneran al Señor de Chalma con bailes y oraciones," (EFE, April 22, 2011): www.elcorreo.com/agencias/20110422/mas-actualidad/cultura/catolicos-mexicanos-veneran-senor-chalma_201104221849.html. A shrine to San Miguel Arcángel, located near the Ocotlán shrine, is also closely associated with sacred water. See Eduardo Báez Macías, *El arcángel San Miguel: su patrocinio, la ermita en el Santo Desierto de Cuajimalpa y el Santuario de Tlaxcala* (Mexico City: Universidad Nacional Autónoma de México, 1979) 39–45.

Index

AA. *See* Alcoholics Anonymous
absolution, 8–9
absorption, 37, 259n59
accessibility, 56, *104*, 104–5
accidents, 90–91. *See also* Marco's miracle
accumulation, 207–11, 313n18, 314n21
Acosta, José de, 228–29
addendum, 232
Adolfo, 46, *163*, *163*, *165*
Adriana, 19, 31, 59, 93, 187
affirmations, 152
agency, 46, 168, 301n22. *See also* sacred
    power and human agency
    of votive offerings, 211–12
alcohol, 183–89, 193–94
Alcoholics Anonymous (AA), 189–90,
    308nn63–64
alcoholism, 188–89, 308nn62–64
Alejandra, 136
ambiance, 21
ambiguity
    God and, 14–15, 248n10, 252n32
    miraculous images and, 11–18
    papal coronations and, 17
    prayer and, 248n12, 248n14,
        249n15
    presence related to, 15–17, 248nn14
    in representation, 15–18, 248n12, 248n14
    of retablos, 225
anatomy, 200–203, *201*, *202*, 310n2
anger, 133
anointment, 196
anomalies, 215, 315n26
Antonio, 26, 64, 71, 133, 143, 191
apparitions, 115–16, 148
Aquinas, Thomas, 155, 295n1
art history, 37
Arturo, 187

"asking place" (pedimento), 68, 101–2, 106
asymmetry, 80–82, 275n40
atrium, 235–36
attributes, 18
    ambiance related to, 21
    emotions, 19–20, 250n18, 250n20
    familiarity as, 24–25
    home as, 23–24, 54–55, 105, 252n31,
        267n10
    movements as, 21–22
    relationships as, 24–25, 252n32,
        253n35
    substitution as, 23
    sweating, 20, 22, 129
    volition as, 22–23, 251n28
Augustine, 171, 257n55

Baltimore Catechism, 248n12
Bartolomé de Jesús María, 239–40
belief, 28, 118. *See also* religious belief
    as reality, 6, 121, 247n7, 284nn15–16
    for support, 213, 314n22
Besançon, Alain, 248n14
blessings (*eulogia*), 178–79
blindness, 128–29
bone relics, 11–12, *13*
Bustamante, Francisco de, 18, 249n17

Caesarius of Heisterbach, 32
cancer, 137
candles, 21, 56, 176, 314n23
canonization, 86, 89, 134, 137, 293n62
captions, 230
Carlos, 84, 160, 169, 182, 186
Carmen, 83
catharsis
    in disclosure, 169–70, 302n25
    of votive texts, 222–23, 318n41